Commissioned Ridings
Designing Canada's Electoral Districts

Where did the idea for nonpartisan constituency redistributions come from? What were the principal reasons that Canada turned to arm's-length commissions to design its electoral districts? In *Commissioned Ridings* John Courtney addresses these questions by examining and assessing the readjustment process in Canada's electoral boundaries. Defining electoral districts as "representational building blocks," Courtney compares federal and provincial electoral readjustments in the last half of the twentieth century, showing how parliamentarians and legislators, boundary commissions, courts, and interested members of the general public debated representational principles to define the purposes of electoral redistricting in an increasingly urban, ethnically mixed federal state such as Canada.

Courtney analyses boundary commissions – their membership, degree of independence, and powers. He explores the participation of the public and politicians in the deliberation of the commissions, as well as the extent to which Canada's ridings have moved gradually toward greater population equality and the prospects for further changes in the way electoral districts are designed. Noting that Canada's electoral boundary readjustments are based on principles markedly different from those in the United States, Courtney examines the impact of various Canadian court decisions based on the "right to vote" protection of the Charter, as well as new concepts such as "community of interest," "minority representation," and "effective representation." Courtney concludes with an examination of the conditions that must be met before changes to other representational building blocks, such as the electoral system, can be made.

JOHN C. COURTNEY is professor of political studies at the University of Saskatchewan, co-editor of *Citizenship, Diversity, and Pluralism: Canadian and Comparative Perspectives*, and author of *Do Conventions Matter?: Choosing National Party Leaders in Canada*.

Commissioned Ridings

*Designing Canada's
Electoral Districts*

JOHN C. COURTNEY

McGill-Queen's University Press
Montreal & Kingston · London · Ithaca

© McGill-Queen's University Press 2001
ISBN 0-7735-2226-3 (cloth)
ISBN 0-7735-2265-4 (paper)

Legal deposit second quarter 2001
Bibliothèque nationale du Québec

Printed in Canada on acid-free paper

This book has been published with the help of a grant from the
Humanities and Social Sciences Federation of Canada, using funds
provided by the Social Sciences and Humanities Research Council
of Canada.

McGill-Queen's University Press acknowledges the financial support of
the Government of Canada through the Book Publishing Industry
Development Program (BPIDP) for its activities. It also acknowledges the
support of the Canada Council for the Arts for its publishing program.

Canadian Cataloguing in Publication Data

Courtney, John C.
    Commissioned ridings : designing Canada's electoral districts
    Includes bibliographical references and index.
    ISBN 0-7735-2226-3(bnd)
    ISBN 0-7735-2265-4 (pbk)
    1. Election districts – Canada. I. Title.
    JL193.C678 2001   328.71'07345   C00-901685-6

Typeset in New Baskerville 10/12
by Caractéra inc., Quebec City

To Joanne and Murray, John and Lesley, Madeleine, William, and Elizabeth, Liam, Jackson, and Quinn

Contents

Tables and Figures

TABLES

FIGURES

Acknowledgments

This is a study of an institution that most Canadians have never heard about – the independent electoral boundaries commissions. That such bodies have maintained a low profile and received relatively little attention since first being introduced to Canada from Australia in the 1950s is testimony to the extent to which theirs is a success story. Although the primary purpose of this book is to gain a better understanding of an institution that has become a part of the federal, provincial, and territorial systems of government, *Commissioned Ridings* is also about other questions of importance to Canadians. These include federalism, representation, and institutional legitimacy; together they form something of a sub-text running through the book.

I trace the origins of my interest in Canada's electoral constituencies to many conversations I had over the years with my late colleague and friend at the University of Saskatchewan, Norman Ward. He, perhaps more than anyone in Canada, had established the topic of parliamentary representation as one deserving of serious attention by political scientists. I regret that he did not live to see the progeny of his scholarly pursuits on representation in Canada, for there are now many in our profession spread across the country who are researching and writing on the representational questions that he was often the first to explore.

When I first began working on this project a number of years ago, there might have been another half-dozen or so political scientists in Canada with a serious interest in how constituency boundaries were designed. A quick glance at this book's bibliography attests to the considerable growth of interest in the subject since then. We may now have to revise the usual quip about Canada's constitutional debates putting the food on the tables of our profession. Research for royal commissions, service on electoral boundaries commissions, and active participation as directors of research in the daily routine of electoral boundaries commissions, have introduced many members of our profession to the study of an important public institution.

I am indebted to all who have helped in some way or another in this project. As I have found on several previous occasions, election officials at the federal, provincial, and territorial levels are invariably helpful and cooperative in providing material and in answering questions. Their knowledge about electoral districts and the boundary commissions that define them reinforces my long-held view that Canadians are as well served by the men and women in their electoral offices as are any people in the world. In the process of gathering my research, I interviewed something in the order of five dozen individuals in Canada and Australia – chairs and members of boundaries commissions, politicians, and electoral officers. Many of them were political science colleagues who had served as boundary commissioners or research directors for commissions, which proved advantageous as it enabled me to interview them as members of my own profession and as knowledgeable participants in the process about which I was writing. To a person, they were willing to share with me their impressions, either favourable or not, of the non-partisan, arms-length institutions that were charged with designing Canada's ridings. Those who were interviewed in the course of researching this topic are thanked collectively. Their names appear in the list of interviews on pages 267-70.

A number of colleagues read drafts of various chapters of the book. I am deeply appreciative of the time they took from their own busy schedules to offer comments, criticisms, and suggestions. They are: Peter Aucoin, Don Blake, David Docherty, Munroe Eagles, Richard Jenkins, Larry LeDuc, Louis Massicotte, Andrew Sancton, Leslie Seidle, Jennifer Smith, Graham White, Melissa Williams, and Lisa Young. Perhaps foolishly, I have not always followed their advice. Nonetheless, I am grateful for their help. Several colleagues at the University of Saskatchewan were, as always, willing to oblige by reading drafts of chapters or pointing me in the direction of needed research material. In particular, I would like to thank Cris de Clercy, Peter Ferguson, Ron Fritz, Andy Hubbertz, David Smith, and Duff Spafford for their assistance. J. Paul Johnston of the University of Alberta and Norman Ruff of the University of Victoria also guided me to helpful sources.

Financial support from the Social Sciences and Humanities Research Council of Canada enabled me to carry out the research, to conduct the interviews, and to visit archives in which collections of papers relating to electoral boundaries readjustments are held. My research assistants, all students in our department at the time, were a great help: Stéphane Audet, Jim Farney, Russell Isinger, Ian Mokuruk, and Erin Tolley. Calvin Hanselmann deserves special thanks, for he handled much of the statistical analysis and crafted many of the tables, graphs, and diagrams with great skill. A Killam Research Fellowship awarded by the Canada Council for 1998–2000 provided me with the time free of teaching and administrative responsibilities at the University of Saskatchewan to devote to the research and writing of this book. I am grateful to both the SSHRC and the Killam Program for their generous support of this work. My department and university have remained fully supportive of my research.

McGill-Queen's University Press has, once again, been a pleasure to work with. I deeply appreciate the efforts that the Press's executive director and editor, Philip Cercone, its coordinating editor, Joan McGilvray, and their staff have made to ensure as expeditious a publication of *Commissioned Ridings* as possible. They have given this book the attention that authors hope for from their publisher. And, of course, nothing has pleased me more than working again with Diane Mew. She continues to demonstrate why she enjoys the reputation as one of Canada's finest, sharpest, and best-humoured copy editors. I also wish to thank Geri Rowlatt for her careful preparation of the index.

As always, my final but greatest debt is to Helen who has, once again, shared vicariously in the writing of a book.

John C. Courtney
Saskatoon, Saskatchewan
September 2000

Commissioned Ridings

1 Introduction

> To change and to change for the better are two different things.
>
> – German proverb

The term "representation" has assumed a variety of meanings in the modern democratic state. It can denote the presence of elected or appointed agents who have been authorized to act on behalf of others with the expectation that at some time in the future they will be held accountable for their actions. It can be used descriptively as a way of comparing the racial, linguistic, gender, or occupational composition of an elected assembly with that of the general population. Or it may in some symbolic fashion embrace myths or images, such as flags and anthems, that have developed as part of a political culture. In each of these three respects, representation applies to an end: actions followed by accountability, socio-demographic attributes of the elected and the extent to which these mirror society, and symbolic threads interwoven into a cultural tapestry.[1]

But there is more to representation than such a tripartite distinction suggests. To imply that it is only about an end product is to miss part of what representation entails. A flag or an anthem are, admittedly, an end product. But those who were authorized to choose such symbols and who will be held accountable for their decisions owe their selection to a more broadly inclusive representational process. A prior stage is no less critical to representation theory than the final stage. There is a point at the opposite part of the representational equation – at the input end of an input-output model of representation – at which the focus is on citizens as electors or, to be more precise, on the institutions designed to ensure that citizens can exercise their rights as electors. An analysis of those institutions requires an expanded theory of representation.

To determine what the initial institutional processes must be before electoral representation can take place, let us give a twist to an old familiar question: what if we held an election and there was no machinery by which to conduct it? There were no statutes or regulations to establish who could vote. There were no political parties to choose candidates and leaders to mobilize voters. There were no districts, geographically-defined or otherwise, within which votes could be aggregated, counted, and distributed to elect members. And there were no laws or regulations by which to govern the campaign, to oversee candidates' fundraising and expenditures, to establish thresholds for electoral victory, or to determine which group of candidates (remember there are no political parties) would be entitled to form the government.

In such a mythical state, elections would be all but impossible. The logical conclusion, therefore, is as obvious as it is simple. For legislative, parliamentary, presidential, or congressional representation to take place, acceptable and legitimate means must first be established to turn the inchoate Hobbesian world of total electoral anarchy into an institutional framework for electing members to an assembly and for holding those members ultimately responsible for their actions. Representatives who are authorized to act on our behalf and who will ultimately be held accountable for their policies can be chosen for office only if there are in place at the outset of the process what I have chosen to label the procedural building blocks of representation.

Representational building blocks are the institutional arrangements that enable citizens to participate in elections, parties to compete for public office, and votes to be aggregated to distinguish winners from losers. In Canada there are several building blocks which are an essential part of our electoral machinery. These include at the macro level the electoral system and the registration of voters, and at the micro level constituency parties and electoral districts. Elections would be impossible to hold without the first two, and difficult, though not impossible, without the second two.

This book is about one of those building blocks, electoral districts, and about how and why our constituencies have come to be designed as they are. It spans a period of Canadian history – the last half of the twentieth century – in which control over the design of electoral districts (or ridings as Canadians like to call them)[2] passed from the hands of the elected politicians to those of independent boundary commissioners. The transformation was unparalleled in Canada and, for that matter, in many other countries in the world. It amounted, to a revolution.[3] In accounting for that transformation, *Commissioned Ridings* is based on the premise that for institutional change to be accomplished certain basic conditions must first be met. Without the most critical of those conditions in place, reform cannot take place.

In public policy theory it is said that the moment is ripe for an institutional or a policy change when certain essential tests have been satisfactorily met at roughly the same time. To apply John Kingdon's analytical terms for agenda-setting, three streams must converge to open a policy window before action can be taken. Problems must be identified, solutions advanced, and political support forthcoming for the change.[4] Without all three being in place, we could predict that the reform of an institutional building block, such as the periodic readjustment of electoral boundaries, cannot be brought about. We will see from the experience of Manitoba in the 1950s and Quebec two decades later, as well as at the federal level in the 1960s, that the origins of independent electoral boundaries commissions in Canada can be traced to the confluence of these three streams. Social scientists played an important part in acquainting the politicians with the severity of the problem by demonstrating how unfair the method of redistributing seats had become to many voters in Canada and by laying out the preferred policy alternative as a solution to the problem. Once they gave their support to the change, the politicians relinquished their direct control over the design of constituencies and ensured that independent and non-partisan electoral boundaries commissions were established. These bodies, in turn, have drawn a good part of their membership from the ranks of Canada's social science community – the very sorts of individuals who had recommended the change in the first place!

At one level *Commissioned Ridings* is a case study of a single institutional building block and the largely successful transformation it has undergone both federally and provincially since the 1950s. At another level the book is a study of the process of designing parliamentary and legislative constituencies in a federal country and a commentary on some of the inherent strengths of a federal system. Federalism has a remarkable capacity to enable politicians and government officials to learn from one another's innovations. That has certainly been demonstrated with the transference from one jurisdiction to another of the idea of turning over to independent commissions the construction of electoral districts.

There is a counter-intuitive aspect to the way in which federalism has played a part in electoral boundary readjustments in Canada. Federalism is often justified as an institutional arrangement that allows for significant policy differences among its various parts in areas that are entirely within their respective legislative orbit. "Unity with diversity" has been one of the standard maxims offered in support of a federal system. As they have developed since the 1950s, Canada's electoral boundary readjustment processes (which are clearly within the orbit of the individual jurisdictions to determine) point not so much in the direction of unity as of similarity over diversity. Rather than seeing the various federal and provincial processes go their own way and bear little resemblance to one another, Canadian federalism has encouraged "copy-cats."

The statutes and the terms of reference for the boundary commissions are understandably not identical, but collectively they demonstrate sufficient similarity to show that throughout Canada there are shared representational values that relate directly to the design of constituencies. The small number of court decisions of the 1990s furthered that "nationalizing" of representational values. Moreover, those court cases helped both to validate some of the principal concepts that have been a part of electoral boundaries readjustments from the 1950s on, and to introduce new considerations for commissions of the future to take into account in the construction of electoral districts.

What follows is devoted to an examination of electoral boundary commissions in the provinces and at the federal level: their origin, composition, powers and degree of independence, and the electoral constituencies they design. Statutes, court decisions, public hearings, and political debates all bear on a boundary commission's decisions. The interviews I conducted for this study and the parliamentary and legislative debates reveal a striking difference in representational attitudes on the part of the major participants in the exercise. On the one side are the politicians who, as a rule, are prone to base their evaluation of a redistribution on its impact on their "servicing" role. Whether they will have a territorially larger or smaller riding, or whether they will have more or fewer individuals to serve matters a great deal to elected members. On the other side are the boundary commissioners who are expected to apply the terms of their governing statute and the guidelines established for their redistribution as fairly and as equitably as possible to all concerned. There is an understandable tension between what elected members and redistribution commissioners, each with differing responsibilities and bases of authority, expect periodic boundary readjustments to accomplish.

Commissioned Ridings shows that many of the principal aspects of electoral boundary readjustments in Canada have converged towards a similar procedural model and a proximate set of electoral values. This is all the more remarkable as it has taken place in a highly regionalized, socially diverse federal system in which commissions operate independently of one another in every province once a decade, and each of the provinces has established its own separate commission. Since the implementation of the Charter of Rights and Freedoms, the courts have become a part of the electoral boundaries process. The number of court challenges to provincial boundary readjustments remains small, especially by American standards, where litigations about the size and shape of congressional and state districts have become a regular feature of decennial redistricting. Nonetheless, the impact of the only case to have been heard so far by the Supreme Court of Canada (in 1991) has been substantial. Concepts sanctioned by the court, such as "effective representation," "minority representation," and "community of interest," have entered the standard vocabulary of Canadian redistributions even though agreement on their substance remains at issue.

The institutional building blocks that emerge from the redistribution process serve a strictly utilitarian purpose: they are the territorially defined units within which we elect members of Parliament or of a provincial legislature. But those building blocks also tell us something about ourselves. The criteria that we employ (or ignore) in setting the terms by which boundaries commissions are expected to draft proposals, hold hearings, adjudicate conflicting demands, and establish electoral districts are the criteria by which we choose to define an essential part of our representational equation. How often should constituency boundaries be readjusted, and should they be drawn according to an area's total population or its number of electors? How big or how small should constituencies be? Should isolated and primarily rural parts of the country be treated differently from the rest, or should all ridings, regardless of their location, be approximately equal in size? By what measures should the fairness of riding designs be judged? Should special efforts be made to design seats for minority groups that might not otherwise be able to elect "their own" representatives? If so, which groups?

These are the questions that the parliamentarians, legislators, commissioners, and, to a smaller extent, the courts and the public have debated since electoral boundaries were first designed by independent commissions in Canada. From the mid-1950s, when the germ of an idea for independent commissions was first imported from Australia, to the end of the last century, the issues that were central to the exercise of designing constituencies have also remained a part of a continuing debate over how they should be resolved satisfactorily. In the 1990s a federal royal commission and a parliamentary committee each attempted to address a number of the issues that they saw as critical to improving Canada's electoral boundaries readjustment process. Their proposed reforms have remained nothing more than that – proposals. The agenda facing the parliamentarians and legislators in the years ahead can be expected to return to those issues and proposals. In the meantime the existing process, which has constituted such a striking improvement over the previous government-controlled method of designing seats, will see independent electoral boundary commissions continue to construct the institutional building blocks that play an essential part of Canada's party and political systems.

2 Electoral Districts in a Federal State

> The way in which redistribution has been carried out in the past is a sorry story.
>
> – Stanley Knowles, 1964

Regardless of whether a state is federal or unitary, the regular readjustment of its electoral boundaries has the same effect: it has the potential to provoke a measure of conflict in both the political and public arenas. The reason is obvious. Institutions permit the marshalling of resources in alternate ways, and what benefits some voters, candidates, or parties in one configuration of territorially defined electoral districts may under an alternative arrangement work against their interests. Elected members of the same party from neighbouring constituencies may be pitted against one another for re-nomination because of changes made to their respective districts. Rural and urban members, quite possibly of the same party, may hold contrary views on such important representational matters as population and territorial size of constituencies and voter equality. Various political or local interest groups may be at odds publicly as they seek to advance opposing positions on the inclusion of a particular community, town, or neighbourhood in one riding and not in another.

These are familiar and understandable issues that invariably come to the fore whenever changes are made to a building block to which there is a degree of political and public attachment. It is natural for politicians or the public to enjoy a certain comfort level with the familiar and to be sceptical of the new and untried. Not surprisingly, elected representatives and party organizers often press for the retention of districts that were first brought into existence at the previous redistribution – districts to which they may well have voiced strong opposition at the time they were created. An old administrative adage helps to describe such a reversal of opinions: "the initial judge becomes the later advocate."

Compared with a unitary system, a federal one could be expected to experience greater conflict over the construction of electoral boundaries. Elected members at one level may oppose what their fellow party members at another level have chosen to do with electoral districts. But such disagreements are inherent in federal politics. Federalism is designed not only as a way of protecting social, regional, and territorial differences; it also ensures that those differences can be expressed, often in opposition to those of other federal units. Federalism enables the various units to establish standards and procedures appropriate to their own circumstances.

Federalism also requires the division of powers between two levels of government and a formula to determine the number of members to which each province and territory is entitled in the federal parliament. Elected assemblies at both levels (and, in Canada, in the territories) need to be established and maintained. Questions naturally arise about the size of these assemblies, the frequency with which their electoral boundaries should be adjusted, and the standards applied in designing their ridings. There has been no "standard size fits all" for Canada's legislative assemblies.

Equally, there are definitial issues to be examined. (What *is* a redistribution? what *are* electoral boundary readjustments?) This chapter begins with a brief overview of some terms that are essential to any study of electoral districting. It then moves to a comparison of the size of Canada's assemblies, a brief review of Canada's first nine decades of federal redistributions, and a description of the constitutional and political factors that have determined the provincial entitlements to seats in the House of Commons. It concludes with a comparison of some of the representational differences in two federal countries, Canada and the United States.

DEFINING TERMS

In a federal country such as Canada or the United States electoral districts in the national Parliament or Congress are reallocated from time to time amongst the provinces or states. *Redistribution* and *reapportionment* are the terms used to refer to that reallocation. Canada redistributes its House of Commons constituencies (301 as of the redistribution of the 1990s) among its ten provinces and three territories, whereas America reapportions its 435 House of Representatives districts among its fifty states. In both cases the allocations are based on a province or state's share of the country's total population. These are subject to guarantees of minimum numbers of districts to each federal unit that are markedly different in the two countries. Once that preliminary stage has been completed, the determination of the actual territorial boundaries of those districts can proceed. That is described in Canada as the *electoral boundary readjustment* process and in the United States as *redistricting*. In spite of these definitional differences, it is clear from the academic literature, the press, and political discourse that the various terms employed in the exercise of allocating seats and drawing boundaries are often used interchangeably.[1]

The adjustment of electoral boundaries has long played an integral role in politics, so much so that politicians have historically used the occasion to try to enhance their own partisan advantage. The time-honoured practice of manipulating district boundaries for the benefit of one political group and to the detriment of another, referred to as *gerrymandering*, was named after Governor Eldbridge Gerry of Massachusetts, who in 1812 signed into law an electoral districting bill establishing oddly-shaped districts whose only purpose was to benefit his own party's electoral interests.

Canada's John A. Macdonald was known to have followed in Governor Gerry's footsteps and to have been instrumental in carefully overseeing the design of parliamentary seats with his own Conservative party's electoral fortunes in mind. According to Norman Ward, "the [Conservatives'] tampering was done with some hesitation and pretence of principle in 1872, with a gay abandon in 1882, and with dignity and persistence in 1892." As is sometimes the case with such manipulations, however, the payoffs were minimal, since the strategy worked to the benefit of the Liberals as often as to the Conservatives.[2]

This process, which we can call *intentional gerrymandering*, has more recently encompassed the deliberate manipulation of district boundaries to enhance the probability of a racially, linguistically, or religiously defined group electing "one of its own" to an assembly. This may be done, as in Northern Ireland, as a way of acknowledging and attempting to address a profound social cleavage. Ulster independent electoral boundary commissions have deliberately sought to construct parliamentary and local government constituencies so as to replicate in the assemblies the presence of two groups deeply distrustful of one another, the loyalist (largely Protestant) and nationalist (overwhelmingly Roman Catholic) communities. Intentional gerrymandering may also be accepted to strengthen the chances of racial minorities winning legislative seats more or less commensurate in number to their share of the total population. In the United States in the final decades of the twentieth century this practice became known as affirmative or inverse gerrymandering and was aimed largely at enhancing the electoral prospects of African-American and Hispanic candidates. It was instrumental in increasing the number of candidates of both groups being elected to House of Representatives, although candidate selection, voter mobilization, party competition, and electoral organization by special interest groups on behalf of minority candidates also played a part in enhancing their congressional numbers. Representation of the two targeted racial minorities jumped from five blacks and three Latinos elected to Congress in 1964 to thirty-eight blacks and seventeen Latinos three decades later.[3]

Unintended gerrymandering describes the partisan bias of electoral districts that comes as a natural by-product of the boundary readjustment process. It is the result of non-partisan boundary readjustment bodies constructing constituencies in which individuals and communities are treated fairly and partisan interests are ignored as much as possible. The effect of the exercise, nonetheless, is to favour one partisan group over another – that is, to "unintentionally" gerrymander the districts. If the impact of boundary readjustments was completely neutral, parties would be expected to win roughly the same share of seats as they do of votes. That is an almost totally unimaginable outcome in a plurality vote system in which single member districts are designed on a territorial basis. At both the federal and provincial levels in Canada, for example, governments are frequently elected with a majority of an assembly's seats without having won a majority of the popular vote, whereas parties gaining as much as 20 to 25 percent of the vote rarely win a commensurate share of an assembly's seats.

Malapportionment describes an unequal distribution of population among electoral districts. If all ridings in a political system had exactly the same population, however impossible that might be to arrange, it could be said that there was no malapportionment in that system. The greater the degree of inequality in their population, the greater the degree to which the districts can be described as malapportioned. With mobility and changing social demographics of population, districts often become malapportioned with the passage of time. The Gini Index, which is a measure of the degree of equality of district populations that will be used in this study, scores complete equality of constituency population size as 0 and complete inequality as 1. The nearer a group of constituencies approaches 0 or 1, the closer it will be to perfect equality or inequality respectively.[4]

The expression *one person, one vote*, first made popular in the United States in the 1960s as a result of a series of Supreme Court decisions, has quite possibly emerged in the boundary readjustment process as the representational term most frequently used and most easily understood by the public. The term derives from the twin premises that one person's vote is the equal of another's and that, as a result, the purpose of constituency redistributions is to ensure that districts contain roughly equal populations. The greater the population variance among electoral districts, the greater the votes of electors in the larger than average population seats can be said to have been *diluted* in relation to those of electors in smaller than average population seats.

The standards of what constitutes equal population districts vary considerably, not only among different countries but within them. Since the landmark voter equality decisions of the 1960s in the United States, courts in that country have generally accepted for state redistricting purposes a variance of up to 10 percent without justifications and up to 16 percent when acceptable reasons have been given. The most extreme application of the one person, one vote principle in the United States came in a 1983 Supreme Court judgment. At that time the court held, "perhaps to the point of caricature" according to one of its critics,[5] that a reapportionment permitting a disparity of only 0.7 percent between the largest and smallest of New Jersey's sixteen congressional districts was found to violate the principle of one person, one vote. In the years since, American courts have become less strict in their application of tight variances. The Supreme Court has accepted the argument, without providing firm guidance about the permissible deviations for district size, that in order to promote *fair and effective representation*, social and racial factors should be weighed in the balance along with equality of population when legislative districts are designed.[6]

In Canada the federal and provincial variances prior to the introduction of independent electoral boundary commissions were considerable. In Quebec by the early 1960s they were actually more extreme than they were in Tennessee at the time when the first successful legal challenge to the malapportioned, rural-dominated legislature of that state was mounted. The variances became markedly less pronounced in Canada after the adoption of legislation by most jurisdictions for the regular review of constituency boundaries by non-partisan commissions and the permissible population limits that commissions would be allowed when designing the ridings. There remain, nonetheless, some notable differences among those jurisdictions in the maximum and minimum population limits that their commissions are permitted.

Issues of apportionment, periodic boundary readjustment, gerrymandering, and malapportionment need never be raised in countries that do not employ a form of territorial representation. Israel, for example, uses a system of proportional representation to elect its Knesset from lists of party candidates on a country-wide basis. The whole country constitutes one giant constituency from which 128 members are elected. This renders redistribution and electoral boundary readjustments unnecessary. Countries whose electoral system requires multi-member electoral districts, such as Ireland and Malta, and those that rely on single-member districts, such as Canada, need to define their electoral boundaries periodically because of shifts in population. The interval between the boundary adjustments varies considerably from one country to another. In Canada and the United States it is a constitutional requirement that district boundaries be redrawn following every decennial census; by contrast, India's last redistribution was in 1973 and its next will not get under way until at least 2001. New Zealand redraws its electoral boundaries every five years and Australia every seven years or sooner in one or more states if population shifts warrant a readjustment. Federal countries that reapportion their seats more frequently than others demonstrate a stronger commitment to the principle of proportionality of seats among the various states or provinces, for they are attempting to track more closely the shifts in population that inevitably occur with time. The contrasting experience of Australia and India speaks directly to that point.

In addition to their frequency, reapportionments in federal countries also vary from one country to another in how they determine the number of seats to which a state or province is entitled in the federal assembly. In the United States the so-called *Method of Equal Proportions* has been employed since 1941, the fifth successive scheme for apportioning districts among the states since 1790. Each of the fifty states receives one seat out of the total of 435 in the House of Representatives. The remaining 385 are assigned a priority value determined by ranking all states according to their respective population, the highest ranked state receiving the fifty-first seat and so on.[7] In Canada, by contrast, a *national quotient* is established for all provinces by dividing the number of seats in the House of Commons in 1976 (282 less three seats set aside for the northern territories) into the national population (minus the population of the territories), then dividing the population of each province by the national quotient to determine its seat entitlement. Canada augments this apportionment through various constitutional or legislated guarantees of additional seats to smaller provinces and those with declining populations than they would otherwise be entitled to. The effect of these "add-on" constituencies in the reapportionment of the 1990s was to boost the Canadian Commons to 301 members.[8]

Legislation is typically used to establish the rules by which the number of seats is determined for the various units in a country, for example for England, Scotland, Wales and Northern Ireland in the United Kingdom, the *Länder* in Germany, and the states in Australia.

In some cases the total number of seats in the lower national house is fixed by law, as it has been since 1929 in the American House of Representatives. In other cases, such as Canada and the United Kingdom, the size of a legislature or parliament changes from one reapportionment to another. This can be the result of changes made to the formula used to determine the number of districts or the application of the existing formula to a population whose distribution has changed. Inclusion of additional population or territory, as happened in Germany following reunification in 1990, can also explain changes in the total number and the relative distribution of seats in a political system.

THE SIZE OF CANADA'S ASSEMBLIES

In *The Federalist Papers*, James Madison wrote that "no political problem is less susceptible of a precise solution than that which relates to the number most convenient for a representative legislature."[9] His words are as apt in the early twenty-first century as they were at the end of the eighteenth. A comparison of the number of members elected to legislative chambers in Canada and in other countries confirms that there are no hard and fast rules governing the size of parliaments and legislatures. Italy and the United Kingdom have roughly equal populations and both have bicameral parliaments with over six hundred members in the lower house. Yet the United States, with a population nearly five times that of either of those European countries, sends only 435 to its House of Representatives. The lower house in New Hampshire, one of the smallest of the American states, has four hundred members; that of California, the largest state, has eighty members.

In Canada the differences may not be so extreme. Nonetheless, both in terms of the variety of sizes of national, provincial, and territorial assemblies and the differences in the size of individual assemblies over time, the Canadian record demonstrates that there is no universally accepted answer to the seemingly simple question: "how large or small should an assembly be?" At Confederation, Canada was composed of four provinces, a population of 3.4 million, and a newly created House of Commons of 181 members. By the early 2000s there were ten provinces, three territories, a population in excess of 30 million, and a Commons of 301 members. The growth in population had vastly outstripped the increase in the size of the Commons. Had the original formula for determining size pegged the number of members elected to the growth in the total population (which it did not), the House would now have an absurdly large membership.

As a general rule at the provincial and territorial levels, those units with the larger populations have established larger legislatures, those with growing populations have gradually increased their legislative size, and those with stable or declining populations have cut back on the number of members elected to their legislature. A fair predictor of an increase in the size of a legislature has been an increase in a province's urban population. Seats have often been added to a legislative assembly to reflect in some measure the growth in a province's cities or its principal metropolitan areas. But in typical Canadian fashion, and as further confirmation of Carolyn Tuohy's description of Canadian policy-making as institutionalized ambivalence,[10] urban seats characteristically have been added without reducing the number of rural seats by a commensurate number. The four largest and fastest-growing provinces, Ontario, Quebec, British Columbia, and Alberta, all followed that custom from the 1950s to the mid-1980s. Possibly the best predictor of a reduction in the size of a provincial legislature in the past has been a severe economic depression. After a post-First World War period of expansion, every provincial legislature, except for those of Manitoba, New Brunswick, and Prince Edward Island, was cut back in size in the 1930s.

As with any generalization, however, there clearly have been exceptions. Table 2.1 shows that Quebec, with a population less than two-thirds that of Ontario, has a larger assembly and has almost doubled its membership since Confederation. On the other hand, Ontario at the end of the twentieth century had only twenty-one MPPs more than it did in 1867. But that modest net increase in Ontario is misleading. It ignores the roller-coaster ride that Queen's Park has taken since Confederation, from a low of eighty-two members in 1871, to 112 in 1919, to ninety in 1934, then gradually to a high of 130 in 1987, and down to 103 at the century's end. Figure 2.1 shows that Ontario has changed the size of its legislature a total of fifteen times since Confederation, or on average once every seven years. That stands as a Canadian record.

Until the 1990s the changes in Ontario could be accounted for by an increase in the province's total population, the growth of its major urban centres, the failure to reduce the number of rural and remote seats to any significant degree, and the impact of a major economic depression. But in 1996 the government of Mike Harris introduced a new rationale for reducing the number of members elected – downsizing of government during times of economic expansion and population growth. As part of the cost-cutting measures contained in the newly elected Progressive Conservatives' "Common Sense Revolution," the Ontario legislature in 1996 approved a 21 percent reduction in its membership. At the same time, it avoided the expense of a redistribution of the province's constituencies by legislating that the boundaries recently established for the 103 federal ridings would also serve as the new provincial ones.

Table 2.1
Size of Federal, Provincial, and Territorial Assemblies, 1867–2000

Assembly and Date of Entry into Confederation	Size	
	At Time of First Election	2000
Canada (1867)	181	301
Ontario (1867)	82	103
Quebec (1867)	65	125
Nova Scotia (1867)	38	52
New Brunswick (1867)	41	55
Manitoba (1870)	24	57
British Columbia (1871)	25	75*
Prince Edward Island (1873)	30	27
Alberta (1905)	25	83
Saskatchewan (1905)	25	58
Newfoundland (1949)	28	48
Northwest Territories (1905)[†]	15[‡]	19
Yukon (1898)	10[‡]	17
Nunavut (1999)	19	19

Source: Canadian Parliamentary Guide 1998, and reports of the provincial chief electoral officers, 1999.
* To increase to seventy-nine seats at the time of the first British Columbia election following 1999.
[†] Reconstituted 1905, 1974 and 1999.
[‡] Until the election of the first legislative assemblies (1909 in the Yukon and 1975 in the Northwest Territories) the territories were governed by a smaller "council" that was both appointed and elected as well as a chief commissioner appointed by the federal government.

Figure 2.1
Size of Ontario Legislature, 1867–1999

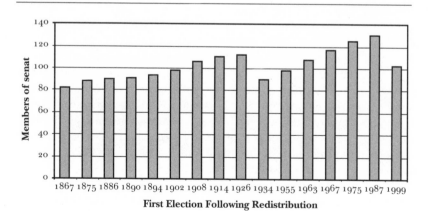

Source: Ontario, Chief Election Officer, *Election Returns with Statistics from the Records 1999*
(Toronto, 1999), xxxvii.

Ontario was not alone in reducing the size of its assembly. Several other provincial governments elected in the 1990s cut the number of members elected to their legislatures. Support for smaller legislatures was found in three different parties (Liberal, Conservative, and NDP) in various provincial capitals. The legislatures of Saskatchewan, New Brunswick, Newfoundland, and Prince Edward Island all accepted a reduction in their size, in some cases by up to 10 percent. In seeking re-election (unsuccessfully, as it turned out) the Conservative government of Manitoba in 1999 pledged to follow the lead of the other provinces and cut its legislature from fifty-seven to fifty-one members. The Conservative premier of Alberta mused publicly in 1999 about reducing the size of that province's legislature, and a legislative committee was appointed in Alberta to examine the issue. In January 2000 a study commissioned by the government of Saskatchewan found in a province-wide survey that opinion was split almost evenly between those who thought the province had "about the right number" of MLAs (45.3 percent) and those who believed there were "too many" MLAs (43.1 percent). The government took no action to reduce the number of MLAs from its current level of fifty-eight, which itself had been reduced from the previous sixty-four in the early 1990s by the new NDP government.[11]

British Columbia bucked the provincial trend of the 1990s by increasing the size of its legislature in its redistribution at the end of the decade. Aware that its proposal ran counter to the current mantra of "less government, not more," the British Columbia commission recommended (and the legislature accepted) increasing the legislature from seventy-five to seventy-nine members. The commission justified its move on the grounds of "preserving regional representation" and "accommodating [areas] of population growth." It was also determined to maintain a legislature with an odd number of seats to avoid the difficulties and uncertainties that face governments and legislatures when, as in Saskatchewan in 1999, an election leads to a tie in the results.[12]

The reduction in the size of provincial assemblies reflected the strength of the populist rhetoric that had become politically fashionable in the 1990s, perhaps best illustrated by the government downsizing agenda that had helped the Reform party achieve considerable success in the federal election of 1993. Advancing its case for sizable cost-cutting in the public sector, the Ontario Progressive Conservatives were blunt in their assessment of the public's current antagonism to politicians: "[Ontarians] have told us we have too many politicians."[13] The title given to Ontario's Fewer Politicians Act was carefully chosen to appeal to those who accepted the claim that legislative size is principally a function of cost.

The size of a legislative assembly has important implications. To be sure, costs should always be borne in mind, but size is not wholly a function of costs. A legislature's size bears directly on its capacity to function effectively and to represent the public interest. In Madison's words, a legislature must be large enough "to possess a due knowledge of the interests of its constituents," yet small enough "to avoid the confusion and intemperance of a multitude."[14]

In a parliamentary system such as Canada's, a critical mass of members is needed to ensure that a prime minister or a premier has a reasonable pool of possible ministers from which to construct a cabinet. Speakers, leaders of the opposition, whips, parliamentary or legislative secretaries, committee chairs, and others required to carry out the operation of parliamentary government add to the total number of members that ought to be elected. So too is there a need for a sufficient numbers of backbench members to staff committees and enable committee assignments and constituent business to be conducted with reasonable dispatch. If the number of backbench members on both sides of a house becomes too small, this can only contribute to the further centralization of power in the hands of the executive and reduce a legislature's capacity to review a cabinet's actions or influence its decisions.[15]

Another factor must be taken into account in any discussion of size of legislative assemblies. The plurality electoral system has a proven tendency when converting votes into seats to over-reward the winning party and to disadvantage (sometimes markedly so) the losing parties. It stands to reason that the larger an assembly the greater the likelihood that votes will be translated into seats equitably. *Reductio ad absurdum*, an assembly composed of every elector would be the most "representative" of the total population. The reverse will almost certainly be the case, given the demonstrated biases of the plurality electoral system. If legislative membership is to be chosen by the first-past-the-post system, elections to smaller assemblies are more likely to produce a greater measure of distortion in converting votes into seats. It is no coincidence that examples of Canadian legislatures in which every seat, or all but one or two seats, were captured by one party, characteristically with a popular vote in the 50 to 60 percent range, are drawn overwhelmingly from those with the smallest legislatures – the four in Atlantic Canada.[16]

John A. Macdonald was the only Father of Confederation to have addressed publicly the issue of the size of Canada's House of Commons. His preference was for a Commons larger than the one eventually decided upon for the 1867 election (181 members). His remarks linked important questions of politics to representation and argued against the two principal reasons often advanced in opposition to a larger legislature – its added costs and an insufficient supply of qualified members to serve in it:

I was in favour of a larger house ... but was overruled. I was perhaps singular in the opinion, but I thought it would be well to commence with a larger representation in the lower branch. The arguments against this were that, in the first place, it would cause additional expense; in the next place, that in a new country like this, we could not get a sufficient number of qualified men to be representatives. My reply was that the number is rapidly increasing as we increase in education and wealth; that a larger field would be open to political ambition by having a larger body of representatives; that by having numerous and smaller constituencies, more people would be interested in the working of the union; and that there would be a wider field for selection for leaders of governments and leaders of parties.[17]

Macdonald's remarks have a Madisonian quality about them. They display a considerable understanding of four factors essential to a healthy democracy: political ambition, citizen efficacy, participation in politics, and the functional needs of governments and political parties. They do not include costs.

CANADA'S FEDERAL REDISTRIBUTIONS

Nine federal decennial redistributions were carried out between 1872 and 1952. Without exception each was carefully managed by the government of the day, whether Conservative or Liberal, in its own interest. The great majority, especially the gerrymander of 1882, were partisan and blatantly self-serving affairs. A few, notably the 1952 exercise, were the work of a government-dominated parliamentary committee on which all parties in the House gained certain favours through a series of political trade-offs. Each redistribution was subjected to editorial and public criticism at the time and led opposition parties, not unexpectedly, to pledge to end the practice of partisan gerrymandering once in office. The history of promised (but subsequently undelivered) reforms to Canada's electoral boundary readjustment process is a long and not particularly honourable one. As the prominent Quebec Liberal MP Chubby Power described it in a Commons debate in 1939, the process of readjusting electoral boundaries in Canada amounted to "an unseemly, undignified and utterly confusing scramble for personal [and] political advantage."[18]

Although Canada's first nine federal redistributions amounted to little more than acts of political expediency, with the passage of time a certain number of "theories masquerading as principles" (in

Norman Ward's words) were concocted by governments, Commons committees, and individual MPs to justify their self-serving moves. By the mid-twentieth century some five "principles" had evolved which, in varying degrees, had been brought into play over the course of ninety years. County and town lines were to be preserved as electoral boundaries; party leaders' seats were to be left untouched; ridings might be added in areas of growing populations; urban constituencies were expected to contain larger populations than rural ones; and, however unfeasible this might be given the other constraints, representation was to be determined by population. The inherent contradictions of this grab-bag of rules proved to be no obstacle to successive governments who were armed with the power of the whip and a parliamentary majority.[19]

Canada's federal redistribution process developed over three stages that closely paralleled the three periods of party development identified by David E. Smith and R.K. Carty.[20] From Confederation to the First World War Canadian parties were characterized by their pervasive patronage and by a preoccupation with constituency politics and localism. That stage corresponded with the dominance of the prime minister and his closest political allies who micro-managed the details of the boundary readjustments between 1872 and the early 1900s.

From the early twentieth century to the mid-1950s, federal parties in Canada increasingly shifted their focus away from a preoccupation with the truly local to the provincial and regional arenas. In the process, the leader entrusted many major political decisions to powerful provincial and regional ministers. Coinciding as it did with the growth of regional protest movements, the emergence of new cleavages in the Canadian social fabric, and the arrival of additional parties in the federal Parliament, the new power structure prompted a more brokered style of management on issues that directly impacted on parties and elected members. That included electoral boundary adjustments. The government's approach to constituency redistributions was more accommodative than it had been previously, to the extent that special all-party committees of the Commons were charged with redrawing the maps. It was in those committees and their regional sub-committees that the real political "horse-trading" took place amongst the MPs from all parties.[21] As the governing party made certain that it maintained the chairmanship and its majority on those committees, the reforms from the first to the second phase of adjusting riding boundaries in Canada were more illusory than substantive. The only major difference between the two stages was that the pool of MPs taking part in what has been described as the unseemly and confusing scramble for political advantage had enlarged from those on one side of the House to both.

The third period of party development dated roughly from the late 1950s. It was again distinguished by the governing party's shift in political focus, this time from the region to the country as whole. Distinguished by a pan-Canadianism that began with John Diefenbaker and was furthered by Lester Pearson and Pierre Trudeau, the first decade of that stage was marked by an unprecedented five federal elections, four of which produced minority governments. Lacking an assured majority, no one party could, as in the past, single-handedly engineer an electoral boundary readjustment without first making major concessions to the opposition parties.

It was during this period that Parliament and parties alike accepted several reforms aimed generally at making the political process more democratic and accountable. Principal among the reforms was the federal election expenses legislation of 1974, which was aimed at controlling and partially subsidizing party financing. A decade earlier the national parties had begun adopting internal procedures, such as leadership review, in an effort to become more participatory, accountable, and open.[22] That spirit of intra-party openness, participation, and reform spilled over to include electoral boundary processes. Beginning in Manitoba in the 1950s and at the federal level in the 1960s, the responsibility for adjusting electoral boundaries was transferred by elected members from their own hands to those of independent electoral boundary commissions. That reform gradually spread to other provinces in the ensuing years.

The possibility of taking redistributions out of the hands of politicians and of turning them over to an independent body had surfaced periodically in Canadian history, only to be lost again in a government's rush to play the partisan card once the opportunity presented itself. The idea of entrusting electoral redistributions to an "independent authority of judges" had first appeared in the initial draft of the 1864 Quebec Resolutions. But once it became clear to the politicians that they would forfeit a seemingly valuable opportunity to influence electoral outcomes, it gave way to section 51 of the Constitution Act (1867) which delegated to Parliament the power to fix the number of MPs to be elected from each province. It did not, however, go the next logical step and determine how boundary readjustments of parliamentary seats were to be carried out *within* the provinces once their decennial entitlement was established. The entire constitution was silent on that point.[23]

Almost every decade in the first half of the twentieth century saw some prominent politician calling for the transfer of the responsibility for decennial redistributions to independent commissions. The list included Robert Borden in 1903, Mackenzie King in 1919, Stanley

Knowles and John Diefenbaker in the 1940s, and George Drew in 1952. Their parties may have been different (Conservative, Liberal, and CCF), but these political notables shared one trait in common: they were all on the opposition benches when they called for reform of the electoral boundary readjustment process. Unless they chose to carry through on their promises once they gained office, history was bound to repeat itself.[24]

At the provincial level, electoral boundary readjustments fared no better. In fact they suffered a worse fate. Without constitutional requirements similar to those spelled out in section 51 for the Parliament of Canada, the provinces were under no obligation to readjust the boundaries of their legislative assemblies at regular intervals. As a consequence, redistributions in a province, if they were held at all, were often decades apart. The ineluctable shifts in populations meant that the long delays between redistributions had the effect of increasing the disparity in the populations of provincial constituencies. When they did occur, redistributions were invariably under the control of the governing party and were frequently introduced in the legislature without prior consultation with the opposition parties. Biases against urban and in favour of rural voters were common to all provinces; they varied only in the degree of their discrimination. Given the legislative majorities that provincial governments typically enjoyed, the approval of a government-sponsored bill by a legislature (often on division and over the objections of the opposition) was a foregone conclusion. As was the case federally, provincial politicians calling for reform of the redistribution system were found exclusively on the opposition benches, and editorialists and academics urging the adoption of non-partisan boundary readjustment commissions received no support among the governing elites.[25]

ALLOTTING SEATS IN PARLIAMENT TO THE PROVINCES

As noted, section 51 of the Constitution Act, 1867 granted Parliament the exclusive power to determine the number of seats to which each province or territory would be entitled. Initially the number of MPs from Quebec was set at sixty-five, with the number from the other provinces determined by the ratio of their population to Quebec's. The plan was designed to appeal to Quebec, by guaranteeing the province the same number of seats that it had had in the pre-Confederation Assembly of the United Canadas, as well as to the rest of Canada, in that the eventual addition of new provinces and probable growth in population outside Quebec would be reflected in a Commons with a gradually increasing membership.

The formula that was put in place in 1867 for redistributing the seats among the provinces and, as a consequence, for determining the overall size of the Commons lasted until 1946, at which time it was replaced by one that capped the Commons at 255 members. In its failure to anticipate future population patterns, the 1867 formula had produced some anomalies. Even though their population increased in absolute terms, the smallest provinces (all in the Maritimes) grew at a relatively slower rate than other parts of the country. As a result, from one redistribution to the next they continued to get fewer commons seats in relation to the total house membership. Nova Scotia, for example, slipped from twenty-one of 206 seats (10.5 percent) in the Commons in the early 1870s to twelve of 245 seats (4.9 percent) sixty years later. Ontario, like the three Maritime provinces, also continued to increase in population in the first half of the twentieth century and grew at a slower rate than both Quebec and Western Canada. But unlike the Maritime provinces, Ontario's number of seats in the House did not decline. Norman Ward explained this paradox:

The one-twentieth clause [contained in the BNA Act (1867)] had saved the province a steady 82 seats since 1914. The operation of this clause was such that unless the population of a province declined [by] one-twentieth *within the ten years between each census*, the province suffered no loss of seats. Ontario's population, although on the increase, was nevertheless becoming a progressively smaller fraction of the total for the country. Yet for several decades it remained within the limits set within the BNA Act, so that Ontario's representation remained unchanged. Strict representation by population would have reduced Ontario's quota of seats to 81 in 1924, to 78 in 1933 [and to 74 in 1946]. If this trend had continued another few decades, Quebec would have been faced with the interesting but disturbing picture of a population equal to or greater than Ontario's, but a representation of sixty-five seats, as compared with eighty-two. The demand for fair representation, which had been so familiar a cry in the mouths of Upper Canadian statesmen before Confederation, was logically taken over in 1946 by Quebec.[26]

The capping of the House in the 1940s replaced one set of anomalies with another and added further proof of the difficulty of forecasting shifts in population over any extended period. Had the 1946 formula not then been replaced by another one in the 1970s, five provinces would have lost seats in the post-1971 census redistribution in spite of their increased population, and two others, Ontario and British Columbia, would have received the same number of additional seats even though Ontario's growth had been three times that of

British Columbia's. James Mallory reflected a widely shared sentiment at the time: "Almost any change [would be] a change for the better."[27]

The plan adopted by Parliament in 1974 was designed to ensure no further loss of seats for slow-growth provinces. Called the Amalgam Method, the scheme grouped the provinces according to three categories of population size. As with the descriptive categories in "Goldilocks and the Three Bears," they were labelled small, medium, and large. The majority of provinces fell in the first category, Alberta and British Columbia in the second, and Quebec and Ontario in the third. Quebec was pegged at a fixed number of MPs (seventy-five) and was to increase by four additional members with each subsequent redistribution. Large provinces (by 1981 British Columbia had joined the other two in that category) were to have their entitlement determined by the ratio of their population to Quebec's. No province was to be assigned fewer seats at a redistribution than it had had following the previous one and no province was to have fewer seats than a province with a smaller population. The number of seats for the Yukon and Northwest Territories was fixed at one and two respectively. Two of the critics of the scheme viewed it as "fundamentally bad," a "crazy-quilt of ad hoc recipes, loose ends, and exceptions" which "conceals grave defects" and "violates the common sense of fair division."[28]

Not surprisingly, the Amalgam Method was abandoned in the 1980s when MPs learned how wide of the mark they had been a decade earlier in anticipating the impact of changes in lifestyle, interprovincial population movements, and immigrant settlement patterns. The Amalgam Method had been predicated on, among other things, the assumptions that Quebec's population would continue to increase at approximately the same rate as it had in the past and that its four additional seats per decade would more or less match its share of the projected growth in Canada's total population. These assumptions proved to be false in that they missed three demographic changes that were already underway in the 1970s: the reversal of Quebec's birth rate from the highest in the country to the lowest, high interprovincial mobility, and the decline in immigration to Quebec relative to that of most other provinces, principally Ontario and British Columbia.

The population projections on which the seat redistribution policy was based were correct at the macro level but markedly wrong at the micro level. The 1971 projections had rightly forecast the country's total 1981 population to within 200,000 people. But on the intra-provincial level, notably in Quebec and Alberta, they were well wide of the mark. The projections for Quebec were over the actual population by approximately 600,000, and for Alberta they were under by roughly the same number. The effect of these miscalculations on the likely size of the Commons after the redistribution of the 1980s was obvious. Instead of increasing by twelve members, as had seemed likely when the Amalgam Method was adopted in 1974, the House would have jumped by twenty-eight in the 1980s from 282 to 310 members. If Quebec's relatively slow population growth compared with that of the next three largest provinces were to continue, and if its automatic increase of four Commons seats with every redistribution were retained, projections showed a Commons of at least 369 members by 2001. This calculation jarred the newly elected Conservative government and led it to usher through Parliament yet another method for determining the size of the House.[29]

Neither the MPs nor the public wanted such an increase that would have resulted from the application of the Amalgam Method. Thus for the third time since the end of the Second World War, the scheme for establishing seat entitlements in the House of Commons was changed. Legislation enacted in 1985 approved the redistribution method that remains in existence in the early twenty-first century.[30] The calculation, as noted earlier in this chapter, is based on dividing a fixed number of seats among the provinces. That number was set at 282 (the base number of the previous Amalgam Method) less one seat for the Yukon and two for the Northwest Territories. (With its creation in 1999, Nunavut was granted one of the two Northwest Territories' seats). A grandfather clause ensures that no province will receive fewer seats than it had at the 1976 redistribution or in the 33rd Parliament (1984–8), whichever is less.

Together with the "senatorial floor" constitutional amendment of 1915 (subsequently entrenched in the Charter in 1982) which ensured that no province would have fewer MPs than it had senators, these two special clauses had the effect in the redistribution of the 1990s of granting seven provinces a total of twenty seats more than to which their population entitled them. Prince Edward Island and Saskatchewan were the biggest beneficiaries of this provision relative to their entire provincial allotment, with three and four "add-on" seats respectively. Only Ontario, British Columbia, and Alberta had their seat entitlement determined solely on the basis of population. Rather than fashioning a House of 282 members, the formula with the various add-on clauses led to the creation of one with 301 members in the redistribution of the 1990s.[31] (See table 2.2 for the redistribution of Commons seats based on the 1991 census.)

Should there be any move to adopt a new formula for allocating Commons' seats (a move that the history of the post-Second World War

Table 2.2
General and Partial Redistributions of the House of Commons, 1867–1996

Year	Canada	Ont.	Que.	NS.	NB.	Man.	BC.	PEI.	Sask.	Alta.	NFLD.	Yukon NWT Nunavut
1867	181	82	65	19	15							
1871*	185	82	65	19	15	4						
1872	200	88	65	21	16	4	6					
1873*	206	88	65	21	16	4	6	6				
1882	211	92	65	21	16	5	6	6				
1887*	215	92	65	21	16	5	6	6				4
1892	213	92	65	20	14	7	6	5				4
1903	214	86	65	18	13	10	7	4				11
1907*	221	86	65	18	13	10	7	4	10	7		1
1914	234	82	65	16	11	15	13	3	16	12		1
1915*	235	82	65	16	11	15	13	4	16	12		1
1924	245	82	65	14	11	17	14	4	21	16		1
1933	245	82	65	12	10	17	16	4	21	17		1
1947	255	83	73	13	10	16	18	4	20	17		1
1949*	262	83	73	13	10	16	18	4	20	17	7	1
1952	265	85	75	12	10	14	22	4	17	17	7	2
1966	264	88	74	11	10	13	23	4	13	19	7	2
1976	282	95	75	11	10	14	28	4	14	21	7	3
1987	295	99	75	11	10	14	32	4	14	26	7	3
1996	301	103	75	11	10	14	34	4	14	26	7	3

Source: Adapted from Elections Canada, "Representation in the Federal Parliament" (Ottawa), 4.
* Partial redistributions occasioned by special circumstances such as addition of territory.

period suggests cannot be ruled out), that would entail as a minimum changes to the 1985 statute. But more than legislative changes would be required if the guarantees contained in the senatorial floor provision were to be altered or, for that matter, if the Senate were to be abolished or if there were changes to the number of senators to which the provinces were entitled. In each of those instances, a constitutional amendment would be required governed by the unanimity rules of section 41 of the Constitution Act, 1982. The amending formula that was added to Canada's constitution in 1982 included the senatorial floor guarantee as one of the five subjects requiring the unanimous approval of Parliament and of all ten provincial legislatures before it could be changed. Could such approval be obtained when the agreement of two provinces whose House entitlement has long been protected by the senatorial floor (Prince Edward Island and New Brunswick) would be needed? Highly unlikely, barring some major political and representational trade-offs.

CONTRASTING FEDERAL
REPRESENTATIONAL INSTITUTIONS

The contrasting experience of Canada and the United States in the apportionment and design of seats for their respective federal units speaks to the ways in which reapportionment and redistricting have evolved in different countries. The American approach to reapportionment of electoral districts among the fifty states underscores a commitment to balancing federalism and representation, with the emphasis on the latter once the constitutional obligation in the assignment of the minimum number of seats has been met. That is less the case in Canada, where special treatment of small and declining population provinces has long been a feature of the reapportionment formula and has effectively led to the creation of districts of much greater population variance than would be allowed since the 1960s, by the courts in the United States. Like other countries attempting to balance representational and territorial factors in their periodic reapportionment/redistricting exercise, these two countries have found an acceptable compromise that would be seen as out of place were it introduced in the other.

Why have Canada and the United States treated the redistribution and reapportionment aspect of legislative representation so differently? Why has Congress remained committed to the principle that population must serve as the basis for allocating seats amongst the states, whereas Parliament has sanctioned moves in the opposite direction? The answers are no doubt complex and rooted deeply in the representational values that are expressed from time to time in court decisions, statutes, and constitutional amendments that result from exhaustive judicial, parliamentary, and congressional arguments. One of the striking differences between the two countries on the matter of representation in the Commons and the House of Representatives is found in the kinds of reapportionment topics debated in the respective legislatures. In Canada the question invariably comes down to the relative weight to be attached to territory as opposed to population and the perceived need to protect those provinces with smaller or declining populations or with large sparsely-populated regions. In the United States the focus tends to be on the accuracy of the Census Bureau's counts, especially in large metropolitan areas, and on the likely impact that population shifts will have on party strengths in the House of Representatives and on the distribution of electoral college votes. Population is at the core of both kinds of debates, of course, but it is approached from different perspectives and used to defend different political and representational interests.[32]

Two possible reasons are worth exploring to account for the contrasting approaches that Canadians and Americans have taken to reapportioning the seats among their provinces and states. The first relates to the relative size and number of units being represented, and the second to the presence of another elected chamber constructed so as to give equal weight to all federal units.

Canadians have long been accustomed to representational protection being granted to provinces with allegedly special needs. "Rep. by pop." may have been one of the rallying cries in Upper Canada in the 1860s, but within a few years of Confederation exceptions were made to that principle when the first new provinces were admitted. Exceptional treatment on a case-by-case basis were inevitably repeated on later occasions. From 1870 to 1949 every new province received more seats (sometimes by a factor of three) than it would have been awarded through a strict application of a population-based formula. As Norman Ward has noted, "initial representation in parliament [has always been] considered one of the negotiable terms of entry."[33] But the entry-level exceptions were only the first of many. They were joined by the one-twentieth clause of the Constitution Act, 1867; the senatorial floor guarantee of 1915; the 15 percent amendment of 1952 (adopted to cut back on Saskatchewan's projected loss of seats from five to three); the 1952 provision foreclosing any possibility of a province having fewer seats than any other province with a smaller population; and the grandfather clause introduced in the 1970s. Since 1867 not a single province has ever failed to qualify for protection against loss of seats under at least one of the special categories that have been created purely on an ad hoc basis to address some particular representational claim of the moment. Typically it has been the smallest provinces that have been the most frequently and the most generously protected.

No equivalent rabbit-warren of representational protection exists in the United States. The closest that Americans have come to addressing similar sorts of reapportionment issues is to debate periodically the relative merits of various formulas that might be used to determine the number of seats awarded each state. But even at that level, as one of the most authoritative works on the subject makes clear, the debate concerns a possible reallocation of only small numbers of electoral districts.[34] In contrast to Canada, concerns in the United States about relatively or absolutely declining state populations or about the impact of population shifts do not lead to legislated or constitutional protection for affected states.[35]

It could be that the seemingly widespread consensus amongst members of Congress on the continuation of the existing floor of one seat per state, and on a reasonably evenhanded redistribution of remaining seats according to population, owes much to the large number of units affected (fifty) and to the small number of districts available for reapportionment (385). The mathematics of any protectionist scenario, either legislated or in a constitutional amendment, would no doubt effectively rule out any realistic chance of sufficient support being marshalled behind any one proposal. Canada faces no similar difficulty. With a substantially larger number of seats on a per capita basis than the United States, one-fifth the number of federal units, an adjustable House membership, and two-thirds of the seats in only two provinces, Canada's approach to reapportionment has been to forego adherence to any permanent formula in favour of particular responses each decade to the demographic and political pressures of the moment. With the passage of time, the cumulative effect of such ad hockery on the allocation of seats among the provinces has been to offend increasingly the principle of representation by population.

But it is equally true that, given the federal structure and membership complement of the American Senate, it would be impossible to mount any serious campaign in the United States to increase the share of seats in the House of Representatives allotted to the smaller states. Expressed another way, the egalitarian federal composition of the American Senate must, by definition, make it easier than it would be otherwise to justify adhering as closely as possible to the principle of representation by population for decennial reapportionments of the House's 435 seats.

The reverse is almost certainly the case in Canada. The absence of a politically-salient upper house composed from the outset of equal numbers of members from each province has had the effect of transferring part of the federal representational task to the House of Commons. This, in turn, has helped to make more persuasive any arguments (stretching back to the senatorial floor amendment of 1915) in support of guaranteed floors far in excess of what strict population figures would award. In the early 1980s, for example, the Canadian equivalent to Alaska (assuredly not in land area) was Prince Edward Island. Both had their respective country's smallest population, yet Prince Edward Island had four times more Commons seats than Alaska had in the larger House of Representatives.

Without its inflated Commons membership, Prince Edward Island's parliamentary presence (reduced as it would be to one seat) would be barely noticeable. With it, however, the province has come to expect (depending, of course, on the political mix of its MPs at the time) that one of its members will serve in the cabinet in Ottawa and will act as the province's federal presence at the executive level. That the same would be true of all provinces because of the federal structure of the country and the concentration of power in a parliamentary system in the hands of the political executive was an anticipated outcome as far back as the debates on the constitutional arrangements under Confederation. During the Confederation debates in Quebec in 1865, Christopher Dunkin, Legislative Assembly member for Brome, voiced strong criticisms of the design of the proposed Senate. His prediction about the role of the cabinet as the federally important institution is worth noting, for it proved in the event to be remarkably accurate:

I have to ask [the] honorable gentlemen opposite how they are going to organize their Cabinet, for these provinces, according to this so-called Federal scheme? I think I may defy them to show that the Cabinet can be formed on any other principle than that of a representation of the several provinces in that Cabinet. It is admitted that the provinces are not really represented to any Federal intent in the Legislative Council [Senate]. The Cabinet here must discharge all that kind of function, which in the United States is performed, in the Federal sense, by the Senate.[36]

CONCLUSIONS

There are clearly no universally accepted rules governing the size of legislative assemblies and the number of representational building-blocks to be created. Each jurisdiction has evolved its own particular representative institution and its own rules governing its construction. Even though a number of such bodies may, in a manner of speaking, have sprung from the same source (as with Commonwealth parliaments fashioned in some way on the Westminster model), each has assumed its own distinctive character. The size of a legislature or parliament can be dictated by constitutional requirements, or it may be the product of a periodic statutory recrafting of the relevant formulas. In either case, the debate surrounding the size of an assembly and the apportionment of its seats can become a highly-charged political one.

The number of members in Canada's Parliament is a product of both constitutional and legislative requirements. Through almost the entire twentieth century, Canada's parliamentarians did not hesitate to change the redistribution formula in response to pressures aimed at shoring up a province's entitlement to parliamentary seats. In so doing, they succeeded either in postponing or reducing a province's projected loss of seats or in protecting in perpetuity all provinces from ever falling below an agreed-upon minimum. In both cases the moves came at the expense of the "one person, one vote" principle. Table 2.3 shows that the average population of federal ridings created in Prince Edward Island and Ontario (the two most extreme provincial

Table 2.3
1985 Redistribution Formula Using the 1991 Census

Province or Territory	Number of seats Established in 1976 and Constituting 33rd Parliament[1]	Population 1991	National Quotient[2]	Rounded Result	Special Clauses[3]	Total	Electoral Quotient
Newfoundland	7	568,474	97,532	6	1	7	81,211
Prince Edward Island	4	129,765	97,532	1	3	4	32,441
Nova Scotia	11	899,942	97,532	9	2	11	81,813
New Brunswick	10	723,900	97,532	7	3	10	72,390
Quebec	75	6,895,963	97,532	71	4	75	91,946
Ontario	95	10,084,885	97,532	103	–	103	97,912
Manitoba	14	1,091,942	97,532	11	3	14	77,996
Saskatchewan	14	988,928	97,532	10	4	14	70,638
Alberta	21	2,545,553	97,532	26	–	26	97,906
British Columbia	28	3,282,061	97,532	34	–	34	96,531
Northwest Territories[4]	1	34,500	–	–	–	1	–
Nunavut[5]	1	23,149	–	–	–	1	–
Yukon Territory	1	27,797	–	–	–	1	–
TOTAL	282	27,296,859	–	–	–	301	–

Source: Adapted from Elections Canada, *Representation in the Federal Parliament* (Ottawa, 1993), 17. Modified to include Nunavut and a reconstituted Northwest Territories, 1 April 1999.

[1] Assign two seats to then Northwest Territories and one to the Yukon Territory (three seats). As of 1999 this was changed to one Yukon, one Northwest Territories, and one Nunavut seat.

[2] Use 279 seats and population of provinces to establish national quotient $(27,211,413 \div 279 = 97,532)$.

[3] Add seats to provinces pursuant to "senatorial clause" guarantee in the constitution and the grandfather clause.

[4] The 1991 NWT population of 57,649 was allocated to the NWT and Nunavut according to their respective portions of the total territorial population in 1991.

[5] Created in 1999 from former Northwest Territories.

examples of the 1990s) varied by a factor of three. In this respect the interpretation that Canada has given to its federal and representative systems distinguishes it from that of the United States.

Canada has two provinces (Ontario and Quebec) that are centrally located, share a boundary in common, and account for some 60 percent of the country's total population. There is no equivalent to that in the United States, where the combined population total of the two largest states (California and Texas) accounts for 20 percent of all

Americans. The domination of central Canada (long the target of complaints from disgruntled Canadians in other provinces) adds a unique dynamic to Canada's federal representational concerns that is not present in the United States. Canadian provinces are far fewer in number and have considerably greater variation among their population than their American counterparts. This lends support to a small province's arguments about the need to prevent sharp drops, and no drops beyond a certain point, in its parliamentary entitlement.[37]

Quebec benefits along with the smaller provinces from the various floors guaranteeing parliamentary representation. That province's gradual demographic decline (now below 25 percent of Canada's total population) has been attenuated by the representational floors. Quebec's present level of 75 seats can, of course, be modified by Parliament in the future, but the political pressures against doing so can be expected to remain strong. Quebec could reasonably expect support in any fight against the change from the other six provinces that benefit from representational floors. While the rules no longer use Quebec as the base for establishing the Commons' size and the entitlement of the other provinces (as they did from 1867 to 1946 and 1974 to 1985), Quebec nonetheless retains a pivotal role in determining that entitlement because of the potentially negative political consequences for any federal governing party choosing to alter the formula.

Given the role that the Canadian cabinet plays as the country's principal federal representational institution, there is little likelihood that the floors that are in place guaranteeing minimum Commons representation to the provinces will be abandoned in the foreseeable future. The potential political costs would almost certainly dissuade any government from removing or reducing the protection offered by the grandfather clause. That floor currently protects seven provinces, including the second largest, and the consequences of ending the "special status" that those seven provinces enjoy in their parliamentary representation would no doubt be feared as being too great. For its part, the 1915 senatorial floor is now entrenched in the constitution. The acceptance of the unanimity amendment provision (section 41) of the Constitution Act, 1982, meant that the consent of all provincial legislatures and of both houses of Parliament would be needed to alter or to abandon the senatorial floor guarantee for Commons representation. It is impossible to conceive of any of the smaller provinces agreeing to end their inflated protection of parliamentary seats when that helps to ensure their presence at the federal cabinet table.

Canada's experience with a series of redistribution formulas underscores the problematic nature of forecasting demographic changes and the precise impact that those changes will have on the future size of the House of Commons. The same can be said of forecasts of intra-provincial population shifts which, though clearly not of the same magnitude as the federal ones, can nonetheless affect the future size of a provincial legislature. Cutting back on the number of members elected to provincial legislatures became part of the populist rhetoric that contributed to shaping the political agenda of the 1990s. It reflected an "anti-politician" sentiment that was used to considerable effect by some politicians and its timing was propitious. It proved to be an opportune moment to embrace the cause of legislative down-sizing, even though the possibly negative consequences of such a move were, at least publicly, barely acknowledged.

3 Institutional Role-Modelling: Canada's First Provincial Electoral Boundaries Commissions

Tradition means giving votes to the most obscure of all classes – our ancestors. It is the democracy of the dead.

– G.K. Chesterton, 1908

A distinguishing feature of federalism is its capacity to enable one jurisdiction to try out institutional arrangements or processes different from those of other jurisdictions. James Bryce, then British ambassador to the United States, noted over a century ago in his classic study of American government that

federalism enables a people to try experiments in legislation and administration which could not be safely tried in a large centralized county. A comparatively small commonwealth like an American State easily makes and unmakes its laws; mistakes are not serious, for they are soon corrected; other States profit by the experience of a law or a method which has worked well or ill in the State that has tried it.[1]

Federalism encourages copy-cats once an institutional experiment wins favourable notice. When the reform of one order of government is judged to have worked successfully, to have gained a measure of public approval, or to be appropriate to circumstances in other jurisdictions, a kind of institutional contagion comes into play. The "diffusion of innovations" studies in political science lend solid empirical support to Bryce's comment. In both the United States and Canada reforms adopted in one jurisdiction characteristically have made their way into others. An analysis of dozens of public policies in Canada confirms that, from medicare to snowmobile regulations, a single provincial legislature has been the first to introduce an idea only to find that in time it has made its way to other jurisdictions in the federal system.[2]

Canadian experience with a number of electoral and representational reforms can also be explained by the diffusion of innovations theory. Twentieth-century Canadian history demonstrated that it was the individual provinces that played the principal role of initiator of electoral and representational experiments that were later adopted at both the federal and provincial levels. For example, for the first two decades of the twentieth century, parties in several provinces (most notably Ontario) broke with the previous practice of allowing legislative caucuses to chose their leaders. They turned that task over to more "representative" and "democratic" conventions composed largely of constituency delegates. In 1919 the Liberals, and in 1927 the Conservatives, followed suit, ushering in the first of many leadership conventions by federal parties in the twentieth century.[3]

In a second instance, Quebec's 1963 legislation to control party and election financing predated steps later taken by the government of Lester Pearson and the Barbeau Committee it appointed to recommend a plan. That committee admitted to being greatly influenced by the Quebec election expenses law and accepted it as the basis for the federal plan. Once in place, this plan, in turn, was later replicated in significant respects by a number of provinces.[4]

Finally, beginning in the late 1980s, several provincial political parties experimented with some variant of a one-person one-vote system of direct election of their leader. The lessons drawn from the provincial experiments with direct democracy for leadership selection (especially those of the Ontario Liberals and the Alberta Conservatives) were deemed a success by party organizers and the media and were instrumental in leading the federal parties (including, most recently, the Canadian Alliance) to put in place some form of a universal membership vote for choosing their leaders.[5]

In each of these examples, institutional changes that in the first instance had been put in place provincially ushered in similar representational reforms in other provinces as well as at the federal level.

MANITOBA POINTS THE WAY

This "role-modelling" made possible by federalism plays a part in the eventual acceptance in Canada of the idea of independent electoral boundary readjustments. A decade before Parliament or any other provincial legislature legislated a process for redistributing constituencies impartially, Manitoba became the first Canadian jurisdiction to establish a system whereby periodic, independent, arms-length redistributions of electoral districts would be guaranteed. Why that province at that time? A confluence of three political developments set the stage for all-party approval in the provincial legislature in 1955 of the establishment of independent electoral boundary commissions: glaring voter inequities resulting from a history of government-controlled redistributions; reform-oriented and innovative opposition parties pushing a novel idea; and a measure of public and political dissatisfaction with the proportional representation and alternative vote electoral systems then used for provincial elections.

The irregular redistributions carried out in Manitoba since its creation as a province in 1870 had been controlled, as had long been the practice federally and in all other provinces, by the party in power. In Manitoba's case, this effectively meant that the maps were drawn by government-dominated legislative committees. For the first decade or so after 1870, the constituency boundaries for Manitoba's twenty-four-member legislative assembly had been drawn to conform to parish lines to ensure equal representation to the province's French and English population. But the demographic changes that took place in the late nineteenth and early twentieth centuries brought Manitoba's linguistic duality to an end and introduced new elements to the exercise of designing electoral boundaries. The most obvious of these was partisan gerrymandering.[6]

The rapid growth of Manitoba's non-francophone population, the arrival of immigrant settlers (many from eastern Europe) to establish homesteads and towns in the southern third of the province, and the substantial increase, both in size and ethnic complexity, of metropolitan Winnipeg changed the linguistic and social composition of the province dramatically. Governments responded by courting the farm vote and by allocating a disproportionate number of electoral districts to the non-urban part of the province. The rule of thumb that was followed by legislative committees in designing electoral maps was simple: for every elector in a rural seat there would be two in an urban one.[7] The distinction between rural and urban electors in Manitoba was never more pronounced than in the early 1950s when the province's 228,280 urban voters were represented by seventeen members in the legislature and the 224,083 in rural Manitoba by forty members.[8] Understandably, the opposition labelled the redistribution in 1949 (the first in the province in twenty-nine years and the last before the switch to independent redistributions) an "old-fashioned gerrymander"[9] based on political "selfishness" and partisan "horse trading."[10]

The opposition not only opposed, they also proposed. This in turn provides the second reason for the move to independent commissions. In an editorial published at the time of the debate surrounding the 1949 redistribution the *Winnipeg Free Press* attacked the continued "denial of the principle of representation by population" and advanced a novel proposal (at least by Canadian standards at the time) for the establishment of a non-partisan, independent commission to ensure that the task was no longer entrusted to a "weighted and compromised committee of the legislature."[11] Nothing further was heard of the idea until three years later when the CCF introduced a resolution calling for the removal of electoral redistributions from partisan politics and entrusting the matter of designing constituencies to "impartial and disinterested persons" who would constitute an independent commission. Although the motion failed, the idea it advanced quickly caught on. The provincial Tories made non-partisan redistributions part of their election platform in 1953; the press gave the suggestion a good deal of favourable coverage; and various civic organizations in Winnipeg endorsed the principle of independent electoral redistributions. By 1954 the premier, D.L. Campbell, had been convinced that Manitoba's entire electoral system of designing constituency boundaries should be referred to an all-party legislative committee for review. The premier and the attorney general signalled the importance they attached to the work of the committee by becoming members of it.[12]

The report issued by the Special Select Committee on Redistribution after more than a year of hearings, research, and debate set the stage for the province's move to independent electoral boundary commissions. The committee clearly did its homework. It consulted books on representation, redistributions, and electoral systems by two noted political scientists of the time, England's David Butler and Canada's Norman Ward. Members corresponded directly with elected officials in other Commonwealth countries. Among them was Australia's prime minister, Robert Menzies, who provided a detailed account of the independent electoral boundary readjustment process that had operated in Australia since 1902. Manitoba's chief electoral officer prepared several background papers on redistributions in other jurisdictions, and written submissions were received by the committee from over a dozen private groups or organizations and a number of interested individuals. The points made in the various submissions and at the hearings differed in their particulars, but the contributions spoke with unanimity on one issue – the need to get electoral boundary redistributions out of the hands of a government-dominated committee and into those of an independent, non-partisan commission.[13]

Among those who prepared a brief for the committee were two respected members of the faculty of the University of Manitoba, historian W.L. Morton and political scientist Murray Donnelly, whose joint contribution appears to have carried considerable weight with the committee. Its basic premise was that "representation by population should be the basis of electoral divisions," but that population should not be the only factor to be considered when seats were designed. Equally important were "community or diversity of interest, means of communication and physical features." Australian experience throughout the twentieth century had demonstrated, they concluded, that all of these factors could be brought into the boundary readjustment exercise successfully. To remove the possibility of partisan gerrymandering, Australia also showed that the entire process could be handled by small non-partisan commissions made up of judges and such senior government officials as the chief electoral officer and the surveyor general.[14]

The legislative committee linked its examination of alternative redistribution schemes to an assessment of the province's electoral system, and herein lies the third, and arguably the most important, reason for the move to reform the process of drawing electoral boundaries. Manitoba, along with Alberta (between 1926 and 1956) and British Columbia (1952 and 1953), had experimented with non-plurality voting systems for provincial elections. Legislation was approved in 1920 establishing the single transferable vote (STV) for electing Winnipeg's ten MLAs from a single city-wide constituency. The alternative vote was added in 1927 to elect the remaining MLAs from single-member districts in the rest of the province. These preferential vote schemes were adopted in a flurry of post-First World War reforms that swept across Ontario and Western Canada. They were aimed at building a more democratic and participatory society and at eliminating the excessive organizational control commonly associated with the established political parties. By the early 1920s, reforming Manitoba's electoral system had become a key element in the Progressive and United Farmers' movements, was supported strongly by farm and labour organizations, and was championed by the influential *Winnipeg Free Press*.[15]

But Manitoba's experiment with electoral reform was not to last. After more than thirty years of coalition governments, Manitoba "politicians of all stripes were [critical of] PR as the main barrier to single-party majority government."[16] In Winnipeg the criticisms levelled at the proportional representation scheme, as well as the calls for a more openly competitive party system, were particularly strong. That city's method of electing MLAs from multi-member ridings had fallen into "disrepute"[17] for three principal reasons: inequality of populations among the ridings; fierce fights among candidates of the same party for election in the multi-member seats; and an allegedly widespread impression that multi-member districts did not encourage the close contacts between elected members and voters that single-member districts were claimed to foster. The first had nothing to do with the electoral system per se, for equal distribution of voters can as easily take place among multi-member constituencies as single-member ones; the second and third are criticisms frequently levelled at electoral systems in which a number of members are simultaneously elected from one multi-member district.

The extraneous, though nonetheless politically potent, argument mounted against STV in Winnipeg was based on the principle of electoral fairness. Quite simply, the number of provincial MLAs elected from metropolitan Winnipeg had not kept abreast of the city's growth in population. When in 1949 only fourteen of the fifty-seven provincial seats were allotted the area that contained roughly one-half of the province's total population, civic groups, newspapers, labour, and business leaders called for an end to STV and a return to single member, simple plurality vote elections based on a more equitable distribution of seats to population. Those in favour of enhanced voter equality linked the number of members of the provincial legislature allotted the metropolitan area to their attack on the electoral system. The connection that they successfully established between a reformed electoral system and a greater measure of voter equality gave the politicians and the press a powerful argument in favour of non-partisan reviews of constituency boundaries.

The two standard criticisms of proportional representation schemes were, like the issue of unequal populations in urban and rural districts, linked to a call to return to the pre-STV system of single-member districts and straight plurality voting. Parties were described as indulging in domestic squabbling during election campaigns under proportional representation, with candidates of the same party fighting "more fiercely among themselves than with the enemy."[18] For their part, voters who lived in multi-member districts were said to have been disadvantaged by being prevented from having closer relationships with an MLA and from "pointing to one of the ... members" as their own.[19] In its brief to the legislative committee studying electoral boundary readjustments to Manitoba, the Winnipeg Chamber of Commerce argued:

Whatever the merits of proportional representation may be, the fact remains that it is impossible for the individual voter in these constituencies to recognize any member of the Legislature as his particular representative. For the Member himself, the effort to maintain contacts with his constituents is beyond the time and ability of most men and the expense of conducting a campaign among such a large number of voters becomes unreasonable. It is perhaps significant that these constituencies have about the lowest voting percentages in the Province. Add to this the fact that in many cases a candidate's running mate often is a greater obstacle to election than his opposition and you have a very practical reason for careful consideration of the abandonment of this Proportional Representation System.[20]

The chamber concluded its brief by recommending decennial redistributions based on census data, the adherence "as closely as possible" to representation by population, and legislation establishing a process whereby a committee of three judges could independently design electoral boundaries.[21]

The case for removing electoral redistributions from the hands of the politicians and turning it over to an independent commission was a compelling one. Winnipeg's unequal treatment in legislative representation combined with the level of dissatisfaction with the electoral system provided two key ingredients for the shift. But the critical variable was the strong support that the principle of independent commissions received from the political elite, specifically the premier, (D.L. Campbell), the opposition leader, (Duff Roblin) and the ccF leader, (Lloyd Stinson). Had the politicians been unwilling to relinquish the control they had long enjoyed over determining the shape and size of the electoral districts, and had they chosen not to play the leading role in advocating change, the reform would not have been implemented. In this instance the public interest supplanted electoral self-interest because the politicians themselves were convinced that the time had come to bring to an end an old and long-discredited practice. The committee and legislative records made it clear that, in Mr Stinson's words, "the main objective of establishing an independent commission on redistribution" had to be obtained.[22]

The Electoral Divisions Amendment Act adopted by the Manitoba legislature in 1955[23] also made it clear that the main objective of the legislation was precisely as the ccF leader had stated: to put in place a system whereby electoral boundary readjustments of fifty-seven single-member districts would be conducted every ten years by an independent three-member panel. What it did *not* attempt to eliminate was the distinction between rural and urban seats, a fact that clearly reflected the strength of the rural faction in Manitoba's governing Liberal-Progressive party. Urban electoral districts (defined as those in metropolitan Winnipeg and Brandon) were to be treated differently from all others and were to be constructed with a quota of seven persons to every four in a rural seat. At best, this amounted to a modest improvement over the urban/rural split that had previously existed in the province. Not until 1968 did the distinctions between the two categories of constituencies and the different population quotas end, and not until 1978 did metropolitan Winnipeg, by then with over one-half of the province's population, receive a majority of the seats. In both the 1988 and 1998 redistributions, thirty-one of the fifty-seven districts were assigned to Manitoba's largest urban area.[24]

Apart from the abandonment of urban/rural distinctions in constructing districts, the principal modifications to the act since 1955 have been first to increase, then subsequently to decrease, the maximum and minimum allowable limits for constituency populations. Initially, the maximum variations were set at +/−5 percent of the average population for each category of seats, urban and rural. Judged by later standards in Manitoba and most of the rest of Canada, this was an extraordinarily tight set of population limits. In 1968, when the urban/rural distinction was dropped, the legislation was changed to permit variations of up to +/−25 percent of the quota established for the province as a whole. (The 25 percent variation was identical to that adopted by Parliament earlier in the 1960s in the first federal legislation establishing an independent electoral boundary process and was later to be picked up by a number of provinces as their standard for population variations.)[25]

Prior to the 1988 redistribution Manitoba's act was amended to establish a new category of seats, those north of the 53rd parallel. For those districts (four in both 1988 and 1998), a variation of +/−25 percent of the seats' total population was allowed, but for the rest of the province the limits were reduced to +/−10 percent of the quota of population south of the 53rd parallel. A province's distinction (in this case Manitoba) between "the north" and the "rest of the province" for the purposes of defining an institutional building-block and in allowing "robust departures" from the provincial quotient has become, in Kent Roach's phrase, "as Canadian as maple syrup."[26]

In other respects, the legislation governing the Manitoba process has remained unchanged since it was first adopted in the 1950s. The population used to determine the quota and limits of constituency size is the "total provincial population" as established by the mid-decade Statistics Canada census plus the estimated population of Indian reserves not included in the federal census count. Public hearings are to be held, following "reasonable public notice of time and place," at which interested organizations or individuals can make submissions or comment on the initial electoral boundaries and constituency names proposed by the commission.[27]

Possibly the most important of the items that remain as originally legislated by Manitoba are the factors, apart from population, to be considered by a commission in making its decisions. With some variations these have become the model for other independent boundary commissions across Canada, and because of that they are worth noting in their entirety. The Manitoba act reads:

In determining the area to be included in, and in fixing the boundaries of, any electoral division, the commission shall take into consideration

(a) the community or diversity of interests of the population;

(b) the means of communication between the various parts thereof;

(c) the physical features thereof; and

(d) all other similar and relevant factors;

and, in so far as possible, shall include the whole area of each municipality in the same electoral division.[28]

With only slight modifications these were precisely the terms presented to Manitoba's special legislative committee studying electoral reform by the Australian prime minister (drawing on his country's legislation), the committee's staff (in a summary of the New Zealand law), and by Professors Morton and Donnelly in their brief to the committee. The Australian role model clearly played a major part in this matter, as can be seen from the almost identical wording of the relevant section of the Australian legislation. According to Australia's act:

In making any proposed distribution of a State into Divisions the Distribution Commissioners shall give due consideration to –

(a) Community or diversity of interest,

(b) Means of communication,

(c) Physical features,

(d) Existing boundaries of Divisions and Sub-divisions.[29]

The Manitoba steps to reform the electoral boundary readjustment process received favourable notice outside the province, particularly among social scientists acquainted with electoral questions and in some of the popular press. Toronto's *Star Weekly*, whose circulation of 910,000 made it the most widely distributed newspaper in Canada, carried a strong editorial endorsement of the reform under the heading "Manitoba Points the Way," in which it drew unfavourable comparisons between the highly partisan manner of redistributing district boundaries in Canada and the practice of referring the matter to independent commissions in Britain, Australia, and New Zealand.[30] The first edition of Paul Fox's widely used introductory text of political science readings, *Politics: Canada*, included the report of Manitoba's first impartial electoral boundaries commission as "an example of the work of such a body."[31] In 1961 Quebec's newly elected government under Jean Lesage's premiership commissioned a study by six distinguished social scientists ("experts désintéressés") to recommend alternative ways of revising the process of drawing the province's electoral map. In their report, the authors included a section on Manitoba's reforms and noted that "le système de 'redistribution' du Manitoba mérite d'être examiné puisqu'il s'agit ici de la seule province à avoir jusqu'à ce jour constitué une commission indépendante pout accomplir cette tâche."[32]

In his 1970 book *The Election Process in Canada*, T.H. Qualter lauded the Manitoba changes. He was particularly impressed with the ability of the commissioners to design seats that were relatively equal in population even though the various factors to be considered in the preparation of the maps might suggest otherwise:

When it is remembered that the *Act* enjoined the Commissioners to take into consideration the usual factors of community or diversity of interest, the means of communication, the physical features of the area, "all other similar and relevant factors" and, as far as possible, to keep the boundaries of municipalities intact, they were remarkably successful ... in producing equality of representation. Their success suggests that the criteria are not as inhibiting as is sometimes proclaimed.[33]

A measure of the extent to which the process was subsequently legitimated in the province of Manitoba can be found in the fact that members of the legislature have neither rejected nor changed the proposals of any of the commissions to have reported to date. According to the act, the provincial legislature is to consider a commission's final report; more important, it also retains the ultimate authority to fix the area and boundaries of the electoral districts. That the de facto power and authority rest with the commission, however, can be judged from the record: not a single detail of the five successive decennial reports issued by the commissions since 1957 has been altered by the legislature prior to its approval and implementation.[34]

The Manitoba legislation, later referred to in countless other provincial legislative and federal parliamentary debates on redistribution, had broken new ground and had become an institutional role model. The particular composition of the commission (the province's chief justice as its chair, with the president of the University of Manitoba and the province's chief electoral officer as its other members) remains unique to Manitoba. But the fundamental principle underlying the establishment of an independent process as well as many of the details of the terms of reference guiding a commission's work served as exemplars for the changes to the electoral boundary readjustment process that were subsequently introduced by other jurisdictions. Manitoba's representational innovation was soon to begin a process of diffusion.[35]

QUEBEC FOLLOWS SUIT

Three elements of the political context in Quebec after the launch of the Quiet Revolution in 1960 played an important part in leading the legislature to adopt a system of independent electoral boundary commissions. They were remarkably similar to those in Manitoba. First, Quebec for many decades had made no fundamental alterations in its electoral map, apart from periodically adding a few seats in areas of population growth. As the additions neither kept pace with the province's growth nor came at the expense of areas with declining or stable populations, the effect amounted to gerrymandering through a combination of neglect and political expediency – what V.O. Key Jr termed a "silent gerrymander."[36] The suburban areas around the city of Montreal were particularly disadvantaged in legislative representation as they had far fewer members of the legislature than their population warranted. Second, the province embarked on a heated debate over reforming the electoral system after the distorted conversion of votes into seats in the 1966 election led to the displacement of the Liberal government by a Union Nationale one. Third, once Quebec's inquiry into electoral reform was launched by referring the issue to a legislative committee in the early 1970s, many sideward glances were cast (from the eyes of academic experts in testimony before the committee and from reform-minded members of the governing Liberal party) at methods of electing representatives and drawing district boundaries in other jurisdictions.

On the first issue, Quebec had no history of regular boundary readjustments of its electoral districts. Unlike other provinces and the federal Parliament, no government-controlled committee of elected members carved up the political map on an established, recurrent basis. The Quebec legislature (by which one should read "the government") simply added more seats or split existing seats into two or three parts as the need (and the political instincts) suggested. Otherwise, constituencies were left much as they had been when they were first designed in 1853 at the close of the seigneurial era. The effect of over a hundred years of arbitrary boundary decision-making was apparent to the six-member committee of experts appointed in 1961 by the Lesage government to recommend reforms to the system.

The committee stated at the outset of its report that "[ces] mesures provisoires [et] partielles" did little more than reduce "les anomalies grossières."[37] The cumulative effect of the ad hoc practices that had been employed for more than a century were obvious in the unequal allocation of seats to population throughout the province. In 1861 the mean electoral population of a constituency was approximately 2,150 voters, with nine districts average in size, thirty-one below average, and twenty-one above average. Constituency populations ranged from a low of 400 (one seat) to a high of 6,500 voters (one seat), with a mode (eighteen seats) of 1,900 voters. Fully three-fifths of the districts in 1861 were within +/−15 percent of the average constituency size. By contrast, in 1960 the mean electoral population of a district had become 27,500 in a much larger legislative assembly. The dramatically increased number of voters reflected the growth in the province's population, the widening of the franchise to include females and non-propertied males, and the lowering of the voting age. Twelve ridings qualified as having average populations in 1960. But with over twice as many (fifty-nine) seats below average as above (twenty-four), and with a mode (eighteen seats) of 12,500, it was clear that the degree of equality that had been achieved a century before had been replaced by a markedly different distribution of seats to voters. Barely one-third of the seats in 1960 fell within 15 percent of the average district size. The range in constituency size in 1961 told a similar story. At one extreme, the three smallest ridings (all rural) contained an average of 6,800 voters, whereas at the other exteme, the three largest (all in the Montreal suburbs) averaged 108,000 voters each.[38]

Measured by the Dauer-Kelsay index (which establishes through an ordinal ranking of constituencies by size the smallest percentage of an entire population that could theoretically elect a majority of a legislature), the share fell from 39 percent in 1861 to 26 percent a century later.[39] By that measure, Quebec was *more* malapportioned in the early 1960s than was the state of Tennessee at the time (1962) that the United States Supreme Court issued its historic *Baker* v. *Carr* decision on appeal from that state and ushered in the principle of one person, one vote.[40] The cumulative biases resulting from a century of silent gerrymandering in Quebec were all too plain to see.

Electoral reform was the second factor to play a part in ushering in Quebec's legislation on independent boundary commissions in the 1970s. Confident of winning their third consecutive election the Liberals under Jean Lesage's leadership called an election for June 1966. In the event, they were defeated by the principal opposition party, the Union Nationale (UN).[41] The results graphically illustrated one of the flaws of the first-past-the-post electoral system – its capacity under certain circumstances to give one party more seats in the legislature with a smaller percentage of the popular vote than were cast for another party.

The spreads in 1966 were considerable. With 40.9 percent of the vote the UN captured fifty-six seats, whereas the Liberals won 47.2 percent of the popular vote but only fifty seats. The Liberals did well (sometimes extremely well) in the larger, typically urban ridings. By contrast the UN did better in the less populated and more rural seats which, in several cases, the party won by relatively close margins. The variation in the two parties' respective share of the popular vote figured in the new premier's election night victory speech. In terms ominously predictive of those used by Jacques Parizeau three decades later, in which the blame for the defeat of the sovereignty referendum was laid at the feet of "ethnics and money," UN leader Daniel Johnson observed in 1966 that "the subtraction of the Jewish and English Liberal vote showed that the Liberals had been rejected by 63 percent of the French-Canadian nation."[42] Understandably the election provoked heated discussions within Quebec's intellectual and political elites about alternative electoral systems.

If the Union Nationale's unexpected majority victory could be at least partially explained by the inequitable conversion of votes into seats in a plurality system, it was also true that it owed something to a constitutional anomaly unique to the province of Quebec. The British North America Act, 1867 contained a provision guaranteeing the continuation of twelve electoral districts that had existed prior to Confederation as part of Quebec's sixty-five-member delegation to the legislative assembly of the United Canadas. These "comtés protégés," as they were known, were located principally in the Eastern Townships and along the Ottawa River and were home to the bulk of the province's English-speaking, Protestant population outside Montreal. Included in the 1867 document largely at the insistence of Alexander Galt, the constitutional provisions guaranteeing the protected status of those districts could only be terminated by the Quebec legislature at some future point with the explicit approval of a majority of the members representing those districts at the time.[43]

In the hundred years after Confederation the socio-demographic mix of the protected ridings changed dramatically in favour of French-speaking Roman Catholics. As well, the number of districts increased from twelve to eighteen as the more populous ones were partitioned into additional seats when their growth (and the government's interests) justified such a move. But the population of other parts of the province, particularly in the metropolitan Montreal region, grew at a faster rate and was rewarded with a relatively smaller share of legislative seats. At Confederation, the twelve protected districts accounted for eighteen percent of the provincial assembly and 17 percent of the province's population. By 1966 the eighteen protected ridings sent 17 percent of the members to the legislature, yet they contained only 12 percent of the provincial electorate. Capturing a majority of those seats in 1966 clearly played an important part in the Union Nationale's electoral success: ten, or nearly eighteen percent, of the party's seats came from protected ridings that in total contained barely 7 percent of the province's electorate.[44]

The inequities resulting from a century of silent gerrymandering and from the translation of votes into seats in 1966 led the Liberals upon their return to power in 1970 to change the province's electoral machinery. Having won an overwhelming majority in the national assembly in the election that year, including victories in eleven of the eighteen protected seats, the new government first obtained approval (unanimous as it turned out) in the legislature to bring an end to the anomalous "comtés protégés." With that done, according to one of the observers of Quebec politics, "la voie est ouverte à la fabrication d'une nouvelle carte électorale plus équitable."[45]

A legislative committee was then charged with investigating and reporting on a variety of questions relating to elections and electoral systems. The inquiry that followed remains to this day one of the most wide-ranging investigations of alternative methods of elections and of drawing electoral boundaries ever conducted by a provincial legislative committee. Among the topics it considered were presidential systems, a permanent voters' list, mixed and plurality electoral systems, alternative methods of voting, the electoral behaviour of Quebecers, and laws governing electoral boundary readjustments. The deliberations of that committee constitute the third element leading to the adoption of legislation establishing electoral boundary readjustments by an independent commission in Quebec.[46]

The hearings of the legislative committee, whose work continued for the better part of six months, commanded considerable media attention. Several historians and political scientists testified before the committee, including such distinguished students of electoral systems as J.-C. Bonenfant, Vincent Lemieux, Jean Meynaud, André Bernard, John Meisel, and Gilles Lalonde. The questions, testimony, and briefs often addressed important theoretical and practical matters and were peppered with references to the work of Alan Cairns, Maurice Duverger, Norman Ward, and S.M. Lipset. The record of the committee hearings reads like an informed and inquisitive academic seminar.

Committee members and many who appeared before them were convinced that Quebec's principal need at that point was to correct the electoral map. In the opinion of several experts, reform of the electoral system might come later, or might not be needed at all, whereas the immediate need was to construct a system for readjusting electoral boundaries on a regular and fair basis. That no doubt suited the political instincts of the governing Liberals who had, after all, recently been elected under the plurality vote system, but with a smaller share of the popular vote than in 1966. They stood to benefit from an electoral map that would increase representation from one of their greatest areas of support, the greater Montreal area. Reform of the redistribution process also appealed to the opposition Parti Québécois who, like the Liberals, had made a pre-election commitment to ensure a more equitable electoral map.[47]

At the time that the legislature of Quebec considered alternate ways of ensuring a fairer and more equitable electoral boundary readjustment process, Manitoba had been the only province to have such legislation in place. But as the Parliament of Canada had adopted the Electoral Boundaries Readjustment Act in 1964, the federal experience with a statute governing the redistribution process and with ten independent commissions to carry out the terms of the act also entered Quebec's deliberations. The province's chief electoral officer, François Drouin, had served as a member of the first federal redistribution commission in Quebec. He testified to the legislative committee about Ottawa's process of electoral boundary readjustments and about his experience with the federal commission in Quebec. Others who appeared before the committee drew on examples of independent bodies outside Canada, notably New Zealand and Australia, as well as from Manitoba. To J.-C. Bonenfant, Manitoba's legislation had ensured that its commission "est vraiment indépendante" and the federal statute had created "le plus parfait" system.[48]

Upon completion of the committee's study of electoral mapping alternatives, the national assembly established the Standing Commission on Reform of the Electoral Districts, a permanent body composed of the province's chief electoral officer and two non-elected individuals approved by a two-thirds vote of the National Assembly. The legislation was passed without dissent and clearly reflected the mood of political reform that had begun a decade earlier. In the premier's words, if the objective of ensuring "une représentation juste et équitable à l'Assemblée nationale" was to be obtained, "il importe donc pour le moment de corriger les faiblesses évidentes de notre carte électorale."[49]

As in Manitoba, Quebec's commission was granted only a recommendatory status and was limited to proposing electoral boundary readjustments to the legislature for its final approval, alteration or rejection. But in other respects the terms governing the redistributions were different from those in Manitoba. Quebec's commission was charged with examining the need for electoral boundary readjustments following every general election in order to ensure that the principle of "fair and equitable representation" for all electors was upheld. Districts were to be composed of 32,000 electors, with a tolerance limit of +/−25 percent, and Quebec became the first jurisdiction in Canada to permit electoral boundary commissions to design constituencies that exceeded the 25 percent limits. For "exceptional reasons," such as "very low population density, the relative growth rate of the population of a region, its accessibility, area or shape," a district could be constructed outside that range. The act included no explicit list of considerations to guide a commission's work, such as community of interest, means of communication, physical features or municipal divisions, but it is impossible to conceive of a commission completing its work without in some fashion referring to those factors to justify their proposals.[50]

Between-election shifts in district sizes were unavoidable in Quebec because of the mobility and growth of the population. An increase in any province's population would have no effect on the distribution of its seats if it occurred evenly. But it does not, as the post-Second World War settlement patterns of both foreign and out-of-province immigrants have made clear. Immigrants overwhelmingly opt for urban and suburban centres over rural parts of a province. Added to that, in Quebec, as in the rest of Canada, approximately 20 percent of all people move at least once a year, with the urban/suburban centres the net beneficiary of those moves.[51]

In practical terms, these demographic trends guaranteed boundary readjustment proposals being presented to Quebec's legislature at least every four or five years. Moreover, as Quebec's legislation based redistributions on a *fixed* number of voters per seat rather than, as had Manitoba, an average number determined by dividing the total electorate by seats available, Quebec's legislature continued to grow with each redistribution during the first decade of the new legislation. From a house of 108 members in 1970, Quebec's Assembly grew to 110 in 1973 and 122 in 1981.

The long-overdue changes wrought by the first boundary readjustment under the new law were massive: only two of the existing 108 constituencies remained untouched. The two parties with the most to lose from a fundamental restructuring of the province's electoral map, the Union Nationale and Ralliement créditistes, mounted an ultimately unsuccessful attempt to block its passage in 1972. They were clearly not misguided in their concern about its impact on their rural power bases: neither party won a seat in the provincial election the following year.[52]

The advisory role that the commission played in the exercise was made apparent in 1976. The legislature was dissolved for an election without having approved the considerable changes to the constituency maps proposed by the commission. It is easy to understand why. A new set of electoral maps would have been the second within less than four years. Furthermore it would have modified sixty-six ridings and created two new ones, and it would have pitted a number of MNAs of the same party (many of whom had been elected for the first time barely three years earlier) against one another for their party's nomination in the newly designed seats. The dislocation and uncertainty that the exercise would have provoked, together with the attendant practical concerns shared by all politicians over constituency-level organization in the months leading up to an election, prepared the way for changes to the original legislation.

Amendments came in two stages. In 1979 the commission (renamed the Commission de la représentation électorale) became the effective decision-making body with the ultimate power to establish the province's electoral boundaries. As was true of the federal Parliament, members of Quebec's legislature would be able to consider, debate, and propose changes to the map but the authority to determine its final complexion would rest with the commission itself. Average district size was increased to 34,000 electors and for the first time the notion of constituencies being composed of "a group of electoral precincts" was introduced. Precincts were to contain no more than 2,500 electors and were to be designed to reflect the "socio-economic homogeneity and the natural boundaries of each locality." The "demographical, geographical and sociological considerations" that were to guide a commission's work included "population density, the relative growth rate of the population, the accessibility, area or shape of the region, the natural local boundaries and the limits of municipalities." As amended in 1979, Quebec's electoral boundaries legislation moved towards an exposition of the principles underlying the design of constituencies that was more akin to those previously adopted in Manitoba. It also advanced the novel idea that, at the micro-level, small socio-economic building blocks could be used in the construction of individual ridings.[53]

A 1991 amendment to the act reduced the frequency of redistributions and replaced the original method of determining the number of constituencies. Henceforth redistributions would be held after every second election, thereby reducing for MNAs the incidence of intra-party nomination fights and constituency party reorganizations. The original statutory requirement of an average of 32,000 electors per constituency (changed to 34,000 and 36,000 in 1979 and 1982 respectively) had meant that there would be no change in the size of the National Assembly so long as the total electoral population remained stable. The same number of seats would simply be distributed among an unchanged number of electors. But with an increasing electoral population, as was the case in Quebec in the 1970s, growth in the size of the Assembly was unavoidable, and the jump from 110 seats in 1973 to 122 in 1981 was a consequence. Only by changing to an assembly of a relatively fixed size, as in Manitoba, with constituency populations determined by dividing the number of seats available into the total electorate, could the problem be overcome. That is precisely what Quebec did, with the introduction in 1987 of a range of the minimum and maximum number of constituencies (between 122 and 125) that the commission had available to it in designing the maps. Had Quebec's legislation not been changed, the post-1998 redistribution would have created an assembly of 154 members, or some thirty more than the range then allowed.[54]

CONCLUSIONS

Several conclusions can be drawn from the Manitoba and Quebec cases. Based on the experiences of those two provinces in introducing independent electoral boundary commissions, at least three variables were present that made such changes possible. Whether the shift to independent commissions would have taken place without those variables (particularly the first two) is doubtful. Before considering them, however, two general observations can be offered.

First, federalism enables institutional role-modelling to take place "close to home." Reforms that one province has successfully experimented with can commend themselves to others. Interprovincial networks form naturally in a federal system through ministerial meetings, bureaucratic contacts, and political parties, and they encourage the exchange of information about possible solutions to common problems. As well, the national media play an educative role in disseminating information about institutional changes in one province that could well seem promising to another.

This is not to say that institutional role-modelling is dependent upon or solely a function of federalism. Rather it suggests that Manitoba's experience with independent electoral boundary readjustments in the 1950s and 1960s spoke more directly to Quebec in the 1970s than would, say, any European country at that point. Their cultures and principal languages may be different, but Manitoba and Quebec nonetheless share similar institutional frameworks, electoral systems, and political values that serve to commend one's experiments to the other. Manitoba blazed the boundary readjustment trail in Canada by borrowing extensively from the two most successful examples of independent commissions, New Zealand and Australia, because it had no choice but to look elsewhere for possible guidance. Once it had its own process successfully under way, it effectively served notice to Canadians that they had in their midst a solution to grossly inequitable, partisan-dominated redistributions.

Designed as a system of institutional arrangements that is premised on the acceptance of social diversity, federalism neither requires nor expects uniformity of laws in matters under provincial jurisdiction. As demonstrated by the Manitoba and Quebec examples, and was subsequently true of other provinces and Ottawa, the policies that were put in place to ensure independent and fairer electoral boundary read-justments differed in many of their details from one jurisdiction to another. The system that evolved in Manitoba requires legislative approval of proposals brought forth every ten years by a three-member commission for a redistribution based on the province's total popula-tion and the construction of all but the northern seats within 10 percent limits. For its part, Quebec granted its commission the final authority to design its constituency maps following every second elec-tion on the basis of electoral populations within 25 percent of the electoral quota, leaving open the possibility that some "exceptional" seats may exceed those limits. Whatever their differences, the prov-inces share in common the acceptance of a fundamental guiding principle: that a measure of voter equality among electoral districts can be achieved by legislating the terms within which periodic redis-tributions will be conducted and by delegating the responsibility to frame the maps to a non-partisan and creditable body.

Second, the changes were accomplished in Canada without any involvement of the judiciary. No court challenges had been initiated to the malapportioned legislatures of Manitoba and Quebec (or any-where else for that matter), and no court-ordered redistributions had forced legislators to recraft electoral districts according to the principle of one person, one vote. If anything, Quebec urban voters in the lead-up to the 1960 election could have pointed to a greater degree of malapportionment in their legislative districts than did their American counterparts in 1962. Yet no court challenge was launched seeking a more equitable distribution of voters to seats.

Why this difference between Canada and the United States in the early 1960s? Part of the answer is explained by the absence of any constitutional hook on which to hang a court challenge in Canada, in contrast to the United States. In a system of government based on the principle of parliamentary or legislative supremacy, the likelihood of any individual or group successfully challenging legislatively approved electoral redistributions, no matter how malapportioned and gerry-mandered the districts may have been, would have been extremely slight. Not until the adoption of the Canadian Charter of Rights and Freedoms in 1982 were the constitutional tools available to mount a case against electoral boundaries. Even so, it was a further decade before the Supreme Court of Canada heard its first (and to date its only) case on such a matter.

The United States, on the other hand, has for much of its history turned to lawyers and the courts to resolve a variety of rights and freedoms issues that in Canada would, until the Charter, have been left to Parliament and to the provincial assemblies. Since the ground-breaking *Baker* v. *Carr*, when the United States Supreme Court reversed its earlier stand that courts had no role to play in the political question of redistricting, American courts have, in Justice Frankfurter's remarkably predictive phrase, entered the "political thicket" of electoral districting in a major way.[55]

In stark contrast to Americans, Canadians have had no history of citizen group involvement in protecting voter rights. Incentives for the creation of public interest groups dedicated to pursuing questions of voting rights have been vastly different in the two countries, as is illustrated by the distinctive approach each has taken to registering voters. In the United States voluntary voter registration provided the opportunity, in particular from the 1950s on when the civil rights movement became politically active, for the creation of countless associations dedicated to advancing the electoral participation of racial minorities and other systematically disfranchised voters. It was a natural extension for many of those groups to extend that involvement by seeking to promote equality of electoral districts through court challenges. The names of many of the groups responsible for those challenges have become increasingly familiar to Americans over the years. They include the National Association for the Advancement of Colored People (NAACP), the American Civil Liberties Union (ACLU), Common Cause, and the League of Women Voters. There have been no equivalent groups with the organizational base, legal expertise, and available funds to challenge redistributions in Canada.

In contrast to the United States, door-to-door enumeration in Canada carried out within a few days or weeks of an election all but removed any need for the creation of equivalent groups, for federal and provincial enumerations captured a far greater share of the total potential electorate than has ever been the case with voluntary voter registration in the United States. Estimates of the share of the total potential electoral population captured by each of the two methods of registering voters confirm that, in spite of the massive registration drives mounted in the United States, the differences between the two countries remain vast. Only between 65 to 69 percent of the eligible American electorate is registered, compared with between 95 and 97 percent of the Canadian under door-to-door enumeration.[56]

Three variables were common to Manitoba and Quebec at the time they shifted to electoral boundary commissions: widespread criticism of the existing electoral system and gerrymandered legislatures, acceptance by the political elites of the need for reform, and an intellectual and practical contribution by social scientists to the debate leading up to the adoption of independent commissions. To generalize on the experience of these provinces, it is difficult to conceive of electoral reforms being adopted without at least a confluence of the first two elements. Arguably the third is important, but not essential.

Manitoba and Quebec both had abundant cause for public concern about the extent to which their legislatures were composed of members elected from districts of vastly unequal populations. In one case, this was the product of periodic gerrymandering; in the other, it was the result of conscious neglect. Whether the gerrymander was deliberate or silent, its effect was the same – to over-represent the rural and less populated parts of the province at the expense of the major metropolitan areas. That, together with the attention devoted by the media, civic groups, and interested members of the public to the faults of their particular electoral system gave the legislative committees appointed in each province the impetus to conduct wide-ranging inquiries into electoral reform. The first necessary ingredient was in place in both provinces: a cause for public concern and a mechanism for examining it.

A common criticism of politicians is that they concentrate power in their own hands (especially those of the executive) and avoid, if at all possible, having to change institutional arrangements that work to their own political benefit. There is much truth in that. Yet the move to establish legislation for the drawing of electoral districts by independent bodies operating at arms'-length from the legislature stands as a notable exception to that charge. The record from Manitoba in the 1950s and Quebec in the 1960s and 1970s suggests that there was a willingness on the part of political elites to forfeit something – in this case the power to determine district boundaries for election to the legislatures – that they would normally be expected to see as benefiting them. Without the clear support of the premiers, cabinet ministers, and opposition party leaders the reforms would not have been implemented. In Manitoba the government and both opposition parties were persuaded of the need to construct electoral districts less differentially and to end a sullied and self-serving tradition. In Quebec the mood of reform that began with the Quiet Revolution at the end of the Duplessis era provided the critical context for the political leadership to push for fundamental changes in electoral redistricting. The second ingredient, the political will, was present in both provinces.

Finally, the role that social scientists played on this issue cannot be discounted. It is not uncommon for experts to be asked to testify to parliamentary and legislative committees. In this instance, the outcome would suggest that their contribution made a difference. At the legislative committee hearings in both Manitoba and Quebec, distinguished members of Canada's history and political science communities presented informed background papers on important questions of electoral reform and independent boundary commissions. Academic literature on electoral institutions published in Canada and abroad was also consulted by committee members and their research staffs. The comparative analysis of political systems helped to shape the discussion about the relative merits of new and different institutional arrangements for readjusting electoral boundaries. There was a clear appreciation on the part of the politicians of the contributions that social science could make to their deliberations. It need scarcely be added that that has not always been the case in policy formation in Canada.

These three elements – the cause, the will, and the knowledge – came together in Manitoba and Quebec and enabled an acceptable and, by Canadian standards, a novel model of adjusting electoral boundaries to be constructed. Expressed in slightly different terms, the three streams that John Kingdon defined as necessary to open a policy window were present in both provinces. The *problem* of vastly unequal populations in constituencies used to elect legislative members was identified. The *solution*, in the form of independent electoral boundary commissions, was available after senior government officials, social scientists, and the media, played an important role in informing the politicians. Arguably the most critical variable, *political* support, came from both sides of the legislatures. Without that, the window would not have opened. That independent electoral boundary commissions were initially adopted by two parts of a federal system meant that with time other jurisdictions, when they too were sufficiently provoked into exploring alternate means of designing seats, could learn from the early experiences of those two provinces and borrow as needed.

4 Going Down Under: Canada Looks to Australia

No debate excites the Chambers as much as the discussion of an electoral law.

– André Tardieu, 1930

By the early to mid-1960s, the three streams needed to ensure the opening of a policy window were in place for changes to the federal electoral boundary readjustment process. The 1962 election had given no party a majority in the House, which meant that for the first time in Canadian history the design of electoral maps based on the latest census would not be firmly in the hands of a majority government. When the Conservatives led by John Diefenbaker were replaced by the Liberals under Lester Pearson following the 1963 election (which, like the one a year earlier, had given no party a majority), the House of Commons found itself in an unprecedented situation. Not only was a government-dominated redistribution out of the question, but both of the major party leaders and the leaders of the smaller opposition parties were in agreement about the need to get electoral boundary readjustments out of the hands of politicians. As well, many of the members were elected for the first time either in 1962 or 1963 and were unfamiliar with the redistribution process. A number of the new parliamentary recruits on the Liberal backbenches in particular sat for urban or suburban areas that had never had their fair share of seats in comparison with rural parts of Canada. They were anxious to reform the electoral laws in a number of respects, including the financing of elections, and they quickly echoed the call of their leader, now prime minister, for a fairer, non-partisan way of drawing constituency boundaries. In Kingdon's terms, the problem had been identified and the political support for change was forthcoming. The solution was at hand. For close to a decade, Manitoba had had legislation in place for constituency redistributions to be carried out by independent commissions. That idea, in turn, had been imported from "down under."

MPs were not only tackling a new piece of legislation. They were also dealing with fundamental representational and organizational principles that are at the heart of constructing any set of territorially-defined constituencies. This called for decisions about riding size, limits on population variance, and whether rural and urban seats should be treated differently from one another. Members needed to decide on matters relating to the appointment and membership of commissions and on the number of commissions. They had to resolve issues relating to the authority to appoint commissioners and on whether or not commissions would have the final say in determining the boundaries. They were entering uncharted waters, and they found much in Manitoba to help them. They found even more in Australia, a federal and parliamentary country with which Canada's political institutions had a good deal in common.

COMPETING PRINCIPLES

Reform of the federal electoral redistribution system was accepted as long overdue in the early 1960s, leading a number of MPs on both sides of the Commons to call for an end to government-controlled redistributions and gerrymanders. For the first time a prime minister took steps to bring the issue of independent readjustments before the House. Late in the life of his 1958–62 majority government, John Diefenbaker introduced a resolution which, had it eventually led to legislation, would have turned over to a single non-partisan commission the power to adjust federal electoral boundaries in Canada every ten years. Diefenbaker claimed to have been the victim of two gerrymanders, or "jimmymanders" as he insisted on calling them after the federal Liberal cabinet minister (Jimmy Gardiner) who was closely involved in recrafting Saskatchewan's federal seats in 1947 and 1952. It is doubtful that the Diefenbaker's proposal in 1962 amounted to anything more than a pre-election ploy, however, as Parliament was dissolved within days of the announcement for the 1962 general election and no action was taken on establishing independent commissions.[1] The minority Conservative government elected in 1962 took no steps to introduce any redistribution legislation before it was defeated by the combined opposition parties early the following year. The ensuing federal election replaced one minority government, the Progressive Conservatives, with another, the Liberals.

The essential institutional element that had always guaranteed passage of a set of maps designed largely in the government's favour was a majority of government supporters on both the parliamentary committee and in the House. But at the very time that Parliament was constitutionally obligated to undertake the redistribution based on the 1961 census, the Commons lacked a majority government. Prolonged and acrimonious debates over a government-sponsored redistribution (the type of redistribution that had been the custom for one hundred years) would have been a virtual certainty in the bitter political climate that marked the Diefenbaker-Pearson years. Passage of a government-controlled redistribution bill could not have been assured in that political climate. This proved to be a powerful incentive for changing the method of designing constituencies. So too did the presence of a group of newly elected, reform-minded Liberal MPs under Lester Pearson's leadership. Anxious to ensure a measure of support for their minority government from the parties on the opposition benches, principally the NDP, the Liberals sought to appeal to their fellow parliamentarians on issues such as electoral reform. They were convinced that changes to the way electoral districts were designed would be attractive to members on both sides of the House. They were right.[2]

There was a large measure of agreement amongst the MPs about the need to abandon party-driven redistributions, but that level of support for independent commissions would never have made the change possible without the agreement of the party leaders. Lester Pearson, John Diefenbaker, and T.C. Douglas of the NDP endorsed the principle and left the details to be worked out by their parliamentary colleagues most familiar with electoral administration, J.W. Pickersgill, Gordon Churchill, and Stanley Knowles. The objective was, quite simply, to ensure that non-partisan, arms'-length bodies would draw the maps and give the process a credibility it lacked when left to the politicians.[3]

The shift in Manitoba a decade earlier to independent commissions was a common reference point for MPs of all parties who favoured a similar move on the federal front. Stanley Knowles, among others, noted in the debate that "the only experience [Canada has] had of boundaries being drawn by impartial commissions is Manitoba's" and that had served as a guide to show that independent commissioners could do the job well. The government house leader agreed, saying Manitoba's experience with independent redistributions "was very satisfactory."[4] Members were also reminded that the shift to independent commissioners was long overdue. Pledges to remove redistribution from the hands of elected politicians and to turn it over to arms'-length commissioners were found as far back as 1903 in the Conservative party and 1919 in the Liberal.[5]

There was far less agreement about the way in which independent commissions should be structured, the powers they should enjoy, and the representational principles that should inform their work. Were seats to be constructed of relatively equal populations or of manageable territorial size? Were identifiable groups entitled to any special protection? What residual power, if any, should Parliament retain to approve, alter, or reject proposals from the commissions? Should there, in fact, be one commission for the whole country or one for each province and territory? Should the selection of committee members be the prerogative of the prime minister and leader of the opposition or should it be turned over to the Speaker of the House or the chief electoral officer? These and other related issues were resolved on terms that had long governed decision-making by Canadian politicians, that is on the basis of compromises befitting a geographically large, sparsely populated and federally structured country with a multitude of competing interests.

The upshot of Canada's longest debate on redistribution (fifty-one days over the first two sessions of the 26th Parliament) was the Electoral Boundaries Readjustment Act (EBRA) of 1964. This act represented Parliament's attempt to address the two historic problems associated with electoral redistributions in Canada: the overtly partisan character of the whole exercise, and the frequently marked discrepancies in both the geographic size and the population of constituencies. The first problem was more easily disposed of than the second, reflecting both the extent to which the principle of independent electoral commissions enjoyed bipartisan support and the degree to which territory, isolation, and sparsity of population had become issues central to any debate over redistribution in Canada.

Diefenbaker's call shortly before the end of the 24th Parliament for an independent commission and for "fair, just and reasonable"[6] redistributions had met with no opposition when it was presented in 1962. Virtually the same words were repeated by the new Liberal government a year later. In introducing the bill for the establishment of electoral boundaries commissions the Pearson government took the unusual step of acknowledging that except for the "fundamental principle of an impartial redistribution" the bill was "open to amendment from any quarter of the house" on any matter or detail it contained.[7] Typical of the many compromises reached during the long debate on the floor of the House (the bill at no point was referred to a standing or special committee as had been the case in Manitoba) was acceptance of the +/−25 percent tolerance limits – that is, the maximum and minimum amounts that the populations of federal constituencies within a province could deviate from the average constituency population size within a province. Some members, principally from urban ridings and the NDP, had pressed for maximum deviations of +/−20 percent;

others, largely from rural seats and the Conservative party, had pushed for +/−30 percent. The 25 percent tolerance limits, like many other compromises, were accepted by all four parties in the House.[8] When it was eventually passed, the EBRA represented a major break with Canada's age-old practice of politicians redrawing the boundaries of their own constituencies.

The basic principle underlying the bill was relatively simple to agree upon. The far more vexing problems surfaced in the debate over the details. The century-long tradition of sanctioning constituency inequalities had created a House of stakeholders. In different ways the representational compromises that had been crafted over time had benefited various regions, different political parties, and individual MPs. The notion of one person, one vote, or of creating federal ridings of equal populations, scarcely entered the parliamentary debate. When it did, it was only supported by the handful of members from high-population urban ridings.

In notable contrast to later years when representational comparisons came to be frequently made in relation to American examples, between 1962 and 1964 fewer than a half dozen MPs even alluded to the recent *Baker* v. *Carr* decision of the United States Supreme Court. Yet *Baker* is often held to be one of the most important cases of the United States Supreme Court in the post-Second World War period, effectively paved the way for acceptance of the one person, one vote principle in the United States. In Canada, by contrast, pragmatism and localism, rather than theories espousing voter equality, marked the parliamentary debates between 1962 and 1964.[9]

Also much in evidence were the cross-party cleavages created between members from urban and rural constituencies. When fundamental reforms to the redistribution process were debated, MPs from urban and suburban seats, regardless of their party or province, made essentially the same points in support of their case for a fairer distribution of population among ridings. Urban voters had long been penalized and had "effectively lost their vote and voice in Parliament." Because urban constituencies tended to be so much more populous than others, their elected representatives complained of having incurred a "disproportionately heavy workload." The sorts of arguments mounted in favour of more equitable distribution of populations by MPs from large metropolitan ridings demonstrated that members from Montreal, Toronto, and Vancouver, regardless of party, shared representational concerns in common with one another that they did not share with fellow caucus members from their own province.[10]

By contrast, MPs from rural and more isolated parts of the country, again irrespective of party or region, claimed that their constituents feared becoming even more marginalized in the policy process and distant from the principal centre of power. They too described their workload as onerous. Their seats were often at considerable distance; travel time between Ottawa and their riding, and travel time within the riding itself, took its toll. The House was told that representing a rural constituency would become an even more difficult task were electoral boundaries designed purely, or even largely, on the basis of equal populations.

Examples were readily produced in support of the opposing positions. Just as the territorial size of vast rural and northern ridings far removed from Ottawa was argued by some members as the basis for allowing wide variations in constituency population size, so did some MPs from the major metropolitan centres call for small population variances among districts on the grounds that it is people, not territory, that are at the heart of political representation. The favourite reference point presented by urban members to confirm the stark contrast in constituency size was drawn from the most recent census in two ridings created a decade earlier: the federal electoral districts of York-Scarborough and Îles-de-la-Madeleine had populations in 1961 of 267, 252 and 12,479 respectively. The debate reinforced the obvious: there was no commonly held set of representational principles that served to unite MPs on both sides of the House and within the respective party caucuses.

THE AUSTRALIAN MODEL

The eventual compromise was made possible largely as a result of a study of the Australian redistribution system carried out by Canada's chief electoral officer, Nelson Castonguay. In a report in 1963 to the minister responsible for redistribution, secretary of state, and government house leader, J.W. Pickersgill, Castonguay commended to the government many of the principal features of the Australian system of electoral boundary determination. Following a visit early in that year to New Zealand and Australia to examine at first hand their redistribution processes, the chief electoral officer concluded that the Australians in particular had brought redistribution "down to a fine art." Theirs was a "more refined and accurate" procedure than that used in Canada, but one which, with appropriate modifications for the Canadian political environment, could well serve as the model for a reformed system. The government agreed, later acknowledging its debt to Australia during the 1963–4 debates on its Electoral Boundaries Readjustment legislation.[11]

The logic of Canada's inquiry into Australia's experience with electoral redistributions could not have escaped the politicians. Both countries were economically advanced, territorially large federations using Westminster-style parliamentary systems, and both had relatively small populations whose location patterns and movements shared striking similarities. Some sparsely populated regions covered land areas that were vast by any comparative measure; the continuing rural exodus and the considerable post-Second World War immigration had combined to increase markedly the urban and suburban populations, particularly in the two or three dominant metropolitan centres of each country; and uneven growth patterns within, but more particularly among, the various states and provinces had invariably prompted criticisms of the redistribution process from the adversely affected areas.

In other respects, Australia differed markedly from Canada. Entrusting electoral boundary readjustments to independent commissions was one of them. This was part of a larger package of electoral reforms dating back to the mid-nineteenth century that had helped to give substance to Australia's democratic and egalitarian values. Described as a country of "collectivist" radical thought (in contrast to the "individualist" radical thought of North America), Australia has for the past century and a half been at the forefront of electoral reform.[12] Beginning in the 1850s with the adoption of universal manhood suffrage in four colonies and the secret ballot in five, Australia's electoral reforms helped to define that country's distinctive political character and to give expression to a particular set of representational values.

Australia's permanent electoral roll, compulsory voting, three-year parliamentary life and preferential balloting suggest a state-driven attempt to ensure a measure of inclusiveness, totality, currency, and fairness to electoral politics. If Australian liberal democracy is to rest on, among other things, elections, then everyone shall be registered to vote at all times and shall be *required* to indicate preferences frequently and exhaustively. On the other hand, Canada's door-to-door voter enumeration (which was used from Confederation to the 1997 federal election), parliaments that could last for up to five years maximum, voluntary voting, and plurality electoral system combine to suggest a different view of government obligations and individual responsibilities. They signify on the state's part a periodic but nonetheless momentary interest in current and complete electoral rolls, and on the voter's part the *freedom* to participate or not in elections that theoretically could be held no more often than twice a decade and with ballots that permit no preferential ordering of candidates. If elements of Rousseau's social contract are to be found in Australia's electoral practices, then there are traces of Locke's in Canada's.[13]

This was not the first time Canadian lawmakers had looked to Australia for guidance on electoral law. A decade earlier Manitoba had copied much of its redistribution system from Australia. But even before that, British Columbia had sent election officials to Australia in 1949 to learn first-hand about that country's methods of voter registration, compulsory voting, and alternative vote. Rejecting both compulsory and alternative voting, but favourably impressed with Australia's continuously updated roll of electors, the officials recommended a similar system for the province. Legislation implementing Canada's first attempt at a continuous voter's list was adopted shortly after by British Columbia.[14]

Australia's experience with extra-parliamentary electoral boundary readjustments had been a long one and clearly qualified as one of its lasting contributions to representational reform. From the beginning of the federal (Commonwealth) electoral system in 1902 several principles had been accepted as basic to fair electoral redistributions in Australia. Although some of the particulars had changed in the intervening period, by the early 1960s the main tenets of the Australian system were much as they had been six decades earlier. According to the legislation in effect at the time of Castonguay's study in 1963 these included:

- A separate three-number commission for each state and territory appointed by the governor-general-in-council. The Commonwealth chief electoral officer or the federal electoral officer for the state was named as one member, as was the surveyor-general of the state or an official with similar qualifications. Customarily a senior federal official familiar with the demography and geography of the state served as the third member.
- A requirement that in no case could the number of electors in a division be greater or less than 20 percent of the state's quota. The quota was obtained by dividing the total number of electors in a state by the total number of seats to which the state was entitled.
- A list of five matters to be considered by the commissions in drawing the constituency boundaries: community or diversity of interest; means of communication; physical features; existing boundaries or electoral divisions; and boundaries of state divisions.
- An opportunity for the public to submit written suggestions or objections to the initial proposals of the commissions before those proposals were submitted to the appropriate cabinet minister.
- A stipulation that both Houses of Parliament consider and approve the proposed redistributions on a state-by-state basis before they could take effect.[15]

The extent to which Canadian MPs in the 1960s accepted these features of the Australian model is striking. After debate and amendment of the government's original bill, Parliament adopted the following key provisions as part of the EBRA:

- A separate four-member commission for each province appointed by the governor-in-council. The chair of the commission was to be selected by the chief justice of the province from amongst superior court judges in his province; two members (in practice this generally came to mean academics and officials such as clerks of the provincial legislature) were to be named by the Speaker of the Commons; and the newly established representation commissioner was to sit ex officio on each of the ten commissions.
- A requirement that no constituency's population could vary by more than 25 percent above or below the provincial electoral quota. The quota was to be determined by dividing a province's population by its number of seats.
- A stipulation that the population of each electoral district was to correspond "as nearly as may be" to the province's electoral quota. Exceptions to that principle were possible where, in the view of a commission, special conditions warranted departure from the average population figure. These included geographic considerations, such as sparsity, density, or relative rate of growth of population, or accessibility, size, and shape of a region and social and economic considerations, such as community or diversity of interests of the inhabitants of a region.
- An opportunity for the public to present written briefs and to make representations at public meetings called by the commission about the maps proposed by the commission.
- An opportunity for MPs to voice comments on the proposed maps once formal objection to a commission's work had been filed with the Speaker by any ten members. The debate precipitated by the objection would, together with the maps as originally proposed, be forwarded to the commission for its consideration. The decision that the commission reached would be final.[16]

The Canadian legislation was, according to Nelson Castonguay, "updated as to how Australia [and New Zealand] would like to have [had] theirs" at the time.[17] Although the Australian +/−20 percent limit was one-fifth tighter than the Canadian one, the instruction to the Canadian commissions to design constituencies with population sizes as close "as may be" to those of the provincial electoral quotas was unknown in Australia at the time. So, too, was the clause respecting the "relative rate of growth" of populations of constituencies – a caveat guaranteed to generate (as it did) heated debate amongst the commissioners, the public, and the parliamentarians in Canada. Unlike Australia, public hearings on each commission's initial set of proposals were to be held in Canada before the commissions prepared maps for parliamentary consideration. Most important of all, in lending support to the principle of truly independent electoral boundary readjustments, the MPs in Canada, unlike their Australian counterparts, transferred the final authority for the maps to the commissions following the "parliamentary objection" stage. No other institution so affects the complexion and, ultimately, the life of the Canadian Parliament, yet the members had relinquished their power to alter, approve, or reject the commissions' final decisions.

THE DIVERGENT PATHS

In 1964 many of the principal features of the redistribution systems in Australia and Canada were similar, but since then the paths taken by the respective laws governing electoral readjustments have diverged. The cumulative effect of the amendments made since 1964 to Australia's Commonwealth Electoral Act has proved to be much more substantial than has been the case with Canada's revisions to the EBRA. Apart from deleting in 1975 the contentious "relative rate of growth" clause from the instructions to the commissioners, reducing in 1979 the size of commissions from four to three members when the office of the representation commissioner was eliminated, and in 1985 permitting commissions to exceed the +/– 25 percent limits in "exceptional circumstances," Canadian MPs have not changed the statute in any significant way.

That is not for want of trying. With the emergence on the political agenda of the reconsideration of electoral boundaries every ten years, the pages of *Hansard* are peppered with speeches by MPs expressing concern, often outrage, about the impact on their constituency or region of the maps proposed by a commission. Calls for changes to the EBRA invariably precede or follow the release of the final maps, often in the form of private members' bills aimed at changing the terms of the governing legislation. In the mid-1970s, for example, MPs introduced legislation to change the membership of the commissions, to alter the instructions to be followed by commissioners in designing seats, and to require each commission to give reasons for every set of constituency boundaries they established. None of these initiatives by backbench MPs (often supported by members from all parties) passed the House.[18] The greatest single attempt to change the law came in the mid-1990s in the government-supported drive to introduce massive changes to the act. As will be seen in chapter 7, the failure to gain Senate approval ended that attempt.

The elimination of the post of representation commissioner in 1979 was not unexpected. MPs had feared from the outset of Canada's move to independent commissions that such an official might "exercise a centralized control over all the maps, with the ten commissions merely acting as rubber stamps."[19] The reality, however, was quite the reverse. Commissions made it clear that they intended to be in complete charge of designing their own set of electoral districts. The representation commissioner was, by law, required to prepare maps for each commission setting out alternate proposals for electoral boundaries. For most commissions this meant that between eight and ten different sets of maps were designed, although for one 1965 commission sixteen separate sets were prepared. Still, "not one commission" adopted them, the representation commissioner admitted. Commissioners found them "useful and helpful as [purely mathematical] guides," but relied on their own "reference [points]" and knowledge of the "local provincial situation" to carry out their task.[20]

For its part, Australia has moved since the 1960s to a two-stage redistribution operation which, in one respect at least, is identical to Canada's. In 1983 the Australian Parliament was removed completely from the process, which means that MPs no longer have an opportunity to debate, approve, or defeat redistribution proposals. The redistribution responsibilities have devolved entirely on two newly constituted groups at the state level. Following the submission of suggestions by the public, the parties, candidates, and MPs, the proposed electoral division maps are designed initially by a four-member redistribution committee composed of the electoral commissioner (a position created as part of the Australian electoral commission to replace the office of the chief electoral officer), the Australian electoral officer for the state, the state's surveyor-general, and its auditor-general. Objections to the proposed map are heard by the "Augmented Electoral Commission" which consists of the four-member redistribution committee for the state plus the remaining two members of the electoral commission, its chairman (a judge), and a non-judicial member. Once the Augmented Commission promulgates its decisions they become final without any debate in, or approval of, Parliament.

Australian parliamentarians were more than willing to give up their formal role in electoral readjustments for several reasons. Since the early 1960s the process had become increasingly politicized. Two redistributions (1962 and 1975) had failed because they were not approved by Parliament. There had been resentment over the fact that electoral divisions adopted in 1955 were in many instances markedly inequitable by the time they were replaced in 1968, and following a royal commission of inquiry, a cabinet minister was dismissed in 1978 for having interfered in an electoral commission's work. In 1983 the call of the newly elected Hawke government for consensus politics struck the right note among MPs of all parties who wished Parliament freed of its last formal role and powers in the redistribution process.

The new two-tiered redistribution process, when combined with the professional and technical expertise of the committee members responsible for redrawing the electoral maps, lends support to the "judicialization" thesis of Australian redistributions. Colin Hughes and Dean Jaensch have noted that at both the federal and state levels Australia "has had an exceptional experience of transferring responsibility for drawing electoral boundaries from the persons most concerned, the members of parliament themselves, to non-parliamentary commissioners drawn almost entirely from the judiciary and the public service."[21] The 1983 amendments removed the last of the redistribution powers from the politicians and transferred them to committee members whose procedural and substantive roles suggest the judicial model. According to a former Australian electoral commissioner, these members learn "to behave and to act like judges."[22] Almost certainly the same could now be said of the Canadian electoral boundary readjustment commissions. Chaired by superior court judges they are presented with written and oral testimony and are responsible for weighing arguments and evidence before handing down their final decisions.

To Canadians, long accustomed to population shifts causing increased disparities in constituency sizes over the ten-year span between redistributions, the Australian system stands in sharp contrast. Australians attach great importance to adjusting for changes in population between their regularly scheduled redistributions. Starting with their first independent boundary readjustments, their legislation stipulated that redistributions could occur in one or more, but not necessarily all, of the states when the occasion demanded. A redistribution could be held whenever the governor-general-in-council thinks fit, or the number of MPs to be elected in a state changed because of changes in a state's population, or one-fourth of a state's constituencies differed from the limits of that state's electoral quota.[23]

Changes to Australia's law have also tightened the provisions governing the conditions under which redistributions would be required. In 1973 the tolerance limits for constituency electoral populations were reduced from +/−20 percent to +/−10 percent of a state's electoral quota, a move which in turn led to pressures for special allowances for large rural constituencies. The adoption in 1977 of a size and population rule addressed that concern. No seat having an area of 5,000 square kilometres or more could contain a greater number of voters than one with an area of less than 5,000 square kilometres. An amendment approved in 1983 guaranteed that Australian redistributions would be held every seven years, instead of every ten. By the end of the millennium the rules stipulated that a redistribution would occur even more frequently if the number of seats to which a state were entitled changed or if the number of electors in more than one-third of a state's constituencies exceeded the 10 percent tolerance limits for more than two consecutive months.[24]

To guard against that latter possibility, the most novel of Australia's electoral population provisions was put into place. It is worth examining for the lessons it offers about the limitations of demographic projections. An "eye of the needle" test was adopted in 1983 whereby redistribution committees were charged with ensuring that "as far as practicable" the number of electors enrolled in each electoral division would be equal three-and-a-half years *after* a state or territory had been redistributed.[25] The purpose of this provision was to keep constituency size as equal as possible over the life of a redistribution by striving for more or less equal electoral populations at the mid-point in a seven-year redistribution cycle. It was felt by supporters of this innovation that it was preferable to aim for population equality part way through the period covering two or even possibly three elections than it was to begin the seven-year cycle with relatively equal populations only to have them move in opposite directions as suburban and new town populations increased and rural and inner city ones declined.

The first test of Australia's new provisions came with the 1984 redistribution. At that time the divisional returning officers (career public servants knowledgeable about local affairs and often in the field at the electoral division level for many years) and local, state, and Commonwealth officials familiar with population statistics and growth patterns presented their best estimates of future electoral figures to the redistribution committees. Possibly more than any other feature of the 1984 Australian redistribution, the three-and-a-half-year rule concentrated the minds of the committee members and electoral commissioners and served as the focal point for comments and criticisms by the parties and interested members of the public. According to one state's principal electoral officer, the rule proved to be "the main limitation" on his committee's work, making more difficult the application of the "community of interest" principle. Redistribution commissioners, particularly in the large states with rapidly growing populations, acknowledged that their "predicted enrolment voter" figures three-and-a-half years hence often amounted to little more than "best guesses."[26]

Some past practices of redistribution commissions clearly had to end under the eye of the needle provision. Chief among these was the placing of slow-growth or declining-population seats (typically large rural ones) on the low side of a state's tolerance limits and fast-growth seats (generally compact urban areas) on the high side in order to minimize as much as possible the differing geographical sizes of a state's districts. The reverse practice is now followed. According to the Australian electoral commission "the most rapidly growing [districts] are started with [voter] enrolments well below the quota while those that are losing population are started well above the quota," in the hope of arriving at relatively equal populations halfway through the seven-year period.[27]

Given the uncertainties inherent in projecting population growth and movement, the difficulties in applying the eye of the needle test became apparent when the first redistribution projections were compared with the actual electoral populations three-and-a-half years later. Four-fifths of the 147 seats were within a respectable +/−4 percent of their respective state's quota. But of the remaining one-fifth, eleven seats were above or below the quota by more than 6 percent, and in the most extreme case the projection underestimated by 14 percent the real growth of a district. Although reasonably close in the majority of cases, the figures nonetheless illustrated how problematic the exercise of anticipating population growth, decline and movement can be. Even in such a relatively short span as three-and-a-half years and with valid and supportable demographic assumptions about births, deaths, migration, and mobility, the exercise is prone to "a degree of rubberiness" and occasional "misjudgment."[28] To try to allow for that, the standards have since been somewhat relaxed. They now permit a deviation of up to +/−3.5 percent from the average of a state's electoral enrolment halfway through the seven-year cycle.[29]

To place these post-1964 changes in their rightful context, it should be recognized that in Australia partisan considerations affected the complexion of electoral and redistribution laws to an extent unfamiliar to Canadians. Soon after the First World War, MPs in Canada began what was to become a seventy-five-year tradition of approving significant amendments to the Canada Elections Act unanimously. That spirit of unanimity spilled over into the early years of independent electoral boundary legislation when, without a dissenting vote from any of the four parties then in the House, approval was given to the Electoral Boundaries Readjustment Act in 1964. Also accepted without recorded opposition were the temporary suspension of the act in 1973 and the "amalgam method" in the Representation Act, 1974 as a new way of allocating seats among the provinces.

The consensual approach to amending electoral laws gained further legitimacy with the adoption of the election expenses legislation in 1974. Officials of the parties represented in the Canadian House began to meet regularly (behind closed doors and with no recorded minutes) with officials from Elections Canada to discuss and approve methods of implementing the new election expenses legislation. The responsibilities of this Ad Hoc Committee (as it styled itself) of party and electoral officials naturally broadened to include the search for ways of improving the Canada Elections Act, with the result that the practice developed of obtaining all-party agreements before electoral law amendments were proposed to the House.[30] That practice of obtaining bi-partisan support prior to the introduction of legislative changes to Canada's electoral law ended when, starting in the mid-1980s, the Ad Hoc Committee was criticized by the press, the National Citizens' Coalition and, after its formation in 1987, the Reform Party of Canada on the grounds that it was a secretive and self-serving structure intent on shaping electoral laws for the benefit of the parties already in the House of Commons.[31]

By contrast, since the 1970s Australia has pursued an openly partisan approach to changing its laws on boundary redistributions. The restriction of the permissible electoral roll variation to 10 percent above or below a state's quota was a change introduced by the Australian Labor Party (ALP) within a year of coming to office in 1972. The ALP had consistently "opposed any attempt to overrepresent areas outside the cities"[32] and was determined, once in office, to abolish the 20 percent tolerance because it favoured the National Country Party (NCP). For its part, the NCP sought to restore the 20 percent limit when it returned to office following the 1975 election, only to be rebuffed by its Liberal coalition partner. The eventual compromise reached by the two parties in the coalition government respected the NCP sensitivities to large rural seats by adopting the 5,000 square kilometre rule. Back in power after the 1983 election, the ALP succeeded in dropping that provision as part of its redistribution package approved by Parliament that year. It added instead a provision much more in keeping with Labor's stated commitment to electoral fairness and egalitarianism – the direction to redistribution committees to construct divisions with populations equal in three-and-a-half years. By prevailing Canadian standards of the time, these measures were controversial. This was illustrated by the fact that they were put into law in Australia over strong opposition objections.

CONCLUSIONS

In one essential respect Canada's debt to Australia was obvious. The authority to determine the boundaries of their own electoral districts had been given up by the politicians, turned over to non-partisan bodies, and decentralized along federal lines. Instead of one commission charged with designing all the Commons seats, as John Diefenbaker had wanted in 1962, Parliament in 1964 approved, at the Liberals' insistence, a structure in which separate commissions would be appointed for each province and territory. This was based on the reasonable presumption that local residents would be better acquainted with the social and physical landscapes of the area for which they were responsible than would a single national body. The decentralized process implied that there could be variations in the application of the terms of the statute among the commissions – one possibly paying greater attention to geographic considerations, another to social or economic ones, yet another designing its seats nearer to the provincial quotient than had neighbouring commissions, and so on. The national standards would be spelled out in the Electoral Boundaries Readjustment Act, but their application would be entrusted to separate institutions created for each province and (where applicable) territory that would operate independently from one another. An explanation offered in 1964 by Nelson Castonguay, as the newly appointed representation commissioner, to the judge who chaired the first federal commission in New Brunswick stressed one of the merits of a federalized process. Commissioners drawn from each province could be expected to know different parts of their respective jurisdiction and to be in a better position to assess the variety of proposals and arguments presented to them than could members of a single national body.[33]

But in another equally important respect, Canada pursued the matter of designing parliamentary seats differently. Lacking the commitment to representational egalitarianism that increasingly distinguished Australian from Canadian politics, Canada has left its process largely unchanged after it adopted the Australian model in the mid-1960s. Compared with Australia, redistributions in Canada permit substantially greater population disparities among electoral districts. The +/-25 percent tolerance limits translate into a possible maximum spread of 67 percent between the smallest and largest seats in a province, a figure that is triple the potential for Australian states. Moreover, as Canadian seats are readjusted less frequently than Australia's and are constructed without an eye of the needle test, there is a far greater likelihood in Canada that disparities in population sizes will increase between redistributions.

With the change in 1964, sociological, economic, and geographic factors, however difficult they might be to define with any degree of precision, displaced political ones as the grounds for drawing electoral boundaries in Canada. Superior court judges, provincial election officials, and academics replaced politicians as the arbiters of competing arguments relating to boundary readjustments. The way was also prepared for the engagement in the redistribution process of those who in the past had merely witnessed the game from afar. For the first time the public, local government officials, defeated candidates, and constituency association executives would be able to participate at one stage of the process by submitting briefs and appearing before the commissions holding hearings throughout their respective province or territory. The *modus operandi* of Canadian redistributions had changed dramatically.

5 Drawing the Maps

Population is the only true basis of representation.
                                            – George Brown, 1853

Canada's Electoral Boundaries Readjustment Act (EBRA) of 1964 represented a fundamental break with the previous practice of designing electoral districts. It took the actual drawing of the maps out of the hands of politicians and entrusted that to a small group of non-partisan commissioners in each province. For the first time in Canadian history it acknowledged the value of public opinion on boundary readjustments by requiring every commission to hold open hearings and to accept written submissions on its initial set of proposed maps. A second set of maps, possibly different from the first as a consequence of the public hearings, was to be submitted to members of Parliament for their consideration, debate and objections. Arguably the most notable feature of the EBRA was its guarantee of the independence of the commissions. They were free to accept, reject, or modify the suggestions of the public and the MPs, and they were empowered to establish the final set of boundaries they deemed appropriate.

Transferring the readjustment of electoral boundaries from politicians to non-political outsiders effectively led to the creation of a new institution in the representational process: the independent electoral boundary commission. This chapter looks at how Canada's federal commissions have gone about their work and at the role that Elections Canada has played in assisting them. The costs of conducting redistribution by electoral boundary commissions are compared, and further reforms that could be introduced to the seemingly innocuous issue of naming constituencies are explored. The chapter begins by addressing a question to which two different answers reflect contrasting views of electoral representation in a liberal democratic state: should Commons constituencies be allocated to the provinces, and should their boundaries be drawn within the provinces on the basis of total population or of eligible voters? In spite of the similarity of so many of their electoral readjustment features, Australia and Canada have reached different conclusions on that issue.

POPULATION OR VOTERS?

Whether constituencies should be drawn according to total population or number of electors is important. Is the purpose of a constituency as a geographically-defined entity primarily electoral or is it representational? The first of these alternatives speaks to a riding as a critical part of the *electoral* process, implying that only electors ought to be counted in the initial building-block stage. The second looks beyond that to its representational role, that is to the constituency as a way of aggregating all those who will be represented by an elected member through the normal workings of the *legislative* process. In Canada, each has its own proponents and set of redistributions.

Part of the justification for seats designed on the basis of an electoral population derives from the fact that they are less likely to compromise or erode the relative equality of constituency electorates than total population. As Munroe Eagles has explained, malapportionment can result when total population is used as the basis for boundary readjustments:

So long as the ratio of eligible or actual voters to total population is spatially invariant, no dilution of vote equality will result from the conventional practice. However, when non-citizens (i.e., those not entitled to vote) or non-voters are systematically concentrated in particular constituencies or types of constituencies, the votes of citizens in these ridings assume proportionately greater values. In fact, whenever the population base used in boundary adjustment is broader (i.e., more inclusive) than the number actually casting ballots, the result is a magnification of the voting power of those residing in districts with high numbers of non-voters.[1]

In other words, there is little likelihood, given the uneven distribution of both eligible voters and the general population, that a constituency boundary readjustment based on total population would generate equal electorates in the ridings. Thus, if the goal of a redistribution is to construct seats in which there will be no "magnification of the voting power" of those who are ineligible to vote, then constituencies based on the roll or list of electors will be the preferred option.

One-fifth of all Canadians move at least once every year.[2] Mindful of that fact and aware that with the passage of time the constant movement of a population reduces the comparability of ridings, the Royal Commission on Electoral Reform and Party Financing appointed in 1989 (styled the Lortie Commission after its chair, Pierre Lortie) recommended that redistributions continue to be held following every decennial census and that, if needed, they also be held more often. These would amount to a kind of mini-redistribution if the population shifts warranted them. The royal commission called for the redrawing of boundaries after each general election in any province where one-quarter or more of the federal constituencies contained a number of voters deviating from the provincial quotient by more than +/−15 percent. It also endorsed a change from total population to number of voters as the basis for constituency design.

The Lortie proposals were part of a larger package aimed at ensuring greater equality of voting power among ridings throughout the ten-year redistribution cycle. Not only would the +/−25 percent deviations be reduced by ten percentage points, but the "extraordinary circumstances" clause of the EBRA would be dropped. Parliament had responded in 1985 to pleas from MPs from isolated, northern, and sparsely populated constituencies to grant commissions greater latitude in the construction of ridings than the 25 percent deviations permitted. The act was amended to allow commissions to depart from its basic representational rule that "each electoral district in the province ... shall, as close as reasonably possible, correspond to the electoral quota for the province" and to "ensure that ... the population of each electoral district remains" within the 25 limits except in circumstances viewed by the commission as being extraordinary.[3]

The Lortie Commission justified the move from constituencies based on general population to ones based on electoral population on the grounds of enhancing voter equality and using the most current data on electors. According to the royal commission's research director, Peter Aucoin, the choice of electoral lists "had nothing to do with democratic theory." It was preferred "for the very practical reason" that voters' lists would permit the readjustment of boundaries more frequently than a general census.[4] This is certainly true, for lists of electors are prepared whenever there is an election (on average every three-and-a-half years at the federal level since 1945) or maintained on a continuous basis in jurisdictions such as British Columbia and, as of the late 1990s, Canada. By contrast, the country's most reliable total population census occurs only every ten years, too long a period, the Lortie commission believed, to ensure a reasonable measure of comparability across constituencies over time.[5] A practical consequence of a more frequent redistribution that appealed to MPs was that the changes would be less disruptive to local polling districts, constituency party organizations, and the members' electoral organizations than a ten-year redistribution.

Seats designed according to electoral populations are also justified on grounds of civic responsibility. The notion is that if some individuals have been given the right to vote because of their citizenship and age and others denied it, then those who constitute the electorate should be counted in the construction of the representational building blocks. Electors, the argument goes, are those who are most directly concerned with voting and its consequences. In Canada, three provinces (Prince Edward Island, New Brunswick, and Quebec) and one territory (Yukon) redistribute their seats according to the number of electors. Asked if he had a preference for either of the two methods of determining riding populations, one Quebec electoral boundary commissioner (who had served on commissions at both the federal and provincial levels in the 1980s and 1990s and who, accordingly, was acquainted with both bases for determining riding size) opted for electoral populations. That method of determining constituency size was fairer to those who, in his opinion, were "charged with the most important civic responsibility of all – voting."[6]

Other jurisdictions in Canada have chosen to determine their electoral boundaries according to total population. This shifts the focus from the voters to the legislative or parliamentary members and to their responsibilities as elected representatives. Redistributions at the federal level, in seven provinces, and in two territories are based on total population figures obtained in a general census. The premise underlying this method is that in their ombudsman role elected members are expected to speak for and to act on behalf of the entire population of their respective riding, not simply those who are eligible to vote or who may have voted for them. Irrespective of their age, citizenship, or political preference, residents of a constituency, so MPs believe, deserve to be helped. The range within which that help may be requested is vast – from passport forms and social insurance information to missing pension cheques and immigration issues.

David Docherty found in his study of members of the House of Commons that of the five duties that MPs serving in the 34th Parliament (1988–93) were asked to rank, they attached the greatest importance to "helping individuals" in their ridings. This was explained by the members' desire to be seen as problem-solvers and as successful trouble-shooters for constituents. The priority that members attached to helping their constituents ran counter, interestingly, to the ranking offered by members of the general public. To constituents, who ranked helping individuals the lowest of their five priorities for MPs, the most important responsibility of members was to keep in touch with the residents of their riding. Still, MPs claim that they have little choice. According to one, "helping people will not get me re-elected. But not doing it will sure get me defeated."[7]

Given the priority that MPs attach to servicing their constituencies, it is scarcely surprising that they have not supported any move away from total population-based redistributions. The most extensive Commons' discussions in the 1990s of the electoral boundary readjustment process (first in committee, then in the House in the debate on the 1994 bill, C-69) confirm that there were no members of Parliament who were seriously interested in considering having redistributions carried out on the basis of electoral lists. Those debates, together with interviews conducted with several members of the 1993–7 Parliament, suggest that the MPs' uneasiness with the number of electors as the base for boundary readjustments stemmed from a variety of different concerns.

These included a belief that "communities of interest" were easier to capture in constituencies designed on the basis of total population; that rural areas, already favoured by having more seats than their population entitled them to, would fare even better from elector-based readjustments because rural parts of the country tend to be composed of disproportionately more eligible voters than urban areas; and that members from large, socially and ethnically mixed urban seats devoted a considerable part of their time and office resources to "servicing" individuals who resided in their constituencies but who, for whatever reasons, were ineligible to vote. The concern behind that last sentiment was that if seats were drawn according to their eligible electorate rather than total population, the service burden of urban members would increase.[8] This approach was in contrast to the tack taken by the Lortie Commission, whose concern was to enhance voter equality by using the most current voter information available.

At a practical level, the number of seats to which provinces are entitled in the House of Commons can vary, depending upon whether the number is determined by total population or by eligible electors. The Lortie Commission was silent on that point, from which one can infer that it would leave the current population-based scheme in place. Jean-Pierre Kingsley, the chief electoral officer, advised MPs against that, however, arguing that either total population or eligible electors be used for *all* parts of the redistribution exercise. According to Kingsley, "the moment you start to mix, I think you're going to create more problems for electoral maps than you solve."[9] If electors were to serve as the basis for the intra-provincial part of the exercise, what would happen if they were used as well in the initial allocation of seats to the provinces?

The current formula for redistributing Commons seats among the provinces, as seen in the previous chapter, is based on the most recent decennial census. By ignoring its senatorial and grandfather clauses for the purposes of this analysis, we find that if a switch were made from a population-based formula to an electoral-based one, it would make little difference to the seven smallest provinces. For the three largest ones it would be a different picture. In the 1996 census Ontario, Quebec, and British Columbia had 75.2 percent of Canada's total provincial population and 74.4 percent of its electorate. Yet that aggregation disguised another reality. Although they had a combined total of 50.4 percent of Canada's population, Ontario and British Columbia had only 48 percent of its voters. This stood in marked contrast to Quebec. That province had 24.8 percent of Canada's population but 26.3 percent of the country's total electorate.

There are two principal causes for Quebec's difference from the other two large provinces. First, along with Atlantic Canada, Quebec has a relatively older population. The population of each of the five most easterly provinces is composed of a greater share of over eighteen-year-olds – the age at which Canadian citizens become electors – than is true of the five other provinces. The differences are most pronounced in the age demographics of Quebec and British Columbia. Twelve percent of Quebec's population is under eighteen years of age, compared with 15 percent of British Columbia's. Second, although Quebec has taken in large numbers of immigrants in recent years, the numbers for Quebec have been much less than either Ontario or British Columbia. Between 1991 and 1996, Ontario received the majority of Canada's immigrants (54 percent), followed by British Columbia with 21 percent. At 15 percent, Quebec ranked third.[10]

The combined effect of age and immigration differentials on provincial entitlements to seats in the House of Commons is obvious from a hypothetical redistribution. If we ignore the grandfather and senatorial floor provisions and compare the redistribution of seats among the provinces under the existing formula by using the 1996 quinquennial census and the 1997 voters' list, we find that the alternative population bases for redistributions would have altered the seat entitlement of a majority of provinces. Had the number of voters been used in place of the general population, British Columbia and Ontario would each have lost three seats. By contrast, Newfoundland, Nova Scotia, and New Brunswick would each have gained a seat, and Quebec would have been allotted an additional five seats. (The two-seat net difference is explained by the rounding of decimal points that the act formula calls for.) This serves as yet another example of the familiar political science maxim that institutional arrangements help to shape outcomes.[11]

One way of addressing the issue without penalizing some provinces and favouring others would be for Canada to follow Australia's lead. At the federal level in Australia, there is a bow in both directions, electors and population. The seats in Australia's House of Representatives are allocated among the states according to their respective share of the country's total population. The boundaries of the electoral districts assigned to each state are subsequently determined according to their share of the state's electorate. An attempt to end this distinction (a distinction that was as curious to many Australians as it was to outside observers) was made in 1974 when a country-wide referendum was held to seek approval for population instead of electors to be used as the base for determining district boundaries.

The Labor party, then in office, strongly supported the change. Its MPs from Sydney and Melbourne in particular pushed for a population-based boundary readjustment on the grounds that their service and representational role as members from heterogeneous urban districts with large numbers of ineligible voters was excessively burdensome. The party, which stood to benefit from the shift because of its considerable political strength in the major cities, urged approval of the change to population-based electoral districts on the ground that "votes are cast *by* electors but they are cast *for* people, for all the Australian people. To guarantee that all people are treated as equals – be they adults or children, migrants or Aborigines – they should receive equal representation in our parliament."[12]

Those who defended the status quo in Australia argued that approval of the change would amount to a denial of the fundamental principle of "equality of voting power." Their case was based on the claim derived from an elector-based theory of democracy that "equal numbers of electors ... is democratic, [whereas] equal numbers of people regardless of whether they are voters is undemocratic."[13] The proposal to make total population the basis for federal boundary readjustments failed in the referendum by a vote of 53 to 47 percent, with massive suppport for the proposed change from the principal cities and considerable opposition in all other parts of the country. The distinction, which dates back to the formation of the Commonwealth of Australia in 1901, remains in force to this day.[14]

While such a scheme as Australia's existing one (assigning population and electors a separate role in the formula) would solve one problem in Canada, it would not address a second. The intra-provincial distribution of voters and non-voters is no more "spatially invariant" (to use Munroe Eagles's expression) than the interprovincial one. Immigrants to Canada settle overwhelmingly in the metropolitan areas in three provinces. In 1991, 62 percent of Ontario's immigrant population lived in greater Toronto, 66 percent of British Columbia's lived in the Vancouver area, and 88 percent of Quebec's resided in metropolitan Montreal.[15]

Ontario and metropolitan Toronto serve as good illustrations of the point that is at the core of the defence that MPs mount against a change from population-based to elector-based boundary readjustments. A comparison of the 1996 census and the 1997 voters' list shows that of the 3.2 million residents in the twenty-nine Toronto area ridings, 59 percent were entitled to vote. By contrast, in the province's remaining seventy-four seats the share of the total population on the electoral lists was a full ten percentage points higher: 69 percent. The difference between the population and number of electors in the average Toronto area constituency was 45,059, compared with a provincial average of 35,318. In two Toronto seats, the total population was more than twice that of the number of electors: Davenport had a population of 103,074 and a total electorate of 42,558, and York-West a population of 104,957 with an electorate of 47,994.

It is difficult to determine precisely the impact that an electoral boundary readjustment would have on the internal allocation of seats in Ontario, for electoral boundary commissions have the statutorily-defined population variances to work with in designing constituencies. That said, it is reasonable to assume that metropolitan Toronto would have forfeited seats to the rest of the province just as the province of Ontario would have lost seats to other parts of the country if the EBRA redistribution formula had been based on number of electors. A change from population to electors might have cost the Greater Toronto Area something in the order of three or four seats in the 1990s; rather than having 30 percent of the province's 1996 population, the metropolitan area would have had 26 percent of the province's 1997 electorate. A changed readjustment process would have meant fewer MPs from the area to service the same total population.

This was scarcely an alternative designed to commend itself to MPs already convinced that they carried a disproportionately heavy service burden. Comments made by members in the 1994–5 committee and House of Commons debates on a modified redistribution process indicated how unattractive MPs found the elector-based idea for designing electoral boundaries. A sample of their concerns includes the following:

– "Members of parliament represent not only the electors in their constituencies. They also represent the other non-electors who approach them for assistance, and others who are not citizens of Canada but [who] live in the electoral district and who go to the

[MP] for assistance in getting citizenship ... Why would you ignore those people in counting who [should be] put into an electoral district?" (Peter Milliken, Liberal, Kingston and the Islands, and chair of the Commons Committee on Procedure and House Affairs.)

– "I want to give you my dilemma. I have 33 languages in my riding and I have 206,000 eligible voters, but 250,000 people. I get 100 telephone calls a day in various languages on visas and immigration." (Carolyn Parrish, Liberal, Mississauga West)

– "A lot of my work, whether it be immigration, whether it be young individuals with family problems, the stuff that a member of parliament has to go through when in office ... is almost as if there is a shadow out there that doesn't exist. But in fact it does, and we get the real impact of it." (Dan McTeague, Liberal, Ontario)

– "My work on the [Commons] board of internal economy indicates to me that population is probably a more accurate barometer of the real service demands of a member of parliament, particularly because it is ... the non-citizen population that is a fairly heavy source of constituent demand." (Stephen Harper, Reform, Calgary West)[16]

According to Charles Caccia, first elected to the House of Commons in 1968 and re-elected in the following eight federal elections of the twentieth century, his responsibilities in the Davenport seat in the 1990s were particularly onerous and were markedly different from those of MPs from rural or suburban areas with relatively few immigrants. One member of Caccia's staff, for example, spent "at least one-half of every day on citizenship matters" for constituents who had been ineligible to vote in the previous election and who would not have been counted in constructing an elector-based constituency.[17]

Comments such as these suggest that for members of Parliament representing seats in the core of a city, the service role that comes with holding office counts far more heavily than enhanced voter equality in determining the correct base for constituency size. For such MPs there would be real consequences following a switch from population to elite-based constituencies, especially for members such as Caccia, with high non-citizen populations in their ridings. For those who represented seats such as Davenport, that contained large immigrant populations, the workload of servicing non-citizens would become even heavier if, as would be likely with a shift from population to citizen-based ridings, the area that their seat covered would be enlarged. The central areas of the large metropolitan areas would forfeit seats to the relatively higher Canadian-citizen areas in the rural and suburban parts of their province, and although the number of constituencies would shift, the non-citizen population would remain largely where it has demonstrated its habit of locating – in the cores of the big cities.

GETTING UNDER WAY

The first federal commissions struck the procedural model in the 1960s that was followed by all later commissions. In keeping with the terms of the EBRA, they drafted a proposed set of maps; advertised them widely in newspapers; convened open meetings at major centres throughout their provinces to which the public was invited to present their views on the proposals; redefined their maps, if they deemed it necessary, in light of the public response; forwarded their reports and maps to the Commons Speaker through the chief electoral officer for consideration and possible written objections from members of Parliament; and gave final consideration and possible modification to the reports and maps following the parliamentary objection stage (see Appendix A). These statutory requirements have been common to all federal commissions since they were first established in the 1960s.

In other respects, each commission in 1964–5 made up its own organizational structure and its own preferred method of operation. All hired a recording secretary, but the salaries they received were at the discretion of the commissioners and reflected the decentralized character of the exercise. Amounts varied from a low of $11.75 per day (!) in New Brunswick to a high of $180 per week in Alberta.[18] Most commissions employed shorthand reporters who produced complete transcripts of commission meetings and public hearings; a few kept little more than abbreviated minutes of their meetings. Some correspondence, draft maps, and submissions received from the public were kept, but the records remain spotty. Much of the material accumulated by the commissions from the 1960s through to 1990s has been deposited either with the National Archives of Canada in Ottawa or with Elections Canada. The net result is that holdings are more complete for some commissions and for some federal boundary readjustments than for others.[19]

Elections Canada has played a key role in the reformed electoral boundary readjustment process. At the outset, at least, the chief electoral officer doubled as the representation commission and, in that capacity, sat as a member of every federal commission. Also, under the provisions of the act, Elections Canada is required to provide a variety of administrative and technical support services to the commissions. This includes liaison with such government departments as Statistics

Canada and Natural Resources Canada, production of the commission reports once they have been finalized, and the go-between for commissions in their dealings with the Speaker of the House of Commons.[20]

Starting in 1965 and continuing with every subsequent redistribution, Elections Canada has convened a meeting in Ottawa of all commission chairs once the Speaker's selection of members had been confirmed by order-in-council. These one-day meetings have been of the standard nuts-and-bolts variety. The agenda is designed to introduce the chairs to their obligations under the EBRA, to the relevant court decisions, to the procedures to be followed, and to the administrative and technical support with which they will be provided by Elections Canada. The merit of such meetings has been confirmed by the commission chairs. The great majority were new to the exercise when they were asked to accept the appointment by their province's chief justice, and they found the time spent learning about the essentials of the boundary readjustment process to be invaluable.[21]

In keeping with the terms of the act, it was clear from the outset that commissions did not report to Elections Canada. In fact, they do not report to any agency or institution. Their decisions, as noted earlier, are final, and once the maps have been finalized by the commissions they come into effect a year after the representation order has been proclaimed in the *Canada Gazette*. What Elections Canada can offer boundary readjustment commissions (as in Walter Bagehot's celebrated phrase about the role of the monarch in the British constitutional system) is "the right to be consulted, the right to encourage, the right to warn."[22] Elections Canada officials accept that they "can only offer advice and support" to the commissions and that the mapping technicians they supply to the commissions are there "to follow a commission's dictates not to make election management easier for Elections Canada."[23]

For the first four decades of the EBRA, the method by which commissions designed their preliminary and final maps was laborious and time-consuming. It required the assignment of an Elections Canada technician to every commission (two in the cases of the larger provinces) and the technicians' presence at all meetings where consideration was given to alternative constructs of constituencies. Elections Canada estimated that for the federal redistribution of the 1990s approximately forty staff worked directly or indirectly in providing support to the commissions. These were made up of technicians and cartographers hired by Elections Canada on a temporary basis and individuals from the Survey General's Office and Statistics Canada to certify descriptions of the boundaries and the population count.[24]

From 1965 until the end of the century, the mapping done for each commission was on a trial-and-error basis at the suggestion of the commissioners. Lines were drawn by a technician on local government maps (such as township, municipality, and city maps) using coloured pencils. Once a plausible configuration was arrived at, the technician would be expected to determine the population of each of the possible ridings. The time that elapsed between the crafting of the alternative ridings and the actual determination of their population often ran to several weeks. Because of the time taken and the consequent limitations of such a process, commissions were limited to a relatively small number of alternative maps that they might want to consider.

With the post-2001 redistribution all that will change. Digital mapping, such as that enabled by Geographic Information Systems (GIS), will greatly simplify the process of designing electoral maps. It differs from traditional mapping in that it is a computer-based information system that allows the composite storage and manipulation of vast amounts of data (socio-demographic, geographic, and the like) and the swift aggregation of such parts of those data as are appropriate to alternative sets of boundaries. Digital mapping will enable commissioners to consider a far greater (theoretically unlimited) array of possible constituencies without undue delay. Commission technicians will be able to overlay on the computer's dataset the various polygons or geometric shapes that commissioners might conceive of for the ridings they are designing. These can be drawn according to rivers, streets, municipal boundaries, highways, and the like. Tried successfully by at least three different provincial boundary readjustment commissions of the 1990s (Manitoba, Alberta, and British Columbia), GIS was judged a great improvement over earlier methods of designing maps and to be an extremely useful technological addition to the readjustment process.[25]

Digital mapping also holds promise for greater involvement of the public in a commission's deliberations. It is entirely possible for a commission's public hearings of the future to have microprocessors and technicians present to enable members of the general public, representatives of political parties, candidates, and MPs to present their particular proposals to the commissioners and to supplement their analysis with almost instantaneously available maps for all to see.[26]

WHAT DOES IT COST?

Comparative federal and provincial cost data of electoral boundary readjustments must be looked at with some caution. Accounting practices vary from one jurisdiction to another. What is included as a cost of redistribution by one electoral agency or government department may be treated quite differently by another. Salaried, permanent staff in the office of the chief electoral officer in some regimes may perform tasks at little or no cost to electoral boundary commissions; in others the same expense might be charged in its entirety to a commission. Temporary secondments to boundary commissions of permanent staff such as technicians, surveyors, and cartographers are often treated differently under one government's methods of bookkeeping than under another.

The variability of redistribution costs is apparent in table 5.1. They spread from a low of $.14 per voter in Quebec to a high of $1.08 in British Columbia. Quebec's chief electoral officer provides that province's permanent Commission de la représentation with all necessary personnel and technical assistance from his own staff and at no cost to the commission. In British Columbia, on the other hand, salaries and benefits of staff seconded from Elections BC are charged directly to the provincial boundary commission.

Commissions also handle their assignments differently. The contrast between Quebec and British Columbia is revealing and helps to explain why one boundary commission may in fact be a good deal more expensive than another. In 1990–2 Quebec's Commission de la représentation held public meetings in twelve municipalities around the province, heard 261 individuals at those meetings, and received 484 briefs or petitions about the maps they had proposed. By contrast, over a five-month period in 1998 British Columbia's commission held forty-six public meetings in forty-four different communities throughout the province. The commissioners took pride in travelling by automobile "to as many hearing locations as was realistically possible in the time available in order to gain a better appreciation of the geography of the province and the communication challenges it poses for the effective representation of British Columbians."[27] Unlike most other commissions at both the federal and provincials level, British Columbia's held a second round on a province-wide basis following the release of its proposed maps. In the first quarter of 1999 the commissioners once again took to the road and visited twenty-four communities where they had scheduled meetings. On that round they heard from 185 individuals and were presented with 265 written submissions.

The efforts that the British Columbia commission made to listen to the concerns of often quite isolated and remote communities are impressive, as are the number of individuals who met with the commissioners. But such efforts are also costly, especially in comparison with Quebec's relatively modest schedule of public hearings. Public meetings require advance staff work, advertising, space rental, travel, and

Table 5.1
Costs of Redistributions, Selected Jurisdictions, 1980s and 1990s

Jurisdiction	Decade of Most Recent Redistribution	Reported Cost ($)	Cost as % of Decennial Government Expenditures	Cost per voter ($)
Canada	1990s	6.5 million	0.000463	$ .32
Ontario	1980s	1.6 million	0.000563	.25
Quebec	1990s	689 thousand	0.000152	.14
British Columbia	1990s	2.5 million	0.001143	1.08
Alberta	1990s	418 thousand	0.000266	.25

Sources: Herschell Sax, then assistant director, Electoral Geography, Elections Canada, to author, 7 June 1999, email correspondence (copy in author's files); Elections BC, *1997-9 British Columbia Electoral Boundaries Commission: Report of the Administrator* (Elections BC, July 1999), Appendix C: Finance; W.A. Sage, deputy chief electoral officer, Office of the Chief Electoral Officer of Alberta, to author, 3 June 1999 (copy in author's files); Warren Bailey, chief electoral officer of Ontario, interview with author, Ottawa, 24 June 1999; Commisssion de la représentation électorale du Québec, *La Carte Électorale de Québec : Rapport des Dépenses* (Sainte-Foy: Octobre 1992), 2; Statistics Canada, *CANSIM Matrices* 2787, 3315, 3781, 3785, 3786. Average number of voters per decade for each jurisdiction estimated from *Chief Electoral Officer Report for 1997 Federal Election* (Ottawa, 1997), table 2.

accommodation. Three of the British Columbia commission's biggest expenditures over its eighteen-month life were a direct consequence of its choice to travel widely, hold a large number of public meetings, prepare verbatim transcripts of every public meeting, have commission staff in attendance at all meetings, and have legal counsel in attendance at some. The total expenditures for per diem fees and expenses of the two outside commissioners were $599,215. Advertising and media relations came to $612,503, and contracts with the Vancouver law firm, McCarthy, Tétrault amounted to $406,000.[28]

Comparative differences aside, it would seem that independent electoral boundary commissions are a bargain for Canadians. Table 5.1 shows the reported costs of the most recent electoral boundary readjustments by independent commissions in the five largest jurisdictions – Canada and the four most populous provinces.[29] With the exception of British Columbia, they came to less than one-third of a dollar per voter. Spread over the normal eight to ten-year life of a set of maps, that works out to just pennies per voter per year. As a portion of total government expenditures over a decade the cost of redistributions falls into the third or fourth decimal place. It would difficult to argue successfully on the grounds of financial costs that the move away from readjustments of constituency boundaries by politicians to independent commissions has led to the creation of a fiscally irresponsible and extravagant process.

WHAT'S IN A NAME?

Americans assign numbers to their electoral districts. Canadians, as a carryover of their British heritage, name theirs. The idea of using geographic place names to describe electoral districts in a parliamentary system modelled on Westminster traces its origins back many centuries to the time when the British House of Commons was to represent, in theory at least, the "commons" or "communities" of the kingdom. These were the counties and boroughs of England and the burghs of Scotland which, until Britain's electoral reforms of the nineteenth century, generally elected two members each regardless of their population. The name given a constituency was commonly taken from the county or borough itself or from the most important city or town within it. With the introduction of single-member districts, those units with sufficient population to warrant more than one electoral district were often subdivided, using directional descriptors as in "Leeds, North East," or "Hull, West."[30]

In Canada the value that inclusion of the name of a neighbourhood, town, city, county, or region in a constituency designation is clearly considerable to some individuals. It is important to local officials, such as a mayor's office and boards of trade, whose responsibilities include promoting a city or region. It is of equal importance to many MPs, who seem determined to ensure that their constituency name is as broadly inclusive of geographic place names in their riding as possible. All of this was made clear from the start of independent boundary commissions when commission proposals came under attack for failing to include certain specific place names. In the first federal redistribution after the implementation of the EBRA, 10 percent of the submissions from the general public to the commissions related directly to the name to be assigned to particular ridings, and 10 percent of the objections filed by MPs called for changes to the constituency names proposed by the commissions. That has remained the custom following every decennial redistribution since the 1960s.[31]

According to the EBRA, the name to be assigned to a constituency was the responsibility of the federal boundary commissions. MPs, along with the public, would be free to make representations to the commissions about riding names, but the final authority to select the name was to remain with the commissions. Unwilling to accept that feature of the act, MPs have "successfully asserted their right to change the names of their constituencies through the mechanism of the private member's bill."[32] They have used that method to change the names of their ridings when it suited their purpose, knowing full well that it was a virtually fool-proof way of getting the alterations adopted. As every member may, at some point, want to alter the name of his or her constituency, no member is likely to object when the batch of several private members' bills calling for name changes comes up for a vote in the Commons. Members respect a tradition that the final choice of a constituency's name is entirely up to the local member and that the approval of changes is assured when it is asked for.

Members have not shied away from using this parliamentary option to alter the descriptions of their constituencies. In the period immediately before and after the 1997 election, the names of forty-four of the recently designed 301 federal seats were changed. This represented an average of nearly two per month and was the largest number of changes in any twenty-four-month period since the adoption of the act. The alterations made by Parliament are typically of the "add-on" variety, although occasionally the order of towns or regions listed with a riding title is changed. (There appear to be no recorded instances of constituency names being shortened by MPs.) Thus, in 1997–8, Quebec's Gaspé-Bonaventure-Îles-de-la-Madeleine became Bonaventure-Gaspé-Îles-de-la-Madeleine-Pabok, and Ontario's Bramalea-Gore-Malton was changed to Bramalea-Gore-Malton-Springdale. These are but two examples of what political scientist Norman Ruff has labelled "galloping hyphenation" of constituency names in Canada.[33]

MPs intent on acknowledging as many communities in their ridings as possible are not the only agents of galloping hyphenation. Redistribution commissions too have resorted to this practice, especially when population shifts within their province have forced them to eliminate existing districts and to join them to enlarged adjacent ones. At the time of Manitoba and Saskatchewan's rapid rural population growth in the first one-third of the twentieth century, name hyphenation was unknown. Of the thirty-eight federal seats in those provinces in the 1920s, not one was composed of two place names. By the end of the century, rural depopulation, combined with the relatively fewer Commons seats assigned to those provinces, had led to over 50 percent of the federal constituencies in Manitoba and Saskatchewan being made up of composite place names.[34]

Concerned about the propensity of MPs to add-on whenever they deemed it appropriate, the Lortie Commission had called for acceptance of a reformed process of naming constituencies. It was particularly concerned with the "costs to the public treasury and to local constituency associations" every time a private member's bill calling for a different constituency name was approved by Parliament. (There will be changeover costs in Ontario too every time the name of a federal seat in that province is altered. The terms of Ontario's adoption in 1996 of the federal electoral boundaries as the provincial boundaries are such as to require a corresponding change in Ontario.[35]) The commission also noted the obvious difficulties in capturing all of a district's principal "geographic areas and communities of interest" in any name "no matter how many hyphenated names are strung together."[36]

Accordingly, the commission called for the clear delegation of the naming authority to commissions and an end to using the private member's bill to alter riding names. It also recommended that changes to riding names be prohibited for the entire period between decennial boundary readjustments, and that the number of hyphenated district names be reduced. The Lortie recommendations were largely ignored. Only one federal electoral boundary commission, that of Saskatchewan, attempted to follow the commission's guidelines in the 1994–5 federal redistribution, and by century's end there had been no signs that MPs were prepared to yield their place in the process.[37]

Provinces have dealt with the matter of naming constituencies in a similar fashion to that followed federally. Geographic place names, often hyphenated in rural seats and frequently coupled with directional modifiers in cities, predominate. Until recently, Prince Edward Island had combined the ancient British practice of naming seats with the American one of numbering them. Thus, the names of the province's three historic counties were subdivided numerically into 4th Prince, 1st Kings, 3rd Queens and so on. That has now given way to geographic naming.

Of all the provinces, Quebec has made the most concerted attempt to get away from geographic names for constituencies. Following the terms of its governing legislation, Quebec's permanent Commission de la représentation électorale consulted with the province's Commission de toponymie to determine appropriate names. The names assigned to most seats have remained overwhelmingly geographic. But Quebec has tempered that by naming seats in honour of famous individuals in Quebec history. The only three new names added to the roster of Quebec's seats in the 1990s were chosen to celebrate distinguished Quebecers: Marguerite-D'Youville (in honour of the eighteenth-century founding sister of the Grey Nuns and the first Canadian to be canonized), Borduas (after the twentieth-century surrealist painter, Paul-Émile Borduas), and Blainville (for an eighteenth-century seigneur, Louis-Jean-Baptiste Céloron de Blainville).

Australia, like Quebec, has given geographic place names to some districts and the names of distinguished Australians to others. Many place names in Australia derive from aboriginal terms. With the exception of territorial districts in Canada's three northern territories, aboriginal terms have been adopted as the names of redistributed seats much more commonly in Australia than in Canada. In Australia, explorers, artists, and former prime ministers have been honoured by having seats named after them, as have female pioneers in politics, medicine, the trade union movement, and social work. As a consequence, there has been far less reliance in Australia on geographic place names. Australians have all but avoided the Canadian disease of "hyphenitis." Of the 148 seats in Australia's House of Representatives at the end of the millennium, only two had combined names. This compares to 134 of 301 seats in the Canadian House of Commons.

Also in contrast to Canada is the fact that in Australia (a country in which three of the six states include a direction of the compass in their name, unlike Canada in which not one of the ten provinces does), not a single federal district has a directional reference in it. In Canada 21 percent of the Commons' seats have a directional modifier of some sort: "northeast," "southwest," and so on. To be sure, directions are always helpful in getting one's bearings. But over-reliance on them suggests an unwillingness to break with the past and a certain lack of imagination in finding suitable alternatives. Of the thirteen federal constituencies in Calgary and Edmonton, for example, eleven combine the name of their respective city and a compass direction. Yet both cities have an abundance of distinctive neighbourhoods and have been home to many distinguished men and women whose names could be commemorated. Why confine the descriptions to a city name and a compass direction?

Canadians often decry their limited knowledge of their own history and fail to recognize the accomplishments of those who have made outstanding contributions to the country. The Lortie Commission urged a shift in naming constituencies away from geographic place names to a recognition of distinguished Canadians and important historic events or locations.[38] There have been a few moves in that direction federally, as in the 1990s when the Saskatchewan commission named one of the province's seats Palliser and another Wanuskewin.

But more could be done. Mayors and boards of trade might be pleasantly surprised how, with time, a neighbourhood, city, town, or region could gain a certain unexpected, but nonetheless deserved, recognition. Possible inclusions might be a LaFontaine seat in the heart of Montreal, a Leacock in the vicinity of Orillia, an Agnes MacPhail for Grey County, a Woodsworth for Winnipeg North Centre, a Poundmaker in Saskatchewan, and an Emily Carr on Vancouver Island. The switch would bring with it a measure of honour for distinguished individuals of Canada's past and help to alert Canadians to the names of important historical figures. It would also be a welcome change from ponderous directional reference points and an excessive reliance on hyphenated place names that have marked Canadian redistributions up to the end of the twentieth century.

CONCLUSIONS

One representational issue that remains unresolved in Canada is whether seats should be allocated *among* the provinces and designed *within* the provinces according to their respective electorates or their total population. Although a few provinces and one territory have chosen the electoral base over population for constructing their own legislature, the majority have stuck with population data from Statistics Canada. Federal electoral boundary readjustments and the allocation to the provinces and territories of seats in the House of Commons have for over 130 years been based on the latest decennial census. It is clear from the opinions expressed by MPs that they are not about to change to an elector-based method.

Keeping a population-based scheme has come at the expense of voter equality, as the Lortie report reminded Canadians and as the Commons' committee looking into EBRA amendments in the 1990s was told by several of its witnesses. It can be demonstrated that provinces and regions within provinces with disproportionately large numbers of non-voters fare better in seat distribution than provinces and regions whose share of eligible voters exceeds their share of population. The contrast is most pronounced in the Commons entitlement of Ontario and British Columbia, on the one hand, and Quebec on the other, and within provinces, such as Ontario, when the number of seats allocated to the dominant metropolitan region is compared to the rest of the province.

The passage of time and the constant shifts of a highly mobile population combine to ensure at the end of a ten-year redistribution cycle that the population of seats and the distribution of seats among the provinces will be less equal than it was at the outset of the cycle. This prompted the Lortie Commission to call for redistributions, when needed, based on the most recent voters' list. The Commons committee charged with drafting a new act accepted the argument that more frequent redistributions, when justified by population shifts, should be held.

The endorsement of more frequent boundary readjustments was matched by an equally pragmatic response by members to the idea of shifting to elector-based redistributions. They countered that proposal by noting that MPs, especially those from large metropolitan areas, were in their view already heavily burdened with constituency servicing responsibilities. A shift to an elector-based method of designing seats would merely add to those burdens.

The contrary views on this subject owed little to democratic theory. "Voter equality," "relative parity of voting power," and "citizen responsibility" were concepts that were far less persuasive for MPs debating the issue in the 1990s than their much more immediate concerns over "servicing constituents" and "minimizing disruptions" at the riding level. The very sorts of points that surface in the public arena in Australia, as they did there in the referendum debate of 1974, have not become part of the political or public discourse on electoral boundary readjustments in Canada. Such notions may engage Canadian royal commissions and their researchers, but they count less with federal members than their more utilitarian preoccupations.

Elections Canada plays a central role in federal electoral boundary readjustments. Its technical and organizational support, coupled with its access to Statistics Canada and Natural Resources Canada, has made the tasks assigned the boundary commissioners achievable. The advances that the Geographic Information Systems technology will make possible in the future will add to the ability of the commissioners and, ultimately, the interested public, to consider a far greater range of alternative options for electoral districts than has so far been possible. This in turn may well increase the pressure for electoral boundary commissions (and the legislation governing them at both the federal and the provincial levels) to design and circulate possibly three or four alternative plans and to hold more than one round of public meetings to consider them. The experience of British Columbia holds promise on that front. Public participation and citizen engagement in the exercise clearly stand to benefit, and the information that commissions glean about local representational concerns and identifiable communities of interest would be enhanced by increased public involvement. The additional costs would be, in relative terms, minimal, and clearly justifiable in terms of an improved consultative process.

With few exceptions, members of provincial legislatures have left the naming of constituencies entirely to their respective boundary commission. Federal members could follow their lead. The intent, in 1964, was to ensure that federal boundary commissions were responsible for the names assigned to electoral districts. MPs, having chosen to overlook that feature of the EBRA, have tacitly advanced a proposition that runs counter to the fundamentals underlying boundary adjustments by independent, non-partisan commissions: that is, that the members' selection of constituency names is preferable to that of the commissions and will take precedence over it. If, as the Lortie Commission recommended, MPs were to return to the original intent of the act, the effect would be to reinforce the independence of the commissions and reduce, however minimal they may be, the costs to the treasury and the political parties of frequent alterations in names.

6 Professional and Independent Commissions

I don't think two political science professors should be on [the commission]. I've dealt with them in the past, and I've found that they really are driven by numbers.

– Andrew Telegdi, MP, 1994

From the 1950s on, support for adopting independent electoral boundary commissions gradually spread across Canada. Some provinces (Ontario and Saskatchewan) moved more quickly than others (notably the Atlantic provinces), but by the late 1990s all federal, provincial, and territorial jurisdictions in Canada had gone through at least one boundary readjustment, some more independent than others. Several had held two or more. With five decadel redistributions by the late 1990s, Manitoba held the record by the end of the 1990s, followed by four at the federal level. By the beginning of the new millennium it was clear that in less than half a century an institutional reform had made its way across a diverse, federal system in which jurisdictional prerogatives are almost invariably closely guarded. The reform had been accepted, however warily by some politicians, as part of the country's changing political and electoral fabric. In the process, the people had gained the right to express their views over how districts should be constructed by the judged-chaired commissions, and the courts, however modestly by American standards, had entered the debate in the last decade of the century over the terms of the process.

The integrity and public acceptability of Canada's electoral boundary readjustment process rest upon several interrelated variables. The impartiality, qualifications, and interests of those appointed to a commission must be unquestioned. Also important are the assumptions governing decisions about the size, composition, and representativeness of the commissions. The independence of a commission can best be assured by a true arms'-length relationship to the Assembly responsible for the legislation under which the terms of the redistribution are conducted, by a set of guidelines that are fair and appropriate to the exercise, and by the freedom to interpret and apply those guidelines without legislated constraints or administrative interference. This chapter examines commissions, for the most part at the federal level but with appropriate examples from the provincial sphere, by looking at their composition and their degree of independence.[1]

PROFESSIONALIZED COMMISSIONS

For a group charged with a major representational responsibility, federal electoral boundary commissioners have been a remarkably unrepresentative lot. From the time that commissions were first created at the federal level in the 1960s they have been overwhelmingly composed of male, white, urban professionals. Among the provinces the same was largely true until the 1990s when, as a break from earlier tradition, women and, in some cases, visible minorities were appointed to several commissions. The federal penchant for drawing its commissions' membership from such a relatively narrow pool is scarcely the result of legislative constraints. The Electoral Boundaries Readjustment Act (EBRA) stipulates only that every commission shall be chaired by a judge named by the chief justice of the province and that the two remaining members of each commission, both of whom are appointed by the House of Commons Speaker, must be residents of the province for which they have been named. Apart from those requirements, the field of potential commissioners is, theoretically at least, wide open.

Speakers have taken seriously their responsibility for constructing politically independent commissions. Consultations with the offices of party leaders and whips on both sides of the House are not unknown, but Speakers have felt under no obligation to follow suggestions put forward by such clearly partisan interests. If anything, they have chosen to ignore them and have relied instead on alternate sources for names of potential commissioners. Only rarely have the speaker's appointees been openly identified with the governing party.[2] With the exception of the occasional businessperson or individual with another occupational background, the selections have been made from lists composed overwhelmingly of provincial election officials and the legal and political science professions. A small number of practising and academic lawyers has been appointed in each of the four decades (twenty-one in total), but that remains the only relatively consistent category. The occupational composition of commissions has changed with time and reflects the important role played by the representation commissioner and Elections Canada in this early stage of the exercise (see table 6.1 for the occupation and gender of federal electoral boundary commission members from 1965 to 1994).

From the outset the Speaker has looked for guidance in making appointments. Suggestions came principally from the office of the representation commissioner in the first decade and a half of commissions and from Elections Canada since then. Between 1964 and 1979 the representation commissioner had been required to sit as a member of every federal boundary commission. Created in 1963 in anticipation of the passage of the EBRA the following year, the office of the representation commissioner was charged with the preparation of alternative maps for consideration by each commission.[3] The first and only representation commissioner, Nelson Castonguay, clearly occupied an authoritative position from which to influence the composition of the commissions by way of his recommendations of possible appointees to the Speaker. As Canada's chief electoral officer for the previous fifteen years Castonguay had come to know the relatively small number of academics and legislative and electoral officials across the country who had an interest in and a knowledge of parliamentary representation and electoral boundaries.[4]

The federal process got under way in the mid-1960s when Manitoba's experience with independent commissions was a decade old. Manitoba's membership mix commended itself to the representation commissioner, just as it had to several MPs who had taken part in the 1963–4 debate on the new legislation. The Manitoba model shaped the complexion of Castonguay's recommendations to the extent that provincial electoral officials and legislative clerks (who often doubled as their province's chief electoral officer) and university presidents were named with considerable frequency to the federal commissions of the 1960s and 1970s. At least part of the Manitoba plan later found favour with three provinces – Quebec, Alberta, and British Columbia – who legislated a requirement that their chief electoral officer be an ex officio member (in Quebec's case, the chair) of their boundary commissions. The abolition of the office of the representation commissioner in 1979, which had the effect of removing ex officio membership of the representation commissioner on all commissions and which brought to an end the preparation of alternate maps for consideration by the commissions, led the Speaker to turn for advice about appointees to Elections Canada.

Reliance on provincial electoral and legislative officers for membership on the federal commissions ended abruptly in 1994 when sixteen university-based political scientists were named, more than half the total of twenty-eight for that profession over the past forty years. Apart

Table 6.1
Occupation and Gender of Federal Electoral Boundary Commission Members, 1965–94 (n = 189)[1]

| | | | | Occupation | | | | | | | Gender | |
| | | | Prov. Chief Electoral Officers, Legis. Clerks, Court Clerks | University | | | | Business-people | Other[2] | | M | F |
Year	Judges	Lawyers		Presidents and Principals	Political Science	Law	Other disciplines[3]					
1965	11[4]	0	10	4	3	1	1	0	0		30	0
1973	11	4	7	4	2	1	1	0	0		30	0
1976	13[5]	2	7	2	1	1	1	2	4		29	4
1983	11	2	4	1	4	3	0	2	5		29	4
1987	10[6]	4	6	2	2	1	1	1	3		26	4
1994	11	1	1	0	16	1	0	2	1		31	2
Total 189[7]	67	13	35	13	28	8	4	7	13		175	14

Sources: Canadian Who's Who (Toronto: International Press, 1965–94); Who's Who in Canada (Toronto: University of Toronto Press, 1965–94); and information provided by federal and provincial elections officials.

[1] For the purposes of this table, two sets of commissions whose task was terminated prematurely and replaced by other commissions (1973 and 1983) have been included. Between 1965 and 1994, 190 individuals were appointed to Federal Electoral Boundaries Commissions. This includes Kenneth Langille who, in 1976, was appointed to the Nova Scotia commission upon the death of initial commission member, Roy Laurence. Laurence, rather than Langille, has been included in this table. Occupational information was not available for one 1983 Alberta Commissioner, Kenneth A. Wark, who has been omitted from the occupational data set (n = 188) but included in the gender and residence data sets (n = 189).

[2] Three homemakers and 1 land claims negotiator (1976); 3 homemakers, 1 nurse, and 1 pastor (1983); 1 chartered accountant, 1 journalist, and 1 real estate appraiser (1987); 1 teacher (1994).

[3] A professor of mathematics and philosophy (1965, 1973, 1976) and a professor of history (1987).

[4] In 1965 and 1973 there were 10 commissions, each chaired by a judge. In addition, a judge served as a second member of the British Columbia commissions.

[5] In 1976 the Northwest Territories had its first boundaries commission. Each of the 11 commissions was chaired by a judge. In addition, a judge served as a second commission member on both Ontario and British Columbia commissions.

[6] In 1987 no boundaries commission was appointed for the Northwest Territories.

[7] Of the 189 members, 155 (82%) resided in their province's capital city or its principal urban centre.

from the judicial chairs of commissions, the political scientists in 1994 constituted by far the largest single occupational contingent in any one year. With the exception in 1994 of the Northwest Territories, every federal commission had at least one political scientist, and in six of the ten provinces both of the Speaker's appointments were drawn from the political science community. Elections Canada played a critical part in that development.

Why the remarkable jump in the numbers of political scientists in the 1990s? The explanation lies in the incontestable fact that the Canadian political science community has paid increasing attention to questions of boundary readjustments, representation, and electoral fairness in the past two decades and, as a consequence, networks between Elections Canada officials and the academic community have become established. The body of popular and academic literature produced by political scientists in the 1980s and 1990s has been impressive (see bibliography), and university course offerings confirm that greater attention has been paid in the classroom to issues germane to electoral boundaries and constituency readjustments than ever before. The media's understanding of such issues has improved, and frequently the press has turned to political scientists to offer explanations of some current representational or electoral question. Accordingly, the public profile of those who have studied and proclaimed on these matters has been raised. It was logical for federal and provincial election officials to look for prospective commission members among those who have written books or articles, lectured, appeared as experts in court cases, testified before parliamentary committees, or been quoted in the media on representational issues. Not surprisingly, the great majority of the sixteen political scientists who served on the 1994–6 federal redistribution commissions had previously researched and published on Canada's electoral system, representation or electoral boundaries.[5]

One illustration of how inter-professional contacts developed between Elections Canada and the academic community is provided by a scholarly conference held at the University of Saskatchewan in 1991. The timing of the meeting was fortunate, coming as it did shortly before the commissions of the 1990s were to be constituted. Devoted to an evaluation of legislative and judicial reasoning with respect to electoral boundaries in Canada, the academic papers and commentaries presented at the meeting by seventeen political scientists and six lawyers from Canada and the United States were published the following year in an edited volume, *Drawing Boundaries: Legislatures, Courts, and Electoral Values*.[6] Officials from Elections Canada attended the conference and subsequently prepared a list of possible appointees for the Speaker's consideration on which the names of several conference participants were included. Of those who made presentations at the meeting, four were named to federal commissions (three political scientists and one university-based lawyer) and a fifth declined an offer because of other commitments.[7]

Another pool of potential academic members to which Elections Canada turned in preparing its list for the Speaker's consideration was made up of political scientists who had conducted research on representational questions for the Royal Commission on Electoral Reform and Party Financing. Appointed in 1989, the Lortie Commission released its extensive report on election financing, party organization, voter registration, representational issues, and other election-related topics in the early 1990s. Twenty-nine volumes of research studies, including several with as many as nine separate papers, accompanied the report. In all, the commission's final report and its research studies represented the largest corpus of literature published on electoral, party, and representational questions in Canadian history.[8] As part of the royal commission's research directorate was based in Ottawa, contacts and transfer of information between them, the university-based researchers, and Elections Canada officials were frequent. It was therefore understandable that the chief electoral officer proposed some of their names for membership on federal electoral boundary commissions. Three who had written research studies were named by the Speaker to federal commissions. So too was the royal commission's research director.[9]

Jean-Pierre Kingsley was named Canada's new chief electoral officer in 1990. Succeeding Jean-Marc Hamel, Kingsley (as is the case with any new head of an organization) brought with him his own managerial style and views of how his organization and its mandate should proceed. As a public servant and a product of Ottawa's professional and bureaucratic milieu, Kingsley has urged in his periodic reports to Parliament that changes be made in the electoral law to enable Elections Canada to select and appoint electoral district returning officers, thereby removing the power from the party in office to use this as a form of patronage. Arguing that the current system of allowing the cabinet to appoint returning officers was anachronistic and that Elections Canada, "like any corporate entity," should have "a competent and experienced work force" selected through public competition, the chief electoral officer clearly opted to have carefully chosen professionals run the elections in each of the 301 federal constituencies.[10]

Kingsley was unsuccessful in wresting this prerogative away from the politicians, but the fact that he thought such a move necessary provides a significant clue about his approach to staffing his agency and, at a larger level, to the membership on the commissions whose responsibilities have such an important bearing on electoral administration. To Kingsley and others who share the view that non-governmental professionals should be appointed to such bodies as electoral boundary readjustment commissions, the political science profession offered a pool of potential commissioners. The basic requirements of the names of possible commission members that Kingsley proposed to the Speaker were simple. He was convinced that he could not "come up with something better" than preparing a list of individuals "with knowledge about the Canadian electoral system" who are at the same time "non-partisan."[11]

The effect of having drawn a large number of members from such occupations as law and political science and, prior to that, from among legislative clerks and provincial electoral officials, has been to professionalize the process of electoral boundary readjustments. By entrusting redistribution to those who have studied the subject most closely (political scientists and academic lawyers) or who have administered elections or legislative assemblies (electoral and legislative officials), Speakers have accepted that professionals who study or work with politicians have some special skills to bring to the task. Social scientists teach, research, and write about such concepts as community of interest, representation, and rates of population growth. Discussing and possibly debating these notions with their fellow commissioners would not be an alien experience.

For their part, judges also bring necessary, but different, professional skills to their position as the chairs of commissions. By the nature of their position on the bench they are accustomed to listening to competing arguments, adjudicating disputes, and handing down decisions. Theirs is a skill of accommodating differences, of balancing competing interests, and of attempting to determine what is fair and right within the terms of the law. Members of the judiciary serving as commission chairs lend a credibility and dignity to the proceedings that helps to legitimize a commission's work. In the words of one chair, judges are "non-partisan decision-makers who are immune from flak."[12] That stands in stark contrast to descriptions that were characteristically made of federal and provincial politicians who, prior to the introduction of independent commissions, recrafted the electoral maps in an atmosphere charged with partisanship and self-interest.

Part of the massive changes to Canada's electoral boundary readjustment system that were considered, but never adopted, by Parliament in 1994–5 in the lead-up to Bill c-69 addressed the question of commission membership. It was proposed that three-member commissions continue to be appointed for each province at the time of federal redistributions and, as at present, be chaired by a judge appointed by the province's chief justice. In a proposed change supported by the chief electoral officer, the remaining two members would have been appointed by the Speaker following an open and publicized competition in which applications would be screened. It was hoped that this change would have had the effect of ensuring, in the words of one MP participating in the House committee's deliberations on c-69, that "the job of the commissions ... be professionalized, [for] they are ... *not professional enough* as things stand."[13]

If that sentiment captured the intent of the legislative proposal, it was misguided, for it is difficult to see how the occupational and demographic composition of the commissions could have been much different under the reformed legislation than it has been since 1965. The very sorts of individuals who would be expected to apply and do well in the competition would be the social scientists and legislative and electoral officials who shared a keen interest in and knowledge of the subject. So long as the operative assumption remained unchanged about qualities needed in appointees, and so long as the Speaker continued to ensure that appointments to such arms'-length agencies be non-partisan, it is reasonable to expect that little would have been different about the composition of the commissions had c-69 been adopted.

UNREPRESENTATIVE COMMISSIONS AND TRANSACTIONAL REPRESENTATION

Professionalization of the electoral boundary readjustment process comes at an obvious price. As noted at the outset, commissions have scarcely reflected the demographic characteristics of the larger population. Of the 189 federal commissioners appointed since 1965, only fourteen have been women. No female judge has ever chaired a commission. More than four-fifths (82 percent) of the commissioners resided either in their province's capital city or, as in the case of Montreal, Vancouver, and Calgary, in its major metropolitan centre. No visible minority or ethno-cultural minorities have been named members of any of the federal commissions, and except for Nellie Cournoyer (Inuit) in 1976, no aboriginals have been appointed to any federal body.[14]

The demographic imbalance of commissions is a consequence of their professionalization, their small size, and the almost total absence of any suggestion that they be treated as agencies to which representatives of various social or interest groups be appointed. By selecting those whose occupational expertise includes studying representational issues or who have worked administratively on elections or in legislatures, Speakers have effectively narrowed the pool of individuals who might be appointed to a relatively small number of potential members. In turn, the professions from which the choices have been made are themselves demographically imbalanced. Although the demographics are changing with each decade, political scientists, legislative officials, and the judiciary remain disproportionately male and white. Given the location of large universities, legislatures, and courts, commission members are also far more likely to be residents of provincial capitals or major metropolitan centres than of small cities, towns, rural areas, or isolated, sparsely populated regions. Since the introduction of independent commissions, there have been no suggestions or attempts on either the federal or (with one exception, as will be seen) the provincial level to construct larger commissions that are deliberately composed of members drawn from different social groups or interests. The record to date confirms that as a building block in the early stages of the representational exercise, an electoral boundary commission has not itself been treated as an institution designed to reflect society's parts.

The demographic balance of commissions could be different if their size were larger, if the instructions issued the commissions were less neutral and more *dirigiste*, and if the underlying principle guiding appointments to the commissions was one of attempting to mirror in some mathematically precise way various segments or interests in society. Women, aboriginals, and members of linguistic or visible minorities might then expect to be named to commissions in greater numbers, possibly even becoming advocates on the commission for their respective community. Given the fairly even distribution of males and females across Canada, it would be idle to think that the appointment of women and men in equal numbers would in itself affect the gender composition of the districts agreed to. Territorially defined, single-member districts composed of a majority of female or of male residents would be impossible to construct in Canada.

But that would not be the case where voters might be grouped according to linguistic, ethnic, or racial characteristics. There the numbers might be sufficiently concentrated as to permit a particular seat to be crafted to ensure that a significant portion, possibly even a majority, of its population is drawn from a defined social group. Both the composition of the membership and the instructions issued the Nova Scotia provincial commission of the 1990s came the closest to that model of any federal or provincial commission yet established. Named by an order-in-council in 1991, the six-member body was carefully balanced. It was composed of three men and three women: two political scientists (one who served as chair), a retired judge, a former small-town mayor, an Acadian, and a Black Canadian. Three were from Halifax, three from other parts of the province.[15]

The commission's terms of reference included no maximum or minimum population limits for constituency size, but they did require consideration of minority representation in constructing seats. To that end the commission was instructed to "seek out the advice, support and cooperation of, in particular, representatives of the Black, Native and Acadian communities of the Province."[16] Each of these three communities has a relatively small share of Nova Scotia's population, varying from between an estimated 1 percent for the Natives and 5 percent for the Acadians.[17] The commission tried to ensure a degree of minority representation in the fifty-two-seat legislature by creating what it called "protected constituencies." This was a term it coined to describe districts created around "minority group population concentration." Three of the four protected seats differed substantially in size from districts elsewhere in the province by having populations well below the provincial average. That was justified on grounds of wanting to "encourage, but not guarantee" the election of three Acadians and one Black to the legislature.[18] The likelihood of their being designed was enhanced by the appointment of a demographically more varied commission than has been usual in Canada. In the words of its chair, "the commission could not have ignored minority representation given the presence of Acadian and Black *representatives* on it."[19]

Nova Scotia's ability in the 1990s to craft seats with the intent of encouraging minority representation in its legislature is explained by several interrelated factors. Size of the commission and of the average population per district were both important, as were the instructions that guided the exercise and the political signals they conveyed. A six-member commission provided considerably more room for constructing a demographically diverse body than a three-member commission. A legislature with fifty-eight seats whose average population was 17,300 provided much greater scope for constructing districts to protect relatively small targeted populations with, to continue with the Nova Scotia example but at the *federal* level, an allotment of eleven Commons' seats with an average population of 81,700. The Nova Scotia legislature's instructions to the commission to seek ways of enhancing representation of specifically named social groups has had no equivalent elsewhere in Canada and could scarcely have been disregarded by the commission without endangering its entire work.[20] The balanced composition of the commission, the absence of a legislated range of average constituency populations, and the acceptance of the proposition that protected constituencies should be constructed, all combined to ensure that the redistribution undertaken in Nova Scotia in the 1990s was unlike any other in Canadian history.

The Nova Scotia example raises an important question about the role that commissioners are expected to play in designing seats. As federal and provincial independent commissions have developed in Canada over the past four decades, the men and women appointed to them have neither been chosen nor acted as instructed agents or delegates on behalf of some delegating body. Nor have they subsequently been held accountable to another group or institution for their actions once they have completed their task. Their appointments have rested on the Burkean premise that rational deliberation will take place and that individual and collective judgments will be made by the commissioners with respect to their assigned task and within their interpretation of the relevant law. They have been given, in other words, the *authority* to act independently of particular interests or group expectations. That authority derives from the *transaction* that has been concluded at the outset of the exercise, that is at the time the appointments are made and the commission is constituted. We can label this "transactional representation." The commissioners' role as transactional representatives has a particular meaning: it is to establish to their satisfaction what constitutes the public interest within the jurisdiction for which they are responsible and to fulfill their obligations by attempting to balance competing social interests.

By contrast, when institutional membership is fashioned to mirror certain aspects of society, possibly creating expectations that the individuals appointed will attempt to protect or enhance the interests of a particular social group through the decisions that are reached, a different representational role comes into play. In this instance a commissioner's appointment rests on the fact that he or she "stands for" others. It may be the case, as Hanna Pitkin has described it, that "what seems important [in mirror representation] is less what the [commission] does than how it is composed."[21] Nonetheless, outcomes are important, especially when the credibility of the process and the widespread acceptability of commissions' decisions are at stake.

If the mirror or descriptive theory of representation for membership on electoral boundary commissions replaced transactional representation in Canada, it would alter not only the demographic composition of the (necessarily enlarged) commissions; it could create private and public expectations about the role that a particular commissioner is expected to play, insofar as it implies that it is part of his or her job to get a seat or seats for a specific community. It could also lead a commission to adopt widely different measures of determining the size of populations of its districts. Thus, in order to ensure that some particular social group received its rightful share of minority representation seats, a mirror view of electoral representation could lead a commission to construct districts much closer to the maximum and minimum allowable limits and to make greater use of "extraordinary circumstances" clauses (or their equivalent) than has so far been the case. The Nova Scotia commission pointed in that direction when it constructed roughly 8 percent of the province's fifty-two seats well below the average district size in order to encourage minority representation of two targeted groups, each with its own representative on the commission.[22]

THE INDEPENDENCE TESTS

The move away from government-dominated redistributions to non-partisan commissions was justified from the outset on grounds that extra-legislative bodies would be independent in a way that politicians could not be expected to be. When the term "independent" is used to describe the membership of an electoral boundary commission, it signals one aspect of the process that the general public readily understands: the commission is composed of members whose vocation and livelihood are not affected by the outcome, who can perform their duties with general as opposed to particular interests as their primary focus, and who can adjudicate impartially among competing demands. But there are other aspects of independence in addition to membership. Independence of commissions is ensured by the absence of legislative or regulatory constraints on commissions' decision-making and on the options they may chose to follow in designing districts. A commission's independence also rests on its decisions being free from ministerial or legislative rejection or override. Thus we can say that there is a three-pronged test of true independence. Commissions should be made up of disinterested and non-partisan individuals who have no personal stakes in the outcome; they should operate free of constraints that would otherwise limit their options to construct districts they deem to be in the public interest; and they should be granted the ultimate authority to determine the constituency boundaries.

Non-partisan outsiders

The process of selecting and appointing commission members varies among the jurisdictions, but with few exceptions the intent is the same. At the federal level and in most provinces the legislation under which commissions are selected aims at ensuring non-partisan and arms'-length appointments. Unique among the jurisdictions is Manitoba's electoral boundary commission law which, since it was first adopted in the 1950s, has spelled out the commission's membership. It is composed of the individuals who, at the time of the redistribution, happened to occupy three senior positions in the province: the province's chief justice, its chief electoral officer, and the president of the University of Manitoba. Quebec, on the other hand, aims at a measure of major party agreement by naming the province's chief electoral officer and two non-politicians approved by a two-thirds vote of the National Assembly as the three members of its permanent boundary commission. Quebec's legislature has signalled its confidence in the two outsiders named to the commission and in the commission's autonomy. Regardless of party in power (federalist or separatist) or the partisan complexion of the national assembly, the same two individuals (a Laval sociologist and a Université de Montréal political scientist) have served since 1983 for consecutive five-year renewable terms. Several other provinces have followed the federal lead and have turned over to the Speaker of the legislature the selection of at least some of their commission members. Judges chair most commissions and chief electoral officers serve ex officio on three commissions (see table 6.2).

Until recently many provincial chief electoral officers were readily-identified, in some cases openly partisan, supporters of the party in office, and they would almost certainly be replaced when their party lost office. Obvious partisanship in the selection of the chief electoral officer at the provincial level is largely a thing of the past. Professional and managerial skills are now needed to oversee the operation of an increasingly high-tech government service, and election laws and party finance regulations adopted over the past quarter-century require a degree of specialized knowledge rarely required before. As well the level of trust in the electoral office from all parties in a legislature or during an election needs to be kept high. The posts are now well beyond the point of being filled by partisans. The province of Saskatchewan moved in that direction in 1998 when it named its new chief electoral officer following an open, public competition. According to the late Jacques Girard, chief electoral officer in Quebec, his province's chief electoral official has had "immense moral authority" over the years and a status that has given the person holding that office an independence largely identical to that of a judge. Girard saw his role as chair of the province's permanent electoral commission as proof of the non-partisanship of his position.[23]

The courts have addressed the issue of independence of boundary readjustment commissions in only two cases. In one, the judge held

Table 6.2
Federal, Provincial and Territorial Redistributions

Jurisdiction	Frequency	Most Recent	Authority to Conduct	Composition	Tolerance Level	Basis of Quotient	Procedure of Enactment
Canada	Following every decennial census	1996 (based on 1991 census)	Electoral Boundaries Readjustment Act	Judge appointed by chief justice of province and two members appointed by Commons Speaker	±25% (or more in extraordinary circumstances)	Population	CEO prepares a representation order that comes into force on the first dissolution of parliament
Nfld.	Every ten years	1995	The Electoral Boundaries Act	Judge, with four others appointed by the Speaker*	±10% (±25% is acceptable in four Labrador seats and one on the southwest coast)	Population	By an act of the legislature
P.E.I.	After every third general election	1994	The Electoral Boundaries Act	Judge or retired judge and two citizens, one nominated by the opposition and one by the government	±25%	Electors	By an act of the legislature

Table 6.2 (continued)

Jurisdiction	Frequency	Most Recent	Authority to Conduct	Composition	Tolerance Level	Basis of Quotient	Procedure of Enactment
Nova Scotia	No later than March 31, 2002 and thereafter every ten years	1992	House of Assembly Act	Appointments made by order-in-council on the recommendation of select committee of the House representing recognized parties	No specific limits; established pattern of ±33 1/3%	Population	By an act of the legislature
New Brunswick	As directed by order-in-council	1993	As directed by order-in-council	As directed by order-in-council	±25% (except for Fundy Isles)	Electors	By an act of the legislature
Quebec	After every second general election	1992	Elections Act	Chief electoral officer, two others appointed by 2/3 majority of the National Assembly	±25% (can exceed in exceptional circumstances, but commissions must justify departures in report). The act guarantees a seat to the Magdalen Islands.	Electors	The boundaries commission devises maps which come into force upon dissolution of legislature
Ontario	See Canada	1996	Representation Act, 1996	See Canada	See Canada	See Canada	See Canada

Table 6.2 (continued)

Jurisdiction	Frequency	Most Recent	Authority to Conduct	Composition	Tolerance Level	Basis of Quotient	Procedure of Enactment
Manitoba	Every ten years	1998	The Electoral Divisions Act	Chief Justice of Manitoba, chief electoral officer, and president of Univ. of Manitoba	±10% for districts south of 53rd parallel, and ±25% for districts wholly or partially north of 53rd parallel	Population	By an act of the legislature
Sask.	After each decennial census	1993	The Constituency Boundaries Act, 1993	Judge, and two residents named by order-in-council	±5% (except for two northern districts)	Population	By an act of the legislature
Alberta	After every second general election	1996	Electoral Boundaries Commission Act	A chair appointed by order in council[†] and four members appointed by Speaker, two nominated by the opposition and two by the government	±25%. The Act allows up to 4 districts to have populations as much as 50% below the prov. quotient, when such districts meet at least 3 geographical and demographic criteria enumerated in the Act.	Population	By an act of the legislature
BC	After every second general election	1999	Electoral Boundaries Commission Act	Judge or retired judge, CEO, and a third person named by Speaker	±25% (may be exceeded in very special circumstances)	Population	By an act of the legislature

Table 6.2 (continued)

Jurisdiction	Frequency	Most Recent	Authority to Conduct	Composition	Tolerance Level	Basis of Quotient	Procedure of Enactment
Yukon	No set time within which electoral districts must be reviewed	1991	By an act of the Legislative Assembly establishing a new commission	To be set out in the act establishing the commission. A judge in 1991.	No specific ± limits	Electors	By an act of the legislature
NWT	By recommendation of the Legislative Assembly	1999	By an act of the Legislative Assembly establishing a new commission	Judge or retired judge and two persons recommendation of the Legislative Assembly	No specific ± limits	Population	By an act of the legislature
Nunavut	By recommendation of the Legislative Assembly	1999	Electoral Boundaries Commission Act, 1996	Judge or retired judge and two persons on the recommendation of the Legislative Assembly	No specific ± limits	Population	By an act of the legislature

Source: Elections Canada, *Compendium of Elections Administration in Canada* (Prepared for the Canadian Election Officials Conference in Winnipeg, 2000), Part B.

* In 1995 a judge only. The report of a 1993–4 commission chaired by a judge and composed of four other members was not accepted by the cabinet. That commission's report was made available to the one-person 1995 commission. No new hearings were held.

† The chair must be one of the following: the ethics commissioner; the auditor-general; the president of a post-secondary educational institution in Alberta; a judge or retired judge of any court in Alberta; or a person of similar stature in the opinion of the Lieutenant-Governor-in-Council.

that "maps need not be drawn by fully independent commissions,"[24] and in another the court noted that although it is *preferable* that electoral distributions ... be carried out by a non-partisan, independent boundaries commission" there is no "constitutional guarantee" that requires their establishment.[25] In his concurrence with the majority decision in the *Carter* reference, Mr Justice Sopinka went so far as to state that "it was not necessary for the Saskatchewan legislature to create an independent commission, and, had it simply legislated the impugned boundaries, the process itself [as opposed to the 1989 act that established the readjusted districts] would not have been subject to judicial scrutiny."[26]

It was understandable that the commission responsible for designing the electoral districts at question in the *Carter* case should not have been seen by the Supreme Court as an issue to be addressed. That body was composed of the retired chief justice of the province, a provincial court judge, and the chief electoral officer for Saskatchewan. But what of other much more blatantly partisan bodies? Is it reasonable to accept the proposition that a group appointed to design a set of electoral maps is in fact independent if it is composed of elected members of an Assembly or extra-legislative partisans and representatives of competing political interests?

Prince Edward Island's first attempt at an electoral boundaries commission can scarcely have been seen at the time as independent. It was composed of a Liberal MLA as chair, three other Liberal MLAs, the Conservative leader of the opposition, a former Conservative MLA, a lawyer active in the Liberal party, and a retired judge. Its unanimous recommendations (calling for a slightly reduced thirty-member legislature for the island) were never adopted. Instead, a private member's proposal for an Assembly of twenty-seven members was accepted as part of a bill to get redistribution out of the hands of politicians and to ensure in the future the regular appointment of three-member electoral boundary commissions composed of a judge and two non-partisan outsiders.

Alberta's two commissions of the 1990s also failed the non-partisanship test, in the first case famously so. In 1991–2 the five-member body was made up of a judge (as chair), the province's chief electoral officer, two non-elected government nominees, and one individual named by the leader of the opposition – with disastrous results. Labelled by Keith Archer a bipartisan rather than an independent commission, the five members agreed to very little and "gained the dubious distinction of being the first electoral boundaries commission to file only minority reports."[27] Upon the failure of the commission to reach agreement, the map ultimately approved by the legislature illustrated how politically charged the atmosphere had become over redistribution. The constituencies were designed by four government MLAs, the three opposition members having boycotted the legislative committee in which the redistribution was carried out. The province's second commission of the decade (named in 1995) was no more independent in its composition, although it was able to agree on a single majority report. Of its five members, two were named by the government and two by the opposition. As that commission demonstrated, multi-member commissions composed of individuals appointed by opposing partisan interests can reach unanimous recommendations.[28]

Yet independence, not unanimity, is not the issue here. Commissioners must be *seen* to have no personal stakes in the decisions they make. In the time-honoured method whereby elected politicians' redesigned their own constituency boundaries, MPs and MLAs were obviously the key players in an exercise that related to their personal and their party's well-being. Non-partisan commissions were introduced to correct that problem. Accordingly, the public would be right in being sceptical about the independence of any commissions whose members had been directly chosen by elected politicians. They were the ones who were to have been taken out of the process in the first place.

Absence of constraints

A commission's membership is not the only criterion by which to judge its independence. It should be free to design constituency boundaries in keeping with its interpretation of the principles contained in the legislation, the evidence and arguments presented to it, and the population data with which it is working. Legislative or administrative constraints imposed upon a commission violate its true independence. Saskatchewan's Electoral Boundary Readjustment Act of 1987 serves as an illustration of the sort of limitation that can compromise a commission's independence. The act specified that the province would have sixty-six constituencies: twenty-nine urban, thirty-five rural, and two northern. The line demarcating the southern boundary of the two most northerly seats had been accepted for some time in the province, but the urban-rural distinction was new to Saskatchewan law in 1987. So was the requirement that urban ridings could not extend beyond municipal boundaries.[29] These stipulations, which effectively meant that the average urban seat would have nearly 1,400 more voters in it than the average rural seat, amounted to an illustration of what Rainer Knopff and Ted Morton have called "legislatively mandated inequality."[30] In reality, the plan amounted to little more than a poorly concealed attempt by the governing, rurally-based Conservatives to tip the redistribution scales in their favour.

In the *Carter* decision the majority of the Supreme Court accepted the proposition that, having established the redistribution commission, the legislature was then "entitled to set tight guidelines for [the commission] to follow in the execution of its responsibilities." To the three judges in the minority, however, the division of the province into a fixed number of rural and urban seats as well as the prohibition on urban districts extending beyond urban municipal boundaries amounted to a constitutionally defective product. The commission was effectively "shackl[ed]" and prevented from being able to "sufficiently accommodate the changing demographic reality" of the province. Thus it violated section 3 of the Charter. Boundaries commissions, the minority declared, should be "completely independent."[31]

It is difficult to accept the Supreme Court's majority ruling on this issue. Without complete freedom to apply the basic representational principles as defined in the statutes governing redistributions – such as a measure of population equality and acceptance of community or diversity of interest, means of transportation and communication, and physical features in the actual design of the ridings – a commission is limited in the options it has at its disposal. An arbitrary statutory provision that mandates the creation of separate rural and urban seats or that prohibits designing hybrid rural-urban seats ignores the fact that social interests are layered in multiple ways and that only one of these is place of residence. Highways and mass transportation have made it easy for some who live in a city to work, seek recreation, or have a social life outside a city. Equally, many who live on the fringes of a city but beyond its actual municipal borders have their place of employment, are entertained, do their shopping, or are educated in the city. For citizens who fall into either category, community of interest is not simply a reflection of where they live. Residents of bedroom suburbs adjacent to cities are far more likely to share values and interests that are akin to residents of cities than to residents of truly rural parts of their province. The point is captured in one MP's explanation of why in the 1990s a constituency boundary should be altered to ensure than one rural township was included in the federal seat of Kingston and the Islands rather than, as proposed, Hastings-Frontenac-Lennox and Addington: "the residents of that area work, play and eat in Kingston. [They] already think they live in Kingston."[32]

Moreover, physical dividers such as rivers, bays, inlets, or straits are not restricted to rural parts of the country. Topographical maps of Halifax, Quebec City, Montreal, and Vancouver reveal how marked an urban landscape can be by physical contours. Some commissions may find a combined urban-rural seat the most attractive way of wedding a particular territorial mass with a particular population *because* of the physical configuration; others may have little choice but to rule that option out because of the transportation or communications difficulties created by the topography. Like physical obstacles, means of transportation such as highways or rail lines can divide a population in ways that bear no relationship to municipal boundaries but that nonetheless create distinctive social or economic communities straddling municipal borders. Similarly, means of mass communications, such as large daily newspapers, radio, and television are distributed or broadcast over vast areas that know no artificial municipal bounds.

The districts designed by the federal commissions of the 1990s in Quebec, British Columbia, and Saskatchewan offer instructive examples of how commissioners faced with particular sets of social, physical, and transportation variables respond differently. In Quebec, the St Lawrence River has assumed a "sacred" quality and has "become both a physical and a psychological divide." For the federal commissioners of the 1990s, this meant that the river could not be touched as a natural boundary within the province. Twenty-eight federal districts were allocated to the regions north of the St Lawrence, twenty-six to the south, and twenty-one to the metropolitan Montreal-Laval area. The commission took some pride in ensuring that none of these seventy-five seats crossed the river. For them the St Lawrence served as a natural boundary.[33]

Because the population of North Vancouver had increased between 1981 and 1991, British Columbia's federal commission had originally proposed that the area deserved two urban ridings instead of the current single district. One would cross an inlet, Indian Arm, for the first time and be joined to a portion of the city of Coquitlam. Objections presented at the commission's hearings made it "abundantly" clear that the public thought otherwise. When it announced in its subsequent report that it was scrapping its proposal in favour of one that did not combine two municipalities separated by a body of water, the British Columbia commission stated:

We heard that the proposed boundaries would not only pose transportation difficulties but would also complicate communication with residents because of multiple community television stations and media outlets. As well, not all of the Indian Arm-Coquitlam constituency would be within the free local telephone exchange. Furthermore, it was asserted that a single member would give more *effective representation* to North Vancouver.[34]

The North Vancouver residents had pressed to remain part of one large constituency (the largest by population in the province after the 1991 redistribution) rather than be divided into two with part of one riding jumping an inlet to link up with a different municipality. Justifying their opposition to the proposal on the grounds of community of interest and effective representation, the residents of North Vancouver (in the words of one federal commissioner) cared not a "diddly-squat" about the notion of voter equality.[35]

For Saskatchewan's federal commission of the 1990s, one of the province's largest rivers, the South Saskatchewan, provided an obvious and relatively simple way by which to create four urban-rural districts in and around the city of Saskatoon that were all relatively equal in population and close to the provincial quotient. The commission justified its move in the following terms:

Historically in Canada the tendency has been to create electoral districts that do not mix rural and urban residents, although in recent times Saskatchewan's federal constituencies have not been drawn rigidly in that fashion. Moreover, rural or primarily rural ridings have tended to contain numbers of residents below the electoral quotient, partially as a reflection of the larger area for members of Parliament to service and of the fact that those areas suffered inadequate transportation and communications networks.

What are the realities of today? Many argue that the interests of the urban and rural residents are different. The Commission is not convinced that the differences are significant. Many urban residents were born and raised in rural Saskatchewan. The economic vitality of urban centres in Saskatchewan is dependent on the economic health of the rural residents. There are significant ties between rural and urban residents. Saskatchewan has the most extensive road system in Canada. Its telecommunications network is likewise more than adequate to enable constituents to have easy access to their representatives ... Thus, the Commission concludes that separating rural and urban residents and designing primarily rural electoral districts with populations below the quotient would be unwarranted.[36]

All of these factors (rivers and inlets serving as natural dividing lines, communities of interest defined by natural or artificial borders, rural-urban ties being stronger than is commonly asserted) underscore the importance of granting commissions the freedom to construct seats that best allow for the complexity of modern identities and the realities of Canada's physical terrain. Should commissioners be persuaded, for example, of the merits of creating "rurban" seats (a term used in Alberta in the early 1990s to refer to the mixed urban-rural seats created provincially), they should not be constrained by statute from doing so.[37] Manitoba ensured a greater degree of independence for its commissions when, in 1968, it dropped from its electoral boundaries statute a decade-old distinction between rural and urban seats. On that measure, its post-1968 commissions could rightly be said to have been more independent than those created in Saskatchewan following the adoption of the 1987 law or in Alberta after the approval of the 1990 legislation. In both those cases the statutes distinguished between categories of municipalities, thereby constraining the commissioners' ability to construct districts that they might otherwise have considered to be in the best interests of their province.

Ultimate authority

Finally, a commission cannot be considered totally independent if the statute under which it has been established permits a minister, the cabinet, or the legislature to amend or reject the commission's maps. The electoral boundaries legislation adopted by Parliament in 1964 went further than the Australian law at the time or the laws that later established redistribution commissions in most provinces and territories. By granting the final authority for the maps to the commissions, Parliament has ensured that it is not involved in that stage of the process. Of the provinces, only Quebec and, since its acceptance of the federal law as its own in 1996, Ontario have done the same.[38] All other provinces and territories specify that the final authority to approve, alter, or reject a commission's final rests with the legislature. (See table 6.2 for a comparison of the principal features of federal, provincial, and territorial redistributions.) Such an option would seem to amount to "an open invitation to legislatures to destroy the independence of the commission."[39] Yet in fact, apart from the occasional name change of a proposed constituency, cabinets and legislatures have rarely used these powers. That there are so few instances of clear legislative or executive interference in the process since the shift to electoral boundary commissions in the 1950s – one each in Ontario, Newfoundland, and the Northwest Territories – demonstrates that the process is now a widely accepted autonomous one.[40]

In Ontario in 1965 the recommendations included in a commission's final report were turned down by the legislature. Composed of a judge, a political scientist, and the chief electoral officer, the Ontario commission had called for changes to eighty-nine of the province's existing 108 seats and an additional nine seats to bring the Assembly to 117 members. Attacked by urban and suburban MPPs on both sides of the House on grounds that rural Ontario would continue to be over-represented in the Assembly at the expense of the urban part of the province (even though the guidelines established by the legislature had made this an entirely appropriate avenue for the commission to follow), the report was returned to the commission with instructions to hold new hearings and to recommend a new set of constituency maps. Adoption by the legislature the following year of a second report containing different boundary proposals demonstrated that the commission, even though it qualified as an independent body because it had been composed of non-partisan professionals who had stayed within the established guidelines, had lacked the necessary degree of authority and independence to see its original maps put into place.[41]

A five-member commission appointed in Newfoundland in 1993 fared even less well. Asked to recommend to the House of Assembly a reduction in the number of provincial electoral districts and to redraw the boundaries accordingly, in its first set of proposals it unanimously called for a House of forty members and in its second for forty-four members, both down from the then current fifty-two. Faced with the prospects of caucus unrest and the uncertainty of adoption by the legislature because of such a dramatic reduction in the number of districts, the premier and minister of justice admitted privately that the Liberal government "would have great political difficulty implementing the report."[42] The commission was effectively terminated when no action was taken on its second report. It was succeeded in 1995 by a one-man commission (a judge) who was appointed by order-in-council to recommend boundaries for an Assembly of forty-eight members. His proposals were adopted by the legislature later that year with nothing more than a few name changes of districts.

In 1998–9 the Assembly of the Northwest Territories received, debated, and ultimately rejected the electoral boundary proposals prepared by the territory's most recent commission. Faced with the reduction of its legislature from twenty-four to fourteen ridings because ten of the Assembly's former districts were within the newly created territory of Nunavut, the boundaries commission recommended an additional two seats to correct for the unfair disparity in the population of urban and rural constituencies. That recommendation was defeated (along with a subsequent legislative motion for an additional one seat) in the Assembly. A successful court challenge (considered later in chapter 8) to the constitutionality of an unchanged fourteen-seat legislature that effectively diluted the votes of urban electors led the Assembly to create five additional seats.

Even though the large majority of provincial and territorial legislatures have retained the power to alter or reject the maps proposed by the commissions, few have used it. The record in Manitoba since the 1950s, Quebec since the 1960s, Ontario in the 1970s and 1980s and, more recently, in the four Atlantic provinces, Saskatchewan, British Columbia, the Yukon and (except for the bi-partisan commission that failed to reach agreement in the early 1990s) Alberta, demonstrates that legislatures have accepted the final set of proposed maps without any, or with only minor housekeeping alterations. Boundary commissioners and provincial politicians alike share the view that there is now no politically safe alternative for a legislature. The media and public backlash that rejection or alteration of commission recommendations would generate helps to ensure legislative acceptance of a commission's final proposals. When, as in the Northwest Territories, it ignores the potency of an organized and determined public that feels aggrieved, it risks a court challenge. Thus it can be said that commissions have come to enjoy de facto independence, although the possibility, however remote, of a legislature changing or rejecting a commission's recommendation cannot be ruled out until provincial and territorial laws are brought in line with the federal and Quebec laws. In those two jurisdictions the final maps as approved by the commissions are those that are put into effect.

Under federal and some provincial statutes elected members have been granted either the opportunity in their Assembly to debate motions addressing their concerns with a commission's proposals or to meet separately with a commission should the commissioners wish to determine the views of the Assembly members about the readjustments to be made to the electoral boundaries. Under the federal law MPS are entitled to debate in a House of Commons committee the proposals of the commission from their respective province in what is known as the "objection stage" of the process. The objections are forwarded to the various commissions for their consideration and, should the commissions agree, for changes to the proposed boundaries before the set of maps is finalized. The British Columbia law, on the other hand, grants MLAS a separate "opportunity to make submissions to it."[43] The 1998–9 commission interpreted this to mean that MLAS could meet individually with the commissioners in meetings that were open to the public – once before the commission's first round of hearings and the issuance of its preliminary report, and once at the end of the second round of hearings prior to the preparation of its final report.

The justification offered for such provisions stems from the vantage point of elected members and from the knowledge that members acquire through "on-the-job-training," as it were, about the social and territorial particularities of their individual districts. Members of legislatures argue that they know possibly better than anyone the areas and people they represent and that they are better qualified than most to voice opinions about the likely impact that different configurations of district boundaries would have on the representational role that they (or their successors) could reasonably expect to play. When called upon to defend MPS, the parliamentary "objection stage," the Procedure and House Affairs Committee of the House of Commons argued in 1995:

Members of Parliament brought an important and indispensable perspective to bear on the process; in many cases, points were raised [in the 1995 parliamentary objection stage] by Members that had been disregarded or overlooked by the electoral boundaries commissions ... Because of their detailed knowledge of their constituencies and communities, Members of the house are in a position to contribute detailed insights and knowledge to the process.[44]

The value of allowing elected members to debate the proposals and to forward their own list of objections to the commissions is questionable in light of the fact that they, like other interested individuals, have an opportunity to make presentations to commissioners. MPS and MLAS can make submissions and appear before the commissions at hearings held at various centres around a province to consider the public's views on a set of proposed maps. The advantages that public meetings in the members' ridings confer on legislators are obvious. Covered by the local press, the hearings invariably address matters of local interest. Proposals dealing with artificial or natural boundaries, communities that deserve to be included in one district or another, and geographic size and configuration of alternative riding maps are among the issues typically pursued. Often accompanied by members of their riding executive or by other party activists, MPS and MLAS can command a measure of attention in the community when they take advantage of the opportunity provided. The local public forum is an occasion tailor-made for politicians who, with few exceptions, seek local media coverage whenever the opportunity presents itself.

The Lortie Commission raised concerns about MPS continuing to have a separate objection stage set aside for themselves. It observed that Australia had terminated parliamentary involvement in 1983. Lortie recommended that the parliamentary review process be discontinued, justifying its recommendation on three grounds. First, it noted that the time allotted for MPS' objections effectively lengthened the redistribution process by at least two months. Second, it concluded that parliamentary review contributed only marginally to the success of the process. As Parliament had forfeited its right to approve, amend, or reject the proposals of the commissions, the objection stage was largely pointless. Finally, and most importantly, it insisted that hearing objections from MPS in a Commons committee raised questions about the independence of the process. The Lortie Commission noted approvingly that in one celebrated incident in 1987 the federal commission in Saskatchewan refused a request from the parliamentary committee to appear before it, stating (in the words of the redistribution commission itself) that "such an appearance would compromise [its] independence."[45]

Members of Parliament accepted the Lortie recommendation. In 1995 they voted to end the objection stage when, as part of a larger package of reforms aimed at changing a number of features of Canada's redistribution process, they approved Bill C-69. That legislation failed to receive Senate approval, however, and the terms of the EBRA (that had remained largely unchanged since 1964) remained as they were.

CONCLUSIONS

Three-member commissions federally and in some of the provinces have been composed overwhelmingly of white, urban males whose occupational training in law, political science, or election administration has signalled a professionalization of the boundary readjustment process. Those provincial commissions with more than three commissioners have demonstrated that it is possible to achieve a greater measure of social diversity among their membership than would be possible with a relatively small body. But, given the task of establishing single-member districts in a territorially-based redistribution process, is it necessary to construct large commissions with diverse memberships?

Electoral boundary commissions are intended to serve as institutions charged with reconfiguring a set of representational building blocks according to certain established guidelines. In one sense, to attempt to mirror parts of the larger society in a commission's membership is arguably not what district boundary readjustments are about. They after all are responsible for crafting constituencies in a large and socially mixed country, which suggests that they ought to have the maximum degree of freedom and assurance of independence to do so. Engaged in a complex endeavour which requires both considerable distance from openly partisan interests and the freedom to conduct their business, commissioners should be able to serve as "transactional representatives" whose authority to act independently of particular social interests derives from the fact that they are both knowledgeable about the subject matter and non-partisan. More than anything, they must have a demonstrated ability to weigh competing representational claims and to resolve them as fairly and as equitably as each particular situation allows. Constructed at the beginning of what will eventually be a long representational process, their principal responsibility is to fulfill their legislative mandate and in so doing to define the "public interest" of the jurisdiction for which they are responsible.

Yet it might well be argued that by creating larger and more socially diverse memberships on the commissions, elected members and the public accept that there is something to be gained from having a broader spectrum of society present on the commission. Whether that would then oblige those individuals appointed to the commission to represent a particular group's interest would be very much determined by the expectations of the elected members, the public, and, especially, the respective group, as well as by the instructions or statutory guidelines issued to the commission. There is no necessary contradiction between the idea that a commission could be given a mandate to use its powers so as to ensure fair or effective representation for identified groups, and the idea that commissioners from those groups may do a better job of carrying out that mandate and in legitimating the work of the commission than others.

This second possibility is central to the case that Melissa Williams makes for what she calls "voice" and "trust" in the representational process. Marginalized groups, especially those who can draw on a long memory of systemic discrimination, need to give expression to their voice and to be able to count on the trust of those they elect to public office. In this vein, Williams supports making greater institutional accommodations (through, for example, specially constructed constituencies) to ensure that a marginalized minority's voice is present in a legislature and that the voters will subsequently be able to hold "their" members accountable.[46] Although not explicitly justified in Williams's terms, the Nova Scotia experiment with the membership of its provincial commission in the 1990s clearly pointed in the direction of voice and trust for groups with memories that had been shaped by a history of social marginalization.

A strict application of the three tests of independence would suggest that few jurisdictions in Canada have established an electoral boundary readjustment process that is completely independent. Yet the overwhelming majority have been non-partisan in membership, empowered by the enabling legislation to design districts as they see fit within the terms of the legislation, and free of statutory or administrative constraints that would otherwise restrict their freedom. Federal and Quebec commissions have also been specifically granted the final authority to determine the boundaries of the districts, and in most other jurisdictions the legislatures have accepted the proposals without any significant changes. These facts suggest that in reality the degree of de facto independence that commissioners have come to enjoy is impressive. It confirms that, along with the professionalization of commissions, the principle of independence has been widely accepted as an essential part of the reformed electoral boundary readjustment process.

7 Participation, Objections, and Delays

> The task of boundary drawing is very much like the "Rubick's Cube" puzzle: every decision made has an impact elsewhere.
> – Electoral Boundaries Commission of the Province of British Columbia, 1998

It would be a mistake to paint an overly idyllic picture of the electoral boundary readjustment process and to leave the impression that the work of the commissions has been carried out without interruption or criticism. The process of designing a representational building block may have been reformed, but that does not guarantee that the efforts of those who do the designing are without their critics. If anything, every statute establishing an independent electoral boundary readjustment process provides opportunities for both the public and elected officials to voice their views on the proposed maps.

With very few exceptions, the participation of the public and the politicians has been directed at criticizing commission proposals, the governing legislation, and (federally at least) the number of seats assigned a province. The great majority of those who appear at public hearings are there to criticize the proposed maps. Some even present alternative suggestions or plans of their own for the design of particular constituencies with which they are most directly concerned. When members of the public offer criticisms or alternative suggestions, however, these are typically given without comment or direction on how the set of constituency maps should be constructed for the entire province. Few submissions or comments presented in public meetings or at the members' objection stage take into account the unavoidable domino effect of boundary readjustments, for changes in one riding's borders invariably involve changes in another's. Even fewer intervenors make presentations supportive of a commission's proposals. Individuals and groups do not attend public meetings and elected members do not participate in their objection stage to congratulate the commissioners on their work.

Backbench MPs and members of provincial assemblies have often been the most vocal critics of the maps proposed by the commission in their particular province. This is understandable for one obvious reason: members have a proven tendency to become proprietorial about "their" constituency. Having won the seat, they are loathe to contemplate having its borders changed or having to square off in an intra-party nomination fight against another sitting member from an adjacent district. In the words of one New Brunswick MP speaking in 1995 about the changes proposed for his constituency: "I am actually quite happy with the status quo. I like my riding. I am very satisfied with it. Politically, I think I would continue to do well there ... if it stayed exactly as it is."[1] That sentiment is echoed by members at both the federal and provincial levels.

In the pre-boundary commission era, members (particularly those on the government side) would try to accommodate one another's concerns as much as possible through more-or-less mutually acceptable trade-offs on boundary lines. These did not always work as planned in the subsequent election, but nonetheless the members could accept, no doubt grudgingly in some cases, the lines as having been of their own making. That option is no longer available to members. Often frustrated by what they perceive to be the naïveté and intransigence of the commissioners, they direct their criticisms at the commissions and at the terms of the legislation under which commissions are required to design seats.

Members of Parliament have a demonstrated history of taking full advantage of the objection stage to debate and object formally to the proposals of the commissions. As they lack the authority to approve, amend, or reject maps proposed by the commissions, MPs have felt they have no alternative but to use the two avenues available to them under the Electoral Boundaries Readjustment Act for voicing their concerns: public meetings in their province, and the parliamentary objection stage in Ottawa. Since the 1970s they have also made a custom of suspending or ignoring the first boundary readjustment of every decade and of changing or, as in the 1990s, attempting to change in a major way, the legislation under which the boundary readjustment process takes place. Regardless of the source of criticisms levelled at a commission's proposals (the general public or elected members), the case made for change in the proposed maps is as often as not argued on the basis of "community of interest." Rarely is a case made by the public or politicians on the basis of constituencies of equal or near equal populations.

This chapter examines public participation, parliamentary objections and government-prompted suspensions and delays of electoral boundary readjustments at the federal level. It also reinforces the distinctiveness of Canada's federal units when it comes to the federal commissions applying the terms of the EBRA, and shows how the public, the MPs, and the commissioners each have a different understanding of what electoral boundary readjustments are intended to accomplish.[2]

PUBLIC PARTICIPATION

One of the aims of the federal EBRA and the provincial acts was to increase the public's awareness of and involvement in the redistribution process. As exact attendance numbers and participation rates are often not recorded or published by all commissions, it is impossible to know precisely the number of individuals who have taken advantage of the widely publicized invitation to the public to attend a hearing and to present a brief or testify before a commission. From the available data it seems clear that the number of participants and briefs presented to commissions has never been large in absolute terms. Commissions in the bigger provinces rarely hear from more than a few hundred individuals, and in the smaller provinces sometimes no more than a few dozen. It is also clear that the numbers fluctuate from one boundary readjustment to another and from one area within a province to another according to the degree of public concern with the possible impact of the proposals on a particular region or riding. When, for example, it appeared likely in the first federal redistribution in Manitoba of the 1970s that the province would lose a seat in the House of Commons, the commission met with or heard from approximately three hundred individuals and received ninety-three written briefs. With the assurance two years later that the province would lose no seats because of the adoption of a new redistribution formula, the newly constituted commission did not have to perform the same drastic surgery on Manitoba's map as had the previous one. The contrast was obvious in the amount of interest that the second redistribution generated. Some of the scheduled hearings were cancelled for lack of public interest and the commission received only three formal briefs.[3]

A comparison of six federal boundary readjustments (four that went to completion and proclamation – 1966, 1976, 1987, and 1996 – and two that were suspended part way through the process – 1973 and 1983 – and then superseded by a second redistribution) shows that the number of written briefs and oral presentations to commissions in Ontario and Quebec varied from one decade to another and

Table 7.1
Written Briefs and Public Hearing Presentations to Federal Commissions,
1965–94 Ontario and Quebec*

Year	Briefs and Oral Presentations to Commissions[1]	
	Ontario	Quebec
1965	75	152
1973	209	99
1975	203	111
1983	392[2]	208[3]
1987	337[4]	305[5]
1994	301[6]	156[7]

*The numbers in this table vary slightly from those in table 7.2. This table is based on numbers as reported by the commissions; table 7.2 is compiled by Elections Canada from material in its files.
Source: Canada, *Reports of the Federal Electoral Boundaries Commissions for the Provinces of Ontario and Quebec, 1967-1994.*
[1] For 1965, 1973 and 1975, briefs only.
[2] According to the commission, "well over 500 notices of intention" to make representations at its public hearings were received. The commission's method of calculating submissions from more than one individual are explained in its 1983 report (p. 7). The figure of 392 is the actual number of individuals who appeared before it.
[3] In addition, 117 "letters and other written communications from various persons or organizations" were received (1983 report, 5).
[4] Composed of 238 oral presentations and 99 written ones.
[5] Composed of 181 oral presentations and 123 written ones.
[6] Composed of 185 oral presentations and 116 written ones.
[7] Composed of 65 oral presentations, 36 briefs, and 55 other written communications.

between the two provinces (see table 7.1). Quebec had twice as many participants in 1965 and half as many in 1994 as Ontario. Ontario's surges in the 1970s and in the 1980s and 1990s were not always matched in Quebec. In fact, public participation in Quebec actually declined in the 1970s relative to what it had been a decade earlier. It picked up again in the 1980s, only to fall back in the 1990s.

Several reasons help to account for these shifts and differences. In Ontario, much of the public participation (and, at a later stage, MPs' objections) derived from the peculiar position of northern Ontario in the larger provincial context. In the 1964–5 redistribution that section of the province (defined roughly as "that part of Ontario north of the French River")[4] had been given twelve of the province's eighty-eight seats in the House of Commons. The region's stagnant growth over the following three decades meant that successive commissions had to face the prospect of reducing the north's representation in both absolute and relative terms. The 1994 commission had little choice but to reduce the number of seats in the area from its 1987 level of eleven of ninety-nine districts to ten or possibly even nine of 103, for in the previous decade the region's share of Ontario's population had slipped from 9.1 percent to 7.8 percent. It could have invoked the "extraordinary circumstances" clause of the EBRA and created a northern seat or two below the −25 percent population limits, as had the Ontario commission a decade earlier when it designed one northern seat with a population 30.5 percent below the provincial quota. But as a matter of principle the 1994 commission agreed at the outset not to use the special circumstances clause in any part of the province. Instead, it settled upon ten districts for the north, all with populations "substantially below the provincial quota."[5]

With each successive redistribution, the issue of northern representation has generated considerable debate in Ontario, not only in the north but in other parts of the province as well. In part this was the result of the steady decline in the region's representation in the Commons. Losing a seat or two in Parliament is seen by the local media and interested members of the public as a reduction in a region's presence on the national political stage and, accordingly, a weakened voice in decision-making. In part the debate was also a product of the "service" concern of members and constituents. Almost all of the northern districts numbered among the largest in area in the province and were composed of the most isolated and remote communities. The province's largest riding in the 1994 redistribution was Kenora-Rainy River. It covered roughly one-quarter of Ontario's land mass but had a population of only 76,320, which was 22 percent below the provincial quota.

Members from the large, sparsely populated and remote ridings have invariably argued in favour of commissions applying the +/−25 percent limits for constituency size (and, as of 1985, the "extraordinary circumstances" option) as generously as possible when constructing northern districts. When the opportunity presents itself to argue in front of a commission the case for constituencies with the smallest population and land mass possible, members take advantage of it. Of course, the issues generated by northern representation were not restricted to residents of the north. The public and members of Parliament from all over the province who participated in hearings understood that if the north was allotted more seats than its population warranted, those extra seats would come at the expense of other areas of the province. That understandably brought some attention to the work of a commission and some increased participation at its hearings that would not otherwise have been forthcoming.

Other demographic shifts within Ontario in the period following the adoption of the EBRA also prompted some attendance at commission hearings and submissions to the commissioners. In order to construct new seats in areas of fast population growth, such as the suburbs of Toronto, the Ottawa-Carleton region, the 905 region around metropolitan Toronto, and parts of western and southwestern Ontario, successive commissions had to reassign seats within the province. This meant in the 1980s removing one seat from northern Ontario and another made up of parts of Huron, Perth, Bruce, Grey and Wellington counties; in the 1990s it meant a further reduction in the north's entitlement and a seat from the core of the City of Toronto. Each of these changes prompted an understandable public reaction although, interestingly, the intended removal of one seat from metro Toronto provoked the least public participation.[6] Attendance at meetings, criticisms, counter-proposals, and objections increased in those relatively isolated areas targeted to lose a seat or destined to have their constituency boundaries altered dramatically. The "domino effect," it might be said, can lead to a "participation effect."

The story in Quebec is in some respects similar to that in Ontario, although Quebec's geography has a different north-south configuration from Ontario's as the St Lawrence River serves as the major divide slicing at an angle through the heart of the province. The region stretching north and west of the St Lawrence as far as Hudson Bay, James Bay, and the Ontario border covers a vast area that includes not only the most removed and isolated parts of the province but also some of its most sparsely populated. In contrast to Ontario's 1994 commission, Quebec's chose not to cut back on the number of seats in the area even though the census data would have supported such a move. Instead it preserved the same number of seats (nine) and "reconfigured" their boundaries.[7] The population of seven of the nine districts fell below the quota but within the 25 percent range; two of those seven came in only fractionally above the 25 percent minimum level. Northern Quebec had no net loss of seats. Accordingly, compared with northern Ontario, public participation in that region was low.

The Quebec commission's use of the lower population limits for northern seats was similar to what the Ontario commission did with the northern part of their province, but with two notable exceptions – the Quebec districts of Abitibi and Manicouagan. Abitibi was designed at slightly above Quebec's 1991 provincial average, and Manicouagan (the only "extraordinary circumstances" seat in the entire province) at 40 percent below the provincial quota. Two factors made the Abitibi seat stand out. Unlike remote and isolated communities in other parts of Quebec and throughout much of the rest of Canada, its population was larger than the provincial average. Moreover, it was designed to cover the largest land mass (841,163 square kilometres) of any federal seat in Canada outside of the territories.[8]

The incongruity (at least by Canadian standards) of a territorially huge riding with a larger than average population was explained by the commissioners to be what the local native population had wanted. At a public meeting the commissioners had been informed in a "compelling and well-documented brief" from a leading Inuit organization in northern Quebec that the Inuit wished to be removed from the commission's proposed Manicouagan riding and given a separate seat of their own north of the 55th parallel. The commissioners did not grant the request on the grounds that the extremely small Inuit population (7,693) did not warrant an individual seat. As a counter-proposal and with the support of the Inuit leadership, Quebec's commission enlarged the proposed Abitibi seat, which already had a relatively large native population in its southern portion, to include the Inuit. Even though it meant they would be part of a riding that was both territorially immense and had an above-average population, the Inuit gave their consent for the move. The idea appealed to them that they, together with the other natives of Abitibi, "would be represented by a single member with whom it [would] be easier for them to deal."[9]

Quebec's 1994 commission received its largest number of public objections in the Gaspé region in response to a proposal to reduce from four to three the number of electoral districts in the area. The commissioners were convinced that they had no choice. The federal commission a decade earlier had preserved the existing four ridings only by ensuring that they were all well below the provincial quota and that one with a population 40 percent below the provincial average, Bonaventure-Îles-de-la-Madeleine, was saved only by the "extraordinary circumstances" clause. Arguing that it needed one seat from the Gaspé region and one from the Island of Montreal (where the population had risen by less than 1 percent in the previous decade and where there were few criticisms voiced publicly about the probable loss of a seat), the 1994 commission stuck to its proposal to create two new districts in the fast-growing areas around metropolitan Montreal.[10]

Commissions in both Ontario and Quebec have faced similar demographic realities from one decade to the next. The sparsely populated, territorially vast constituencies of the provinces' northern fringes have been in a state of continuous decline in relation to the total provincial population. So too were the cores of their largest cities, Toronto and Montreal. Depopulation in rural areas of southwestern Ontario and in Quebec's Gaspésie accounted for the vulnerability of seats in those areas. The dynamic growth in the areas around the major urban centres could only be addressed in terms of their parliamentary representation by the addition of new seats to those areas. Those new seats, in turn, could only come from two sources: additional electoral districts being created by virtue of the redistribution formula, or an internal reallocation of the existing allotment of seats. The Ontario commission benefited from having both to draw on; Quebec's had to make do with the second.

The experience of recent federal boundary readjustment commissions in Quebec and Ontario offers an important clue about why participation rates vary within a province and from one redistribution to another. The prospects of losing a seat in an area, such as northern Ontario and the Gaspésie, that already has relatively few districts and that is well removed from the principal urban centres of a province provokes more criticism, local interest in the work of a commission, and participation at public hearings than does the pending loss of a seat in the core of a large metropolitan area. Cities such as Toronto and Montreal are part of a much greater urban conglomeration that in itself is experiencing a both net population gain and an increase in its total seat allotment. The loss of a seat from a downtown area can be seen as a transfer within a metropolitan area. For northern Ontario and the Gaspésie, there is no possibility of internal transfers.

The issues that the Ontario and Quebec commissions addressed were faced by other federal commissions as well. The majority of Canadian provinces share four geographic and demographic variables in common: a vast northern terrain populated by relatively few inhabitants and dotted with isolated communities; steady population shifts from the farms, villages, and small towns to the cities; rapid growth of suburban communities and satellite towns or cities near the principal metropolitan centres; and either declining or relatively stagnant population growth in the core of the major urban centres. These factors have become the stock-in-trade of every commission's "Rubick's Cube." Every decade commissioners have been forced to address them at the same time as they tried, on the one hand, to respect the representational claims of the elected members and the public and, on the other, to apply the principles set forth in the EBRA.

The 1987 Newfoundland commission seized upon the new addition to the act and created not one but two of its seven seats with populations outside the +/−25 percent limits. Labrador, with only 6 percent of the province's population, was given a seat of its own. At 61 percent below the provincial average, the district's size gave real meaning to the new concept of "extraordinary circumstances." It also prompted a greater than normal amount of public participation in commission hearings (118 presentations); stimulated intense public discussion at the meetings and in the press; led to the issuance of a minority report by one of the three commissioners; and prompted the standing committee of the Commons charged with examining the proposals to call on the commission to abandon its plan and to continue instead with the ridings that had been in existence for a decade.[11]

In rejecting the attacks on their proposal, the majority of Newfoundland's 1987 commissioners argued that the special provision of the act were intended for precisely the kind of isolated, sparsely populated and, in this case, physically removed, area as Labrador. It was, in their view, an inherently "difficult district … to represent."[12] The trade-offs involved in creating the Labrador seat were obvious in the populations assigned to the province's other six seats. All were constructed with above average populations. The largest of these was St John's West, whose population was three-and-a-half times that of Labrador's. At 29 percent beyond the provincial quota, it became Canada's only "extraordinary circumstances" district with an above-average population.

Public uncertainty about the wisdom of making Labrador a separate constituency changed markedly over the next decade. Public participation in 1994 dropped significantly from what it had been in the 1980s. Seven hearings were scheduled throughout the province in 1994, but only fourteen presentations were made.[13] One of these came from the mayor of one island town who proclaimed that her council was "pleased to see Labrador being accommodated," and the commissioners concluded from the absence of criticism that "retention of Labrador as a separate federal district ha[d] met wide public acceptance."[14] Accordingly, the 1994 commission also set aside one of its seven seats for Labrador (this time with a population 62 percent below the provincial average), but changed the boundaries sufficiently of St John's West to bring it back, once again, into the +/−25 percent range.

At the other end of the country, British Columbia's federal commissions have never chosen to use the "extraordinary circumstances" clause of the act even though it might well be justified by the province's rugged and mountainous terrain, its uneven distribution of relatively small numbers of people throughout parts of the interior and the north, and its heavy concentration of population in the lower mainland and Vancouver Island areas. Participation in 1994 was spotty around the province. It was, in general, described as "disappointingly low" by one of the federal commissioners.[15] The commission received 121 submissions and added a second day of hearings in Vancouver, where it received fifty-four briefs from twenty-three ridings from around the province. But it cancelled its scheduled hearings in Victoria and Prince Rupert for lack of public interest.[16]

A theme common to commission hearings in all provinces was highlighted by British Columbia in its 1994 report: "Most of our informants exhibited a general disposition to leave boundaries unaltered as much as possible."[17] This possibility was dismissed by the commission. It noted by way of illustration two extremes in population in federal constituencies that had been created only a decade earlier. Surrey North had a 1991 population 48 percent greater than the provincial average, and Kootenay West-Revelstoke a population 29 percent below. Drawing on the analogy of the jigsaw puzzle, the commission noted that "whichever way the exercise is performed, the addition of new pieces into the jigsaw will necessarily alter the shape of the remaining pieces."[18]

The British Columbia commission's original set of proposals called for "ridings that were much closer to the provincial quota than what was finally implemented."[19] The commissioners were very explicit on the reasons for the change. The "criticisms," "adverse reactions," and "anguished objections" to their initial plan persuaded them to reconsider.[20] The principal reason for accommodating parts of the province's interior and its north, according to one commissioner, "was just plain geography."[21] The distances between settled communities in remote parts of the province, the mountain ranges, rivers, and lakes all factored into the commission's decision to rethink its earlier commitment to try for a substantial measure of population equality throughout British Columbia. Convinced as a consequence of the public meetings that they had good reason to be more generous with the act's statutory limits, the commissioners maintained their resolve not to invoke the extraordinary circumstances provisions. The closest they came was to construct one seat (Cariboo-Chilcotin) within a percentage point of the floor of the range.

The work of all federal electoral boundary commissions appointed in 1993 was abruptly interrupted early the following year when parliamentary approval was given to Bill C-18, a bill to suspend the redistribution for twenty-four months and to abolish the existing commissions. Bill C-18 was justified by the newly elected Liberal government on grounds of affording Parliament the opportunity to review the existing EBRA, to consider alternatives to its main provisions and principles, and to replace the existing act with a new one if that were deemed necessary. The real reason for the suspension lay in the fact that between the time that the commissions had been appointed in 1993 and they issued their preliminary reports early in 1994, a federal general election had been held and had produced massive changes in the membership of the House of Commons. More than two-thirds of the members elected in 1993 were new to Parliament (203 out of 295 MPs). Largely unfamiliar with the decennial electoral boundary readjustment exercise, they were astounded to learn upon assuming office that in the majority of cases the boundaries of the constituencies they had won only months before were soon to be altered. Liberal and Bloc Québécois members, particularly those from rural or northern constituencies, "strongly objected to the proposals that involved major changes in some provinces, a general transfer of seats to urban centres, and an addition of six seats" to the Commons.[22] The Reform party MPs (all but one newly elected to the Commons in 1993) were, at least publicly, less concerned with the impact that the decennial redistribution would have on their own seats than they were with the prospects of the Commons growing even larger from one decade to the next. The government was easily persuaded to introduce, via C-18, a delay in the process to allow time for MPs of all parties to reflect on alternative courses of action.

The confusion that the suspension caused among MPs, the public, and the commissions was obvious throughout the period that it was in place. The bill had been introduced shortly before the commissions were to begin their public hearings. Uncertain as to how they should proceed, the chairs of all federal commissions discussed their options in a telephone conference call. Though clearly dismayed at what they perceived to be gross interference in the work of independent bodies and an attack on the integrity of the process, the commissions, with one exception, continued in accordance with the terms of the EBRA under which they had been appointed. This meant that they would hold their scheduled round of public hearings and revise their maps accordingly before presenting them to the chief electoral officer for the parliamentary objection stage.

The exception was the Newfoundland commission. Through its chair, Mr Justice William Marshall, it registered its strong objections and suspended its work until such time as the fate of C-18 was known. The chair outlined his commission's views in a letter to the chief electoral officer. Believing that the process they had been engaged in was "soon to be made obsolete" by the passage of the bill, the Newfoundland commissioners judged that any public meetings or further work would be futile and would amount to "nothing more than an ineffective and expensive charade." The introduction of C-18 had the effect of ensuring that the process was "so irretrievably marred and impaired that further involvement seemed quite pointless."[23]

Amendments to the bill were agreed to in a compromise between the Liberal-controlled Commons and the Conservative-dominated Senate. The suspension was reduced from two years to one and the work of the existing commissions was to proceed in accordance with the terms of the existing EBRA. The commissions' final reports would stand unless a new act were adopted before 22 June 1995. "In spite of serious reservations about the over-all integrity of the process," the Newfoundland commission reluctantly resumed its hearings.[24] By September 1994 all commissions had completed their public hearings and had transmitted their reports to the chief electoral officer for submission to the Speaker and consideration by the MPs. The suspension ended without the Senate and Commons agreeing on a new EBRA, which had the effect of leaving the commissions appointed in 1993 free to complete their final reports once the MPs' objections were taken into account.

This episode, in the view of many commissions, cost them dearly. Only British Columbia's federal commission reported in 1994 that it thought otherwise.[25] The vast majority of commissioners were convinced that the uncertainty that the introduction of C-18 had created with the media, the public, and the MPs had lowered appreciably the participation at hearings and the presentation of briefs. The public was ambivalent about taking part in a process that seemed likely to be repeated in the following year or so, and most elected members operated under the assumption that new legislation was on its way and that a different redistribution would get started some time after June 1995.

There can be little doubt that the suspension had a negative impact on participation. In Canada as a whole the number of submissions made to commissions was down to 641 in 1994 from 928 a decade earlier, and the number of public hearings slipped to sixty-eight from ninety-six. In only two provinces were the submissions up: Ontario and New Brunswick. As table 7.2 shows, in Newfoundland, Quebec, Manitoba, Saskatchewan, and the Northwest Territories the numbers fell dramatically (see table 7.2).

Attendance at public hearings in Quebec in 1994 was little more one-third of what it had been in the previous redistribution. In 1986–7, 181 individuals had been heard by Quebec's commission, including twenty-seven federal cabinet ministers and MPs; in 1994 only sixty-five, including seven MPs, showed up at its ten scheduled public hearings. One Quebec commissioner, who described the public participation stage as normally being the most rewarding part of the whole process because of "the alternative ideas it generated," faulted C-18 for the disappointing public turnout in his province. To the Quebec commission as a whole, the public hearing stage was frustrating because of the doubts on the part of the public and the politicians about its utility.[26] Even though it received nearly one hundred more submissions than had been filed a decade earlier, the Ontario commission reported that it "believe[d] that it would have received additional submissions if Bill C-18 had not been introduced."[27] That sentiment

Table 7.2
Number of Written Submissions
by Province to Federal Commissions,
1987 and 1994

Province	1987	1994
Newfoundland	118	6
Prince Edward Island	6	1
Nova Scotia	16	4
New Brunswick	30	33
Quebec	230	123
Ontario	238	325
Manitoba	39	8
Saskatchewan	51	9
Alberta	50	32
British Columbia	128	97
Northwest Territories	22	3
TOTAL	928	641

Source: Elections Canada.

was echoed by commissioners in Alberta, Manitoba, Newfoundland, New Brunswick, and Nova Scotia. In the last two provinces, the commissions received written or oral submissions from only thirty-three and twenty individuals or groups respectively – possibly a new low in both provinces.[28]

Regardless of the differences among the provinces and over time and the uncertainty created by c-18, the data that are available on participation at hearings or by way of written communication to the commissions suggest that the public is not massively engaged in the exercise. It can be safely said that public consultation on proposed electoral boundaries is not the political equivalent to Hockey Night in Canada. In the words of the chair of the 1994 New Brunswick federal commission, the "vast majority of people simply don't give a damn" about the public hearings.[29] It might be asked, then, what public is interested in participating in a commission's deliberations? The answer is clear. The kinds of individuals and groups who present briefs and who appear before commissions vary far less from one redistribution to the next than does the number of participants. Since they first got under way in the 1960s, federal redistributions, regardless of the province, have at the public hearing stage attracted testimony, briefs, and other written communications from essentially the same types of individuals and groups.

The year 1994 saw an atypically small number of public hearing participants. An analysis of the testimony and briefs to earlier federal

boundary commissions shows that the largest single category of intervenors has been that of "elected local authorities." They made up
roughly one-third of all who met with or who submitted briefs to the
commissions. These are the mayors, reeves, and councillors of cities,
towns, villages, counties, parishes, school boards, and municipalities
who, as part of their representational role, feel compelled to urge
changes in the proposed constituency boundaries because of the
impact that an intended boundary configuration could be expected
to have upon residents of their particular authority. This group was
followed, with between one-quarter and one-third of all participants,
by local commercial associations and voluntary organizations, such as
boards of trade, chambers of commerce, historic societies, and service
clubs, who voiced similar concerns to those of the elected authorities.

Members of Parliament and executives of party constituency associations generally accounted for about one-fifth to one-quarter of all
participants, but if a commission's proposals proved to be particularly
controversial, as they were in Ontario in the 1970s, for example, the
numbers of MPs and constituency association executives who met with
a commission went up appreciably. At the public hearings in Ontario
in 1975, fifty-one of the province's eighty-eight MPs and thirty-five of
its federal riding associations testified or presented briefs. Categories
composed of private individuals and of "former or present candidates,
provincial legislative members, provincial parties, and party activists"
rounded out the list with the smallest numbers of participants –
anywhere between 5 and 15 percent each. The number of private or
unaffiliated individuals who appeared before any commission in their
own right was, at most, in the single digits.[30]

Regardless of the type or numbers of intervenors, the sorts of arguments presented in briefs and oral testimony at the hearings were basically similar from one redistribution to the next. Fewer than 1 percent
of the types of arguments presented at hearings of all commissions lent
support to the proposals. The rest all called for the drawing of constituency boundary lines differently from the plan put forward by a commission. At 50 percent, community of interest, which includes cases
argued primarily on the economic, transportation, and communication dimensions (and less often, on the social dimensions) of proposed
ridings, topped the list of expressed concerns. This was followed by
claims based on the historic (18 percent) and geographic (12–15 percent) considerations of an area. Population factors, which were calls
for commissions to pay greater attention to a riding's rate of growth
and to make more frequent use of the population variances allowed
under the EBRA, accounted for between 6 and 15 percent of the arguments. Changes to the proposed names of ridings were called for in

Table 7.3
Electoral Boundaries Commissions, 1994: Number of Revisions to Proposed
Constituencies Following Public Hearings*

	Number of Ridings	Number revised	% revised
Newfoundland	7	4	57.14
Prince Edward Island	4	0	0.00
Nova Scotia	11	9	81.82
New Brunswick	10	7	70.00
Quebec	75	40	53.33
Ontario	103	76	73.79
Manitoba	14	9	64.29
Saskatchewan	14	5	35.71
Alberta	26	20	76.92
British Columbia	34	29	85.29
Northwest Territories	2	0	0.00
TOTAL	300	199	66.33

Source: Elections Canada, Electoral Geography division, 30 September 1997.
*Does not include the single seat in Yukon.

between 5 and 10 percent of the briefs. In what must constitute the most marked contrast to the kinds of arguments that would be made in the United States with respect to reapportionment, fewer that 1 percent of the public submissions to federal commissions in Canada made any reference to egalitarian or one person, one vote principles.[31]

Do commissioners act on suggestions that are made at public hearings? The evidence from 1994 suggests that they do, but only up to a point. Two-thirds of all proposed ridings were altered in some way by the commissioners after they considered the arguments made at their scheduled open hearings (see table 7.3). This, plus the fact that twenty-seven of eighty-one objections filed by MPs were partially or entirely accepted, led Louis Massicotte to conclude that 1994, as was true of previous redistributions, "proved [that commissioners are] quite responsive to complaints from the public and [m]embers."[32]

As impressive as such figures may sound, caution should be exercised in reading too much into them. The two-thirds revision rate refers to constituency boundaries that are adjusted subsequent to a set of hearings, not to the number of requests for changes that commissions accepted. It can safely be said that many requests for changes go unanswered, and of those that are answered, the degree to which they alter the original proposal varies considerably. Changes range from the relatively low-level ones, such as a modified constituency name or the movement of a small portion of a proposed border to accommodate the request of a village, town, or city neighbourhood to be in one seat rather than another, to a major recrafting of several constituencies to ensure a different configuration of seats in one region of a province.

With the exceptions of Ontario, British Columbia and, to a lesser extent, Alberta, the description of the changes listed in the 1994 reports suggest that minor, relatively peripheral revisions outnumbered the major, more extensive ones. Interviews with commissioners confirm that the two greatest reasons for their reluctance to make large-scale revisions are the impact that the domino effect would have on a whole set of seats once one was changed, and the inherent contradictions of many of the calls for changes. One riding's plea for a substantially lower population, smaller territory, or considerably revised set of boundaries impacts in a reverse fashion on another riding. In the words of one commission, the conflicting and irreconcilable views presented at public hearings leave commissions with little choice but to reject the great majority of them.[33]

PARLIAMENTARY OBJECTIONS

The question of parliamentary review of the proposed boundaries received little attention from MPs in 1963–4 when the federal electoral boundaries legislation was debated by the House. Norman Ward noted shortly after that this was an odd oversight in light of the many objections that members soon registered to the maps of the first independent boundary commissions.[34] In 1965 well over one-half of the MPs (158 out of 265) signed a total of thirty-five different objections to the proposed constituencies. Although the number of objections has since fluctuated from one redistribution to another, they have all confirmed a measure of unease bordering on outright hostility on the part of at least some members toward the process and the work of the commissions.

A record eighty-one objections were filed in the 1995 parliamentary consideration stage. This high number signalled profound discontent on the part of certain members with the proposals coming from the commissions. It also reflected the fact that a large number of MPs who would otherwise have appeared before a commission when it held public hearings in their province had chosen not to. They had believed that the one-year suspension of the process under c-18 would lead to the passage of a substantially revised EBRA and to a whole new redistribution. The failure to adopt a new act, because the Liberal-dominated Commons and the Conservative-controlled Senate could not reach agreement on it before the expiration of the one-year suspension, only added to their frustration with the whole electoral boundary readjustment process. As Munroe Eagles and Ken Carty concluded, "the firestorm of controversy and criticism unleashed by this exercise in electoral cartography was quite remarkable."[35] Despite the misgivings of some members and the highly publicized objections of several new ones (especially Liberals from Ontario), a survey of members by Eagles and Carty found that by no means were "all MPs opposed to the proposed new riding maps." In fact, over half of the members believed that the electoral boundaries adjustment process had worked well.[36]

Why the divergence within the ranks of the parliamentarians? The answer reflects squarely the self-interest of politicians. MPs who sense their interests to be largely unaffected by a redefined constituency, or who judge the proposed changes as possibly working to their advantage, have little or nothing to gain from opposing the maps of their respective commissions. For those members who judge the proposed maps as likely working against their perceived interests, however, the process provides an opportunity to voice their concerns. Couched in the language of an MP's service role (too large a territory to cover adequately, too large a population to service properly, and so on) or in terms relating to the communities of interest contained in or excluded from the proposal for their seat, members' objections are guided by their political instincts. Of the fourteen variables they used to determine an MP's satisfaction with the 1994 redistribution, Eagles and Carty found the only statistically significant relationship was with the extent to which a member's existing constituency was affected by the boundary readjustment. They concluded that "those MPs whose ridings were most affected by the adjustment process were the least satisfied" with the proposed boundaries.[37]

Members nonetheless had a variety of other reasons for disliking the proposals of the commissions. In its 1995 report to Parliament summarizing the MPs' objections, the Commons committee listed several causes for concern among the members. Principal among these were: the excessive attention paid by commissions to constructing seats with populations approximating the provincial quota; the failure of commissions to make sufficient use of the +/−25 percent margins; the insufficient attention paid to the protection of communities of interest and to the need to ensure effective representation; the need for more information and more clearly stated reasons on the part of commissions for the proposals they advanced; and the general neglect by commissions of anticipated population growth (a provision that had in fact been dropped from the legislation by Parliament in the 1970s) in fast-growing areas. At the root of those concerns, however, was the issue that MPs care most about in a boundary revision: whether and how it affects their own riding.[38]

The 1994–5 parliamentary committee was mindful of the inherently contradictory nature of its list of objections. In a particularly revealing passage in its report, it recited the two sides of a perennially familiar issue among MPs but without offering any suggestions for its resolution:

[The] problems of representing urban and rural constituencies were frequently raised [by members] ... [R]ural constituencies place special demands on an MP; they are more difficult to serve because of their large size, difficulty in transportation and communications, and the number of municipalities, organizations and counties. Moreover, rural constituencies tend to make great demands of their elected representatives because of the absence of services that are more readily available in urban areas. There was also a concern that rural constituencies were losing ground to the urban counterparts, either because of their unmanageable size or because of an increasing number of mixed urban-rural ridings where the interests of rural voters tend to be overshadowed by those of urban voters. Against this, it was strongly argued that urban ridings, while geographically small, are often very diverse and carry their own particular types of problems and challenges. They often possess large and growing populations, high rates of mobility, and a diverse ethnic and cultural make-up. It was argued by many members that the workload created by uniquely urban issues, such as immigration and unemployment, was very heavy, and should result in smaller urban ridings in order to counter the cynicism about the political system that exists among many urban voters. *Obviously, the conflicting demands of rural and urban Canadians and members cannot be reconciled, but these concerns must be taken into account.*39

Members of Parliament from Ontario and New Brunswick were among the most outspoken of the parliamentary critics of the 1990s redistribution. New MPs are initiated to a fast learning curve at the best of times. But when, as in early 1994, they come face-to-face with proposals to alter their own ridings, that has the effect of introducing an unexpected and unwanted uncertainty early in their new job about the possible consequences of the riding changes at the next election.

Fresh from winning all but one of Ontario's ninety-nine federal ridings in the 1993 federal election, the Liberals from that province were, in many cases, unfamiliar with the extent to which electoral boundary readjustments might alter existing constituencies. Almost half (thirty-nine of eighty-one) of the objections filed by MPs were from Ontario members, and over one-third (forty-three of 118 pages) of the report of the House committee that considered members' objections was devoted to Ontario. The difficulty of adjudicating those objections was hinted at in the committee's report: the Ontario "objections tend to be clustered in specific regions of the province, such as the Ottawa area, Metropolitan Toronto and the Windsor area, ...

[and] *they often interact with each other.*"[40] To add a seat to suburban Toronto by sacrificing one in northern Ontario, for example, was bound to create interregional tensions within the Ontario Liberal caucus in Parliament, just as it had at the public hearing stage.

Few Ontario MPs had brought their concerns to the commissions in the 1994 public hearings; they seemed, to the commissioners, to have organized a boycott of the public hearings because of the C-18 suspension. As they had not heard (at least officially) the views of the members on the proposed maps, the Ontario commissioners took the complaints that were raised in the parliamentary objection stage particularly seriously.[41] They found that the most helpful of the members' objections contained detailed recommendations for addressing the problems that members had with the maps. In some cases the recommendations amounted to calls for relatively minor adjustments, as was the case of the request (which was granted) of the two directly affected MPs to transfer a small island with a population of 401 from one riding to another. In other cases the requests were more substantial, as was true of one from the two MPs from the Kitchener and Waterloo seats who proposed a different configuration for three ridings in their area. The commission accepted this as an improvement over its own plans. In all, twenty-two changes were accepted by the 1994 commission for Ontario, which accounted for half of the forty-five changes adopted by all the federal commissions.[42]

The 1994 federal redistribution in New Brunswick was unlike that of any other province. As in Ontario, the Liberals had captured all but one of the province's ten federal seats in 1993. The New Brunswick redistribution, the only federal one to date to have led to a court challenge, provoked outrage amongst the province's Liberal MPs. Objections were filed to five of the ten federal proposed seats. In the view of the chair of New Brunswick's federal commission of the 1990s, the difficulties that his commission's proposals encountered were the result not only of the uncertainty created by C-18 but also of the failure of earlier federal commissions to make the changes to the constituencies that the circumstances in the province had called for at the time. As a result, unpopular decisions that should have been made in the 1980s or earlier became even more unpopular in the 1990s. Two of the three commissioners signed a majority report in which they argued that successive years of minor changes to New Brunswick's federal ridings meant that a major revision of the province's map was overdue. [43]

The commission's majority proposed changes to most of the province's ten seats to reflect the population shifts to the southern and more urban areas by making both Fredericton and Moncton more geographically compact urban districts and by enlarging and changing quite dramatically the configuration of several other seats. A minority report disagreed, saying that the population shift that had taken place did not require such "substantial changes ... to the existing electoral districts," nor did it oblige the commission to "deprive the northern part of the province of one seat in parliament" as had been proposed by the majority of the commissioners.[44]

At the next stage of the process a majority of the province's Liberal MPs agreed with the commission's minority report and filed a total of five different objections to the commission proposals. In spite of the criticism of its work at the parliamentary objection stage, the three New Brunswick commissioners remained unchanged in their views of the degree to which constituency modifications were called for in the province. None of the five parliamentary objections was accepted and the maps remained as they had been when first proposed by two of the three commissioners at the close of the public hearing stage. The minority commissioner remained opposed.

The contrast between the treatment accorded the objections raised by Ontario and New Brunswick MPs is illustrative of one fundamental feature of the federal electoral boundary process – the independence of the commissions. The unique character of each commission is confirmed by the fact that they are part of a highly federal process and are therefore free to interpret the governing legislation and the particular circumstances in light of their own reading of their own province. Commissions are issued the equivalent of the same book of prayer in the EBRA but, like the clergy, they are then at liberty to deliver sermons (which is to say, reports) that differ one from another.

Designing parliamentary constituencies is a very practical activity with consequences that impact directly on the elected politicians. The outcome of the process is determined by, among other things, the degrees of freedom the various commissions have in relation to the job at hand. Ontario's commission could afford to be more accommodative of the concerns of parliamentarians than New Brunswick's; it had ten times the number of electoral districts to work with. In a province of such immense geographic and demographic diversity as Ontario, a commission has more latitude on the macro-scale than any other commission in the country. But on the micro-scale, the objections consequent to the readjustment of one region's entitlement in relation to another's are not significantly different from those of smaller provinces. Northern Ontario lost a seat to another part of the province just as northern New Brunswick did. In neither case did the public protestations and the parliamentary objections persuade a commission to abandon that goal. But in New Brunswick the removal of a seat from the north was *the* issue in the province; in Ontario it was only of many.

The regional factors that were at play in the New Brunswick redistribution (north/south, rural/urban) disguised a more profound issue that was at stake in that province in the 1990s redistribution. The linguistic character of New Brunswick is markedly different from that of any other province. Composed (as of the 1991 census) of two-thirds anglophones and one-third franchophones, New Brunswick is the only province to have been included in the Charter of Rights and Freedoms in 1982 as officially bilingual, and it was the linguistic composition of the ten federal seats that was at the heart of the dispute. It prompted the great majority of the thirty-three submissions to the commission, figured prominently in the objections of three of the five MPs who filed objections, and led to the issuance of a final minority report by a member of the commission. Roger Ouellette proposed his own set of maps, and saw the majority's proposals as damaging to the representational interests of New Brunswick's francophone population. Under the majority proposal, several francophone communities were slated to become parts of larger anglophone ridings with which, according to Ouellette, "they [had] absolutely no cultural, historical, economic or administrative ties."[45] The number of federal districts composed of a majority of francophones would drop from three out of ten seats to two. Unsatisfied with the maps that were eventually accepted, the Société des Acadiens et Acadiennes du Nouveau-Brunswick launched a complaint with the official languages commissioner in Ottawa and initiated a court action to have the electoral districts designed in 1994 declared invalid.

Ontario, by contrast, has no linguistic minority of equivalent proportions to New Brunswick's. Sizable non-official language groups such as Italian and Chinese are concentrated for the most part in Ontario's major urban centres, particularly the greater Toronto area, but they do not come close to making up a third of the province's population. On a province-wide basis, francophones account for about 5 percent of the total population and are concentrated for the most part in the Ottawa region and parts of eastern and north-eastern Ontario. Constituencies such as Ottawa-East (now Ottawa-Vanier) and Prescott and Russell (now Glengarry-Prescott-Russell) have long been known for their history of choosing only francophone members. Other regions with sizable francophone populations have been less consistent, but in general something in the order of five to seven MPs at any one time have been from Ontario's francophone community.[46] In part because of the francophones' long history of having won a handful of parliamentary seats roughly commensurate with their share of the province's population, in part because of the relatively small portion of the total population made up of francophones, and in part because of the considerable linguistic and ethnic diversity of the province, the issue of parliamentary representation of francophones has not provoked the same kind of public and parliamentary response in Ontario as in New Brunswick.

Some MPs have gone further than raising objections to boundary proposals in Commons committee. They have introduced private members' bills aimed at repealing the EBRA or, less drastically, amending it to try to ensure that the provisions they find offensive are changed. This dates back to the early years of the act. Dissatisfied with what the first federal boundary commission had done with his party's ridings in rural Quebec, Réal Caouette, the leader of the Créditistes, introduced a bill to repeal the EBRA within a year of it having been adopted. His bill found no support in the House and did not get beyond first reading; but it was indicative of the length to which some members would go to express their displeasure with independent commissions and the way they carried out their assigned task.

Other MPs have attacked parts of the legislation, the size of the House of Commons, or the formula for allocating seats to the provinces. There have been private members' bills calling for acceptance of (a) a special category of northern seats that would be exempt from the +/−25 percent population limits; (b) an increase in the tolerance limits to, in one case, +/−35 percent and, in another, +/−50 percent; (c) a guaranteed minimum number of seats for northern Ontario; (d) a cap on the membership of the Commons; (e) a suspension of a current redistribution; and (f) a guarantee of 25 percent of the seats to the province of Quebec. None has been adopted by Parliament. Perhaps not surprisingly, no bill to date has been introduced calling for a reduction in the tolerance limits on constituency size from the current 25 percent.

A number of members of Parliament from British Columbia and Saskatchewan objected vehemently to the proposals for new constituency boundaries coming from the commissions in their respective provinces in 1987. The British Columbia MPs scheduled an unprecedented meeting in Vancouver of the Commons committee charged with hearing members' objections. There they called as witnesses the three boundary commissioners. The members' aim was to air their concerns with the commission's proposals in a location that would be close to their own constituents and to the local media. As was expected, they wanted substantial changes to the maps that the commission had proposed. The MPs from Saskatchewan issued a call (the first of its kind in the history of electoral boundary commissions) for the commission members from that province to appear before the Commons committee in Ottawa so that they might be questioned directly about their proposals. The Saskatchewan commissioners refused, citing the need to preserve their independence from parliamentary pressures and pointing to the absence of any such requirement in the procedures as spelled out in the EBRA.

Following the parliamentary objections stage, the British Columbia commission made minor changes to six urban ridings after it met with the parliamentary committee in Vancouver. The Saskatchewan commission joined five other provincial and territorial commissions in making no changes to its proposed maps. The first federal boundaries commission for Saskatchewan had set a tone that was replicated by the one twenty years later. The minutes of the 1964–6 commission, of which Norman Ward was a member, acknowledge receipt of the four objections filed by the Saskatchewan MPs, of whom John Diefenbaker was one. The commission considered the objections and found it could accept none of them. The first "could not be sustained;" the second "was unfounded;" the third it "could not accede to;" and the fourth was "found to be unacceptable." The commission had found four different ways of saying "no."[47]

SUSPENSIONS AND DELAYS

Backbenchers have not been the only ones who have been concerned with the interpretation that commissions have given to the terms of the EBRA. Governments too have got into the act. Readjustments of electoral boundaries begun after the census of 1971 and 1991 have been suspended with parliamentary approval of government-sponsored legislation. The first post-1981 redistribution commissions completed their task only to have Parliament ignore it, amend the EBRA, establish a new formula for determining the number of members to be elected, and appoint new commissions. The stated purpose of these moves has invariably been the same: to allow the government and all parties in the House time to consider more fully and to possibly recraft either the formula for distributing seats or the boundary readjustment process.

According to Stephen Harper, a Reform MP from 1993 to 1997 who served on the Commons committee charged with designing a new electoral boundaries readjustment process, the unstated goal of a number of MPs who succeed in persuading a government to legislate a suspension is "not to redo the redistribution process" so much as it is "to scuttle the redistribution then underway." Delays, according to Harper, are the "direct result of the self-interest of those MPs" who, once elected, take a "proprietorial view" of their riding. Many have little or no understanding of the electoral boundary readjustment process, are unwilling to accept judges and academics as knowing much about about drawing riding maps, and are intent on preserving what they are most familiar with by introducing barriers to change.[48] Harper's views were shared by a federal electoral boundary commissioner from Ontario who attributed the hostility of some Liberal MPs from that province to the 1994 boundary proposals to their ignorance of the process and to their "fear of losing their seats."[49] These views lend further support to the Eagles and Carty findings about a member's satisfaction level with a boundary readjustment being a function of the extent to which the member's own riding is affected by a redistribution.

Before electoral boundary readjustments were turned over to independent extra-parliamentary commissions, governments had a vested interest in making certain that their redistribution bills were approved by Parliament in advance of the first possible election to be called using new constituencies. Accordingly, redistributions were handled expeditiously. All of Canada's nine redistributions from 1871 to 1951 were completed and approved by Parliament within three years of the decennial census.[50] The consequence of this swift action in every decade before the 1960s (save for the wartime delay of the 1940s) was that federal elections were much more likely to have been held nearer the time of the redistribution than has been the case since the introduction of electoral boundary commissions. The first general election following the redistribution was invariably the first one following the assembling and publication of the census statistics, and the last election was never more than a decade later (see table 7.4).

The suspensions and longer readjustment process under independent commissions have meant that speedy redistributions have ceased to be the norm, although, admittedly, that has come at the cost of being a highly partisan "norm." The redistribution of the 1960s was delayed because the legislation needed for the establishment of commissions was not in place until 1964. In both the 1970s and 1980s the first boundary readjustment of each decade was abandoned then eventually succeeded by a second one because of strong opposition to the formula used to determine the number of members from each province. In the 1990s there were actually two delays – one sponsored by the Conservative government in 1992 and the other by the Liberals in 1994. The first, for twelve months, was prompted (ostensibly, at least) by the general unease that MPs felt with proceeding with the redistribution at the same time that Parliament was considering the recommendations, including those on electoral boundary readjustments, of the Lortie report. The second, as we have seen, was prompted by the unease of many MPs with the actual proposals of the commissions.[51]

Table 7.4
Years of Census, Redistribution, and First General Election Following Redistribution

Census Year	Redistribution Completed and Proclaimed	First General Election Following Redistribution	Last General Election Held under Redistribution
1871	1872	1872	1878
1881	1882	1882	1891
1891	1892	1896	1900
1901	1903	1904	1911
1911	1914	1917	1921
1921	1924	1925	1930
1931	1933	1935	1945
1941	1947	1949	1949
1951	1952	1953	1965
1961	1966	1968	1974
1971	1976	1979	1984
1981	1987	1988	1993
1991	1996	1997	–

Whatever their reasons, the delays resulting from the suspensions have meant that the elections of the past four decades have been waged on outmoded constituency boundaries and population figures. The first election of the 1960s to be fought on the basis of the 1961 census was the fourth, and last, of that decade – 1968. The first of the new constituency elections of the 1970s was the third, and last, of that decade – 1979. The only elections of the 1980s and 1990s fought on seats designed on the census figures of those respective decades were in 1988 and 1997. The general elections of 1974, 1984, and 1993 were held on constituencies that had been drawn on population data that were then twelve or thirteen years old.

The delays have come at the cost of some of the egalitarian gains that commissions have aimed to achieve by designing constituencies, as the EBRA instructions read, "as close as reasonably possible" to their province's population quota. Many illustrations could support that conclusion, but the case of Quebec in the 1993 general election will make the point. The boundaries of the seats contested in 1993 had been proclaimed in 1987 on the basis of the 1981 census. The extent to which the population had changed in the twelve-year interval between the census and the election was apparent in the numbers of electors in Quebec's seventy-five seats in 1993. Seven had electoral populations greater than 25 percent of the provincial quota and eight fell below the 25 percent level. The seats ranged from 36,853 voters in Bonaventure-Îles-de-la-Madeleine to three times that number

(111,511) in Terrebonne. In all, one of every five Quebec constituencies in the 1993 election exceeded the +/−25 percent tolerance limits. That compared with only two of seventy-five seats (both "exceptional circumstances" seats, of which Bonaventure-Îles-de-la-Madeleine was one), in 1987.

The delay that ensued following the passage of C-18 in 1994 was unlike any previous one. The Commons called upon the Committee on Procedure and House Affairs to conduct a complete review of the existing process and to draft legislation for a new electoral boundaries readjustment act for Parliament to enact before the expiry of the twelve-month suspension. Chaired by MP Peter Milliken, the committee, after several months of hearing witnesses and debating alternative proposals for reforming the electoral boundary readjustment process, presented its bill to the House. Although approved by the Commons, Bill C-69 died on the order paper in 1996 after the Senate and the House of Commons failed to agree on several Senate-sponsored amendments. The chronology of the events from the time of the appointment of the commissions in 1993 until the federal election of 1997 is given in appendix B.

The concerns of the MPs that emerged from the committee hearings and debates were predictable, given the typical reaction of members to commissions and to the ridings that have been designed since the 1960s. The Milliken Committee was composed of Liberal, Bloc Québécois, and Reform members who shared many similar reservations about the electoral boundary readjustment process. Its final report, however, failed to receive the unanimous support of all committee members. As Richard Jenkins has noted, the members disagreed "on what the bill did not do rather than what it did."[52] The BQ had wanted Quebec to be guaranteed 25 percent of the House seats, and Reform members had pressed for a smaller House capped at 265 members. Reform also preferred a reduction in the maximum deviation from 25 to 15 percent on the grounds that the smaller number would be sufficient "to ensure the primacy of equality of voting power *over* sociological considerations" in the construction of seats.[53] The Liberals, with a majority on the committee, wanted none of these proposed changes.

Several recommendations did receive the unanimous, or near unanimous, support of committee members. Of these, the following were the among the most important:

- Retention of the +/−25 percent variance limits;
- a definition of "community of interest" that included references to the economy, existing electoral boundaries, and access to means of communication and transportation;

– quinquennial redistributions to be held in provinces where the quinquennial census showed that more the 10 percent of the ridings varied by more than 25 percent of the provincial quotient;
– a requirement that boundary commissions publish three alternate maps and give reasons for their preferred options before holding public hearings;
– removal of the parliamentary objection stage from the redistribution process; and
– the principle of "effective representation" to be of "paramount importance" in guiding commission decisions.[54]

Bill c-69 was testimony to the ability of MPs to reach a compromise agreement on most of the principal items on a complex and politically sensitive issue. That no doubt reflected the fact that many members saw their own interests at stake. But it also reflected the fact that the cleavages that were created cut across parties and regions and pitted rural against urban members. A Liberal MP from the rapidly growing fringes of Toronto shared more in common on this issue with a Reform MP from the burgeoning suburbs of Calgary than with a Liberal member from northern Ontario. This suggests that the probability of inter-party compromises being reached on an issue such as redistribution increases dramatically when caucuses do not speak with one voice and when interests are shared across region and party rather than within them. If it also suggests that no change in the existing legislation is the solution that will satisfy more MPs than any other option, then the ultimate fate of c-69 cannot have displeased a sizable number of members.

When c-69 failed to be adopted by Parliament, the process of drawing the maps that had been interrupted twice in one decade was then completed. The time and resources that Parliament had spent examining the whole process had delayed the process and left the public, the parliamentarians, and the commissions in some considerable doubt about what the outcome would be. But it also had the effect of allowing those MPs who had felt sufficiently aggrieved to vent their concerns and frustrations with the process, with the commissioners, and with the proposed constituencies. In that sense the suspension was judged by at least one MP to have had a beneficial effect on members, for it gave those newly elected ones, particularly from Ontario, parts of Quebec, and New Brunswick, time to appreciate more fully some of the complexities of constituency readjustments and some of the compromises that ultimately are required if competing interests are to be accommodated.[55]

CONCLUSIONS

The depoliticization of electoral boundary readjustments that has been the mark of independent commissions has not been matched at the parliamentary level. Successive parliaments have remained key participants. They have either scrapped or altered parts of the legislation governing the commissions or changed the formula used to determine the number of members elected to the House of Commons. Recent parliaments have followed a pattern established shortly after the Second World War. Faced with large shifts in the population since the redistribution of the 1930s, Parliament changed the formula for allocating seats among the provinces for the first time since Confederation through a 1946 constitutional amendment to section 51 of the BNA Act. This was followed in 1952 by the introduction of the "15 percent rule," whereby no province would lose more than 15 percent of the seats to which it had been entitled at the previous redistribution, and a provision that no province would have fewer seats in the commons than another province containing a smaller population. These changes served as a precursor of what was to come from the 1960s on.

Since 1964 Parliament has amended the EBRA several times; suspended two redistributions in mid-stream; ignored, then replaced, another at the completion of its work; and adopted in succession three different formulas for determining the number of seats to be awarded the provinces and territories. Six starts at electoral redistribution in thirty years suggests that the process of independent electoral boundaries commissions has yet to win the measure of support and confidence of parliamentarians needed to ensure its long-term institutional independence. In that respect members of Parliament in the last decade of the century were no different in their political instincts as they related to redistributions from MPs in the pre-boundaries commission era of the 1940s and 1950s. Those of the 1990s harboured, in Stephen Harper's opinion, a "pre-1964 attitude" toward redistribution.[56]

Parliament's actions over the life of the EBRA are only the latest in a series of manoeuvres designed, at least in part, to protect political interests of the moment. No doubt, part of the motivation for seeking to change the act also has stemmed from a genuine desire on the part of some MPs to improve the system. Whatever the reason for weighing alternative proposals for electoral boundary readjustments, it is clear that MPs have yet to establish a consistent and widely accepted representational theory underpinning electoral boundaries readjustments.

Parliament's insistence on having one stage of the redistribution process reserved for members in which they can present and debate their objections to commission proposals is also reminiscent of the earlier, highly partisan involvement of MPs in the redistribution exercise. By definition, constituency boundary readjustments will be treated differently by politicians with electoral interests to protect than by appointed commissioners.

The parliamentary debate and objection stage delays an already long process and grants special representational standing to a small group of Canadians with a vested interest in the outcome. It also raises a question which, when couched in democratic terms, points to an uneven playing field: why should MPs be entitled to two opportunities to press their claims on the commissioners when all other Canadians are limited to one? It is true that the way a constituency is constructed is of more direct relevance to MPs than to most Canadians. But it is also clear that when given a choice of addressing public hearings in their ridings or raising objections in a parliamentary committee, MPs have a demonstrated preference for the first. Accordingly, the utility of the second is doubtful.

8 "A Full and Generous Construction": The Courts and Redistribution

Without the right to vote in free and fair elections, all other rights would be in jeopardy. The Charter reflects this.
– Madam Justice Beverley McLachlin, 1989

The debate over the relative weight to be attached to population and territory in the design of electoral districts will almost certainly never disappear from the floors of legislatures and parliaments in Canada. It has raged since Confederation, and it seems unlikely in the foreseeable future that the debate will end. The issue is simply too close to the hearts (and self-interests) of politicians to expect members to become disinterested observers in the exercise. MPS and MLAS, however, are no longer the only players in the game. The circle of participants in the electoral boundary readjustment exercise first began to enlarge in the 1950s at the provincial level and a decade later at the federal level when independent commissions were charged with designing seats and members of the public were invited to express their opinions on the proposals of the commissions. The circle of participants expanded again in the early 1980s as a consequence of the introduction of the Canadian Charter of Rights and Freedoms. Court challenges drawing on the charter's guarantee of the right to vote opened up for the first time the possibility that judges would also become players in the boundary readjustment process.

The few decisions on electoral boundary disputes handed down by Canada's courts since the introduction of the charter have pointed to a jurisprudence different from that of the United States. "Voter parity," "one person, one vote," and "affirmative gerrymandering" have formed the cornerstones of American jurisprudence on redistricting and have been the subject of countless American court challenges since the 1960s. By contrast, the Supreme Court of Canada's sole decision on electoral boundary readjustments deliberately eschewed strict American notions of voter equality. In its place the court advanced the notions of "relative equality of voting power," "better government," and "effective representation" as the principles underlying the periodic readjustment of electoral boundary readjustments.

Those principles have since played out in various ways in the choices that redistribution commissions have made. They have been invoked by some commissions in support of their decisions, but not by others. The uses to which they have been put at the federal, provincial, and territorial levels serve to remind us once again of the inherent flexibility of Canada's federal system and of the variety of ways that judicially promulgated, but nonetheless ambiguous, concepts can be applied in a federal system. As background to chapter 9, this one briefly describes the principal court cases and takes a closer look at the most important of these, the Supreme Court of Canada's ruling in the *Carter* reference case. The uniqueness of Canada's process of readjusting electoral boundaries is an obvious and consistent theme in the court decisions. That is also true of the value that the courts have attached to the concepts of effective representation and relative parity of voting power. Both of those principles have, through the courts' generous interpretation of the charter's guarantee of the right to vote, emerged in little more than a decade as basic to designing constituencies in Canada.

THE ROAD NOT TAKEN

Robert Frost's evocative phrase "the road not taken" usefully distinguishes the handling of redistricting issues by American and Canadian courts. Judged by recent American standards, Canada's courts have scarcely entered the game of adjudicating electoral boundary disputes. The US Supreme Court decision of 1962 started the judicialization of electoral districting in America when, in a sharp break with its past history, the court held that legislative apportionment was a "justiciable question." Courts subsequently accepted the equal protection of the laws clause of the Fourteenth Amendment to the American constitution as grounds for overturning municipal, state, or congressional districts whose construction violated the principle that one person's vote should equal another's. Outdated or malapportioned districts (which tended to favour rural voters over urban) were no longer permissible. "One person, one vote" became the new mantra of American legislative apportionment.[1]

Numerous cases have since been decided by American courts. They, together with the Voting Rights Act (initially passed by Congress in 1965 and amended in 1975 and 1982), have served to ensure that districts at all levels have been constructed as equitably as possible. As we have seen earlier, and as Bernard Grofman reminded a Canadian audience in the early 1990s, the standards applied to the construction of congressional districts in the United States have been far harsher than those for state and local redistricting.[2] In addition, American courts have attempted to ensure that a racial minority whose population is sufficiently large and concentrated as to constitute a majority of a geographically defined area could turn to the courts to have district boundaries drawn. Accordingly, "majority-minority" districts (composed of a numerical majority of an identified minority population) were added to the list of judicially sanctioned apportionment principles.

The application of that principle meant that, in order to capture a "majority of a minority," some districts had to be created with unnatural and particularly odd configurations. One was likened by its critics to a bug splattered on a car windshield; another was widely described as having the shape of a snake. Beginning with *Shaw* v. *Reno* in 1993, however, the US Supreme Court stepped back from a strict application of the majority-minority principle. According to the court, districts that were so highly irregular in shape could rationally "be understood only as an effort to segregate voters by race." Thus began a new era, this time of interpreting each case on an individual basis to determine if affirmative gerrymandering had taken place and, if so, if it could be justified by "sound districting principles."[3]

In no other country does the frequency of redistricting litigation even approximate that of the United States. By American standards, Canadian courts have only begun to scratch the surface of adjudicating cases that allege discriminatory treatment of voters under a particular set of electoral boundaries. The approach to redistricting in the United States since the early 1960s, as Robert Dixon described it, has been kaleidoscopic. It has amounted to constantly changing patterns of "new cases, new doctrines, new possibilities, and new insights" with each round of redistricting.[4] To another expert on American redistricting, nearly four decades of court decisions have been "riddled with irony, confusion, and, sometimes, contradictions."[5] As a consequence of turning to the courts as often as Americans have, their judges have now become regular players in the seemingly unending game of redistricting politics, with a few cases having dragged on through trial and appeal for the better part of a ten-year redistricting cycle.

Malapportionment was found to be in violation of the Fourteenth Amendment because it devalued or diluted the votes of some individuals in relation to others. Unequal population districts in the same state were struck down by the US Supreme Court because individuals living in above-average population districts had votes that were "worth" less than those of others who lived in below-average districts. The clear focus of the court in propounding such a principle is on the rights of the voters, the idea being that equality of numbers translates into equal protection of individual rights. In Howard Scarrow's terms, "equal population districts [in the United States] are justified in terms of equal vote worth."[6] By contrast in Canada, the notions of better government, effective representation, and relative parity of voting power introduced different concepts to be fitted into Canada's representational jigsaw.

Some Canadians had hoped that American case law and jurisprudence would bolster their claim for a close approximation of one person, one vote in Canada. They were to be disappointed. The Supreme Court of Canada has made it clear in the only case it has yet heard on the question of electoral districting that the one person, one vote principle counts for less in Canada than what the court called the "more pragmatic approach" to electoral representation that had developed earlier in England and Canada. It was never, according to the majority in the Saskatchewan reference case (the *Carter* decision), the ultimate goal of the framers of the charter to reject "the existing system of electoral representation in this country" and to aim for "the attainment of voter equality."[7] Instead of accepting a reasonably strict measure of voter equality as the fundamental constitutional principle contained in section 3 of the charter, the court based its decision on the principles of effective representation and relative parity of voting power.

WADDELL AND DIXON

Two cases, both in British Columbia, were heard between the time the charter was adopted in 1982 and the Supreme Court of Canada's handed down its decision in *Carter* in 1991. The first was unusual in two respects. It was launched by a member of Parliament, and its arguments were not based on any sections of the charter. The 1985–7 federal redistribution prompted Ian Waddell, a British Columbia member of Parliament, together with the city of Vancouver, to challenge the formula for determining the size of the House of Commons contained in the Constitution Act, 1985 (Representation). British Columbia's federal commission had readjusted the province's constituencies by giving additional seats to rapidly growing parts of the province and by cutting the city of Vancouver from five to four seats. In the process it eliminated Waddell's constituency.

The 1985 legislation had replaced the amalgam method for determining the number of seats to which each province was entitled with a formula based on a fixed number of seats: 279 + three for the territories plus the add-ons for the provinces saved by the senatorial and grand-father clauses. The add-on clauses for the provinces had the effect in the 1985 redistribution of granting six provinces (British Columbia was not one of them) a total of twelve seats more than to which their population had entitled them. Although it gained seats, British Columbia was awarded fewer additional ridings under the amended formula than it would have received under the amalgam method, whereas the six provinces that benefited from the special provisions received the same allotment of seats under either method. That led the plaintiffs to argue that British Columbia, along with the other growth provinces of Alberta and Ontario, had been disadvantaged relative to the other provinces by the new formula.

The plaintiffs acknowledged in their factum that "unlike the US cases [this was] not one involving equality among ridings" within a province. Accordingly, they did not base their claim on the charter. Instead they questioned the constitutionality of the 1985 formula on the grounds (a) that it had been adopted by Parliament unilaterally without consultation with or approval of the two-thirds of the provinces containing at least 50 percent of the population as, they argued, the amending formula of the *Constitution Act* 1982 required, and (b) that it violated the "proportionate representation of the provinces" provision of section 52 of the Constitution Act 1867. The challenge was unsuccessful at both the trial division and on appeal. The British Columbia courts concluded that (a) the principle of proportionate representation of the provinces in the Commons is not equivalent to pure representation by population; (b) the senatorial and grandfather clauses were necessary to protect provinces with declining populations and were in keeping with a modified view of representation by population; and (c) the power to change the representation formula rested exclusively with the Parliament of Canada, meaning that the approval of the provinces was not necessary and their consent need not be sought. Waddell's application for leave to appeal to the Supreme Court of Canada was denied.[8]

The first constitutional challenge to electoral boundaries based on the Canadian Charter of Rights and Freedoms was the 1989 case of *Dixon v. British Columbia (Attorney General)*, so named for the petitioner, John Dixon who, as president of the BC Civil Liberties Association, had launched the case.[9] British Columbia's existing and controversial redistribution legislation had grouped the province's ridings into different categories and assigned a separate population quota to each: metropolitan, suburban, urban-rural, interior-coastal, and remote. There was no minimum population for a district, but for those with populations in excess of 60 percent of their category's quota two members were elected to the legislature. At the time the case was heard there were seventeen "dual-member" ridings in the province. The variations in population of the fifty-two electoral districts (electing a total of sixty-nine members) were considerably more extreme than under the boundary readjustment legislation in place federally and in a number of provinces, including Manitoba, Quebec, Ontario, and Saskatchewan. On a population-per-MLA basis, the range went from 68,347 in suburban Surrey-Newton to 5,511 in remote Atlin, which amounted to deviations above and below the provincial average constituency population of +63.2 percent and −86.8 percent. In all, ten districts were more than 25 percent above the provincial average and nine were more than 25 percent below it. As Norman Ruff noted in his study of the *Dixon* case, "the province had only partially moved out of the 19th century in its redistribution process."[10]

The case was heard by the chief justice of the British Columbia Supreme Court, Madam Justice Beverley McLachlin, later named to the Supreme Court of Canada, and, as of early 2000, appointed that court's chief justice. She considered the petitioner's claim under the "right to vote" guarantee of section 3 of the charter and applied that section to evaluations of electoral boundaries. She also based her judgment on the distinctiveness of Canadian constitutional principles and practices. The court ruled that the purpose of section 3 is to preserve "to citizens their full democratic rights in the government of the country and the provinces." However it rejected a strict one person, one vote interpretation of that right by noting that "democracy in Canada is rooted in a different history [whose] origins lie not in the debates of the founding fathers, but in the less absolute recesses of the British tradition." Canada's was a tradition of evolutionary democracy and pragmatism, in contrast to that of the United States. To McLachlin, "American jurisprudence, at least at the congressional level, requires virtually absolute equality of voting power ... [I]t would be simplistic and wrong to infer, without more, that the Canadian concept of democracy dictates the same result. It is vital to recognize that it is *Canadian*, not American constitutional history, values and philosophy which must guide this court."[11]

British Columbia's electoral boundaries were found to be unconstitutional on the grounds that they violated the right to vote (section 3). As section 3 cannot be overridden by section 33(1) of the charter, McLachlin concluded that it constitutes "a preferred right."[12] She ruled that the section 3 guarantee means that "the dominant consideration in drawing electoral boundaries must be population," but that that does not require "absolute equality of voting power." Instead, it is "relative equality of voting power [that] is fundamental to the right to vote." Acceptance of that principle in turn meant that deviations from strict equality in constituency size were permissible so long as they did not go beyond certain limits, and were justified.[13]

Although the court chose not to provide an exhaustive list of possible grounds for justifying deviations, it did note that they would be permissible if they contributed "to better government of the populace as a whole, giving due weight to regional issues within the populace and geographic factors within the territory governed." Declining to stipulate any specific limits on the range within which deviations from a population quota would be permitted, McLachlin allowed that this was a matter for a legislature to establish. She offered the suggestion, however, that the +/−25 percent limits that formed part of the proposals contained in the report of the then current provincial redistribution commission (the Fisher Commission) appeared "reasonable" and "within tolerable limits." Accordingly, the provincial electoral boundaries then in place were ruled unconstitutional and the legislature was instructed to adopt a scheme "similar to that proposed" in the Fisher report.[14]

CARTER

To date, the only section 3 challenge to have been heard by the Supreme Court of Canada came in 1991 in what has become commonly referred to as the *Carter* decision. Named for Roger Carter, QC, who was appointed by the Saskatchewan Court of Appeal to present the case for the Society for the Advancement of Voter Equality (SAVE), the reference (whose questions were formulated by the provincial government) sought the court's opinion on the constitutional validity of Saskatchewan's recently adopted electoral boundaries. SAVE had been formed in response to the new constituency maps. Its members (about thirty-five in all) were Saskatoon and Regina voters sufficiently concerned by the maps that resulted from the application of the Representation Act, 1989 to seek a court ruling on it. The act had empowered Saskatchewan's three-member independent commission to create seats in all but the northern part of the province with tolerance limits of +/−25 percent. For the two northern seats the limits were set at +/−50 percent. It made a further distinction among the seats in the southern part of the province by dividing them into rural and urban categories. The 25 percent limits for southern seats represented a switch from Saskatchewan's previous population limits of +/−15 percent, and the urban/rural distinction was a first in the province's history.[15]

The issues at hand, as defined by the Saskatchewan Court of Appeal, were whether the electoral distribution scheme adopted as a consequence of the enabling legislation were consistent with equality of voting power and what it termed "fair and effective representation of all citizens." The court aimed at avoiding a narrow or technical view of the right to vote. Recognizing that the section 3 right "does not entail absolute equality," the court nonetheless accepted the proposition that the idea of equality is inherent in the right to vote and is the guiding ideal in evaluating electoral distribution schemes. Thus the right to vote included "a substantive right to full and effective participation in the political process." Determining that section 3 of the charter was violated by the +/−25 per cent population variances, the "arbitrary" apportionment of seats into rural and urban categories, the predetermination of the number of seats that fell into rural and urban categories, and the resultant smaller than average population in rural as opposed to urban seats, the court struck down those provisions of the Representation Act, 1989. Accordingly, the maps drawn were ruled invalid.[16]

Only the province's two northern seats were accepted as justifiable under section 1. In attaching particular weight to the term "effective representation," the court stated that "the concept of two northern constituencies is 'rationally connected' to the notion that this area needs effective representation. The exigencies of geography, very sparse population, transportation and communication warrant deviation from the ideal."[17] With the court's acceptance of claims relating to effective representation, possibly the single most important element of the larger representational debate of the 1990s had been broached.

The province immediately appealed to the Supreme Court of Canada, where intervenor status was granted to ten federal, provincial, territorial, and municipal governments, and eight individuals and groups. The case had attracted national attention, and several governments clearly felt they had a good deal at stake. At the Supreme Court level, the Saskatchewan court's judgment was overturned in a six to three decision. According to the majority, whose opinion was written by Madam Justice McLachlin, the issue was not whether the Representation Act, 1989 was unconstitutional but whether the electoral boundaries created pursuant to its passage violated the charter. The validity of the act came into question only insofar as it defined the constituencies. The Supreme Court's majority departed from the Court of Appeal's ruling to the extent that it placed its focus on the results obtained rather than the process employed to arrive at them, although it concluded that the process used in the Saskatchewan instance did not in fact violate section 3. To the Supreme Court, the basic question was "whether the variances and distribution reflected in the constituencies themselves violate[d] the Charter guarantee of the right to vote." They found that they did not. The majority's line of reasoning, similar to that in *Dixon*, was that in enshrining the right to vote in the written constitution, the framers of the charter had never intended to adopt the American model. The more pragmatic, pluralist, and group-based notions of effective representation could be traced back to 1867 when Sir John A. Macdonald gave "due weight to voter parity but admit[ted] other considerations where necessary."[18]

To the court's majority, the right to vote guaranteed by the charter was "not equality of voting power per se [the Court of Appeal's definition], but the right to 'effective representation.'" In the words of Madam Justice McLachlin, "effective representation is at the heart of the right to vote." Recognizing that absolute equality of voting power is impossible (because "voters die, voters move"), the court accepted "relative parity of voting power" as the principal condition underlying effective representation. That said, however, the court was clear about not countenancing the "dilution" of one citizen's vote as compared with another's. Drawing on *Dixon*, McLachlin held that deviations (on the grounds of practical impossibility or the provision of more effective representation) should be admitted only when they could be "justified on the ground that they contribute to better government" of the population as a whole. Deviations from strict parity of voters could also be justified by population growth projections for the period during which the maps will be in force.[19]

Such relative parity as is possible to achieve may, according to the majority, prove to be undesirable because it can detract from the primary goal of effective representation. The judgment gave illustrations of the kinds of factors that made for effective representation: "Factors like geography, community history, community interests and minority representation may need to be taken into account to ensure that our legislative assemblies effectively represent the diversity of our social mosaic. These are but examples of considerations which may justify departure from absolute voter parity in the pursuit of more effective representation; *the list is not closed.*"[20]

The Appeal Court had found the Saskatchewan act flawed and arbitrary because the commissioners were required to produce a fixed number of rural, urban, and northern seats. The Supreme Court rejected that argument, finding instead that the discrepancies between urban and rural constituencies were small and could be justified on the basis of geography, community of interest, and population growth patterns. It also concluded that it is a "fact that it is more difficult to represent rural ridings than urban," even though no evidence had been presented in support of this claim when it had been presented to the courts.[21]

The dissenting opinion, delivered by Mr Justice Cory, held that "each vote must be relatively equal to every other vote" and that deviations should be permitted only where they "can be justified on the ground that they contribute to better government of the populace as a whole." To the three dissenting judges the right to vote is too important to be diluted in the absence of valid justifications. They found no such justifications in this instance. Instead, they found that the previous provincial redistribution (carried out in 1981) was better suited to their reading of the meaning of section 3 than the impugned redistribution. In 1981, unlike the legislation establishing the commission whose work was now the subject of the reference case, there had been no strict number of urban and rural ridings imposed, the urban seats were not required to coincide with existing municipal boundaries, and the +/−15 percent variance levels (for the construction of all but the two northern ridings) had amounted to an "eminently reasonable accommodation of the greater difficulties" of representing rural ridings. The right to vote is "so fundamental" that the "interference[s]" caused by the 1989 act were sufficient to constitute a breach of section 3. In their view, only the two northern seats could be justified under section 1 of the charter.[22]

THE ALBERTA REFERENCES

The *Dixon* case had been followed closely by the province of Alberta, whose variations in riding sizes "made British Columbia's system pale by comparison."[23] At the time of the *Dixon* decision, some 51 percent of Alberta's eighty-three constituencies (compared with 37 percent of British Columbia's fifty-two districts) fell outside the +/−25 percent range. Given the *Dixon* ruling, a court challenge to Alberta's ridings was highly probable. In fact, in the following five years the Alberta Court of Appeal was twice called upon to rule on the constitutionality of the province's electoral laws. The *Carter* ruling only served to heighten the interest in Alberta over the constitutionality of the existing ridings and the government's plans to revise them.

Within months of *Dixon*, the Alberta legislature approved a new Electoral Boundaries Commission Act. The cabinet prepared to appoint a five-member bipartisan commission composed of a judge, the chief electoral officer, and three persons not members of the Legislative Assembly, of whom two were to be chosen by the government and one by the opposition. Prior to the commission's appointment, the government referred the new act to the Alberta Court of Appeal for a ruling on its constitutionality. The act called for the commission to design eighty-three electoral districts. Forty-three were to be single-municipality, urban ridings, and the remaining forty were to be multi-municipality, rural, districts, of which five could be hybrid seats containing parts of certain specified municipalities. The act included population limits of

+/−25 percent and the commission was to be given the option of allowing up to 5 percent of the districts to vary by as much as 50 percent if they satisfied at least four of seven criteria relating to area, population, and distance from the provincial capital.[24]

Basing its ruling on the then recent *Carter* decision, Alberta's Court of Appeal expressed its understanding of what section 3 of the charter was intended to mean:

(a) the right to cast a ballot;
(b) the right not to have the political force of one's vote unduly diluted;
(c) the right to effective representation; and
(d) the right to have the parity of the votes of others diluted, but not unduly, in order to gain effective representation or in the name of practical necessity.[25]

The court limited its ruling to the 50 percent population limits, the urban or rural/hybrid categorization of districts, and the legislated allocation of forty-three and forty seats respectively to the two categories. It accepted as reasonable the use of a 50 percent tolerance limits for a small number of districts, but expressed reservations about restricting a commission's discretion by allocating a fixed number of rural and urban seats. Nonetheless, it concluded that the manner in which the redistribution was proposed to be carried out under the act "seem[ed] not to offend section 3 of the Charter in the sense that the general scheme of the 1989 Act is of the sort approved by the Supreme Court of Canada in *Carter.*"[26]

The failure of the five-member boundaries commission to reach any agreement on its report, together with the release of the 1991 census which showed that the existing boundaries "were even more vulnerable to a successful challenge under the Charter,"[27] prompted the government to name a special committee of the legislature to propose new boundaries. The legislation that ensued establishing the new constituencies led the town of Lac la Biche in 1993 to seek an injunction against the act's proclamation. It argued that the town's community of interests had been violated by the new district boundaries.

The province responded by directing a reference to the Court of Appeal to determine the constitutionality of the act establishing the new constituencies. The court ruled against the town stating, that the "balance of convenience militated against the granting of the injunction."[28] In its response to the government's reference, the court allowed that it was unable to answer the constitutional questions that had been posed due to the absence of satisfactory records of the legislative committee's reasons for the boundary proposals. Stepping "back from the brink" as it had in the earlier reference case by not finding the constituencies in violation of section 3, the Alberta Court of Appeal nonetheless re-emphasized the need for committees charged with designing constituencies to justify the deviations from the electoral quota. It reaffirmed its conviction that "there is no permissible variation if there is no justification. And the onus to establish justification lies with those who suggest the variation."[29] The province adopted new electoral boundaries commission legislation following the judgment of the Court of Appeal.[30]

PRINCE EDWARD ISLAND CASES

No redistribution had taken place in Prince Edward Island for twenty-five years when, in 1991, Donald MacKinnon, a resident of Charlottetown, relied on section 3 of the charter to apply to have the province's electoral boundaries declared invalid and to have an order issued for the redrawing of the electoral districts. The city of Charlottetown intervened on his behalf. There were at the time sixteen electoral districts, each electing two members. The province's three historic counties, Prince, Kings, and Queens, were each divided into a number of districts. The cumulative effect of years of neglecting to readjust boundaries had led to the over-representation of rural and under-representation of urban parts of the province. The range of deviations of the electoral districts was even more extreme than in British Columbia at the time of *Dixon*: from 63 percent below the provincial average to 115 percent above it. Every one of sixteen districts fell beyond the +/−30 percent range, and twelve of them exceeded the +/−40 percent level. The spread amounted to 486 percent between the smallest and largest ridings.

In issuing a judgment that the section 3 provisions of the charter had been infringed, the Prince Edward Island Supreme Court rejected the province's defence that the variations could be justified on the basis of effective representation in order to better protect rural and more sparsely populated regions. The court's interpretation of effective representation rested clearly on the geographic and demographic differences between two provinces. The court held, in the words of the deciding judge, that McLachlin's thinking in *Carter*

was controlled by the specific situation in the Province of Saskatchewan, a province of extreme vastness in comparison with Prince Edward Island, in which very large areas are characterized by sparse population and long distances to any population or urban centres. That is not the situation in this province ... [Prince Edward] Island is by far the most densely populated province in the country ... [N]o matter where one is located, the distance to any other point on the Island cannot be considered great.

Contrary to the [government's] submission, the evidence in this case does not establish that as a practical reality it is more difficult to represent rural than urban ridings in this province. Quite the opposite, in fact.[31]

The judgment, which was never appealed, had the effect of leading to the appointment of the first boundaries commission (composed for the most part of MLAs) in Prince Edward Island's history and its first redistribution in nearly three decades.

The city of Charlottetown in 1996 unsuccessfully challenged the new boundaries that had been adopted by the legislature following the completion of the commission's report. The legislated boundaries were, in fact, based not on the commission's recommendations but on a private member's bill. The new ridings all fell within the 25 percent range, in spite of the fact that the judge in the *MacKinnon* case had observed that deviations greater than 10 percent appeared to be unnecessary in Prince Edward Island. The plaintiffs in *Charlottetown* alleged that the continued allocation of a certain number of seats to each of the three counties violated section 3 of the charter and that the variance (ranging from +21.5 percent to −19.92 percent) were larger than the province needed. For the appeal, the claim was also made that the enumeration for the 1996 provincial election had demonstrated the extent to which population deviations had increased since the 1993 redistribution. At both the trial and appeal levels, the claims were not deemed to be sufficient as to constitute a section 3 infringement. The courts concluded (by a two-to-one majority on appeal) that the urban/rural allocation of seats among the three counties fairly reflected the distribution of population.[32]

NORTHWEST TERRITORIES

Preparing for the establishment of Nunavut, the Northwest Territories Legislative Assembly in 1998 passed legislation that led to the naming of an electoral boundaries commission to design the constituencies for the remaining Northwest Territories. That commission recommended two additional seats be added to the fourteen that would remain after Nunavut was created. Both additional districts were intended for Yellowknife, the largest urban centre in the territory. The Assembly rejected the recommendation and amended existing legislation to provide for the continuation of the existing fourteen districts. The population variances for these districts ranged from +152 percent for one Yellowknife seat (with a 1996 population of 7,105) to −70 percent for Tu Nedhe (an Aboriginal settlement with a population of 842).

A group of Yellowknife citizens calling themselves Friends of Democracy, together with the mayor of the city, filed a motion with the NWT Supreme Court to have the constituencies declared in violation of the section 3 guarantee of the right to vote. Five intervenors, each representing a different Aboriginal group, were granted status to oppose the declaration. Together with the government, they sought to uphold the legislation approved by the Assembly to keep the districts as they had been constituted. The Aboriginals argued on the basis of two constitutional provisions dealing with their rights: section 25 of the charter and section 35 of the Constitution Act, 1982. They claimed that the status quo should be maintained until ongoing Aboriginal land claims and negotiations over self-government were resolved.

A court decision early in 1999 ruled in favour of the plaintiffs by declaring the legislative representational allotment for all districts with a variance above 25 percent to be invalid. This affected two of the four seats in Yellowknife and the one in Hay River. The "undue dilution" of the vote and the "gross under-representation" of the territory's principal urban areas constituted a clear violation of section 3. Moreover, the court ruled, the charter's guarantee of the right to vote was not qualified by either section 25 of the charter or section 35 of the Constitution Act, 1982. According to the court, "it is entirely unacceptable that such a fundamental right of citizenship ... should be held in suspense" during government negotiations over "the future self-government of Aboriginals." That said, the court was prepared to acknowledge that the size of electoral districts can differ within a broad interpretation of section 3. It noted that Canadians have a demonstrated history of tolerating a "measure of over-representation from thinly populated and relatively remote regions." That, together with such factors as "geography, community history and interests, language difference, difficulties in communication with remote communities and minority representation" enabled the court to accept the over-representation of remote communities. The remedy granted by the court was to instruct the Assembly to add seats so as to reduce the undue dilution of the vote to 25 percent or less in the larger urban areas, but to leave the over-represented areas much as they were in order not to "alter the historical imbalance in representation" that had long favoured voters in those parts.[33]

The legislature moved swiftly. By the end of July 1999 it had approved a new set of electoral boundaries for an assembly of nineteen members. In order to comply with the court ruling that no seat should be exceed the territorial quota by more than 25 percent, the five new seats were all added to the urban areas. The other districts, some encompassing little more than a remote Aboriginal settlement, remained much as they had been. Of these, three had populations below the 25 percent variance. The smallest seat remained Tu Nedhe, with a population 60 percent below the new territorial quota. By including a sunset clause as part of the legislation, the Assembly agreed to return to the issue of electoral boundary readjustments during the life of the next legislature when, it was hoped, discussions would get under way for a new constitution for the territory.[34]

A FULL AND GENEROUS CONSTRUCTION

The tone was set in the *Dixon* case for what McLachlin called a "full and generous construction" of the right to vote.[35] For the first time in Canada, a court allowed that strict equality of population among ridings was never intended to be a part of the Canadian constitutional fabric, and that with justifications for any deviations from equality, acceptable differences among constituency populations would be permitted. The grounds, including better government from *Dixon* and effective representation from *Carter*, have enabled commissions and legislatures considerable leeway within which to define electoral boundaries. So too have the limits that are most widely used in Canada (+/−25 percent) allowed commissions great room within which to construct seats of varying populations.

The critical contribution to the doctrine of electoral representation that the majority opinion of the Supreme Court made in *Carter*, drawing on *Dixon*, was fourfold: (a) eschewal of American egalitarianism as the model for constructing electoral districts in Canada; (b) validation of the proposition that the purpose of the right to vote in the charter is the right to effective representation, not the equality of voting power; (c) establishment of relative, not absolute, parity of voting power as the primary condition of effective representation; and (d) justification for deviations from strict voter equality on grounds of projected population changes, practical impossibility because of the geographic size or shape of a riding, or the provision of more effective representation.

A fifth, arguably more debatable, conclusion might be taken from the *Carter* decision: acceptance of the +/−25 percent population variances for the construction of electoral districts in all but the northernmost ridings. This can at best be inferred from the decision, for at no point does the majority explicitly embrace any population limits. It might be argued that had the Supreme Court been expressly asked to rule on the +/−25 percent limits as specified in the Saskatchewan legislation of 1989 for southern seats, such limits would have been found unacceptable. However, that is far from certain. McLachlin, in her judicial capacity in British Columbia, had looked with favour in *Dixon* on the possibility of introducing 25 percent limits. Here she had drawn from the Fisher Commission report which, in recommending that British Columbia adopt 25 percent as the variance limits to be spelled out in its legislation, noted that +/−25 percent had become "the standard that defines the acceptable limits in this country."[36]

It is entirely possible that McLachlin would have remained as consistent on that point in *Carter* as she did on others, such as the inappropriateness of American representational theory to Canada and the need to ensure better government through the act of redefining constituency boundaries. Unlike the three dissenting Supreme Court judges in *Carter*, who in ruling against the province had seized upon the replacement of the 15 percent limits in the earlier legislation with 25 percent limits, the Supreme Court majority devoted no part of its decision to a consideration of the wider limits. This can be seen in a variety of ways, including the failure to find any need to comment negatively about such limits or to strike them down. Does having *not* done so confirm that the court implicitly accepted the 25 percent limits? Quite possibly, but that cannot be known with complete certainty until a charter-based challenge to the 25 percent limits is decided by the Supreme Court of Canada.[37]

Whatever standing the 25 percent limits may have in case law, they have surfaced in informed commentary, provincial and territorial statutes, and court decisions as acceptable and definitive reference points. Six jurisdictions (the federal and five provinces) have legislation that establishes the 25 percent limits, in some cases subject to exceptional circumstances. Rainer Knopff and Ted Morton claim that Alberta wanted "to Charterproof the province's new constituencies" by legislating "the now familiar 25 percent deviation limit" for the great majority of Alberta's constituencies in its 1990 act.[38] Following the *MacKinnon* case, Prince Edward Island, as we have seen, chose to ignore the judge's suggestion of 10 percent limits. By accepting 25 percent limits in its 1994 act, it joined Quebec, Ontario, New Brunswick, Alberta, and British Columbia in the "25 percent club." In *Charlottetown* the judge did not order the legislature to revise downward the 25 percent variances to 10 percent, as had been suggested in *MacKinnon*. Without the 25 percent limits being the subject of an explicit court ruling, however, it is best to fall back on Judge (and one-member boundary commissioner) Ken Lysyk's observation in his 1991 Yukon electoral districts report. Working from a territorial statute that was without any reference to population quotas or constituency limits, Lysyk introduced his own limits based on his understanding of the current law:

Most Canadian jurisdictions [have] directed that, save for stated exceptions or undefined extraordinary circumstances, boundaries must be drawn in such a way that deviations do not exceed a specified range, typically plus or minus 25 percent. In making my recommendations I have viewed that range as supplying a useful guideline, not a rigid standard.[39]

The way had been cleared with *Carter* for acceptance of "factors like geography, community history, community interests and minority representation" being taken into account to ensure that legislatures and parliaments "effectively represent the diversity of [Canada's] social mosaic."[40] Such terms as "community history, "geography," and "community of interest" had first appeared in provincial legislation as early as the 1950s and in the federal Electoral Boundaries Readjustment Act in the 1960s, where they served as guidelines to be applied by independent commissions or legislative committees when drawing boundaries. By the late 1990s they, together with the wider illustrative list included in *Carter*, also guided courts, as we have seen in the Northwest Territories decision in which the judge drew almost verbatim on the language of *Carter*.

There is one important, but generally overlooked, distinction between the court's ruling in *Dixon* and *Carter*. In *Dixon*, McLachlin accepted in principle that "the majority of elected representatives should represent the majority of the citizens entitled to vote."[41] She relied on data produced by a measure of egalitarianism (the Dauer-Kelsay Index that had first found favour in American courts after *Baker v. Carr*) to criticize British Columbia's impugned electoral boundaries. Their then current design would have made it theoretically possible for a majority of the legislature to be elected by only 38.4 percent of British Columbia's electors.[42]

This majoritarian representative principle, which was one of the essentials *Dixon* offered in support of the relative equality of voting power, does not appear in *Carter*.[43] Instead, the Supreme Court of Canada ruling shifted the argument in the direction of representing minorities. According to Duff Spafford, in *Carter*

a theme [that] can be read into the Court's discussion of effective representation without much difficulty is that of minority representation. The Court's references to "the diversity of our social mosaic," "cultural and group identity," and "citizens with distinct interests," suggest such a theme. This implied conception of representation as something belonging to groups as well as to individuals is not found in the lower court judgments; even in *Dixon*, representation is cast in individualist terms.[44]

Dixon had accepted the classic Canadian typology of interests expressed in terms of their geographic and regional dimensions as suitable grounds for deviating from absolute equality of voting power. The only proviso was that they had to contribute to better government. At no point in the entire *Dixon* ruling did the newer, and now more familiar, terms of group identity, mosaic, and minority representation appear. Their addition to the Canadian lexicon of court-defined representational concepts had to await the *Carter* decision.[45]

What had gone on in the two years between *Dixon* and *Carter* may help, in an admittedly speculative way, to understand the shift in emphasis. The representational agenda had undergone an important change in Canada in the period between the two cases. The Lortie Commission, appointed in late 1989, held hearings across the country throughout much of the following year. That had the effect of bringing considerable media attention (both local and national) to questions relating to elections and electoral institutions. The hearings also proved to be a useful public forum for representatives of several Aboriginal organizations to voice their concerns about their exceedingly low representation in Parliament and legislative assemblies.

Senator Len Marchand appeared at one of the Lortie hearings and called for greater Aboriginal presence in Parliament. Asked by the royal commission to pursue the question with the Aboriginal community, Marchand began consultations with Aboriginal leaders in January 1991, barely months before the Supreme Court of Canada was to hear the *Carter* appeal. These gained considerable press coverage at the time. Marchand and four other Aboriginals, who were current or former MPs, established an Ottawa-based Committee for Aboriginal Electoral Reform the month before the *Carter* ruling and released their report shortly after the court decision. Their recommendations served as the basis for Lortie's call for the establishment of one or more Aboriginal electoral districts (or AEDs as they became known) in a province where numbers of registered Aboriginal voters warranted. Also early in 1991, the province of New Brunswick's electoral boundary commission was asked to consider the question of guaranteed Aboriginal representation in the legislature "similar to the model used by the state of Maine." Nova Scotia soon followed New Brunswick's lead in exploring the issue of guaranteed representation for its Mi'kmaq peoples, and reports from Quebec indicated that the government in that province was considering a similar move.[46]

Clearly, in the months immediately preceding and following the *Carter* ruling, Canada's representational agenda had been broadened to include questions of Aboriginal representation. *Carter*, of course, was not a case that called upon the courts to address the question of Aboriginal representation or to rule on the constitutional validity of AEDS. But the logic of the Supreme Court's ruling as it related to minority representation was such that members of groups that were either able to argue successfully for changes in the electoral boundary readjustment process to help to address their concerns about demonstrably inadequate representational presence, or had a small but nonetheless historically significant presence in a province or region that could be recognized by the construction of specially designed ridings, would turn to *Carter* for support. When the Supreme Court chose in *Carter* to favour minority representation over *Dixon*'s majoritarianism, it was tacitly acknowledging what in fairly short order had become part of a widely discussed issue; it was possibly anticipating legal challenges of the future that might be launched on either side of the issue of accommodating minority groups through guaranteed electoral districts; and it introduced through a full and generous construction of the law the notion that Canada's social mosaic constituted one of the foundations of the relative parity of voting power.

CONCLUSIONS

Unlike the United States, Canada has never had any sustained, well-financed, and powerful interest groups with a strong sense of political or constitutional grievance dedicated to protect those whose votes had been diluted or were worth less than others simply because of where they happened to live or what their racial origins might be. In distinction to the United States, "where unsuccessful attempts to strike down districting schemes had been going on for over thirty years before *Baker v. Carr*,"[47] Canada had no cadres of indignant city dwellers or equivalent organizations as powerful in defending citizen rights as the National Association for the Advancement of Colored People, who were determined to use the courts to claim their fair share of electoral influence. In consequence, by the time *Dixon* was heard in 1989 there had never been an "extensive public debate or entrenchment of positions" to which the court might refer or on which litigants' arguments might draw.[48] This virtual absence of activist electoral organizations meant that legal challenges to constituency boundaries were left up to the occasional civil liberties association (British Columbia and Alberta), instant groups with a focus on one set of maps that would dissolve once their case had been heard (SAVE, Friends of Democracy), rare individuals (MacKinnon), and, with the exception of Vancouver in the mid-1980s, small towns or cities (Charlottetown, Yellowknife, and Lac la Biche).

The charter, which was barely seven years old at the time of *Dixon*, was used by the court not as a way of introducing a revolutionary new concept of egalitarianism to electoral boundary readjustments. Rather, it proved to be the document that enabled the courts to establish redistribution principles that were open to differing interpretations and applications. The road taken by Canadian courts in the relatively few charter cases concerning electoral boundary readjustments heard to date has been in direct contrast to that followed since the 1960s in the United States. The doctrine of one person, one vote has been declared by Canadian judges not to be a part of our constitutional history. In its place, a more pragmatic and generous interpretation of the meaning of the right to vote has been accepted. With it, terms such as effective representation, relative parity of voting power, and minority representation have become important parts of many of the statutes governing electoral boundary readjustment and of the reasoning behind boundary commission designs of constituency maps.

Of these terms, arguably the most critical is effective representation. Not only is it of vital importance to settle the context within which the arguments may be presented to justify deviations from relative parity of voting power. It is also, given its lack of precision, open to widely divergent applications. Effective representation was the term seized upon by Nova Scotia immediately after the *Carter* decision to instruct its electoral boundaries commission to try to ensure representation for the province's Acadian, Black, and Mi'kmaq minorities. In order to do so, Nova Scotia's commissioners in 1992 did not establish any deviation limits, preferring instead to justify each of their handful of considerably underpopulated seats on its own terms. For its part, the newly elected NDP government in Saskatchewan the following year invoked *Carter*'s effective representation to support its legislated reduction in the allowable population variances in the southern constituencies to the lowest in the country: +/−5 percent. These are but two of many examples since *Carter* that reinforce the variability in population limits that the decision has been interpreted as enabling and two of the myriad uses to which effective representation can be put.[49]

By constructing an illustrative list of the factors that contribute to effective representation, the court left open the possibility of entertaining future claims on behalf of aggrieved individuals and groups advancing their particular claims to effective representation. As well, *Carter* makes it clear that legislators and boundary commissioners have a responsibility "to recognize cultural and group identity and to enhance the participation of individuals in the electoral process and society." This obligation on both their parts "requires that other concerns [than equality of votes] be accommodated" in the construction of electoral districts.[50] In the words of two legal experts, this opened the door to the possibility that "an electoral map that scrupulously adheres to the concept of 'one person-one vote' may [at some point be found to] be unconstitutional ... because it fails to reflect the other kinds of considerations necessary to ensure a system of effective representation."[51] Their assessment was echoed by Ron Fritz: "Ironically, by defining the right [to vote] as the right to 'effective representation' which entails a consideration of a number of factors other than 'parity of voting power,' [*Carter* means that] constituency boundaries which are drawn having regard only to 'parity of voting power' would be unconstitutional."[52]

The courts have been clear about the need to justify deviations from relative parity of voting power. The record of the 1990s has varied to some extent, but for the most part territorial, provincial, and federal commissions have made greater efforts than had been the case in the past to provide reasons for the choices they have made. These naturally have not always satisfied the local populations or the politicians (who, on the federal level as part of Bill c-69, called for much more explicit explanations by commissioners in future redistributions), but at a minimum they have helped to put on record what a commission's reasoning has been. That stands in marked contrast to one of the first federal boundary commissions (1965–6) which, in the words of its chair, consciously chose *not* to give any more reasons than necessary, for reasoning "only provokes controversy and gives 'fodder' to the MPS to argue about irrelevant matters." In his capacity as a judge, the chair had learned that it was "a sound principle when exercising discretion not to give any reasons."[53] *Dixon, Carter*, and other decisions interpreting the application of the charter's section 3 to the readjustment of electoral boundaries establish a different, and unquestionably more advanced, interpretation of accountability. The courts now clearly expect commissions to honour their obligations to explain the choices they have made.

9 Life with *Carter*: Commissioned Ridings in the 1990s

Somewhere on the belt there's got to be a buckle.
– Judge Thomas K. Fisher, 1988

With the 1991 Supreme Court of Canada decision in *Carter*, Canada entered a new phase of electoral boundary readjustments. By a six-to-three majority, the court had held that the purpose of the right to vote enshrined in section 3 of the charter was not equality of voting power per se, but rather relative parity of voting power and the right to effective representation. In addition, the ruling allowed for deviations from relative parity of voting power when the move could be justified on grounds of minority representation and cultural and group identity.

How, if at all, did *Carter* influence the subsequent commissions and the legislation governing them? Was there any uniformity in the way it was applied in the 1990s? Were the constituencies that were designed by commissions closer to or further away from population equality than had been the case in previous redistributions, or did they remain the same? What principles, terms, and arguments, if any, did commissions invoke from the court's ruling to justify the kinds of decisions they made? These questions lend themselves to an impact assessment of the *Carter* ruling in the 1900s.

When examining impact, effect, and possible changes resulting from the 1991 decision, there are three distinct possibilities that the evidence might support. The first, along the lines of American experience since the mid-1960s, would be that Canadian electoral boundary readjustment practices have become a highly politicized and judicialized process, marked by numerous court rulings, interest group involvement, and legislative and executive manoeuvring aimed at maximizing partisan advantage. The second, and contrary, would be that legislative, administrative, and judicial norms and practices as well as public attitudes and expectations have remained unchanged and unaffected by the 1991 Supreme Court ruling. The third, somewhere between those two, would be that modest changes have resulted and that these changes would most likely be reflected in the work of the commissions charged with redrawing electoral maps and in the reasons presented in their reports to explain their decisions.

Of these possibilities, only the third seems reasonable in this context. Canadians, either individually or through the establishment of highly charged and well-financed special interest groups, have eschewed the American model of actively intervening in the districting exercise. As we have seen, public participation through attendance at commission hearings or submission of briefs to commissions continued to remain low in the 1990s. There have been few court challenges subsequent to *Carter,* and public involvement in interest groups promoting fairer electoral districts has scarcely changed from the immediate pre-*Carter* period when the BC Civil Liberties Association and the Saskatchewan Association for Voter Equality were instrumental in getting, respectively, *Dixon* and *Carter* before the courts. In the post-*Carter* period, groups or individuals have been responsible for court challenges or government references to courts in only four jurisdictions: Alberta, Prince Edward Island, the Northwest Territories, and New Brunswick. As we know, neither the number of court cases nor the participation of electoral reform interest groups has come close to approaching the levels achieved in the United States. By transferring the power to design constituency boundaries from federal and provincial politicians to independent electoral boundary commissions, Canadians legislators have effectively headed off the most partisan abuses, the need for continuous vigilance on the part of special interest groups, the tug of war between executive and legislative branches of the government, and the plethora of court challenges that has marked the representational history of American redistricting.

Has this meant that the second possibility now applies? Have the legislative, administrative, and judicial norms and practices, as well as public attitudes and expectations, remained unchanged since the 1991 Supreme Court ruling? This seems unlikely, given the record of the decade following *Carter.* Although they have had to decide few electoral boundary cases, the courts have applied *Carter*'s principles in the few rulings they have made. On the statutory front the federal Electoral Boundaries Readjustment Act remains unchanged, though it was scarcely for lack of trying on the part of the majority of the House of Commons in 1994–5, and many provincial boundary adjustment acts in the 1990s were either newly adopted or amended to reflect the language of *Carter*. As a consequence, terms such as effective representation and minority representation have become part of the statutes governing provincial, but not federal, boundary readjustments. The exercise of drawing constituency boundaries in Canada can scarcely be said to have been totally unaffected by the Supreme Court decision of 1991.

That leaves the third possibility. Judicially defined norms and values that emanate from high court rulings over statutory provisions would, with rare exceptions, be expected to shape the norms and values of the institutional players charged with applying those provisions. Thus, alternative three seems the only realistic one in the circumstances. The question is, to what degree have those norms been taken into account, and to what extent can they be said to have shaped the outcome?

To answer that question we turn to the reports of the federal and provincial electoral boundary commissions of the 1990s, to the reasons commissioners have given for the choices they have made, and to a comparison of the levels of population equality in the pre-and post-*Carter* redistributions. We will also look at four provinces where changes have, to varying degrees, introduced principles contained in the *Carter* decision into the appropriate legislation. It could reasonably be expected that in a highly federalized political system with pronounced regional differences, a court decision that leaves such open-ended concepts as effective representation and relative parity of voting power to the various commissions to interpret and to apply will no doubt play differently with different commissions and in different legislation. That has indeed been the case.

FEDERAL BOUNDARY COMMISSIONS OF THE 1990S

The constituency maps designed by the ten post-*Carter* federally appointed electoral boundary readjustment commissions became effective on 27 April 1997, the date Parliament was dissolved for the country's thirty-sixth general election.[1] The reports accompanying those maps, which were the first to be written in the post-*Carter* era, confirm the variety of uses to which that decision was put. Commissions in six provinces specifically invoked at least part of the court's terminology or reasoning in explaining their boundaries; the remaining four (Canada's two largest and two smallest provinces) did not.

Of the six, the references varied from a general one by the British Columbia commission "to provide for effective representation within and among electoral districts," to Nova Scotia's discussion in some detail of the *Carter* ruling and the commission's reasoning, based on that decision, for the boundaries it established. Both Manitoba and Nova Scotia made it clear in identical phrases that the +/−25 percent deviation from the population quota permitted by Canada's EBRA was not, in light of *Carter*, a "license to be used without justification."[2] Accordingly, Manitoba constructed all but one of its fourteen seats and Nova Scotia all but two of its eleven within +/−5 percent of the quotient for their respective province's population. This was a first for both provinces. Two commissions, Saskatchewan and Nova Scotia, emphasized minority representation. Saskatchewan created a northern electoral district with a "high proportion of Aboriginal residents," which in the commission's view was designed to enhance "the possible election of a member of Parliament of Aboriginal ancestry for the riding,"[3] but neighbouring Manitoba, with an equally large northern Aboriginal population, made no such explicit attempt. By constructing Nova Scotia's smallest riding at 11 percent below the province's quotient, the commission "hoped to promote effective representation for the Acadian minority in this constituency," and in another they moved a boundary to better promote Acadian representation.[4] None of the other six provinces that drew in some way on *Carter* did the same, even though a number of them had larger minority linguistic or ethnic populations.

The Saskatchewan provincial legislation that had been at issue before the Supreme Court in 1991 had included as one of the conditions that could be used to justify deviations from the quota "the sparsity, density or relative rate of growth of any proposed constituency."[5] The Supreme Court ruling said, in effect, that anticipated rate of population growth was a criterion that could properly be included in boundary readjustment legislation. But for commissioners working with legislation that did *not* specify rate of population growth as one of the factors to be considered in designing seats (as was the case with federal commissions), it is at best arguable whether they could properly use projected population growth in their decision-making. After all, if it is absent from the law, how can commissioners apply it?

Whatever doubts commissioners may have entertained about invoking expected population growth, this did not deter five of the six federal commissions that drew on *Carter* from justifying their decisions on the grounds of "projected population growth," "anticipated population shifts," or "growth or decline in population." *Carter* was seen as providing them with the window of opportunity to do so.[6] To the Manitoba commission, for example, "where population growth ha[d] already occurred since the 1991 census and there [was] a strong possibility of future growth, the boundaries of the constituencies [were] drawn to take these developments into account." For its part, the Alberta commission relied on "future population growth" to justify the low population it gave to one Edmonton seat and the high population it put into another one in Calgary.[7] The post-*Carter* use of population growth by half of the commissions stands in stark contrast to the last pre-*Carter* federal redistribution. In 1987 not one of the ten commissions accepted anticipated population growth as a legitimate reason for constructing seats of a certain size, even though they were called upon at public hearings to do so. Those that gave reasons for declining to do so cited its absence from the EBRA as a factor to be taken into account.[8]

Bill c-69 was debated in Parliament a little more than three years after the Supreme Court decision was handed down. It in effect acknowledged what the five post-*Carter* commissions had done with anticipated population growth. It widened the list of factors that commissions should consider in determining electoral district boundaries to include "the probability that there will be a substantial increase in the population of an electoral district."[9] Had c-69 been adopted by Parliament, this particular clause would have had the effect of reviving a provision of the original 1964 act which was dropped a decade later.[10] The issue will no doubt return. The chief electoral officer has more than once called on Parliament to revise the EBRA in the context of the rapid population growth in various parts of the country, MPs have been enthusiastic about adding that feature to the act, and the post-*Carter* record demonstrates that at least some commissions have already accepted population growth as a factor to be considered.[11]

In contrast to the federal commissions in six provinces invoking *Carter* in some way, the Ontario, Quebec, Newfoundland, and Prince Edward Island commissions made no explicit reference to the court ruling. Nor did they use the terms or language of *Carter* or justify their decisions on the basis of future population shifts. In a limited fashion, Ontario and Quebec were mindful of minority representational concerns, but without reference either to the substance of or the reasoning advanced in *Carter*. Indeed, according to one Ontario commissioner, his group found *Carter* irrelevant to their work. Ontario's commission attempted to ensure no adverse effect of the boundary readjustments for Ottawa's and the province's most northerly francophone populations. What the commission did on those fronts, according to another Ontario commissioner, was well within what *Carter* sanctioned and would have permitted had they chosen to invoke the court's decision. For its part, the Quebec commission fashioned one seat at the request of the province's Natives within which all the Inuit and other Aboriginals were grouped. It also designed eight Montreal ridings so that their populations were "balanced and their linguistic communities respected." Like Ontario, Quebec's commission carried out both of those moves without drawing on *Carter* for support. In fact, according to one Quebec commissioner, the term effective representation was deliberately not used by his group because the commission was unsure how to interpret it. Beyond those few instances of boundaries in Ontario and Quebec being readjusted to enhance minority representation, there were no signs in the reports of the four commissions that a Supreme Court decision had been handed down.[12]

Table 9.1 looks at the federal redistribution of the 1990s in an historical and comparative framework. It presents the range of variances from population parity within each province for the four redistributions carried out by independent commissions. One of the points it makes most clearly is that there is considerable variation among the commissions and over time. Another relates to the share of each province's seats at the two extremes. These are grouped at one end around the population quota for each province (+/−0.0 to 4.99 percent) and at the other end in the top range (+/−20.0 to 24.9 percent and above). In the first instance the share has gone up in every province from 1966 to 1996. In some cases the shift has been dramatic, as in Ontario, Nova Scotia, Prince Edward Island and, most markedly, Manitoba; in others it has been only modest, as in British Columbia and Quebec. At the upper limits a less consistent pattern emerges. Even so, the number of commissions availing themselves of the upper limits declined from eight to five in the thirty years and the share of seats in the +/−20 percent range or more (including those constructed beyond the 25 percent limit) has declined from 10 percent in 1966 to 6 percent in 1996. This thirty-year development stands in marked contrast to the vastly less equitable electoral readjustments that took place throughout the pre-EBRA era. In the last of the partisan, government-dominated electoral readjustment exercises, in 1952, for example, only 17 percent of the districts were created within 5 percent of their province's average population, whereas 35 percent were designed in excess of a 25 percent variance.

A measurement of equality of constituency population size shows similar features. Table 9.2 presents the Gini Indexes (in which a score of 0 would indicate complete equality and a score of 1 complete inequality) for each federal redistribution in all provinces from 1966 to 1996. For the majority of provinces (six of ten, with a seventh unchanged) the 1996 figures were lower than those thirty years previously, demonstrating a greater measure of equality among their seats with the last redistribution. In some cases (Manitoba being the most extreme example), the change was quite pronounced. Two of the three provinces whose movement had been in the opposite direction over

Table 9.1
Federal Electoral Districts – Percent of Districts within a Given Range
of Absolute Percent Variance from Provincial Parity
(totals may not equal 100 due to rounding)

| Province | Year | n | Range of Absolute Percent Variance from Provincial Parity | | | | | |
			0.0–4.99	5.0–9.99	10.0–14.99	15.0–19.99	20.0–24.99	25.0+
BC	1966	23	22	52	17	4	4	0
BC	1976	28	29	18	29	18	7	0
BC	1987	32	28	31	13	28	0	0
BC	1996	34	29	44	9	15	3	0
AB	1966	19	16	21	5	47	11	0
AB	1976	21	19	38	24	10	10	0
AB	1987	26	23	23	23	19	12	0
AB	1996	26	42	35	8	15	0	0
SK	1966	13	31	23	0	31	15	0
SK	1976	14	36	29	29	7	0	0
SK	1987	14	100	0	0	0	0	0
SK	1996	14	79	14	0	7	0	0
MB	1966	13	0	0	38	38	23	0
MB	1976	14	7	57	29	7	0	0
MB	1987	14	50	43	7	0	0	0
MB	1996	14	93	7	0	0	0	0
ON	1966	88	17	18	36	15	14	0
ON	1976	95	14	15	36	25	11	0
ON	1987	99	37	38	16	3	4	1
ON	1996	103	49	39	3	5	5	0
QC	1966	74	30	38	15	9	8	0
QC	1976	75	13	19	20	40	8	0
QC	1987	75	35	21	20	11	11	3
QC	1996	75	39	16	20	13	11	1
NB	1966	10	30	20	20	20	10	0
NB	1976	10	30	0	20	30	20	0
NB	1987	10	10	20	10	40	20	0
NB	1996	10	40	0	20	30	10	0
NS	1966	11	36	18	36	9	0	0
NS	1976	11	18	36	18	9	18	0
NS	1987	11	18	36	27	9	9	0
NS	1996	11	82	0	9	9	0	0
PE	1966	4	0	0	75	25	0	0
PE	1976	4	75	25	0	0	0	0
PE	1987	4	50	25	25	0	0	0
PE	1996	4	50	50	0	0	0	0
NF	1966	7	29	14	14	29	14	0
NF	1976	7	43	14	14	14	14	0
NF	1987	7	29	14	29	0	0	29
NF	1996	7	43	0	0	14	29	14

Sources: Representation Orders.

Table 9.2
Federal Electoral Districts: Gini Indexes, 1966-96

Year	BC	AB	SK	MB	ON	QC	NB	NS	PEI	NF
1966	0.056	0.087	0.081	0.104	0.078	0.060	0.073	0.060	0.100	0.086
1976	0.071	0.068	0.054	0.060	0.080	0.081	0.098	0.073	0.037	0.074
1987	0.063	0.077	0.013	0.035	0.051	0.072	0.098	0.073	0.042	0.140
1996	0.056	0.057	0.032	0.013	0.044	0.072	0.083	0.036	0.039	0.159

Number of Electoral Districts

Year	BC	AB	SK	MB	ON	QC	NB	NS	PEI	NF
1966	23	19	13	13	88	74	10	11	4	7
1976	28	21	14	14	95	75	10	11	4	7
1987	32	26	14	14	99	75	10	11	4	7
1996	34	26	14	14	103	75	10	11	4	7

Sources: Representation Orders.
Note: Five Ginis differ in the third decimal place from Ginis previously published by Harvey Pasis
in 1972. Pasis uses data from the Reports of the Commissions.

the period (Newfoundland and Quebec) availed themselves of the extraordinary circumstances clause for the second time in a row. The effect was particularly pronounced in Newfoundland's case, where the Ginis were substantially different in the last two redistributions from what they had been in the earlier two. That is best understood as the Index reflecting the facts that the Labrador seat was created 62.7 percent below the province's quota (a Canadian record) and that there were only seven seats in Newfoundland's equation. With Quebec having more than ten times the number of seats of Newfoundland, its commission's use of the extraordinary circumstances clause to construct one riding had comparatively little effect on its Gini score.

The extent to which the *Carter* decision played a part in these developments cannot be established with certainty, but the data are suggestive of various possibilities. The evidence shows that movement had already been under way in the three earlier redistributions toward an increasingly larger share of seats being grouped within 5 percentage points of a province's average population. The first post-*Carter* redistribution simply followed that trend. The Gini Indexes by province for the last pre-*Carter* and the first post-*Carter* redistributions indicate that, with a couple of exceptions, there was continued movement toward greater voter equality after the court decision. But as a similar movement also marked the first two federal redistributions after the implementation of the EBRA, it is difficult to ascribe that particular feature of the 1990s redistribution to *Carter*'s influence and to commissions paying particular heed to that part of the court's ruling that held that "dilution of one citizen's vote as compared with another's should not be countenanced."[13]

What may help here is a somewhat different configuration of the data presented in table 9.1. Table 9.3 aggregates the range of variances from provincial parity into three columns: up to 15 percent, between 15 and 25 percent, and over 25 percent. The 15 percent level was recommended by the Lortie Commission as the maximum allowable deviation from provincial electoral quotients for seats constructed by federal commissions. Table 9.3 also groups the provinces into two categories: whether they explicitly invoked *Carter*'s reasoning and/or language or did not. It shows that of the six provinces that invoked *Carter*, all but one, Saskatchewan, increased or maintained their share of seats within the +/−15 percentage range from 1987 to 1996 and that none employed the extraordinary circumstances clause. On the other hand, the four commissions that did not invoke *Carter* all decreased their share of electoral districts coming within +/−15 percentage points of their provincial average, except for Prince Edward Island which remained constant. Two of those four were the only provinces to have availed themselves of the extraordinary circumstances option.

At this point, it is useful to speculate on why *Carter* was used differently, or not at all, by the various commissions. The appearance of Ontario and Quebec on one side, and the majority of the remaining provinces on the other side of the *Carter* categorization, provides an important clue about the different treatment accorded the court ruling by federal commissions when it comes to the questions of minority representation and equality. Ontario and Quebec, the two largest provinces in both land mass and population, clearly have their own distinctive social, ethnic, and linguistic configurations. Could it be that Ontario in creating districts in the multilingual and multi-ethnic core particularly in Toronto, and Quebec in drawing boundaries to reflect the largely anglophone sections of Montreal, did not have to invoke *Carter* explicitly because the relevant populations were already so geographically concentrated that the boundaries drawn along neighbourhood lines would ensure in any event some measure of effective representation for the relevant groups? Alternatively, those two post-*Carter* federal commissions may have chosen not to draw constituencies in such a way as to include sufficiently sizable minority populations because of the inherent difficulties such deliberate constructions would present the commissioners as they attempted to construct a satisfactory map for a entire province.

Table 9.3
Federal Electoral Districts – Percent of Districts within a Given Range
of Absolute Percent Variance from Provincial Parity
(totals may not equal 100 due to rounding)

| | Province | Year | n | Range of Absolute Percent Variance from Provincial Parity | | |
				0.0–14.99	15.0–24.99	25.0+
Commissions Using Carter	BC	1966	23	91	9	0
	BC	1976	28	75	25	0
	BC	1987	32	72	28	0
	BC	1996	34	82	18	0
	AB	1966	19	42	58	0
	AB	1976	21	81	19	0
	AB	1987	26	69	31	0
	AB	1996	26	85	15	0
	SK	1966	13	54	46	0
	SK	1976	14	93	7	0
	SK	1987	14	100	0	0
	SK	1996	14	93	7	0
	MB	1966	13	38	62	0
	MB	1976	14	93	7	0
	MB	1987	14	100	0	0
	MB	1996	14	100	0	0
	NB	1966	10	70	30	0
	NB	1976	10	50	50	0
	NB	1987	10	40	60	0
	NB	1996	10	60	40	0
	NS	1966	11	91	9	0
	NS	1976	11	73	27	0
	NS	1987	11	82	18	0
	NS	1996	11	91	9	0
Commissions Not Using Carter	ON	1966	88	72	28	0
	ON	1976	95	64	36	0
	ON	1987	99	92	7	1
	ON	1996	103	90	10	0
	QC	1966	74	82	18	0
	QC	1976	75	52	48	0
	QC	1987	75	76	21	3
	QC	1996	75	75	24	1
	PE	1966	4	75	25	0
	PE	1976	4	100	0	0
	PE	1987	4	100	0	0
	PE	1996	4	100	0	0
	NF	1966	7	57	43	0
	NF	1976	7	71	29	0
	NF	1987	7	71	0	29
	NF	1996	7	43	43	14

Sources: Representation Orders.

Note: Use of *Carter* was determined from the Reports of the Commissions.

Both of those possibilities came into play in the post-*Carter* federal redistributions. In Ontario, there was an informal understanding among the commissioners about the need to accommodate northern Ontario. Accordingly, all ten of that region's seats were constructed with populations well below (between 15 and 25 percent) the province's population quota. As the EBRA allowed for that possibility, the commissioners felt no need to invoke *Carter* in their defence. Unlike Ottawa-Vanier and Glengarry-Prescott-Russell, where the commission could with some confidence craft the borders so as to enhance minority representation and the probability of francophones being elected, the ethnic and linguistic diversity of greater Toronto was described by one commissioner as a nightmare. The metropolitan area is composed of a variety of different linguistic and ethnic groups whose habitation patterns may lead to the establishment of distinct neighbourhoods but do not always lend themselves to reasonably clean lines of demarcation that would enable minority ridings of roughly similar populations to be constructed. The irony, according to the Ontario commissioner, is that the "GTA [Greater Toronto Area], contains the country's most ethnically diverse population," yet because of the "complexity of the issue and the sheer number of seats that would be needed to make sense of the demographic jigsaw puzzle," the commission chose to pay little attention to the issue. *Carter* was of no use to the commission.[14]

For its part, the Quebec federal commission of the 1990s also fell back on the 25 percent variances permitted by the act. Seven of northern Quebec's nine seats were constructed near the lower end of the limits and the extraordinary circumstances clause was used for an eighth. The commission made a point with the ninth northern riding of including widely dispersed Native settlements. In the greater Montreal area, the eight ridings it designed with their "linguistic communities respected" were composed largely of the anglophone and allophone minorities or, in the case of Rosemont, were drawn "in order to accommodate the socio-economic homogeneity of that neighborhood as a whole." As the commission made a point on the Island of Montreal of following, whenever possible, the municipal boundaries of the island's "many cities" and of using Statistics Canada language statistics for each urban municipality, the commission had a relatively easy task of constructing ridings containing definable linguistic groups. Like Ontario, the Quebec commission felt no need to invoke *Carter* to justify its moves.[15]

On the reverse side of this speculation, were smaller provinces more likely to be faced with relatively small and more dispersed numbers of minority voters? Would this therefore make it more likely that they would find in *Carter* the support needed to create electoral districts relatively equal in size or with some identified minority population in mind? Here the evidence is, at best, mixed. The special treatment singled out in 1996 for Acadian voters in Nova Scotia and Aboriginal voters in Saskatchewan are two obvious cases where commissions drew on the court decision in their attempt to ensure some measure of representation for a defined minority in their province. In Nova Scotia and Saskatchewan, the only seats created substantially (that is, more than 10 percent) below the provincial quotient were the two that were justified on *Carter*'s principles of effective and minority representation. Saskatchewan and Nova Scotia, in other words, found in *Carter* what they needed to design the seat that each crafted with a minority population in mind.

But British Columbia, unlike the other five provinces to invoke *Carter,* found nothing in the decision to support its constituencies, apart from a very general nod in the direction of the need "to provide for effective representation." The British Columbia commission was, in a sense, closer to the other two big non-*Carter* provinces, Ontario and Quebec. It made a point, according to one of its commissioners, of "taking ethnic distribution in the 1991 census into account" in constructing seats in the metropolitan Vancouver area. But it did this without mentioning *Carter.* Such efforts helped to ensure that racial minorities (primarily East Indian and Chinese) constituted a sizable portion of several Vancouver area seats, although in none were the numbers sufficient to "constitute a clear majority" based on the 1991 census. Three seats in isolated and sparsely populated parts of the province were designed below the 15 percent quotient level, and three in metropolitan Vancouver were given populations above the 15 per-cent level. In every case, the EBRA was judged by the commissioners to be sufficient justification for those population deviations. *Carter* was as inconsequential to British Columbia's stated reasons as it was to Ontario's and Quebec's.[16]

PROVINCIAL BOUNDARY READJUSTMENTS OF THE 1990S

In contrast to their federal counterparts, electoral boundary readjust-ment bodies at the provincial level showed greater willingness in the 1990s to draw on *Carter.* That was no doubt because independent commissions were new to the game in several provinces, notably the Maritime provinces, and they sought guidance from a recent decision at the Supreme Court level (a case in which a number of provincial governments had gained intervenor status) that dealt with provincial legislation. We know that until the 1970s or 1980s, redistributions in some provinces were still conducted in a highly partisan fashion by legislative committees and provincial cabinets. As a number of provinces had a good deal further to go than others, it was natural for at least some of the commissions to look closely at *Carter*. As we will see, a number of provincial cabinets and legislatures became involved in redefining the terms of the legislation governing boundary readjustments in their province. Some relied heavily on *Carter*, others all but ignored the ruling.

Every province has redistributed its legislative districts since *Carter* and many provincial legislatures have passed new laws covering boundary readjustments or amended existing ones. In one case, Ontario, the process could not have been much more easily and swiftly accomplished. With the passage of its delightfully named Fewer Politicians Act in 1996, Ontario redistributed its seats without holding a redistribution. At one fell swoop, and in keeping with the newly elected Conservative government's "Common Sense Revolution," Queen's Park adopted the recently redistributed federal map as the basis for electing its own legislative members.[17] Ontario's move to downsize its provincial legislature stood in stark contrast to the arguments mounted two decades earlier (in a non-common sense revolutionary time) by the Ontario Commission on the Legislature headed by Dalton Camp. The Camp Commission called for an expansion in the provincial legislature from 125 to 180 MPPs – a kind of More Politicians Act. Camp's move was justified in part because it would have provided more effective representation to Ontario citizens! Writing in 1975, the commission expressed the view that "there was renewed recognition in the past twenty years that more members and ridings were needed, essentially in order to give *more effective representation* at the local level, to compensate for immense urban concentration and to provide some elasticity for regions with wide population scatter."[18] The language of *Carter* had been anticipated over a decade and a half before the decision was handed down. By contrast, the Harris government did not attempt to justify its downsizing of the Ontario legislature and its wholesale adoption of the federal maps, nor did the opposition attack the legislation, by referring to *Carter* or to the principles advanced by the Supreme Court in that ruling. In the debates on the bill in Queen's Park there was not a single instance of a reference to *Carter*, the Supreme Court of Canada, minority representation, or relative parity of voting power. Instead, the package was justified strictly as a cost-cutting measure and one that met the public's supposed preference for fewer politicians. By its opponents it was criticized for hurting rural, northern, and relatively isolated parts of the province.[19]

Of the nine other post-*Carter* provincial redistributions in the 1990s, all commissions drew to varying degrees on the Supreme Court decision. In some cases, provincial legislation or terms of reference assigned to a commission were crafted to capture *Carter's* reasoning or terminology; in others, the commissions themselves chose to invoke parts of the decision. At one extreme of legislative action was Quebec which, within months of *Carter* being handed down, amended its Election Act to include the the concept of effective representation as one of the principles underlying the delimitation of electoral divisions in the province, but drew in no other way from *Carter*.[20] At the other extreme was Nova Scotia which legislated the establishment of the province's first independent electoral boundary commission and defined its terms of reference with phrases directly out of Carter:

In keeping with the constitutional right to *"effective representation"*:
1. The primary factors to be considered by the Boundaries Commission to ensure *"effective representation"* are:
   (i) of paramount importance, *relative parity of voting power* achieved through constituencies of equal population to the extent reasonably possible;
   (v) *minority representation,* including, in particular, representation of the Acadian, Black and Mi'kmaq peoples of Nova Scotia; and
   (vi) *population rate of growth projections.*

The commission is to be guided by the principle that deviations from *parity of voting power* are only justified on the ground that they contribute to the *better government of the populace as a whole.*[21]

Even the title chosen by the commission for the report it issued in 1992 was, appropriately, derived from the Supreme Court ruling: *Effective Political Representation in Nova Scotia.*

In the province responsible in the first place for the reference being decided by the Supreme Court, dramatic changes were made in legislation governing electoral boundary readjustments. But in contrast to Nova Scotia, those in Saskatchewan were done, ironically, without any specific invocation of *Carter's* principles. Instead, Saskatchewan's Constituency Boundaries Act, 1993 reduced the number of constituencies from sixty-six to fifty-eight and imposed strict +/−5 percent tolerance limits on all but the two northern ridings. This remains the tightest maximum percentage deviations of any jurisdiction in Canada. Given such a constraint (the 5 percent tolerance amounted to 859 persons either way of the provincial quotient), and without an option of designing seats outside the limits on grounds of extraordinary circumstances, the Saskatchewan commission had neither need nor opportunity to apply *Carter's* reasoning. Indeed, it opted for an even stricter application of the one person, one vote principle than the legislation required. Forty-five of the fifty-six southern constituencies were designed within a 1 percent margin of the provincial quotient. The extraordinary tautness of the new law and its application in Saskatchewan can be seen when measured by the Dauer-Kelsay index. In theoretical terms, 50.9 percent of the electorate would be needed to elect a majority of the members of the Saskatchewan legislature. This compares with 47.5 percent in Ontario at the time of the 1996 provincial redistribution, 46.1 percent in Nova Scotia in 1991–2, and 44.5 percent in Quebec in 1992.[22]

The Saskatchewan experience of 1993 stood in marked contrast to the *Carter* decision, which had left considerably more room to legislators and boundary commissioners to define the terms of the statutes and to design electoral districts. It is not inconceivable that a challenge to a set of electoral boundaries with as little variance as Saskatchewan's might be mounted, where it could be successfully argued "that boundaries which too closely adhere to 'parity of voting' and give insufficient recognition to the other factors identified [in *Carter*] undermine effective representation and are therefore unconstitutional."[23] It would be ironic if a son-of-*Carter* were born of a challenge to the very legislation and its application that had been crafted in response to the initial reference.

What accounts for the different reactions of the provinces to the *Carter* decision? The answer is no doubt multi-faceted and would draw on the distinctive political culture and political dynamics of each province. One element that would be common to most, if not all, of the provinces' handling of redistribution legislation is political self-interest. Politicians, like the stock markets, do not like uncertainty. Anything governments can do to try to reduce the uncertainty of having such essential institutional building blocks as electoral districts designed by non-partisan, extra-legislative bodies would, in their minds, be worth the effort. Most critically, that includes the legislation setting out the terms on which the redistributions will be carried out and the districts that the commissions eventually designed. But if the issue is politically charged for the government, it is no less so for the other parties competing in the elections. As T.H. Qualter wrote in one of the earliest books on Canada's electoral process, "no system of distribution of constituencies is neutral in its effects."[24] Government and opposition parties are highly attuned to that fact. It is understandable that they will attempt to define the rules to their advantage if the opportunity presents itself.

The differing ways in which four provincial governments dealt with the rules governing their redistributions in the 1990s illustrate the point. *Carter* proved a useful tool for some, but not all, of the governments to use in justifying their moves or modifying the appropriate electoral boundaries readjustment legislation. But in each of these four instances the governments had a political incentive for ensuring the legislated changes were approved. In some cases that prompted intense political opposition to the move; in others, strong support.

Ontario's Conservatives under Mike Harris had pledged, if successful in the 1995 election, to scrap the pending provincial redistribution, reduce the size of the legislature, and adopt the federal maps of the 1990s in their entirety. Once in office, the Tories implemented that proposal, but over strong opposition. According to Donald C. MacDonald, a former leader of the Ontario NDP who had served in the provincial legislature for twenty-seven years, the move by the Harris government threw the issue of electoral redistribution directly into "the cauldron of partisan politics."[25] There were a variety of reasons for the opposition to the change, including a "governance" concern that Graham White and others expressed. Simply put, it argued that a reduced number of MPPs would harm the ability of the members to perform their duties, whether in opposition or on the government backbenches, and that the ultimate effect would be to increase the power of the cabinet vis-à-vis the legislature.[26]

But part of the opposition in Ontario was also prompted by fears of the partisan implications of the change. Those hostile to the Harris Conservatives could see as well as the government that the reduction from 130 to 103 MPPs would not cut evenly across the province. One of the hardest hit areas would be northern Ontario, going from fifteen to ten seats, while the areas that would benefit most from the change would be the burgeoning "905 area" surrounding Toronto, the Niagara Peninsula, and the Golden Horseshoe. Based on the support given the various parties in the 1995 election it did not, as they say, take a rocket scientist to figure out which party stood to gain the most at the time of the next election from the intra-provincial shift in seats (the Tories) and which ones stood to lose the most (the NDP and the Liberals). That is precisely what transpired in the 1999 provincial election. The Conservatives were returned to office (in the smaller legislature) having won every one of the twenty seats in the 905 area around Toronto but winning only one of the ten seats (the premier's) in the north. The downsizing move of the Harris government was successfully carried through without any direct references to *Carter*, except for the occasional allusion to effective representation. But even that, as was demonstrated by the Camp Commission, was scarcely a term coined in the 1990s by the courts.[27]

Quebec's Commission de la représentation électorale had all but completed its latest redistribution when, in late 1990, its work was unexpectedly suspended for twelve months by the legislature. The commission's proposals had caused a negative reaction among MNAs, particularly those on the governing Liberal side. Among other things, the commission had planned to reduce the number of seats in the Gaspésie from four to three in consequence of that region's declining share of the province's population. The intensity of the reaction (both from the public in that region and from their MNAs) was far greater than the commission had anticipated. All four Gaspé MNAs were, at the time, Liberal, and the province's second most influential cabinet minister (after the premier), finance minister Gérard D. Lévesque, was one of them. A Gaspé member of the Assembly since 1956, sometime leader of the opposition and interim leader of his party on two occasions, Lévesque was known as a political heavyweight in Quebec City and in his region.

The government's dissatisfaction with the prospects of having a seat taken away from one of its areas of strength, together with concerns expressed by other MNAs on both sides of the House at having their own seat rearranged or eliminated within less than five years of the previous redistribution, prompted the unexpected suspension. The Supreme Court's decision six months later provided the government with an opportunity to amend the legislation. Two changes were introduced. Boundary readjustments would follow every second election, rather than every one, as had been the case, and a statement was added to the legislation to the effect that the purpose of electoral boundary readjustments was "to ensure that the principle of effective representation of electors is respected." *Carter* was not the reason for the suspension or the amended legislation, but it provided the government with the excuse needed to direct the commission to start the process anew.

The commission was subjected to great pressure from the politicians and in the public hearings to abandon the proposals made in its 1990 report. It was called upon to reinstate seats that were slated for removal from the Gaspésie and other regions. In its subsequent public hearings and in drafting its new maps, the commission went out of its way to refer to the "new legal context," the "different weighting of the criteria that the commission must take into account," and the "more flexible application" of the criteria. In the event, it restored the fourth seat to the Gaspésie and generally left the entire map substantially less altered than it would have been had its earlier proposals been implemented.

As the Quebec illustration later demonstrated, boundary readjustment chickens almost invariably come home to roost. The 1992 map of Quebec's 125 ridings, which, following the suspension, was designed largely the same as the previous one, had two seats with populations lower than the 25 percent tolerance limits. Population shifts continued, however, irrespective of constituency borders. The effect of those shifts was so pronounced that by 1994 the number of ridings below 25 percent had increased to twelve; by 1998 it had reached nineteen. All four Gaspé seats fell into that group, but the region had a different political complexion at the end of the decade from what it had at the outset.

In fact, both the province and the region wore different political colours. Gérard Lévesque was no longer a member of the National Assembly, the Parti Québécois (PQ) had replaced the Liberals as the government, and the PQ held three of the four Gaspé seats. Faced with a considerably different electoral map after the pending redistribution in 1999, the legislature approved a one-year suspension of the process in response to the government's stated intention of holding "public consultations on the voting system and electoral representation." The fundamental problem of the legislative entitlement of a region of declining population such as the Gaspésie remained as unresolved at the end of the decade as it had been at the beginning.[28]

But there was now a new political twist to the debate in Quebec about constituency populations. The PQ had emerged by the late 1990s as the dominant party in many of the non-metropolitan regions of Quebec, such as the Gaspé, that were continuing to suffer population losses. This complicated the issue for the sovereigntist government. Thirty years before, when the PQ was almost entirely urban in its support base (except for the Saguenay and the Côte nord), it had been a staunch advocate of voter parity and of constructing electoral districts with roughly equal populations. But support for sovereignty and for the PQ underwent an important shift at the time of the 1980 referendum, and the party became stronger outside Montreal than within. As a consequence, the PQ took up the cause of protecting the regions, within both the government and the party, and became more sympathetic to claims of maintaining rural seats even if their populations were dwindling. Like the Liberals a decade or more earlier, the PQ (and the Bloc Québécois federally) have come to defend rural over-representation ostensibly on the grounds of protecting the regions. In reality, it has had much to do with the party's electoral fortunes but virtually nothing to do with *Carter.*[29]

The *Carter* decision was handed down by the Supreme Court of Canada in June 1991. Seizing the opportunity that the decision presented, Nova Scotia was the first of the provinces to respond. Within a month the legislature approved the establishment of Nova Scotia's first independent electoral boundaries commission and its terms of reference. Composed of six members, the commission was described by supporters of the new Conservative premier, Donald Cameron, as part of his government's reformist agenda. Cameron had succeeded John Buchanan, who had resigned late in 1990 as leader of a patronage-laden and scandal-ridden government. Cameron had promised during his campaign for his party's leadership to ensure that the redistribution of electoral districts would be carried out in a nonpartisan manner.

Once chosen premier, he set about trying to establish his credentials as a political reformer. Changes were introduced to election campaign finance laws, to methods of screening prospective appointments to the bench, to practices relating to letting tenders for government con-tracts, and to electoral institutions that could help to make the Assem-bly more representative of Nova Scotia's society. It was in response to that last item, following a unanimous recommendation of a select committee of the legislature, that the boundaries commission was established and charged with promoting Nova Scotians' "constitu-tional right to effective representation." *Carter* had provided the lan-guage for the terms of reference and lent support to the expressed opinions of the MLAs on the all-party select committee that effective and minority representation were achievable and desirable goals for the province. That suited the new premier's stated objective of reforming his province's governing institutions.[30]

According to the chair and vice-chair of the commission, the group found *Carter* extremely helpful in designing the provincial ridings. They described the court's approach to effective representation and to the representation of minorities as a creative one that "used for-ward-looking language to elaborate it."

Carter's finding that the primary condition of effective representa-tion rested on the the relative parity of voting power led the commis-sion to design constituencies on what it called an entitlement basis. Working with county-based population figures, the commission com-puted the number of seats to which a county was entitled according to its share of the total provincial population. Those with less than the per county average population were combined in some fashion with adjoining ones; those with a greater than average population received commensurately more seats. The commission saw this as a way of honouring both the longstanding practice of allotting provincial leg-islative seats on the basis of county boundaries, and also the principle of relative parity of voting power. Four "protected constituencies" were also designed to encourage the election of Acadians (in three seats) and a Black (in one Halifax seat). In only two Acadian seats did the minority constitute a majority of the population. Nonetheless, the commission's hope was that by designing the ridings well below the average constituency size, the election of minorities to the legislature would be encouraged. The smaller than average size of the protected seats represented a clear departure from the entitlement method, but it was justified in terms that the commission was certain would meet *Carter*'s goal of ensuring that a legislature "represent the diversity of our social mosaic."[31]

The plan as devised by the Nova Scotia provincial commission sat well with the politicians. The governing Tories liked the respect shown for historic communities defined according to traditional county lines, and the opposition Liberals and New Democrats were attracted to the possibility of the province's historic minorities increasing their presence in the assembly. (The Mi'kmaq leadership was unwilling to accept the creation of a separate additional seat at that time, so nothing materialized on that front.) All protected constituencies had populations well below the provincial average. The populations of four of the five (one sparsely populated and territorially large seat was also deemed a protected constituency) ranged from between 8,700 to 9,700 per riding compared with the provincial average of 17,300. Having constructed 73 percent of its fifty-two electoral districts within +/−15 percent of the average, and having justified the creation of the protected constituencies on the grounds of legislative instructions to the commission and the *Carter* ruling, the commission drew the exercise to a close confident that its proposals would be approved by the Assembly and could withstand a court challenge. The subsequent election, which brought defeat to Cameron's government and the election of the Liberals under John Savage, saw the election of three Acadian members and the province's first Black MLA in the four protected ridings.[32]

In something of a reversal of the pattern that obtained in Ontario, whereby the provincial government adopted the federal map, Nova Scotia's federal commission of the 1990s looked to the provincial one for guidance. The three federal commissioners (one of whom had served as chair of the provincial commission) were sufficiently impressed with the logic of the entitlement model of seat allocation for Nova Scotia that they applied the same principle to the federal map. With only one-fifth the seats of their provincial counterparts, however, and with the minority populations relatively small and often dispersed, the federal commission concluded that it had no opportunity for constructing protected constituencies in the same fashion as their provincial counterparts.[33]

In the shadow of the *Carter* decision, the newly elected NDP government of Saskatchewan justified its 1993 electoral boundaries readjustment legislation on the grounds that it moved the province "closer to the principle of one person, one vote" (which was most decidedly *not* in *Carter*), and that it ensured "fair and effective representation for all

Saskatchewan citizens" (which was an almost exact quote from the Court of Appeal ruling on *Carter*).[34] The NDP had reason to complain about the unfairness of both the first-past-the-post electoral system and the disproportionate allocation of seats to rural Saskatchewan. At the time of the previous election in 1986 the NDP had won a slightly larger share of the popular vote (45.1 percent to 44.8 percent) but had come out with thirteen fewer seats than the governing Conservatives (twenty-five to thirty-eight). These figures disguised an even more marked and increasingly persistent feature of Saskatchewan politics – an urban/ rural split. In 1986 all but two of the twenty seats in Regina and Saskatoon were won by the NDP; for their part the Tories were almost totally dependent upon the rural and smaller population seats in the province for their electoral success.[35]

The electoral reform proposals that the NDP adopted while in opposition made no mention of changing the electoral system. (The NDP too had a proven history of winning office in the province with a comfortable majority of seats but only a plurality of the votes. The party leadership sensed, rightly, that their time would come again.) Instead, their target of electoral reform was the province-wide set of constituencies. It was plain to many observers following the 1991 defeat of the Conservatives that after its election the NDP would ensure that a new set of constituency maps would be in place before another election. The 1993 legislation that they introduced to accomplish that was clearly aimed at righting past political wrongs. The changes effectively reduced the value of the rural vote in determining the outcome of a provincial election. By definition, that was expected to help the NDP.

The legislation owed nothing to *Carter*. Indeed, the Supreme Court ruling was at no point publicly invoked by a government minister or an NDP backbencher in support of the changed law. It was clear from the contents of the new law and from the language that the government used to defend it that had they been asked which of the two court decisions on *Carter* they would have preferred, the Saskatchewan Court of Appeal ruling would have won out. Ironically, the government effectively replaced the law that the Supreme Court of Canada had upheld with one that invoked the principles espoused in the court ruling that had been overturned.

Saskatchewan's new Constituency Boundaries Act, 1993 was justified by the NDP government on populist grounds. "People have told us government is too large," and "we can save in excess of $1 million per year" were part of the NDP's pitch to the legislature and to public opinion in support of the new act's reduction in the size of the legislature from sixty-six to fifty-eight members.[36] These were the same points that would soon be made by the Harris Conservatives in their push for electoral victory in Ontario. The new Saskatchewan legislation ended the previous act's "arbitrary" apportionment of seats into rural and urban categories – categories to which the Supreme Court had had no objection. It also reduced the maximum population variance levels to +/−5 percent for all but the two northern seats (which had to be maintained as they had previously existed). The 5 percent limits became the tightest of any in Canada.

The 1993 commission noted in constructing the boundaries for the new fifty-eight-member legislature that "the loss of eight seats was borne entirely by rural Saskatchewan."[37] Regina and Saskatoon were divided into eleven ridings each, which gave them 39 percent of the province's non-northern seats compared with 31 percent at the time of the 1986 election and 34 percent in 1991.[38] Predicting on the basis of past voting patterns is, in isolation, a risky business. Nonetheless the NDP had reason to believe that the legislated changes and the maps produced by the three-member independent commission would work in their favour. The cities, from which the party drew the bulk of its members, had become relatively more important in elections to the legislature, whereas the Tories and Liberals, heavily dependent in the past on the rural parts of the province for their strength, had fewer seats available to contest.

The opposition in 1993 was powerless to stop the change. Neither party dared to oppose changes justified on populist, cost-cutting grounds. The best the Tories could do was to demand an even greater reduction in the size of the legislature. In a novel suggestion advanced by their acting leader and anticipating to some extent Harris's scheme for Ontario, the Saskatchewan PCs called for adoption of the federal map for the province. Their plan was to divide the fourteen federal electoral districts into four provincial ridings each, thereby producing a fifty-six-member legislature and saving the taxpayers part of the expense of holding a total province-wide redistribution. The Tory proposal was rejected by the government.[39] But it served notice, as did the attraction of the provincial idea of entitlement to Nova Scotia's federal commission and the adoption of the federal map by the province of Ontario, that linkages between federal and provincial redistributions might be possible and could be more fully explored in the years ahead.

The Saskatchewan NDP could count their lucky stars for having introduced the smaller legislature, the tighter population limits, and the relatively greater share of the seats for the province's urban areas when, in 1999 they barely held on to power. The party slipped to twenty-nine seats and fell behind their principal opponents in popular vote. The Saskatchewan Party (formed from the remains of the scandal-ridden Tory party and dissident Liberals and NDPers) won twenty-six ridings and the largest share of the popular vote, and the Liberals came away with three seats and one-fifth of the vote. A three coalition with the Liberals assured the NDP of retaining power. Twenty-five of the NDP's seats were in the province's four largest cities, and every one of the Saskatchewan Party's seats came from either a rural or a small-town district. It seemed likely that had the same rural-urban split taken place in the context of a decade earlier – that is for a sixty-six-member House whose constituencies were designed according to 25 percent tolerance limits and a strict allocation of relatively fewer seats to the urban parts of the province – the NDP would have lost power and the Saskatchewan Party would have formed a majority government.[40]

The Gini Indexes for almost all provinces show a reduction in the degree of inequality of voters in the post-*Carter* era (see table 9.4 and figure 9.1). Of the ten provinces, only Quebec saw an increase in its Ginis, and that would not have been the case had the 1990 redistribution not been suspended then repeated a year later with greater population disparities among the ridings than had originally been planned. For several provinces (notably Alberta to its second post-*Carter* redistribution and the Atlantic provinces) the reduction was quite marked. For Prince Edward Island it was extraordinary, dropping from .341 to .09. By adapting the federal maps, Ontario almost halved its measure of inequality. British Columbia shows virtually no change from its last pre- and first post-*Carter* redistributions. This is explained by the fact that the Fisher Commission recommendations, which formed part of the British Columbia court's advice to the legislature in *Dixon*, were put in place before *Carter* was decided. The two decisions shared much in common, not least because they had been handed down by the same judge. In British Columbia, at least, the more accurate comparative measure is the last pre-*Dixon* redistribution, rather than the last pre-*Carter* one. Curiously, the province from which *Carter* sprang had, except for Manitoba, the lowest Gini score of any province in the pre-*Carter* era. As Duff Spafford has noted, "numbers were the weak side of the case against the Saskatchewan electoral map" that led to the court reference. The Saskatchewan numbers, he concluded, "were not the stuff of which horror stories are made" in challenges to electoral boundaries.[41] One can only wonder what the Supreme Court of Canada ruling might have been had the reference it had been asked to rule on come from, let us say, Prince Edward Island rather than Saskatchewan.

Table 9.4
Provincial Electoral Boundaries: Gini Indexes, Pre- and Post-*Carter* Decision

Redistribution	BC	AB	SK	MB	ON	QC	NB	NS	PEI	NF
Last Pre-*Carter*	0.072	0.162	0.031	0.025	0.082	0.074	0.158	0.175	0.341	0.130
QC 1990 (aborted)						0.055				
First Post-*Carter*	0.071	0.094	0.013	0.023	0.044	0.082	0.077	0.089	0.090	0.055
Second Post-*Carter*		0.062								

Number of Electoral Districts

Redistribution	BC	AB	SK	MB	ON	QC	NB	NS	PEI	NF
Last Pre-*Carter*	75	83	66	57	130	125	58	52	16	51
First Post-*Carter*	79	83	58	57	103	125	55	52	27	48

Sources: Reports of redistribution commissions and legislative committees. As Nova Scotia and Prince Edward Island did not have redistribution commissions before *Carter,* these ginis are calculated on the basis of enumerated electors for the last pre-redistribution provincial general election; for Nova Scotia, 1988 and for Prince Edward Island, 1993. Sources for these data are the Reports of the respective Chief Electoral Officers.

Table 9.5 paints a similar picture of a general move among the provinces (Quebec remaining the exception in the 0 – 4.99 range) toward voter equality. The share of seats in the under 5 percent range jumped by a factor of three in Alberta and over five in Newfoundland. At the other extreme, all provinces with a substantial number of seats in the 25 percent and over category before *Carter* had a marked decrease after. In Alberta and Newfoundland that drop was from nearly one-half of the provincial seats to the low single digits. Measured by the Lortie standard of 15 percent variance, the share of seats in that range jumped sevenfold in Prince Edward Island, tripled in Alberta, and doubled in New Brunswick, Nova Scotia, and Newfoundland. The move in the direction of greater voter equality at the federal level with the introduction of independent electoral boundary commissions and the EBRA had anticipated a generally similar, possibly even more pronounced, move in that direction among the provinces in the post-*Carter* redistributions.

THE POST-CARTER CONUNDRUM

The *Saskatchewan Reference* case of 1991 added new elements to the representational puzzle in Canada. It confirmed a role for the courts in defining equality of the vote and the factors to be considered in

Figure 9.1
Provincial Redistributions, Pre- and Post-*Carter* Gini Indexes

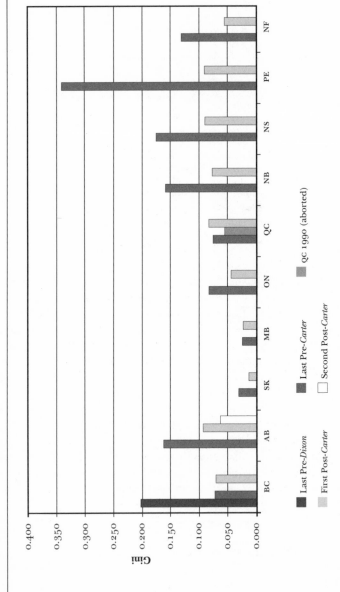

Source: Reports of redistribution commissions and legislative committees, except Nova Scotia 1988 and Prince Edward Island 1993, which use enumerated electors.

Table 9.5
Provincial Electoral Boundaries: Percent of Districts within a Given Range of Absolute Percent Variance from Provincial Parity (totals may not equal 100 due to rounding)

			Range of Absolute Percent Variance from Provincial Parity					
Province	Redistribution	n	0.0–4.99	5.0–9.99	10.0–14.99	15.0–19.99	20.0–24.99	25.0+
BC	Last Pre-*Carter*	75	12	31	36	11	11	0
BC	First Post-*Carter*	79	29	33	16	10	4	8
BC	Second Post-*Carter*							
AB	Last Pre-*Carter*	83	10	11	14	8	8	48
AB	First Post-*Carter*	83	18	17	25	17	18	5
AB	Second Post-*Carter*	83	29	31	27	10	1	2
SK	Last Pre-*Carter*	66	77	20	0	0	0	3
SK	First Post-*Carter*	58	97	0	2	0	0	2
SK	Second Post-*Carter*							
MB	Last Pre-*Carter*	57	79	19	2	0	0	0
MB	First Post-*Carter*	57	95	2	0	2	2	0
MB	Second Post-*Carter*							
ON	Last Pre-*Carter*	130	28	25	22	12	5	8
ON	First Post-*Carter*	103	49	39	3	5	5	0
ON	Second Post-*Carter*							
QC	Last Pre-*Carter*	125	29	20	26	17	6	2
QC	1990 (aborted)	125	39	34	18	6	0	2
QC	First Post-*Carter*	125	21	26	21	18	12	2
QC	Second Post-*Carter*							
NB	Last Pre-*Carter*	58	12	14	10	9	9	47
NB	First Post-*Carter*	55	31	24	20	13	11	2
NB	Second Post-*Carter*							
NS	Last Pre-*Carter*	52	13	15	6	12	12	42
NS	First Post-*Carter*	52	37	17	19	15	2	10
NS	Second Post-*Carter*							
PE	Last Pre-*Carter*	16	0	0	6	0	0	94
PE	First Post-*Carter*	27	4	19	19	52	7	0
PE	Second Post-*Carter*							
NF	Last Pre-*Carter*	51	10	20	18	25	6	22
NF	First Post-*Carter*	48	54	42	0	0	0	4
NF	Second Post-*Carter*							

Sources: Reports of redistribution commissions and legislative committees. As Nova Scotia and Prince Edward Island did not have redistribution commissions before *Carter*, these variances are calculated on the basis of enumerated electors for the last pre-redistribution provincial general election; for Nova Scotia, 1988 and for Prince Edward Island, 1993. Sources for these data are the reports of the respective chief electoral officers.

constructing electoral boundaries. The charter, in turn, provided the courts with the section 3 grounds necessary to decide questions of electoral fairness and equity. The courts addressing the *Saskatchewan Reference* case wrestled with competing notions of strict voter equality and relative voting power. The former won at the Court of Appeal level in Saskatchewan, the latter at the Supreme Court of Canada level. The Supreme Court's ruling could be interpreted as reinforcement of the legislated norms that had, for over three decades at that point, characterized electoral boundary readjustments under independent commissions in Canada. Terms such as "community of interest," "extraordinary circumstances," and "sparsity, density or relative rate of growth" had, starting with Manitoba in the 1950s, become part of the redistribution lexicon in Canada. The *Carter* decision reinforced the balance that Canadian legislators and parliamentarians had attempted to strike up to that point between social pluralism and equitable electoral representation as the principal elements behind electoral boundary readjustments.

What *Carter* left unanswered, however, is as great, if not greater, than what it answered. Ambiguities abound in the decision. Language and terms as imprecise as "effective representation," "fair representation conducive to good government," "relative parity of voting power," and "dilution of voting power," are open to varying, possibly even contradictory interpretations. The Prince Edward Island decision of 1993 speaks directly to that point. It gave a different interpretation to effective representation than to the undocumented fact of the greater difficulties of representing rural than urban areas that the Supreme Court accepted. The result, to contrast the implications of the Prince Edward Island ruling with those of *Carter* two years earlier, is that the distribution of voters was likely to be on a more egalitarian, one person, one vote, basis in one jurisdiction than in another. *Carter* did little to sort out that issue.

Unlike most other representational questions that have been placed before the courts under a section 3 challenge (the successful right to vote cases of prisoners, judges, and the mentally handicapped are the most notable of these), the ambiguities and uncertainties that marked the *Carter* ruling were in keeping with those that marked the history to that point of the acts leading to the establishment of independent electoral boundary commissions. If the language and expressions used in *Carter* left unanswered questions, so had that of the enabling legislation for three or four decades before. "Community of interest," "relative rate of growth" and "extraordinary circumstances" were no more precise or less open to differing interpretations than *Carter's* language. The politicians had been no more explicit in laying down precise guidelines for factors to be used in redistributing seats than the courts.

Jennifer Smith, a political scientist who has served as a redistribution commissioner and written about the process, points out that the representational and institutional stakes involved here are considerable. She places the onus for resolving the lack of clarity over representational terms and conditions squarely on the shoulders of legislators and parliamentarians. It is their responsibility and in their interests, she claims, "to deliberate and decide on the precise reasons for which they deem departures from voter equality to be desirable, and to instruct the independent boundaries commissions accordingly."[42] Andrew Sancton, another political scientist who has both served as a commissioner and written about redistributions, draws a similar conclusion about northern, isolated, and sparsely populated regions and how variable their treatment may be at the hands of different commissions. The federal seats of Labrador in Newfoundland and Abitibi in Quebec illustrate his point. The latter is over three times the size of the former, but it was created in the 1990s with an *above* average population; by contrast, Labrador was classed as an exceptional circumstances seat with a population 63 percent *below* the quota for the province of Newfoundland. Sancton sees such an outcome as a failure of parliamentarians "to decide which remote areas (if any) deserve special treatment outside the +/−25 percent range."[43] Again, *Carter* did little to help sort out that kind of issue.

Whether legislators and parliamentarians view the issue in the same way remains an open question. Bill c-69 which, we learned, was never approved by Parliament, would have added "effective representation" as the "paramount consideration in determining reasonable electoral districts" in a province.[44] Yet no definitions or guidelines were included in the legislation to help the commissions put this principle into effect. That was not a hopeful sign.

Carter offers no firm guidance for reconciling voter equality – which it accepted as fundamental to the whole exercise – with other principles it also accepted as basic to the Canadian representational experience, such as cultural or group identity as critical components of community of interest. The first provincial redistribution carried out in the province of Alberta after the *Carter* ruling illustrated the predicament this can present to commissioners. Attempting to reconcile voter equality with community of interest simply confounded the commissioners and made it impossible to arrive at consensus. Their failure "to agree on the principles of representation led to their [subsequent] failure to agree on how to draw the constituency boundaries."[45] This left the Alberta government with no alternative but to legislate new districts without the help of an outside commission and over the objections of the opposition. In this instance, the reasons presented in *Carter* did nothing to facilitate the work of the boundary readjustment commissioners.

CONCLUSIONS

Judged by the reports of the electoral boundary commissions at both the federal and provincial levels, the maps that commissions produced, and a handful of subsequent court cases, the third of three possibilities posited at the beginning of this chapter has been borne out in the post-*Carter* era. Changes to electoral districting, neither as massive as in the United States over the last four decades nor so negligible as to be undetectable, have been effected in varying degrees at both the federal and provincial levels in Canada. At the aggregate level, combining all federal and provincial statutes and the ridings designed by commissions in Canada in the 1990s, the changes in the 1990s attributable to *Carter* can, most accurately, be described as minimal. To some, the court decision meant presenting carefully reasoned justifications for constituencies deviating from the provincial quotient; to others, *Carter* was all but ignored.

Although overwhelmingly in the direction of increased voter equality, the post-*Carter* changes have been neither uniform in their magnitude nor necessarily for the same stated reasons. More important, it is difficult to attribute them to *Carter*'s influence alone. At the federal level in particular, the maps produced in the 1990s simply continued a trend toward increased voter equality that had followed the adoption of the Electoral Boundaries Readjustment Act in the 1960s. The role *Carter* played in prompting commissions to move toward greater equality of populations in their ridings clearly varied from one federal commission to another, but on balance it cannot be judged to have been extensive.

Of the provincial redistributions, the great majority have seen an increased level of voter equality since *Carter*. In some cases this has been dramatic, in others less so. The magnitude of the shift has depended, of course, on the starting position from which each provincial redistribution of the 1990s had begun. The contrast in the Gini Indexes of the pre- and post-*Carter* redistributions in Manitoba and Atlantic Canada, for example, demonstrate how different the results are in a jurisdiction with an established, independent commission redistributing seats regularly within reasonably tight variance limits and those in a jurisdiction with no history prior to the 1990s of truly independent, non-partisan commissions working with guidelines established by a legislature. All said, as with federal commissions, the degree to which the *Carter* ruling played a conscious or explicit role in provincial legislation or redistributions was not consistent.

Why such differences among the commissions? The variations among the ten federal bodies are understandable given the process through which electoral boundary readjustments are carried out in Canada and by the *Carter* decision itself. Since 1964, federal electoral boundary commissions have operated independently of one another. Created anew every ten years as a result of a federal legislative requirement, each commission is responsible for a limited jurisdiction and a limited task – one province and one redistribution. Apart from the issuance by Elections Canada of a small compendium of academic writings and court cases on redistribution to each commission, a one-day briefing session with the chairs of the separate commissions with Elections Canada officials in Ottawa, and the provision by Elections Canada of technical staff trained to assist the commissions in preparing the maps, the commissioners are on their own.

The independence of the commissions has, from the outset, been reflected in their decisions. These have varied from one province to another and from one commission to another in the same province over time. Some have chosen to construct seats more or less around their province's population quotient; others have opted to use much wider margins. Three commissions, as we know, have availed themselves of the extraordinary circumstances option since it was first added to the federal act in 1985. Seven have not, even though a no less compelling case could have been made in some of them for designing at least one seat below the 25 percent limits.

But the differences among the commissions reflect not only the varying ways in which each commission has defined its mandate. They also attest to the diversity of the social and territorial landscapes that each has confronted. Some have chosen to weigh similar variables differently from others, which in itself speaks volumes about the flexibility that is inherent in the Canadian redistribution process. The statute that leads to the creation of each body and the terms of reference within which it defines its mandate is federal, but once under way the process becomes a decentralized one. Expressed another way, had Canada only one commission – a single body composed of three or four members – to design the parliamentary boundaries for the entire country, it is far more likely that the uniform set of criteria contained in the EBRA would be applied uniformly.

A comparison of the four decades since the introduction of independent electoral boundary commissions at the federal level shows that, in spite of the variations among the provinces, commissions have become less likely to create seats at the margins of their provincial population quota and more likely to design them closer to the quota. *Carter*, in a sense, is a court decision that lends itself to a continuation of that trend, for the ruling stressed relative parity of voting power as the primary goal of redistributions except where deviations can be justified. On the other hand, *Carter* is also perfectly suited to commissions (either federal or provincial) that choose with justifiable reasons to interpret effective representation, relative parity of voting power, and minority representation generously and to construct a greater share of their seats at the margins than they might otherwise.

In the absence of strict court-ordered or legislated standards with respect to one person, one vote or majority-minority principles, as in the United States, Canadian commissions at both the federal and provincial levels demonstrated in the 1990s that they will act very much on their own in crafting electoral districts. As in the past, they will continue to make selective use of what is made available to them in the legislation, terms of reference, submissions, and objections. Since 1991 they have been able to add *Carter* to that list of principles and representational objectives from which to draw.

Carter, in other words, was only one of several influences on legislators, parliamentarians, and electoral boundary commissions in the 1990s. There were many other important parts of the debate over electoral redistributions in that decade: the Lortie report; the preparatory committee work in Parliament to Bill c-69, and the bill's final unravelling through a stand-off between the Senate and the House Commons; the two suspensions in Quebec, one at each end of the decade; the actions taken by some of the provincial legislatures to redefine their boundary readjustment law; and the court cases launched in a few of the provinces against either the relevant statute or the proposed redistribution of seats.

To that should be added another factor that helps to account for the way that governments treated redistributions in the 1990s: possible party advantage. We saw how in Ontario the Harris Conservatives stood to enhance their subsequent electoral chances by following through on their ideological commitment to reduce the Ontario legislature's size by shifting a relatively greater portion of the legislative seats into areas of PC strength. Early in the decade the Quebec Liberals fought to protect at least one area of traditional strength by arranging, together with the PQ who had their own electoral interests to protect, the suspension of the boundary readjustment process. The new Conservative premier of Nova Scotia sought to establish his (and his party's) bone fides as a reformer and a progressive by applying *Carter's* principles to his province's unique social setting. The NDP, once back in office in Saskatchewan, resolved to move to a highly egalitarian boundaries law the effect of which would be to reduce the chances of a rural-based party winning office through a repeat of something equivalent to the 1986 election. In each of these instances, a hoped-for party advantage helps to understand why changes took place, in some instances explicitly invoking *Carter* in the 1990s, in others not. At that level, *Carter*'s utility derived from the fact that if it served a government's purpose it was invoked; if it did not, it was not.

But *Carter*'s legacy can be seen in more than its direct impact on federal and provincial legislation or on the maps designed by commissions. As we will find in the next chapter, some of the concepts that formed a part of the Supreme Court's reasoning lent support to representational arguments advanced for the first time in the 1990s. In this respect, the *Carter* decision can be said to have contributed to a shift in the debate over territorially defined representational building blocks, moving it in a direction not previously a part of constituency redistributions in Canada.

10 Community of Interest and Effective Representation

> It may be termed the representation of minorities; it may be termed the representation of separate interests and pursuits; but give it what name you like, there is no doubt that by means of one member districts you will obtain a very large diversity of representation.
>
> – William Gladstone, 1885

Manitoba, the first of the Canadian jurisdictions to establish independent commissions for the redistribution of electoral boundaries, introduced the concept of community of interest to Canadian electoral boundary readjustment legislation in the mid-1950s. Borrowed from Australia where it had been a part of their Commonwealth Electoral Act for many years, the term (or some variation of it) has since become a staple of most statutes governing boundary readjustments in Canada. It is now familiar coinage to politicians, boundary commissioners, and interested members of the general public who follow the periodic reconfigurations of electoral districts.

We have noted how federalism both enables and encourages social diversity and permits a measure of flexibility in the interpretation of legislated guidelines. The same is no less true of the expression "community of interest." It lends itself to multiple interpretations and applications. It is at one and the same time viewed as a necessary counterweight to an unbridled application of the principle of population equality among electoral districts; as one of the least clearly defined and most subjective of the criteria of electoral districting; and it is not always easy to apply or to respect. For the Lortie Commission the term clearly opened up, on the heels of the *Carter* decision, the possibility of crafting seats with minority representation in mind. For some who looked to ways of increasing the number of natives elected to Parliament, community of interest served to justify the creation of Aboriginal electoral districts that would be separately constructed and whose members would be separately elected from Canada's other parliamentary seats. From the changes proposed in Bill c-69 to the electoral boundary readjustment process, it was obvious that for members of Parliament, community of interest has become a concept far more closely tied to place than to people.

Effective representation is the relatively new kid on the electoral block. Dalton Camp's commission of 1975 had used the expression to justify a larger Ontario legislature. But it was another decade and a half before it was introduced to Canadian electoral boundary readjustments in a slightly more elaborate form in the judgement issued by the Saskatchewan Court of Appeal. When that court decided against the government in the *Carter* reference, it ruled that the redistribution at issue was inconsistent with the notion of "fair and effective representation of all citizens."[1] That exact phrase had been popularized in the United States some twenty-five years earlier when the Supreme Court held in *Reynolds* v. *Sims* that "fair and effective representation for all citizens is concededly the basic aim of legislative apportionment."[2]

With the Supreme Court of Canada's decision in *Carter*, effective representation entered the vocabulary of boundary readjustments in Canada in a major way.[3] Described by Jennifer Smith and Ron Landes as an "arresting phrase"[4] that emerged as the principal reason offered by the court for good governance, effective representation joined community of interest in the 1990s as part of the standard language of Canadian redistributions. Indeed, in some applications of "effective representation," as in the construction of seats in Nova Scotia aimed at enhancing the probability of electing Acadians and Blacks, it is clear that "effective representation" embraces and incorporates "community of interest."

COMMUNITY OF INTEREST

When consideration was first being given to adopting a method for redistributing electoral districts by independent commissions, the Manitoba legislative committee charged with looking into the subject heard from Professors W.L. Morton and Murray Donnelly about the Australian electoral boundary commissions. In their 1954 brief they argued that representation by population should be the basis of electoral divisions, but that two elements of representation should also be factored in. These they called "community" and "territory." In an analysis that anticipated *Dixon* and *Carter*, community and territory were described as the two "clear and intelligible principles" under which departures from equal population districts could be justified.

By community the professors meant that the people represented by a member of the Assembly "should possess certain common interests, neighborhood, the same, or similar, local government, and, perhaps in some measure, generally common economic interests. This is an ancient principle, the one on which parliamentary representation first rested, for the House of Commons was originally the House of Communitates, the counties and boroughs of England." By contrast, they argued that territory was a "recognition of the need of communication between the voters and the representative." They saw this as "particularly important in [Manitoba] as in Canada, for here we attempt to work representative institutions in a very large territory containing a relatively small population. The problem ... is one of low density of population." On its own, they contended, representation by population "is not an adequate basis for just and effective representation." Community and territory must also be carefully factored into the representative equation in order to ensure that the "representative is in touch with his constituents through common interests and personal contact."[5]

From the outset, community of interest was seen as a way of recognizing and accepting a shared attribute as an integral part of a representational building block. That attribute might be defined according to location, as with a neighbourhood or a set of municipal boundaries; or as the product of a common pursuit, such as an economic interest; or as the presence of a common trait, such as a social characteristic. If the interest were judged to be sufficiently paramount or if dividing it among two or more constituencies would in some sense harm the interests of that community, then, so the theory goes, it could justifiably be kept intact and made a part of a particular riding even if it compromised the ideal of equal population districts.

The phrase "community of interest" appears in most electoral boundary readjustment legislation in Canada is some form or another. A few provinces, Newfoundland for example, avoided the expression entirely in the terms establishing a particular commission.[6] Quebec has preferred to rely on the concept of a "natural community," a term that combines the community and territorial factors to which Morton and Donnelly made reference. According to the most recent version of Quebec's Election Act: "An electoral division represents a natural community established on the basis of demographical, geographical and sociological considerations, such as the population density, the relative growth rate of the population, the accessibility, area and shape of the region, the natural local boundaries and the territories of local municipalities."[7]

There is no one term that is used by all other jurisdictions to capture the concept. Some provinces have chosen "community or diversity of interests," others "community interests" or "community of interests." The federal legislation has retained "community of interest" since the

EBRA was adopted in 1964. In its latest manifestation the expression appears in the following form: a federal commission may depart from constructing a riding as "close as reasonably possible" to the provincial electoral quota when it considers it necessary

(a) in order to respect the community of interest or community of identity in or the historical pattern of an electoral district in the province, or

(b) in order to maintain a manageable geographic size for districts in sparsely populated, rural or northern regions of the province.

Community and territory have been combined in that section of the federal act as they have in various provincial acts as well. The intent is to establish population parity as the fundamental objective of electoral boundary readjustments, but to permit departures from that principle when either the community of interest or the geographic size of a district warrants it.[8]

Does it make a difference what term is used? In theory, yes; in reality, no. Community of interests or community interests, often accompanied by diversity of interests, suggest a variety of possibly competing factors. That is even more the case when both identity and historical pattern are added to the principles that commissions are called upon to respect in constructing electoral districts. In theory, the list of possible factors is wide-ranging. It could include such variables as municipal or regional boundaries; transportation and shopping patterns; and some of the leading demographic variables, such as race, occupation, religion, and language. When used in the plural, the expression community of interests accepts the heterogeneity of modern Canadian society while, at the same time, implying that the different interests and identities of an area can be satisfactorily aggregated in such a way as to ensure that the design of a constituency can accommodate them. This is a Herculean task for any commission. Not least among the difficulties that commissioners face in attempting to judge the relative weight to be accorded to often conflicting interpretations of what constitutes a community of interests is the fact that they are also expected to take into account the geographic sizes of the districts they construct.

To speak of a community of interest in the singular is to presume that individuals who happen to live in a territorially defined area either can agree upon a single interest that so clearly defines their geographic proximity, or that one of their interests can be deemed by an outside commission to be paramount for the purpose of defining electoral districts. Not surprisingly, that too creates difficulties for electoral boundary commissioners. It is somewhat easier to manage when a single occupation, such as ranching, farming, fishing, or forestry is widely accepted within a region as an apt general descriptor of the area and when the residents are willing to forego placing higher priority on other factors rather than the occupational one by which they wish to be defined. But the reverse of that holds true as well. Facing multiple occupation categories and widely diverse social characteristics in a region, a commission may find it impossible to design a riding that is entirely satisfactory to all concerned – residents and politicians alike.

The periodic debates in Parliament and the legislatures on electoral boundary legislation, the briefs presented to commissions, and the arguments made at public hearings on district proposals all suggest that there is no essential difference between the singular or plural form of the expression. The terms are often used interchangeably and are rarely defined with much precision. As well, community of interest has subsumed such terms as identity and diversity, with the result that only infrequently do identity issues surface as explicit elements of the redistribution exercise. When they do, as we will see with one issue of linguistic representational entitlement in New Brunswick, they are as likely to surface under effective representation as under community of interest.

There is no question about the value that politicians and the general public attach to community of interest. It is far and away their favourite reference point in constructing ridings. As we saw in chapter 7, of the arguments presented in submissions and at public hearings calling for changes in commission proposals, 50 percent were based on community of interest, 18 percent on historic grounds, and 12–15 percent on the basis of geography. The objections later raised by MPs were presented in much the same ratios.

Four reasons might be offered to account for the importance attached to community of interest. The first, in a sense, is a negative reason. If community of interest were *not* taken into account, and if electoral districts were constructed solely on the basis of largely equal populations, the results could be both absurd and unfair to individuals, groups, and communities. An illustration from the United States makes the point. The American legal scholar and judge, Robert Bork, was named by a Connecticut court to redistrict the state in 1972 with an allowable maximum population deviation of 1 percent from the state average. Unable to disaggregate census tract data, and mindful of the wide disparities in population among the tracts and the uneven population distribution across the state, Bork found that the new districts he created "utterly ignored geographical and demographic facts. Small towns were split into two districts [and] people on opposite sides of rivers were lumped into districts." Given the strict population stipulation and unable to temper it by appropriate accommodations for community interests, Bork had no choice but to draw a map that took practically no account of community. Understandably, the reaction in the state to what was dubbed "Bork's Fiasco" was often furious.[9]

Second, a great number of individuals identify with geographically defined communities of some sort. These might derive from a personal and family attachment to, say, a local church or a synagogue. They might stem from membership in a fraternal organization, a club, a community hall, or a sport team. The list is as vast as it is variable. Based as it is on the principle that neighbourhoods are valuable to maintaining a civic society, the concept of community of interest captures a citizen's identification with a place where an individual and others who live in the same vicinity share a similar interest. Out of that comes a sense of belonging and of sharing an identity with others. It is natural to want to extend that sense of being part of a community to ensuring that that community becomes a part of a larger electoral district with which there is also some affinity.[10]

In some cases the community is natural, as with members of an ethnic group whose settlement pattern has led them to live in close proximity to one another. In other cases the community has resulted from an artificial and totally arbitrary creation of the state. Ken Carty, among others, has noted how a line drawn in one direction rather than another has given rise to what is subsequently deemed a community of interest. Carty uses the example of two prairie provinces carved out of the former Northwest Territories at the same time:

The idea that there is something out there that is a natural political community is often a myth, and very often the product of some former boundary commissioner. The distinction between Saskatchewan and Alberta is in some sense the creation of Laurier's decision to draw the border between them up and down instead of across. You can imagine if in 1905, when they divided the territory between these two new provinces, they decided to have a northern and a southern province ... we would now talk about the natural, normal, historical inevitability of those communities. They evolved in other ways because some boundary commissioner decided to draw the line. In this case it was the prime minister and it was a province. But the same principle works even for electoral districts.[11]

Carty's analysis reminds us that boundaries not only encompass communities; they can also help to create them. Elected members and members of the public are particularly mindful of that fact when they oppose changes to the boundaries of districts they had objected to being created at the previous redistribution! One study of federal and provincial redistributions of the 1980s found that the most frequently mentioned of thirty-one factors referred to in public hearings on boundary readjustments (cited in 30.6 percent of all submissions or testimony) was the importance of preserving the existing electoral boundaries.[12] Alan Stewart explained the obvious advantages those politically aware individuals at the local level gain from maintaining a large measure of continuity in riding boundaries:

The enactment of a particular set of boundaries creates a community of interest among those who participate in politics at any level (including voting) in that jurisdiction. Partisan constituency organizations are organized along these lines, [and] voluntary associations and citizens seeking to influence public policy must organize themselves along these lines in order to influence members and candidates. The maintenance where possible of these established networks and channels of participation is a legitimate goal.[13]

That said, however, the concept of community of interest in some urban settings, particularly those in the larger cities given to high rates of mobility in their population, remains problematic.[14] It stands to reason that it is more difficult to construct communities of interest on, for example, the basis of occupation or employment in an urbanized/suburbanized context than in rural areas. It could be expected that a significant portion of the population of a small town or a farming community would draw their livelihood from one or two local industries, thereby creating among that population a clearly sensed community of interest. But the same would be expected to be less the case with suburban dwellers who commute some distance to a variety of jobs. Higher rates of mobility among urban and suburban populations than among rural ones would compound this. To take one illustration, in parts of the federal district of Vancouver Centre, where the voter turnover between elections is in the order of 50 percent, there would be far less likelihood of attachment to a community than in a more stable rural setting.[15]

Third, community of interest can enhance citizen involvement in politics. It has been demonstrated that political participation, as measured by voter turnout statistics, is positively affected when boundary readjustments leave voters in a riding with which they share a strong community of interest. It is negatively affected when boundaries are redrawn in such a way as to place voters in a seat with which they have less in common. A comparison of voter turnout in the Ontario provincial elections of 1985 and 1987 (between which a redistribution of provincial seats had taken place) showed that turnout increased in 1987 by an average of 1.2 percent in ridings in which voters said that they shared the greatest community of interest, but that it declined by an average of 1.3 percent in areas where voters had been removed from a riding with which they had indicated a stronger community of interest attachment.[16]

Fourth, electoral districts for federal, provincial, or territorial assemblies are frequently constructed to accord with local district boundaries. This makes a good deal of sense, for the local district, in turn, constitutes a perceptible and understandable community of interest for the majority of its residents. City, municipal, or county boundaries may never change in the lifetime of the residents, but electoral district boundaries may be altered every decade or so. It is far easier for an individual to identify with the former than with the latter.[17]

The local districts may be counties, as in Ontario and Nova Scotia, rural or urban municipalities and townships, as in parts of the prairies, or county regional municipalities, as in Quebec. They may be school districts, hospital or health regions. These are known to the residents of an area who, typically, have their most immediate and frequent contacts with government at the local level. They can relate to the city or town hall, the county court house, the local hospital, or the nearest school. That is part of their community. To fail to take full measure of the relevance of local districts is a risk that boundary readjustment commissions try to avoid if at all possible. Repeatedly in interviews, commissioners stressed the critical importance of using these local building blocks as constructively as possible in their exercise. They are mindful of the value of making use of existing district lines and of the attraction of using existing government district lines. The second and third most frequently mentioned of the factors referred to in public hearings on boundary readjustments (cited in 25.1 percent and 23.6 percent respectively of all presentations) were the importance of adhering to county and regional boundaries and the need to respect local municipality or ward boundaries in constructing electoral districts.[18]

The adoption of the federal electoral districts by the province of Ontario in 1996 raises some potentially important issues of representation for elected members insofar as it relates to communities of interest. The community of interest criteria for constructing seats for a provincial assembly from local government districts are different from those of the federal Parliament. This stems from the fact that the division of powers presents different issues for consideration and legislative action at the federal and at the provincial levels. That affects, obviously, the representational demands placed on elected members by constituents and the various local districts contained in a riding. How this will play out for Ontario MPPs is uncertain at this stage, but it could present them with some problems.

Unbeknownst to either Queen's Park or the Ontario federal commission at the time, the seats for the Ontario Assembly were drawn by commissioners who had been charged with designing federal seats for the 1990s. Yet federal and provincial communities of interest as they relate to representational responsibilities are not necessarily the same. What is a community of interest for an MPP is different from that for an MP. For example, it does not really matter to a federal member how many school boards there are in his or her riding, since a federal member has very limited dealings with them. As a result, an MP can have one full school board and parts of several others in the riding he or she represents without much impact on the member's constituency duties. To a lesser extent, possibly, the same is true of hospital boards or health districts. But for the MPPs, education and health by definition are highly important issues. The scope of their representational duties is directly affected by the shape of their ridings and by the various communities of interest defined by municipal district boundaries of school and health boards that they are expected to speak for and to deal with. Without a separate provincial process that ensured that proposed maps would become the focus of public scrutiny and of members' objections, Ontario forfeited, in effect, its control over how ridings were designed to accommodate communities of interest based on district boundaries relevant to members of the provincial legislature.[19]

In combination, these are powerful reasons for wanting to ensure that a community of interest, which might be read as a "commonality (or likeness) of interest," is honoured to the fullest extent possible when constituencies are designed. The difficulty that commissioners face, however, is in meeting that objective as satisfactorily as the public and the politicians want. They face a variety of obstacles. Communities of interest are not always well-defined, agreed upon, or capable of being factored into the redistribution equation.

Independently of one another, the chairs of two federal commissions of the 1990s compared the concept of community of interest to "a blank cheque."[20] The Quebec chair elaborated on his description: "You can write anything that you want on it and take it to the bank. But that's no guarantee that it will be cashed."[21] The bankers, in this case electoral boundary commissioners, are presented with a variety of completed, often competing, cheques about communities of interest. It is up to them to determine if there is sufficient reason for cashing them. The principal difficulty that commissioners have in determining the value of those cheques stems from the absence of objective standards by which to judge a community's interest(s). As a result, the matter is reduced largely to making an informed, subjective judgment.

Sometimes what is claimed to be a community of interest is, in fact, nothing more than barely disguised political self-interest on the part of a politician or a highly parochial understanding of the concept on the part of interested members of the public. Elected members are noted for objecting to changes in their existing constituency boundaries. They prefer the known to the unknown, and their lives are made simpler when they can preserve, if at all possible, their constituency and campaign organizations and personnel. For an MP to object under the guise of community of interest, as one did, to a constituency design change because, in his words, "it moved my constituency office into a different riding," is to miss the point about what community of interest is intended to mean. To some members of the public, community of interest has amounted to nothing more than "the district served by the local sewage treatment plant," or "the area ministered to by the Ukrainian Orthodox but *not* (!) the nearby Ukrainian Catholic church," or "the territory included in the annual music festival."[22] The concept gives rise to limitless varieties of claims.

The same boundary may even be described differently by the principal players in the redistribution exercise. In objecting to the proposed redefinition of her riding, the MP for St John's West from 1993 to 1997 claimed that the TransCanada Highway constituted a natural division line between the western isthmus of the Avalon Peninsula and eastern parts of the proposed district. The federal commission rejected that view. In turning down the member's objection it noted that the highway served as the "principal communication *axis joining* the communities ... rather than as a factor dividing them."[23] As is often the case, highways, roads, and streets are described, depending up who is doing the describing, as either connectors or dividers of communities.

Electoral boundary readjustment laws turn commissions into highwire balancing acts. Commissioners are required to construct seats as close as reasonably possible to the population quota; yet they are permitted to depart from that principle when an area's community of interest, community of identity, or geographic size are deemed to be sufficiently compelling. In some jurisdictions they are even allowed in extraordinary circumstances to go beyond the maximum population variances. It is clear from the record how commissions have interpreted their responsibilities.

If the politicians and the public had had their way, the reverse would have been the case. With particular and local interests to advocate, rather than general and province-wide interests to balance, politicians and interested citizens have a far narrower and more parochial view of what the redistribution process is intended to accomplish. In the description it provided at the conclusion of its work, one federal commission said that "almost invariably those making representations were preoccupied with their local communities of interest and quite unconcerned with the electoral quota ... Perhaps this is as it should be. All the more reason why the commission itself must be responsible for overseeing the process and for maintaining the principle of 'representation by population' within the province."[24] That observation was confirmed by one study that analysed the 470 representations presented to Ontario's federal and provincial boundaries commissions in the 1980s. It found that almost three-quarters (74.2 percent) of the proposals from the public and the politicians would have resulted in greater population *inequality* among the electoral districts. At the other extreme, only 2 percent of the proposals explicitly recommended population equality be given more weight in constructing ridings.[25]

Mindful of the difficulties surrounding the concept, the Lortie Commission concluded that "community of interest cannot be interpreted other than on a case-by-case basis." At the same time, it recommended that commissions be empowered to consider communities of interest and that they "justify their boundary proposals with reference to community of interest objectives." This could be accomplished if commissions were directed by the EBRA to consider electoral districts as representing communities established "on the basis of demographic, sociological and geographic considerations" and if commissions took into account "the accessibility, area and shape of a region, its natural local boundaries and ecology, and the boundaries of local government and administrative units, as well as treaty areas." It favoured the idea that sociological and demographic profiles of constituencies should be examined by commissions because minority groups stood to "maximize their electoral influence" whenever their "community of interest is respected in drawing constituency boundaries."[26]

When the Milliken Committee of the House of Commons examined Canada's electoral boundary readjustment process in 1994–5, it explored alternative ways of improving on the EBRA's provisions with respect to community of interest. It considered the Lortie recommendation and entertained a version proposed by Reform party members of the committee. Those two interpretations of community of interest, together with the one that was finally contained in Bill C-69, are given in figure 10.1.

Unlike the more wide-ranging definition of the Lortie report, the Reform party's take on community of interest was, in Richard Jenkins's phrase, "limited to the landscape and [to] historical boundaries."[27] It

Figure 10.1
Alternative Versions of Community of Interest Proposed in the 1990s

Lortie Commission	Reform Party Proposal	Bill c-69
Community of interest means a community of interest formed on the basis of demographic, sociological, economic, and geographic considerations, taking into account the accessibility, shape, and ecology of a region, the boundaries of local government and administrative units, as well as [Indian] treaty areas. (1991)	Community of interest includes such factors as the existing or traditional boundaries of electoral districts, the boundaries of municipalities, natural boundaries, ecological considerations, and access to means of communication and transport. (1994)	Community of interest includes such factors as the economy, existing or traditional boundaries of electoral districts, the urban or rural characteristics of a territory, the boundaries of municipalities and Indian reserves, natural boundaries, and access to means of communication and transport. (1994)

Sources: RCERPF, *Reforming Electoral Democracy* I: 158; Richard W. Jenkins, "Untangling the Politics of Electoral Boundaries in Canada, 1993–1997," *ARCS*, (Winter 1998), 525; and Bill c-69, An Act to Provide for the Establishment of Electoral Boundaries Commissions and the Readjustment of Electoral Boundaries (1994). s. 19(4).

made no mention of either sociological or economic variables, and was more closely tied to existing boundaries and to access to means of communication and transport than Lortie's proposal. Members of all parties, especially those representing non-metropolitan areas, speak with authority about the reach of television, radio, and print media in their regions. Those from predominantly rural seats know all too well the airline and (possibly) train schedules to cities or towns in their ridings, the proximity of towns or villages to the various means of transportation, and the distances to be covered by automobile within their district. The Reform members' definition of community of interest was understandable given the party's parliamentary membership and ideological bent at the time. All but one of the party's MPs elected in 1993 came from the regions most distant from Ottawa outside of the northern territories: the western prairies and British Columbia. They shared a common distrust of "old politics" and of Canada's "old parties," and they pressed for an un-hyphenated Canadianism that sought to end differential treatment of groups and communities. They subscribed to a populism that called for, among other things, a smaller House of Commons, more free votes in Parliament, and a greater reliance on such non-traditional consultative mechanisms as initiatives and referendums. Given their ideological predisposition, Reform MPs had little reason to favour guidelines for electoral boundary commissions that accepted references to demography and sociology.[28]

The compromise definition accepted by MPs on both sides of the House combined elements of the Lortie and Reform proposals, but it leaned more in the direction of Reform's view of community of interest. The provision agreed to was a good deal more explicit than the terms of the existing EBRA. Bill C-69 contained references to municipal and natural boundaries, Indian reserves, and access to means of communication and transport. It included existing or traditional boundaries of electoral districts and the economy as factors making up a community of interest, but it made no mention of either sociological or demographic factors as part of the definition. The members of the Milliken Committee, not just those from the Reform caucus, were opposed to Lortie's recommendation to use electoral redistricting to enhance the representation of minority groups. They feared that ghettos or ethnic enclaves would be created and that the implementation of a provision adding a reference to Canada's plural society would lead to a form of segregation.[29]

A major concern of the MPs was to make certain that the "spatial characteristics of the single-member plurality system" were included in the guidelines that formed a part of the legislation.[30] They did this by ensuring that C-69 obliged commissions to consider in determining electoral boundaries both "manageable geographic size" and the "probability of ... substantial future population growth" in an electoral district. The thrust of the re-crafted definition of community of interest, which could be seen as a way of fending off groups' claims to their own representation, was, as Jenkins concluded, "place-related as opposed to people-related."[31]

ABORIGINAL ELECTORAL DISTRICTS

"The primary reason for Aboriginal under-representation in Parliament stems from the failure of current electoral laws to recognize the Aboriginal community of interest." With these words a committee of five Aboriginals under the chairmanship of Senator Len Marchand recommended to the Lortie Commission that up to eight separate Aboriginal Electoral Districts (AEDs) be created at the federal level in Canada.[32] The committee, composed of sitting and former MPs, had been asked by the royal commission to consider institutional reforms in the electoral system that could be introduced to redress the structural inequalities blocking the participation and representation of Aboriginal people in the Canadian political system.

Early in its work, the Lortie Commission had identified increased Aboriginal representation in parliament as an issue of concern. According to the commission's final report, Aboriginal peoples comprised approximately 3.5 percent of the Canadian population, but in 125 years only twelve self-identified Aboriginals had been elected to the House of Commons. To the commission this represented "one of the most significant challenges to our electoral democracy."[33] The situation has not demonstrably improved since the commission reported in the early 1990s. In the 1997 election persons of Aboriginal ancestry won a record five seats, but even that represented only 1.7 percent of the 301 seats available. Between 1867 and 1999, a total of twenty-three parliamentarians were of Aboriginal ancestry. Fifteen had been elected to the Commons and eight appointed to the Senate. Since Confederation, no more than half a dozen of the fifteen Aboriginals (including Métis) elected to the House of Commons have been chosen in seats other than those in which Aboriginals constituted a majority of the electorate.[34]

The Marchand committee reported that these low success rates had contributed to "a general feeling among Aboriginal people that the electoral system is so stacked against them that AEDs are the only way they can gain representation in Parliament in proportion to their numbers." AEDs would help to overcome the longstanding concerns of Aboriginals that "the electoral process has not accommodated [their] community of interest and identity." If for elections to the federal Parliament there were constituencies set aside for Aboriginal voters only, this would then ensure that those chosen (who also would be Aboriginal) "would represent them and be directly accountable to them." Aboriginal MPs would "understand their Aboriginal constituents, their rights, interests, and perspectives on the full range of national public policy issues." By creating AEDs, Canada would show that it was prepared to "redress the structural inequality within the present electoral system."[35]

The Lortie Commission needed little persuasion to recommend changes aimed at accommodating Canada's Aboriginal peoples. It considered two options for enhancing "the effective representation of Aboriginal peoples" in the Commons. The first, and discarded, one would have seen electoral boundary commissions "give the effective representation of Aboriginal people much greater weight in the drawing of electoral boundaries than has been the case."[36] This was similar to the initiatives taken by Nova Scotia in the early 1990s to enhance the probability of Acadian and Black minorities electing members to the provincial Assembly. Lortie's second, and preferred, option would be the creation of Aboriginal constituencies along the lines proposed by the Marchand committee. The commission's preference was for AEDs because that change to electoral redistricting "would build upon the Canadian tradition of accommodating both individual and collective rights."[37]

Lortie offered four compelling reasons for its recommendations. Canada could justifiably introduce AEDs because of the unique constitutional status of Aboriginals dating back to the Royal Proclamation of 1763; the expressed desire of Aboriginal peoples to preserve their separate identity; the special responsibilities of Parliament to legislate under section 91(24) of the Constitution Act, 1867; and the opportunity AEDs presented to promote political equality by ensuring, in keeping with *Carter*, effective representation for Aboriginals.[38]

The Lortie proposal called for the creation of up to eight AEDs. Unlike New Zealand, where at the time the Maori had a guaranteed four of the ninety-nine seats in the Parliament, the number in Canada would vary according to Aboriginal voter registration.[39] An AED would be established in a province where the number of Aboriginal voters on a provincial Aboriginal voting register met a minimum requirement of 85 percent of the provincial electoral quotient under the terms of the EBRA. Given the distribution of native population in Canada, this would mean one AED for each of Quebec, Manitoba, Saskatchewan, and Alberta, two in Ontario, and one or two in British Columbia. Additional AEDs would be established in a province where the growth in the Aboriginals' share of the province's total electorate warranted it.

Where two or more AEDs were to be established in a province, these could be designed on a province-wide or on a geographical basis providing the electoral quotient was respected. In provinces with one Aboriginal seat, it would be established on a province-wide basis. No province would gain or lose a seat, but all provinces with an Aboriginal district or two would have their remaining constituencies drawn according to the province's total electoral population less the number of Aboriginal electors. An Aboriginal would have the right to choose whether or not to register on the Aboriginal voters roll. Those who did not opt for inclusion on the Aboriginal registry would still be entitled to vote in the regular manner in the constituency in which they lived.[40]

Roger Gibbins prepared a background study for the Lortie Commission in which he addressed a number of critical issues with respect to the introduction of AEDs. Gibbins was concerned that if electoral districts were created on the basis of identity this would require a significant shift in Canadian political values from concern for "the basic equality of individuals" to "provid[ing] expression for collective differences." He was also of the view that the creation of AEDs could open the door for "analogous claims by other groups." On a practical level, Gibbins noted that there could be difficulties surrounding the logistics and practicalities of Aboriginal voter enumeration, constructing voting lists for AEDs, organizing political campaigns within AEDs, and administering elections within AEDs. Parliamentary government would present difficulties for MPs elected from AEDs as they would have to choose between, on the one hand, the independence but ineffectiveness of being independent members of the House and, on the other, the constraints of party discipline that come with access to power within a party caucus. Finally, with respect to the potential impact of AEDs on Aboriginal aspirations for self-government, Gibbins concluded that AEDs might artificially impose limitations on the scope and character of Aboriginal government. It was his view that

selling the merits of a racially segmented electoral system to Canadians would be a difficult task. It could only be accomplished if the proposal had the strong, vigorous and unanimous support of Aboriginal leaders, if the operational problems could be solved, if the proposal could be rooted in the existing constitutional recognition of Aboriginal rights, and if it could be shown that AEDs were a necessary condition for the achievement of Aboriginal aspirations and the protection of Aboriginal interests.[41]

In spite of such concerns, the Lortie Commission proceeded to recommend the creation of up to eight AEDs.[42]

The Marchand committee had argued for AEDs because Canada's electoral laws had failed "to recognize the Aboriginal community of interest."[43] Lortie shifted the justification for AEDs much more in the direction of effective representation. The reasons were obvious. Effective representation is so open-ended and imprecise that it can be seen, as Lortie implicitly did, to combine both the first and the second stage of the electoral/representational process. Such an interpretation blends who is entitled to take part in an election and the complexion of the district designed to include that individual with what happens when an election is over and the act of representing constituents begins. Many Canadian Aboriginals share a number of common policy goals, including the successful negotiation of land claims, the protection of treaty rights, and the implementation of social, health, educational, employment, and housing policies that would greatly enhance both their standard of living and their life expectancy. But those, as stated, are policy goals. They are part of making representation effective. They cannot be explained as being part of a community of interest in the usual sense in which that term has been used in Canada.

If AEDs worked according to plan, they would undoubtedly lead to an increase in the number of Aboriginals elected to Parliament. Depending upon how many registered on the separate roll, the number of Aboriginal MPs could reach or even surpass the proportion of Aboriginals in the total population. But community of interest by itself offers neither an intellectual foundation on which to build a case for an increased number of Aboriginal MPs nor a framework by which to judge the effectiveness of the act of representation once it gets under way.

At the obvious level, Lortie saw the issue as a *numerical* challenge. But in a more profound way, the argument presented by the royal commission also became a *representational* one. It signalled acceptance of the notion of mirroring a particular part of society in Parliament. Justification for using the concept of effective representation in this way drew on the *Carter* decision and on the commission's claim that Aboriginal people are not "simply one among many communities of interest." Rather, according to Lortie, they are "unique and [enjoy a] special status."[44]

The construction that has long been given to the concept of community of interest in electoral districting in Canada derives directly from the single-member district, simple-plurality voting system that has been used, with few exceptions, at both levels of government since Confederation. It is a system rooted in place, in a territorially defined area. The task as set forth in electoral boundary legislation since the

1950s is to try to ensure that commissions are mindful of the socio-demographic and economic variables of a region as they go about designing their ridings, and that they respect those communities and their interests to the extent possible by placing them within appropriately drawn constituencies.

Carter offered a way out of granting some measure of special treatment to a fragmented, relatively small community that had ample reason to complain about its past treatment and about its current economic and social plight. Aboriginal people did not, in the conventional sense, constitute a relatively compact, territorially bounded community of interest. As Tim Schouls has pointed out, "the diversity of Aboriginal peoples is far deeper and more complex than the categories of 'Indian,' 'Inuit' and 'Métis.' There are status and non-status Indians, urban and rural dwellers, a diversity of tribes, nations and linguistic groups, treaty and non-treaty Indians, and men and women. The interests of many of these groups overlap but also diverge in significant ways."[45]

The Aboriginal community in Saskatchewan illustrates his point. A single province-wide AED in Saskatchewan, such as the kind Lortie contemplated, would stretch from the 49th to the 60th parallel and would be six hundred kilometres across at its widest point. It would include sixty-nine Indian bands, ranging in population from 6,350 to eighty-four persons, and 151 Indian reserves. The two largest cities contain one-quarter of the province's total Aboriginal population of 111,245, of whom close to one-fifth do not identify with the province's Aboriginal community. Saskatchewan's Aboriginals range from Dene in the far north and Woods Cree in much of the Precambrian and Cambrian Shield, to Dakotah, Cree, Sioux, and Saultaux on the grasslands and prairies of the south. It is unlikely that the Dene who tracks caribou or the Indian who works as a trapper, fisherman, logger, or in a uranium mine in the north shares the same community of interest with the Indian or Métis employed in the southern part of the province as a cattlehand on a ranch, a hired man on a grain farm, or a nurse or lawyer in a city. It is understandable from such a complex and disparate portrait of one province's Aboriginal population why Lortie opted to employ effective representation over community of interest as the basis for recommending AEDs.[46]

Community of interest would presumably carry greater weight if it were clear that the so-called community was subjectively, rather than objectively, defined (as Lortie's Aboriginal electoral roll had been defended) *and* if individual hierarchies of interests were widely shared by members of a community. If, for example, the Dene, the Plains

Indians, and the Métis in Saskatchewan attached greater weight to their Aboriginal ancestry than to geography or occupation in their self-identification, then that presumably would lend considerable support to the argument for community of interest. As that is uncertain, however, community of interest gives way more easily to effective representation.

As it transpired, AEDS soon became an academic question. Three events followed closely on the heels of the release of the Lortie report in February 1992. They had the effect of shifting the Aboriginal representational agenda in a different direction. First, the Charlottetown Accord of August 1992 was the latest attempt by the prime minister, the provincial and territorial premiers, and Native leaders to "renew" Canadian federalism with a package of constitutional changes. It called for guaranteed Aboriginal representation in the Senate and supported further discussions on the issue of Aboriginal representation in the House of Commons. As with the Lortie recommendation, David Smith has noted that "the principle [of the Accord] was to bring Aboriginal people into existing institutions."[47] The accord's rejection in the country-wide referendum later that year brought that particular proposal to an abrupt end.

Second, when members of the Milliken Committee in 1994 examined the electoral boundaries act and the parts of the Lortie report relating to constituency boundary readjustments, they did not consider the possibility of introducing AEDS at the federal level. Instead, as they weighed alternative definitions of community of interest, it was clear that their preoccupation was with place rather than persons. As we saw in the previous section, MPS were opposed to Lortie's recommendation to use electoral redistricting to enhance the representation of minority groups. Their views (and the government's) were reflected in the final contents of Bill C-69, which contained no reference to guaranteed Aboriginal representation.

Finally, with the release of the report of the Royal Commission on Aboriginal Peoples (RCAP) in 1996, it was clear that the question of Aboriginal representation had moved well beyond a guaranteed presence for Aboriginals in the House of Commons. The RCAP concluded that it was "clearly in the interests of all Canadians that Aboriginal peoples be represented more adequately and participate more fully in the institutions of Canadian federalism."[48] Notwithstanding Lortie's conclusions, the members of the RCAP shared many of Roger Gibbins's concerns. According to RCAP commissioner Peter Meekison, "the commissioners' greatest concern was how separate Aboriginal representation would fit with the current rules and operation of the House of Commons, the realities of the party system, and cabinet government.

Moreover we also questioned the implicit assumption that Aboriginal members would act as a single cohesive group." The issue of AEDs, so far as the commissioners were concerned, was dead. They took note of the fact that the idea of guaranteed Aboriginal representation in Parliament did not "surface during [their] hearings," and that there was no "great enthusiasm for [AEDs] either in the Aboriginal community or within the government."[49]

Instead, RCAP recommended a radically different proposal based on the idea of a third chamber of Parliament. An Aboriginal parliament, elected by Aboriginal nations or peoples, would constitute a third chamber of Parliament alongside the Senate and the Commons. It would ensure representation to Aboriginal peoples, and its principal function would be "to provide advice to the house of commons and the senate on legislation and constitutional matters relating to Aboriginal peoples." Such a proposal was not intended to act as a substitute for self-government; its purpose was to ensure that more than symbolic representation of Aboriginals took place at the federal level. As with AEDs, no action had been taken to implement RCAP's proposals at the beginning of the new millennium.[50]

EFFECTIVE REPRESENTATION

We saw in chapter 8 that one of *Carter*'s most significant contributions to Canada's electoral boundary readjustment process was its acceptance of effective representation. Justified on the grounds that Canadian redistribution practices dating back to 1867 had been pragmatic exercises aimed at accommodating different interests in a plural society, effective representation was seen by the Supreme Court of Canada in a purposive light. Its purpose was to "contribute to better government." The factors that could be taken into account in ensuring effective representation included geography, community history, community interests, and minority representation. But, as Justice McLachlin expressed the majority opinion, "the list is not closed."[51]

It is clear from the post-*Carter* record that the concept of effective representation is neither definitive nor exclusionary. It has served, for example, as part of the rationale offered by Lisa Young for an electoral reform that would guarantee gender parity in Canada's Parliament and its provincial legislatures. Young's proposal, modelled after a similar one that was turned down by Nunavut voters in a referendum held prior to the new territory's first elections, called for the establishment of two-member constituencies in Canada. Parties would be expected to nominate two candidates in each riding, one male and one female, and electors would be entitled to vote twice – once for the male and once for the female candidates of their choice. *Carter's* concept of effective representation provided the opening needed for such a recommendation. For Young, the court ruling "cannot be interpreted as *requiring* measures to ensure the representation of previously underrepresented groups, [but] it certainly can be understood as allowing for the possibility of such measures."[52]

The proposal's intent was to guarantee a legislative presence for a numerically under-represented part of society. Women have never come close to winning half of the seats in Parliament or in any provincial assembly. The best that female candidates did federally in the twentieth century was to be elected in sixty-three of the 301 Commons' seats (21 percent) in 1997. The record tended to be no better than that, and often worse, at the provincial level. A switch to dual-member constituencies commended itself to Young as a way of correcting this problem in part because it would ensure gender parity, in part because few institutional changes would be needed to implement it, and in part because traditional Canadian representational theory would be honoured.

The plurality-vote system would continue unchanged, apart from electors having two votes rather than one, and territorially defined constituencies would be retained as the basic representational building block. Moreover, such a method of electing members would not represent a sharp break with the theory that has long supported Canadian electoral democracy. The existing direct links between constituents and elected members would still be ensured, and members and their parties would still subsequently be held accountable by voters at election time. The ridings, however, would be twice their current size, unless the assemblies were enlarged. The prospect of representing a larger territory, even though a second member would have been elected to help with that task, would not appeal to a great many members who already had territorially large ridings.

The Nunavut scheme drew on an earlier period of the country's history when Canadians relied on dual-member constituencies as a way of addressing some of the then-present social cleavages. For some time Prince Edward Island had used two-member ridings to permit landholders to elect assemblymen and non-landholders to elect councillors to the same legislative chamber. At the federal level, dual-member elections existed at one time or another in as many as ten districts as a way of enabling parties to accommodate religious differences at the local level. The federal practice, which came to an end in the last two dual-member ridings in 1966, had ensured that each party nominated a Roman Catholic and a Protestant candidate in much the same way as Nunavut had proposed that male and females could be nominated, and elected, in equal numbers. As with AEDs, by the end of the twentieth century no action had been taken on any proposal (dual-member ridings or otherwise) to increase the number of females elected to public office in Canada.[53]

The term effective representation plainly is full of interpretive room. On occasion it encompasses, as the Supreme Court had seemingly allowed that it could in its broad-brush approach to the term, the concept of community of interest of linguistic, ethnic, or racial minorities. This was evident in the case that the Marchand Committee had mounted on behalf of AEDS. It was also clear from the way in which the term was applied in the 1990s in Nova Scotia where, as we know, both the legislature and the boundaries commission sanctioned the creation of generally small population ridings in an attempt to enhance the likelihood that two of the province's minority populations (Acadian and Afro-Canadian) would gain a legislative presence. Yet as if to reinforce the selective use to which the concept may be put, in other provinces where Canada's social mosaic is vastly more evident than in Nova Scotia, effective representation has not been seized upon by minority populations to push for special boundary readjustment considerations.[54]

Affirmative gerrymandering has not become a rallying cry to push for specially constructed seats. Why this should be so is no doubt a complex matter requiring far more analysis than can be given here. One possible clue can be found in the way in which effective representation proved to be a useful tool for Nova Scotia's Black and Acadian communities to advance their representational claims, but the concept was apparently of no utility or interest to the principal minority groups of metropolitan Toronto.

The Black and Acadian communities of Nova Scotia point with pride to their lengthy presence in Nova Scotia. Both regard themselves, along with the English and, prior to European settlement, the Aboriginals, as two of Nova Scotia's "four charter peoples."[55] Acadian Nova Scotians can trace their presence in the province to at least the early seventeenth century when Port Royal was colonized by the French, and Black Nova Scotians to the mid-eighteenth century, at which time over one hundred Black residents were counted in a colonial census.[56] Large numbers of Blacks entered the Maritimes as part of the Loyalist immigration of 1782–4, to be followed by others from Jamaica a decade later and from the United States at the time of the war of 1812. In any account of their current standing in Nova Scotia, both Acadian and Black communities are quick to refer to their long association with the province.

Both can also point to incidents in their history that have helped to shape their respective community's insistence on recognition and acceptance by the province as a whole. For the Acadians, the single most critical event of their history in the Maritimes was their treatment at the hands of the English for much of the first half of the eighteenth century and their eventual deportation between 1755 and 1763. The "forced travel, their prisoner-of-war camps and the ravages of smallpox and typhoid epidemics severely reduced their numbers, but their sense of independent *community* remained undiminished."[57] In the years that followed, when large numbers of their exiled population returned to the Maritimes, the Acadians once again began to protect and to nourish their distinctive culture. At the end of the twentieth century, effective representation became a useful tool in the Acadians' quest for recognition.

For Nova Scotia's Blacks, their history was one marked by poverty, social isolation, racial prejudice, and discrimination. In addition to their ancestors' suffering from countless acts of willful personal discrimination, Blacks in the province can point to a host of incidents over a two-hundred-year period that demonstrated systematic discrimination against their community by public authorities. The list includes the withholding for over thirty years of land grant deeds to Black settlers in the early nineteenth century; the exclusion of Black children from Halifax common schools in the 1870s; a prohibition on Black burials in some municipal cemeteries in the early twentieth century; separate seating facilities for Blacks and non-Blacks in movie theatres for many years; and, starting in 1964 and lasting for a decade, the enforced relocation of several hundred Blacks from the Africville section of Halifax.[58]

The frustrations and anger of the Black community contributed, in the summer of 1991, to a race riot in central Halifax. That, in turn, prompted Black leaders, civic officials, and provincial politicians to explore alternative ways of addressing the concerns of the province's Blacks. One of those concerns was the fact that no Black Nova Scotian had ever been elected to the Assembly. Armed with the recent *Carter* decision, and prompted by a new premier determined to establish his progressive credentials, the legislature set up the province's first independent electoral boundaries commission. The commissioners were instructed to respect the constitutional right to effective representation and the "factor of minority representation for the Black, Native and Acadian communities of the province."[59] Out of the commission's deliberations came four constituencies designed to "encourage, but not guarantee" the election of one Black and three Acadian representatives to the Assembly. No agreement could be reached with the Mi'kmaq leaders, so only the other two minority group had efforts made to construct seats on their behalf.

Minority groups in metropolitan Toronto have not, on the other hand, seized effective representation as presenting them with an

opportunity to press for the construction of affirmatively gerrymandered ridings that would possibly increase their numbers in Queen's
Park or in the House of Commons. There are several striking features
of their respective minorities that point to a plausible explanation for
the contrast between Ontario and Nova Scotia.

First, in Ontario, the great bulk of the province's francophone population lives outside the Toronto area and generally in such sufficiently
concentrated pockets that the election of at least five or six francophone MPs on a province-wide basis is ensured each time. In 1997 seven
francophone MPs were elected from federal electoral districts that held
sizable francophone populations – anywhere between 29 percent and
60 percent of a district's total population. That is slightly greater than
the proportion (4.5 percent) of Ontario's total population made up
of francophones. Those figures would make any case for affirmatively
gerrymandered seats for Ontario's French-speaking population difficult
to sustain.[60]

Secondly, there is clearly a difference in size (or critical mass) of the
visible minority populations. The minority populations of greater Toronto are vastly larger than those of Nova Scotia in general or Halifax
in particular. Ontario's twenty largest visible minority electoral districts
(defined for the purposes of this comparison as seats having at least
25 percent of their population composed of visible minorities) are all
located within the boundaries of the metropolitan Toronto area. Visible minorities make up a clear majority of the residents in five of those
seats. In aggregate, those twenty districts contain three-fifths of the
province's 1.7 million visible minorities. Nova Scotia, by contrast, has
a far smaller share of its total population composed of visible minorities. The 1996 census figures showed 3.4 percent of Nova Scotians were
visible minorities, which compared with 16 percent in Ontario. At
18,100 (the majority being located in the greater Halifax area), the
largest single visible minority group in Nova Scotia is the Black population. The 350,000 Blacks in Ontario are slightly outnumbered by
both the Chinese (391,000) and South Asians (390,000).

Thirdly, close to three-quarters of Ontario's 1.7 million visible
minorities have arrived since 1961, with the great bulk of these settling
in and around Toronto. A comparison of the Black community of
Ontario and Nova Scotia demonstrates a telling difference in the two
groups. Nearly three of every five (58 percent) Blacks in Ontario has
immigrated to the province since 1961, whereas only 5 percent of
Nova Scotia's 18,105 Blacks are post-1961 immigrants.

It follows that Black immigrants who have arrived in Toronto in such
numbers from the 1960s on have neither the sense of historical roots
in Canada stretching back over two hundred years nor the shared experience that came from having had Canadian authorities systematically

discriminate against them for prolonged periods of time. Nova Scotia's Black community has both of those memories. Accordingly, when the opportunity presented itself the Blacks of Nova Scotia sought representational changes to enter the political system of which they had never been a part.[61]

Expectations on the part of visible minorities in the two provinces also help to explain why one Black community would press for a representational district to be designed to help it to gain representation and another would not. Blacks moving to Toronto from Caribbean countries, as is true of other immigrant populations in Ontario, generally attach top priority to securing employment, locating housing, and furthering their own or their family's education. Partisan politics is not high on their list of priorities at the outset.[62] Once established, however, there are immigrants who share the expectation that personal career advancement and service to their community come through participation in politics: not simply as voters, but as organizers, candidates, elected members, and, possibly, cabinet ministers. Along with members of other immigrant ethnic groups in the metropolitan Toronto area, such as the Chinese, Portuguese, Sikh, Italian, and Greek communities, some Blacks also have expectations of participating in partisan politics. That has been missing in Nova Scotia where Blacks have a long history of seeing themselves as marginalized with virtually no chance of advancement in the political system. Only recently has that begun to change among the Nova Scotia Black community.[63]

Fourthly, starting in the 1960s, political parties at the provincial level, but even more so at the federal level, have played a greater socializing role in Ontario in bringing immigrants and visible minorities into the party organization than has been true of parties in Nova Scotia. Ontario parties have had a vastly larger pool to work with, and consequently larger political incentives to engage immigrant Canadians and to solicit their support by nominating candidates from their midst. The federal Liberals in Ontario have been particularly skilled at developing ethnic connections, which has been apparent from many events staged by the party and (since 1993) the government. That was amply demonstrated by Jean Chrétien's trade mission to Italy in May 1998. Accompanying the prime minister were twelve MPs, all Liberal, of whom eight were born in Italy and a ninth was born in Argentina of Italian parents. Six of the twelve held Toronto area seats, four were from other parts of southern Ontario, and two were from the Montreal area.[64] Inter-ethnic rivalries throughout the 1980s and 1990s often distinguished the contests in Ontario for control of the local party apparatus, party nominations, and the election of candidate slates in leadership campaigns. In the Ontario provincial election of 1999, one Scarborough seat was contested by four candidates, all visible minority immigrants: two (including the winner) were born in Jamaica, one in Pakistan, and one in Haiti. There is no equivalent in Nova Scotia to the ethnic penetration of political parties or of the inter-ethnic rivalries that had become a feature of partisan politics in the metropolitan Toronto area by the end of the twentieth century.[65]

The Blacks in Ontario can point to the election of the first member of their race to a Canadian legislature when, in 1963, Toronto-born Len Braithwaite won a seat at Queen's Park as a Liberal. Five years later Progressive Conservative Lincoln Alexander, born in Toronto to West Indian immigrant parents, became the first Black to be elected to the House of Commons. Both Braithwaite and Alexander established another first when they were later appointed to the cabinet in their respective jurisdictions. Alexander went on to become the first Black to be appointed a provincial lieutenant-governor in Canada. It was not until three decades after Braithwaite's first success in Ontario that a Black was elected to the Nova Scotia Assembly, and that came only after the seat (Preston) had been crafted with Black community in mind and, for the first time, all three major parties nominated Black candidates to compete against one another for that seat.[66]

Collectively these factors point to an explanation of why effective representation would resonate with a minority in one province but not necessarily in another. The causal relationship includes as a minimum the length of a minority's presence in a community; the history, if any, of minority participation and involvement in the political system; the treatment of a minority group, either as a community marginalized from the social and political mainstream or as a group whose support is solicited and whose leadership is co-opted into a partisan organization; the critical mass of the respective minorities and their concentration or dispersion within the province as a whole; the expectations, both at a cultural and an individual level, that a minority population has for participating in a political system; the electoral success in non-affirmatively gerrymandered seats of minority population candidates and their subsequent career advancement; and the socializing factors at play through such important partisan and potentially integrative institutions as political parties. Given that range of variables, it is easy to understand the appeal in the 1990s that "effective representation" held in Nova Scotia for the construction of seats that would encourage the election of minority candidates and the absence of any serious interest in Ontario for doing the same thing.

New Brunswick provides the final illustration of the use to which effective representation was put in the 1990s. Arguing that effective representation, dilution of the vote, and community of interest all provided grounds on which to mount a challenge under sections 3 and 15(1) of the charter to a federal redistribution in their province, the Société des Acadiens et Acadiennes du Nouveau-Brunswick (SAANB) petitioned a New Brunswick court to have the 1994–6 federal redistribution in their province declared invalid. They also sought an interlocutory injunction that would have exempted New Brunswick from the application of the 1997 representation order in the federal election to be held that year and that would require a new set of federal boundaries to be drawn in the province.[67]

At issue was the alleged linguistic discrimination that resulted from the way that boundaries had been reconfigured in the 1990s. In prior redistributions, the province's francophone minority (roughly 35 percent of New Brunswick's population) had been able to point to at least three of the province's ten seats in which they constituted a clear majority of the population. Over the objections of one of the three federal commissioners and the province's francophone MPs, the boundaries commission of the 1990s drew the map in such a way as to reduce the number of seats with a francophone majority from three to two. The francophone population, according to the Acadian community's leadership, would as a result of the new map have less effective representation in the House of Commons than they had had in the past and would have their vote, in effect, diluted by having been placed in greater numbers than in the past in predominantly anglophone ridings. In their arguments the Acadians made full use of the new lexicon of redistribution terms that had entered the boundaries readjustment process in the early 1990s with the *Carter* decision. They also alluded to the fact that in the terms established by the New Brunswick legislature in 1992 for the redistribution of provincial seats, the provincial commission was instructed to take into account the linguistic composition of the districts they designed.[68]

The SAANB had preceded its court petition with a complaint in 1995 to Canada's official languages commissioner. The New Brunswick group argued that by reducing the number of MPs from the province's Acadian region, and that by, in effect, transferring a number of French-speaking communities to largely English-speaking ridings, the changes ran counter to the obligations assumed by the government of Canada through the Official Languages Act. It was, SAANB argued, one of the responsibilities of the official languages commissioner to assist and support minority-language communities throughout Canada. Those responsibilities included, in their view, oversight of the linguistic mix of federal electoral districts. The complaint pitted one officer of Parliament, the official languages commissioner, against another, the chief electoral officer, which was certainly a first in federal electoral boundary readjustments.

In his findings on the issue, the official languages commissioner came to the defence of New Brunswick's Acadian minority. He faulted the boundaries commission for not having given "greater consideration [to] the possible effects of the redistribution ... on the province's French-speaking community." In a report to the New Brunswick boundaries commission, the official languages commissioner recommended that full account be taken of the impact of boundary changes on the province's Acadian population, in accordance with what he called the boundaries commission's *obligations* under section 41(a) of the federal Official *Languages Act*. That part of the act states that the government of Canada is committed to "enhancing the vitality of the English and French linguistic minority communities in Canada and supporting and assisting their development."[69]

No corrective action could be taken by the New Brunswick commission at that point, as the official languages commissioner's report arrived after the completion of its work. Nonetheless, the obligation to which his report referred, and to which there is no equivalent reference in the EBRA, together with the force of the official languages commissioner's ruling, introduced the possibility that commissions of the future in provinces with sizable minority-language populations will have to pay closer attention to a province's linguistic composition when designing seats. As part of their presumed obligation to enhance the vitality of Canada's minority language groups and to ensure effective representation, they could be expected to ensure that an official language's share of a province's seats is roughly equal to its share of the province's population. Failing that, they could also be expected to provide reasoned explanations when they depart from a distribution of seats among a province's two official language groups roughly equal to their share of the total provincial population.

The official languages commissioner also found that Elections Canada had failed to advise the boundaries commissions of "their obligations concerning the advancement of English and French." His report noted that Elections Canada has in the past made a point of reminding boundary commissioners of the need to ensure that they provide services to the public in both official languages. There was, however, an equal need for Elections Canada to "review its responsibilities [to all boundaries commissions] in order to ensure that commissions, as federal institutions, are aware of all linguistic obligations in conducting their business." In his comment on these findings and recommendations, the chief electoral officer replied that boundaries commissions are independent organizations and that it was "beyond the scope of his authority" under the act to ensure that they were aware of their linguistic obligations. The matter between these two officers of Parliament remained, at the end of the twentieth century, at an impasse.[70]

The court challenge launched by the SAANB also remained unresolved as the century closed. The interlocutory injunction to exempt New Brunswick from the application of the new electoral districts in the 1997 election was rejected by the court for the "inconvenience" and the "electoral confusion" that would have ensued. The court declined to decide on the charter issue, specifically sections 15(1) and 3, on equality and democratic rights, as they might apply to the linguistic composition of newly designed electoral districts. Instead, the court found the matter constituted a serious question and called for arguments to be presented at a future court hearing on the issue. The official languages commission has gained intervenor status on behalf of the SAANB, no doubt in the hope that a sufficiently broad interpretation to section 15(1) would ensure that language would be accepted by the court as a right to be protected under equality rights and that that protection would extend to the drawing of electoral boundaries. Should the case eventually be heard, the court decision will be looked to as possibly providing guidance about the extent, if at all, that boundary commissions must factor in the linguistic composition of the population of their province. The arguments relating to such guidelines will undoubtedly draw on both the community of interest of a linguistically defined group and the way that district borders should be constructed so as to ensure its effective representation.[71]

CONCLUSIONS

The debate in the 1990s concerning electoral boundary readjustments was unlike that of any previous decade in Canada. MPs wrestled with competing notions of community of interest and settled on one that focused on economic and territorial factors. Sociological and demographic considerations were eschewed, even though they had been championed by the Lortie Commission. The debate among parliamentarians and provincial legislators over what was appropriate to include in a definition of community of interest revealed an epistemological difficulty with the concept. The sense of place that characterized the approach that MPs took to community of interest distinguished it from other approaches that stressed the human side of electoral districts. To boundary commissioners, the open-endedness of community of interest meant that they were dealing with something akin to a blank cheque. Others who favoured the establishment of separate electoral districts for Canada's Aboriginals found that they too could turn to the concept of community of interest for support.

Both community of interest and effective representation are now widely accepted as essential parts of the electoral boundary readjustment process. But while they may be essential, their future application remains uncertain and open to further debate. If representation is deemed to be effective for one group, why not another? If one minority gets its interest accepted as critical to the construction of territorially defined seats, how about another? If gender, race, and language can be factored into the equation, why not religion? Given the interpretive room created by the *Carter* decision, the politics of cultural and group identity together with the claims to group representation that follow logically from the emergence in the recent past of identity politics open up a range of possibilities.[72]

It is with respect to that range of possibilities that effective representation may well be found to have greater resonance with the courts, the public, and possibly even the politicians than community of interest. Effective representation is a more powerful concept than community of interest in one respect. For those pressing a case for corrective measures to be taken to overcome chronic under-representation of a particular group, effective representation at least implicitly acknowledges something basic to the representational process: numbers. Community of interest appears now to be understood, certainly by many politicians and members of the public, in a territorial sense. Effective representation, on the other hand, has come to assume a more sociological and demographic character.

The shift in the premise underlying support for AEDs that the Lortie Commission made to the Marchand recommendation illustrated a difficulty that the royal commission must have sensed with the concept of community of interest. It would be hard to square the notion of a territorially dispersed population as varied as Canada's Aboriginals with an idea that relied so heavily on a territorial justification. Instead, the Lortie Commission implied, it would be preferable to use the historical reality of Aboriginal under-representation in the House of Commons as one of the necessary proofs that Aboriginals should be present in Parliament in greater numbers. That is, they should be present in numbers that would more accurately reflect their share of the total Canadian population.

In ruling that effective representation "is at the heart of the right to vote" and that "the relative parity of voting power," in turn, is at the heart of effective representation, the Supreme Court of Canada in *Carter* gave legitimacy to the notion that effective representation is also about numbers. That point was not lost on the Reform party. The arguments of its MPs during the debate over the preliminaries to Bill c-69 reflected an understanding of the numerical side of effective representation. Without referring explicitly to effective representation in seeking to have the deviations reduced from +/−25 percent to +/−15 percent, Reform members nonetheless seized upon "relative parity of voting power" as the principal rationale for avoiding the socially and demographically based concept of community of interest. They explicitly contrasted relative parity of voting power to sociological considerations as factors to be used in constructing federal constituencies.[73] By preferring the former to the latter, they wanted to avoid problems they foresaw of ghettos, ethnic enclaves, and the like, that they felt would flow from designing seats according to communities of interest or of basing the concept of effective representation solely upon the determination of a riding's sociological and demographic character. The Supreme Court decision gave them the opportunity to make that argument.

When it is seen as containing a numerical component, effective representation is justified on grounds familiar to Canadians. Since the mid-nineteenth century when George Brown and other reformers first began to press for "rep by pop," a large measure of the representational debates in Canada has revolved around numbers. How many seats should be allotted to the provinces or to regions within provinces? What is the right mix of territory and population? Should the electoral or total population be used as the base for designing constituencies? And so on. As arguably one of its most important streams has developed in Canada so far, effective representation is rooted in the rep by pop tradition in a way that community of interest is not. Drawing on, among other things, a clearly and readily understood quantitative justification for constructing seats in a certain manner, effective representation could well prove to be the more potent of the two concepts in the years ahead.

11 Looking Back and Looking Ahead

After a while, there is nothing new to be heard.
                                    – An old priest at confessional.

When a new Canadian prime minister and cabinet are sworn in, media reports and public comment typically focus on the representational composition of the cabinet. How many women and visible minorities were appointed? Will all the provinces be present at the table? How many ministers are from Quebec? Ontario? Did a coastal province get fisheries? Alberta resources? Did Finance go to Toronto or Montreal? And so on. Such questions relate to the territorial and demographic variables of the cabinet as a representative body in Canada. They are raised without reference to the varying size of the electoral constituencies of the members who have been named to the cabinet. It has been that way since John A. Macdonald named his first post-Confederation cabinet when, in addition to province and language group, religion was also a major consideration to be taken into account.[1]

The questions that have been central to representation in Canadian institutions, such as the federal cabinet, have revolved almost entirely around issues other than one person, one vote and strict equality of the vote. Electoral equality, which in the United States since the 1960s has been at the core of representational debates over district size, and in Australia since the 1980s has played a considerable role in determining the boundaries of electoral districts, has been less likely to be a part of the way Canadians define their elected assemblies as representative. Instead, territory, region, language, and (more recently) gender and race, have been the principal variables applied by Canadians to judge how representative their elected assemblies are. Americans, under the watchful eye of the courts, turned to affirmatively gerrymandered districts in the final decades of the twentieth century to increase the number of racial minorities elected to office; but even here, the appropriateness of such schemes was always subject to the more established principle of one person, one vote.[2]

Federal cabinets are only one of thousands of boards, councils, panels, agencies, voluntary and professional associations that are constructed in such a way in Canada. Those who have sat on any such body could not have failed to note its representational makeup. They may even have been apprised of how they were appointed or elected to it. They might have been told that the committee or organization had need of more francophones, westerners, women, or visible minorities to flesh out its pan-Canadian representational character and that they were seen to have the necessary attribute(s)! Reflecting the principal characteristics of society in its public and private institutions constitutes an obvious and, arguably in the context of a diverse, multilingual, and regionalized country, highly salient form of "mirror representation." This measure of an institution's representativeness derives from the idea that it is the principal social and territorial characteristics of the general public that should be replicated in the legislature through the election of members who share those characteristics. It is to be distinguished from what I chose earlier to call "transactional representation."[3]

In Canada, two distinctive varieties of mirror representation have become well established. The first, as illustrated by the federal cabinet or other bodies whose membership is composed of individuals drawn from a variety of distinctive groups and regions, is designed to reflect social and territorial *diversity*. The second, in which two different sets of institutional arrangements are followed, is intended to acknowledge and preserve *duality*. Some political institutions are structured in such a way as to capture both diversity and duality. National political parties, most successfully the Liberals, have made concerted efforts to diversify their membership, candidates, and support base at the same time that they have played up the linguistic and bicultural duality of Canada's history. Recognition of the importance of the country's linguistic, cultural, and legal dualism is sometimes found in legislation, as with the guarantee that three of the nine Supreme Court of Canada positions shall be filled by members of the Quebec bar trained in civil law. More commonly, the country's duality is captured informally through a set of well-understand conventions. The governors-general, the Speakers of the House of Commons, and the leaders of the federal Liberal party are but three examples of positions that normally alternate between predominantly French- and English-speaking Canadians, often between Quebecers and non-Quebecers. This alternation principle is justified largely on grounds of ensuring representational balance to the two main groups responsible for the agreements reached in the 1860s that led up to the adoption of the British North America Act.[4]

What this book has been about, however, is a different, narrower and, in a temporal sense, earlier stage of representation. Its focus has been on an institutional building block constructed to ensure that at a preliminary, but necessary, stage of the representation process, units will be designed from which members can then be elected and become a part of an institution. The institution, of course, is a legislature or parliament, and the unit is the electoral district. Without ridings having been created, members could not be elected to an assembly under a single-member district system. What we have learned about the creation of electoral building blocks to date should serve to inform us of the outstanding issues that legislators, commissioners, and the public will likely have to address in the years ahead.

LOOKING BACK

Independent electoral boundary commissions stand as one of the success stories of the last half-century of Canadian political institutions. Prior to the 1950s, when Manitoba became the first province to pass legislation requiring its constituency boundaries to be readjusted every ten years by a non-partisan, arms'-length commission chaired by a judge, every federal and provincial government had redistributed its Assembly's seats in basically the same fashion. For decades, redistributions had been carefully managed, irregularly timed, and self-interested exercises controlled by the party in office. They often amounted to little more than thinly disguised gerrymanders. Gross inequities in populations of constituencies were not unusual, and boundaries were drawn to try to distribute the governing party's supporters to best advantage for future elections.[5]

In the mid-1960s Parliament adopted legislation similar to Manitoba's, and a decade later Quebec followed suit. By the end of the century every province and territory had in some form or another conducted at least one redistribution by an independent commission. Whatever the mechanisms for setting up the various bodies, it was the eventual acceptance of the principle of delegating responsibility for designing electoral districts to non-politicians that stands as the important breakthrough. An institution new to Canada – an independent electoral boundaries commission – had a successful initial try-out in one province before it gradually spread to the rest of the country.

The credibility of political representation in federal, provincial, and territorial assemblies had been enhanced by the shift to a new representational building block that was compatible with the parliamentary and federal systems. Partisan gerrymandering as it was once practised in Canada was relegated to history. The dramatic impact of the switch that took place federally in the 1960s with the replacement of government-dominated redistributions by independent commissions responsible for applying the terms of the Electoral Boundaries Readjustment Act can be seen in figure 11.1. In seven provinces, the equality of the vote increased sharply. The two provinces in which constituencies were characteristically the most equal before the 1964 legislation, Alberta and Saskatchewan, have since remained about the same or slightly closer to equality in riding size. Only in Newfoundland has the Gini coefficient moved markedly in the opposite direction, a reflection of the province's small number of federal seats (seven) and its two most recent commissions' generous use of the extraordinary circumstances clause.

There was a time lag of close to thirty years before equally dramatic drops in the Gini scores were seen at the provincial level. Some provinces had further to go than had ever been the case federally in the twentieth century. British Columbia, Manitoba, Quebec, and Prince Edward Island all had had Ginis in the range of 0.3 to 0.4 before they shifted to non-partisan boundary reviews and adopted rules establishing the factors that were to guide their respective commission. With the exceptions of Manitoba (because of its move to the new redistribution method in the 1950s) and British Columbia (because of the *Dixon* ruling), the markedly lower Gini scores at the provincial level came only after the *Carter* decision in 1991. For the last decade of the century, the provincial and federal scores as a group were more or less in line: except for Newfoundland's federal Gini coefficients, they were all lower than 0.1 on the scale. (Compare figures 11.1 and 11.2).

Over a four-decade period, there had been a demonstration or copycat effect at work as support for the adoption of non-partisan boundaries commissions spread amongst the various federal, provincial, and territorial jurisdictions. Even so, variations in the size and powers of different commissions as well as in the rules to be applied and their application were bound to occur. From its inception in 1964, the federal Electoral Boundaries Readjustment Act had provided considerable scope for interpretation by commissions, a fact which in the lead-up to Bill c-69 in the mid-1990s concerned many MPs who were critical of both the act and the commission proposals. Differences have been evident at the federal level in, for example, the way in which some commissions have turned to the extraordinary circumstances clause to help them to solve a problem of isolated and sparsely populated areas in their respective province, whereas others, even though they could have made just as compelling a case, have not. This variability

Figure 11.1
Federal Redistributions, 1903–96, Ginis

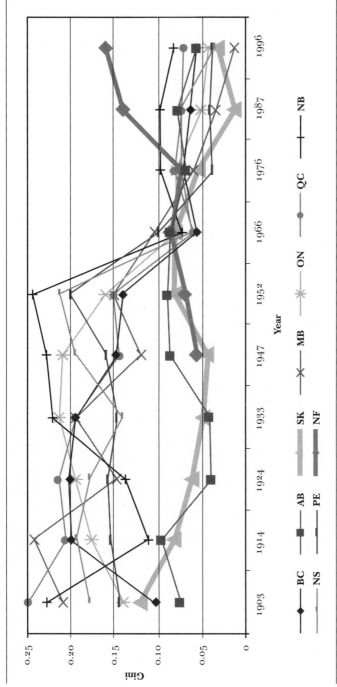

Sources: For 1903–52, John C. Courtney, "'Theories Masquerading as Principles': Canadian Electoral Boundary Commissions and the Australian Model," p. 163; data for 1966–96 from Representation Orders.

Figure 11.2
Provincial Gini Scores, 1911–99

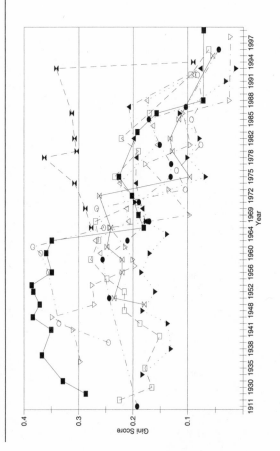

Sources: For 1911–87, Harvey E. Pasis, "Electoral Distribution in the Canadian Provincial Legislatures," in *Representation and Electoral Systems* (eds. J. Paul Johnson and Harvey E. Pasis), Scarborough: Prentice-Hall, 1990, 252. Pasis uses enumerated voters and does not explain his incomplete dataset. For 1988–99, data are from reports of provincial redistribution commissions and legislative committees, with the exceptions of Nova Scotia, 1988, and Prince Edward Island, 1993, which use enumerated electors.

is natural in a process structured to make allowances for the country's federal character and for discretion and judgment to be exercised by commissioners in the application of the rules to their own locality.

It is now fair to say that independent, arms'-length commissions have become established institutions in the Canadian political system. Their institutionalization can be traced to several factors that converged at approximately the same time. There was acceptance of the need to reform a process that had been long abused by parties in office. Public opinion, media commentators, social scientists, and influential interest groups such as trade unions and business organizations often spoke with one voice on why partisan redistributions should give way to something else. Political elites gradually came on side – first, understandably, on the opposition benches, then, more critically, on the government side. Social scientists helped to pave the way for the reform by looking in a comparative context for an acceptable alternative that would fit well with Canada's federal and parliamentary systems. In other words, the "policy window" at the heart of John Kingdon's agenda-setting theory had been opened by the intersection of the three essential streams: identification of a problem, advancement of a solution, and emergence of multi-partisan political support.[6]

Over the course of four decades the idea spread. By the mid-1990s, when Prince Edward Island became the last province to make the change, the first stage of the revolution to which Ken Carty had referred had been completed.[7] At that point all jurisdictions had had experience with at least one non-partisan review of their electoral boundaries, and although the decisions of the commissions did not always sit well with elected members, candidates, or some of the public, the process nonetheless had shown that it grafted well onto Canada's federal and parliamentary systems and offered a more acceptable method of drawing electoral districts than had been employed in the past.

For the first time, public participation in the consideration of electoral boundaries was welcomed at open hearings and through briefs and submissions. Although the attendance has never been large in absolute numbers, an opportunity has been created for members of the public to air their views to the decision-makers on changes in electoral constituencies. By distributing populations more evenly among the constituencies, commissions have interpreted the statutory terms or orders-in-council under which they worked so as to ensure a greater measure of population equality than had ever been the case under partisan-controlled redistributions. It did not match the post-*Baker* v. *Carr* standards in the United States, but it was an improvement over what had earlier prevailed in Canada. For their part, governments and political parties stood to benefit from the fact that they no longer became directly locked into a partisan activity that reflected poorly on the political system.

In all, the civic values essential to any democratic political system have been bolstered in Canada by the change. The list of reasons in support of that claim is impressive. Partisan redistributions widely seen and easily understood as working in favour of some parties and voters at the expense of others were brought to an end; political elites on all sides came to accept, if not always without some reluctance, the need to reform the system; parties in office have been removed as the ascendant players in the exercise; participation has been widened to include the public; non-partisan commissioners have lent a credibility to the process; voters, however wide the discrepancies in constituency size may still remain, have been treated more equitably than under government-dominated redistributions; and territorially large and isolated parts of the country have been sheltered in a variety of ways from the strict application of the principle of one person, one vote. In the view of the Lortie Commission, Canada's "process of designing constituencies by independent boundaries commissions ... has worked well."[8]

The adoption of the Electoral Boundaries Readjustment Act in 1964 was the first of several moves on electoral boundaries taken by Parliament in the last third of the twentieth century. Prior to that, for almost the entire first one hundred years after Confederation, there had been remarkably few legislated or constitutional changes to Canada's redistribution process. The senatorial floor clause was added as a constitutional amendment in 1915, and was later included as part of section 41 of the Constitution Act, 1982. By guaranteeing that no province would ever elect fewer MPs than it had members of the Senate, the provision, along with the grandfather clause added in 1986, has awarded more seats to some provinces than their population warranted and has contributed to an increasingly greater spread in average constituency population sizes among the provinces with each successive redistribution. The formula for assigning Commons' seats to the provinces was changed shortly after the Second World War from one that determined the number of MPs according to a pegged number of seats in Quebec to one that established a fixed number of Commons' seats. That was replaced by the amalgam method of 1974, which in turn was replaced a decade later by a fixed membership in the House of Commons plus various add-ons for constitutionally or legislatively protected provinces. The changes to the EBRA in the 1980s also empowered commissions to draw on exceptional circumstances in designing their seats. Collectively, these shifts by parliamentarians from one decade to the next suggest that the political agenda of the moment has taken priority over consideration of what the long-range consequences of the alterations might be for the size of the House of Commons and for interprovincial variations in constituency populations.

Figure 11.3 shows that, for a period of a few years near the end of the twentieth century, the federal agenda relating to electoral boundaries readjustments became crowded in a way that it had never been previously. The Lortie Commission was appointed in 1989 and reported in early 1992. The *Carter* decision was handed down by the Supreme Court of Canada in 1991, two years after the *Dixon* ruling in British Columbia. The EBRA was suspended twice by Parliament, in 1992 and again in 1994. The Milliken Committee of the Commons was called upon to examine the EBRA and to rewrite the act shortly after the release of the federal boundaries commission proposals early in 1994. That in turn was followed by the introduction, debate, and ultimate death of Bill C-69 in 1995–6. Sandwiched in with these events were several other constitutional or consultative initiatives that touched on parliamentary representation. These included the Meech Lake Accord (1987–90), the Marchand Committee recommendations for Aboriginal Electoral Districts (1991), the Charlottetown Accord, as well as its preliminaries in federal-provincial negotiations and parliamentary committees (1991–2), and the Royal Commission on Aboriginal Peoples (1992–5). In all, it was a congested and often confusing diet of representational proposals, with recommendations or agreements of one year often being supplanted by others in the following year.

It was against this background that several scholarly works addressing important questions of group representation first appeared. Discussion of such topics as the politics of difference, politics of recognition, differentiated citizenship, and democratic exclusion were relatively new to Canada. They soon became a part of discussions in classrooms, the media, and political circles, and they entered constitutional negotiations. The academic literature included contributions that searched for ways to include within the political system groups and minorities that had fared poorly in competitive elections, that could point to a history of exclusion from centres of power, or that had a clearly established sense of being different from or separate from the rest of the country. The literature cast a wide net. The groups examined, depending upon the author, were women, Aboriginals, Québécois, ethnic minorities, and visible minorities, with the arguments mounted for the accommodation of these groups varying from one scholar to another. A theme common to much of the literature was that the prevailing conceptions of citizenship and representation were challenged by identity groups which, in some instances at least, had gained status and had drawn strength from the 1982 Charter of

Figure 11.3
Timeline: Electoral Boundary Readjustments in Canada, 1867–2000

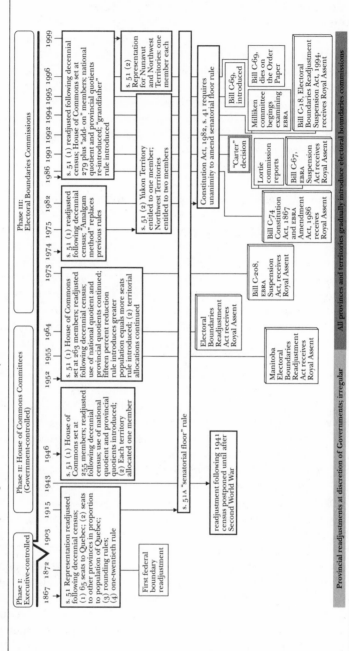

Constitutional provision: Solid-walled box. Legislation: Three-dimensional box. Judicial decision: Double-walled box. Important event: Plain-walled box.

Rights and Freedoms and, in others cases, had a long, established history in the country.[9]

Alan Cairns, for example, in a widely-cited essay on "constitutional minoritarianism" referred to the fact that minorities in Canada had grown "suspicious of theories and practices of representation that imply or assert that representatives can be trusted to speak for citizens/constituents when they *lack the defining characteristics* of the latter."[10] That analysis appeared only months before the Marchand Committee reported and the Supreme Court of Canada was to hear the appeal on *Carter*. It introduced a decade in which the debate over identity politics figured prominently. Will Kymlicka echoed Cairns' reading of the changed representational agenda. In his view, Parliament "has a special symbolic role in representing the citizens of the country" which, in turn, means that those who do not "*see themselves reflected in parliament*" run the risk of becoming "alienated from the political process and question its authority."[11] Mirror representation had taken on an added explanatory power in the academic literature analysing representational questions in the early 1990s.

Richard Sigurdson entered the debate by observing that there were two alternative conceptions of citizenship in contemporary Canada. These were the older "liberal-individualist notion of universalist citizenship" and the newer "cultural-pluralist notion of differentiated citizenship."[12] Drawing on Sigurdson's distinction, we can better understand the context within which electoral districts were considered in the 1990s.

Undifferentiated, or "liberal-individualist" citizenship holds that all citizens are equal and that differences among them (racial, ethnic, and the like) should not count. All citizens should be treated equally. Differentiated citizenship, on the other hand, maintains that equal citizenship is a myth, for it denies historical and contemporary realities in terms of power, inclusiveness/exclusiveness, and access to resources. In the context of electoral boundaries, this plays out essentially as a conflict between territorial conceptions (undifferentiated) and alternative conceptions (differentiated) of how districts should be designed. From the standpoint of those who subscribe to the differentiated citizenship model, if there is adherence to a strict application of the notion that seats should be constructed with equal numbers of voters in the districts, and if there are no compensatory mechanisms available to allow affirmative gerrymandered districts of different sizes, the equality of the vote can be said to have resulted in unequal treatment of the citizens. The group with which those citizens identify has not properly been taken into account.[13]

Is it a coincidence that the concept of effective representation came along and was taken up in various quarters at roughly the same time that prevailing conceptions of representation and citizenship were being challenged by identity groups such as Aboriginals, Acadians, and Nova Scotian Blacks? Almost certainly not. Their claim to representation in an elected assembly rested on the premise that they could most adequately be represented by members of their own group. In this sense, what was being argued was precisely the blending of districts constructed in a certain fashion and the subsequent representation of their constituents that we saw in the Lortie Commission's shift in the rationale offered for Aboriginal electoral districts. Their preference was for effective representation over community of interest. Implicit in their argument was the recognition that effective representation brings together both elements of differentiated citizenship as it applies to electoral districts – that is, who is entitled to vote in specially designed ridings and what is expected to happen after the vote in terms of representing the interests of the constituents.

In *Carter*, the Supreme Court of Canada signalled its acceptance of something amounting to a "politics of difference." According to the court, relative parity of voter power could be tempered by minority representation and effective representation when the application of those concepts was justified on the grounds of contributing to better government. Would this sort of ruling have been possible in the years before the advent of identity politics? That cannot be answered assuredly one way or another, not least because the charter itself had arrived only a decade earlier and pre-charter challenges to electoral boundaries had never materialized. But it is conceivable that the concept of effective representation would not have found its way into the court's reasoning in an earlier era. It emerged in the early 1990s when the country was preoccupied with questions of whether and how best to accommodate differences within the Canadian polity. Perhaps more than anything this helps to explain the change in Madam Justice McLachlin's reasoning. She moved from accepting in *Dixon* in 1989 that the principle that "a majority of elected representatives should represent the majority of citizens" to accepting in *Carter* two years later that "cultural and group identity" and "citizens with distinct interests" should have their identities and interests accepted as part of the electoral boundary readjustment process. These need not be mutually exclusive, of course. What makes them important for our purposes is that each was featured as a major part of the reasoning in one case but not in the other.

The reasons offered by the courts in their decisions, as it turned out, were very much in keeping with what might loosely be called the Canadian tradition of constructing electoral districts. McLachlin had posited her analysis in both *Dixon* and *Carter* on the distinctive character of the boundary readjustment exercise in Canada. She was right. The country had never had a history, in either the pre- or post-independent boundaries commission period, of designing its ridings with equality of the vote as the absolute and sole standard to be adhered to. Consideration of countervailing factors in the drawing of riding boundaries had been a part of that history as far back as 1867. Canada's constituencies had always been designed according to a number of variables, some more subjective and elusive of precise definition than others, and the courts were not about to change that. These included geography, relative isolation, sparsity of population, community of interest, and community history. Effective representation and minority representation were simply the latest concepts to join that list – a list that the chief justice herself admitted was not closed.

LOOKING AHEAD

In spite of the advances that have been made since the 1950s, there remain several unresolved issues in Canada's and the provinces' electoral boundary readjustment processes that suggest further work remains to be done.

Among the provinces, the degree of acceptance and of institutionalization of non-partisan reviews of electoral boundaries varies widely. Some provinces, such as those in Atlantic Canada, are relatively new to the game and have yet to develop any institutional memories of regular, non-partisan boundary readjustments by independent bodies. Alberta's recent history of redesigning ridings has been ambivalent and has lacked the sense of permanence and regularization that is now a feature of its neighbouring provinces' redistributions. Ontario, at least for the time being, has foreclosed the possibility of designing its own seats. How long that will continue once the province's "revolution" is no longer "common sense," or once the number of federal districts from Ontario begins to creep up to the previous provincial level, remains an open question.

Still others, such as Manitoba, British Columbia, and Quebec have as regularized and as independent a process as exists at the provincial level, although the book-end suspensions in Quebec in the 1990s qualify that statement to the extent that the province's commission could only resume its task when the Assembly said it could. The suspensions in Quebec, like those on the federal front from the 1970s on, demonstrates that elected politicians are willing to step in when they foresee political dangers ahead because of a commission's decisions. They are prepared to risk public displeasure by using the instrumentalities of the state to call a temporary halt to the proceedings.

Suspensions, delays, and changes in the governing statutes will continue to occur until such time as there is widespread and deeply held attachment to independent commissions by politicians and the risks of provoking the public outweigh the advantages of delaying the redistribution. It is fair to say that neither of those two conditions is likely to be met in the foreseeable future.

Saskatchewan, in the wake of the *Carter* decision, seems headed in the same direction as Manitoba and British Columbia, with legislation in place that ensures automatic decennial boundary readjustments. It has also adopted the smallest population variances in the country, with Manitoba next. In spite of the legislatures of Manitoba, British Columbia, and Saskatchewan retaining the power to amend the riding proposals that come from their commissions, all three provinces also have an established tradition of accepting those proposals without modification. Quebec alone among the provinces has, like the federal Parliament, yielded the legislative authority to change the proposed maps. There were no signs at the beginning of the twenty-first century that other provinces would follow suit. The true measure of the extent to which independent commissions will have been accepted as the final authority and will have unquestioned institutional autonomy awaits that addition to the provincial electoral boundaries laws. In the meantime, a high level of de facto independence of the commissions can be inferred from the largely unfettered treatment accorded the final commission proposals by the respective legislatures.

The record shows that there is no one institutional model for redesigning ridings that plays out in all parts of Canada. This is also true in Australia and is a feature of redistricting in the United States. Federalism allows differences, enables experimentation, and encourages the various federal units to make the best fit of the institution into their political system. In a reverse fashion, it also implicitly serves to discourage provinces (or states, as the case may be) from stepping back to an earlier model – one that, like the government-controlled and gerrymandered exercises of the past, has been discredited. A return some time in the future to government-controlled redistributions is simply not an alternative in Canada. However varied and, at least for some jurisdictions, relatively non-institutionalized, independent electoral boundary commissions may be, they have an established presence in the country's various political systems that will be impossible for politicians to try to bypass in the years ahead.

At the federal level, a difficult and, as yet, unresolved issue pertains to the number of seats in the House of Commons' should be allocated to the provinces. This question is scarcely new to elected members, which suggests that it may well be so layered with complexities that it

precludes an entirely satisfactory answer. From the guarantee early in
the twentieth century that no province would have fewer MPs than
senators, to the acceptance of the grandfather clause in the 1980s,
the topic has surfaced on the parliamentary agenda with a certain
regularity. The various measures that have been taken over the years
have always been in response to MPs' (and provincial governments')
expressed concerns about how the then-current formula would impact
on their particular province's membership in the Commons. It has
proven to be an extremely difficult matter for members to address
satisfactorily, for populations, by definition, grow and shift at different
rates, and anticipating those changes with precision is far from a
foolproof science. What appears to be the solution to today's problem
can often create an unexpected and unwelcome consequence ten years
down the line.

That said, the issue cannot be expected to disappear in the future
when people are reminded by the press, as they will be whenever
federal redistributions are discussed, and by critics of whatever the
then-current formula happens to be, that the votes of some Canadians,
depending upon the province in which they live, are worth less or
worth more than those of others. The problem is manifestly obvious
when the most extreme examples are contrasted. Prince Edward
Island and Saskatchewan, with their respective guarantees of four and
fourteen seats in the House of Commons, have a larger number of
seats than their population warrants when their parliamentary allot-
ments are compared on a per capita basis with those of Ontario,
British Columbia, and Alberta.

Even with the additional seats to be granted to the provinces whose
population will grow faster than the national average, the contrast
between provincial per capita populations will become more dramatic
in the years ahead. This stems from the fact that although the senatorial and grandfather guarantees apply to all provinces, in reality they
only assist those with low populations, or, those with relatively modest
growth, such as Quebec, that fail to keep abreast of the faster-growing
provinces. Assuming the current redistribution formula is maintained
for establishing provincial entitlement to Commons' seats, and applying Statistics Canada population projections into the early twenty-first
century, we find that the number of MPs is expected to increase from
its 301 following the 1991 census to 322 by 2021 (see figure 11.4).
The only changes among the provinces, all in the form of additional
seats, are expected to be in Ontario, British Columbia, and Alberta
(see figure 11.5). The upshot of this is that the per capita population
of federal electoral districts after the 2021 census is projected to be in
the order of 126,500 persons per district in Ontario, British Columbia,

Figure 11.4
Size of the House of Commons Applying the Redistribution Formula Actual, 1981–91, and Projected, 2001–21

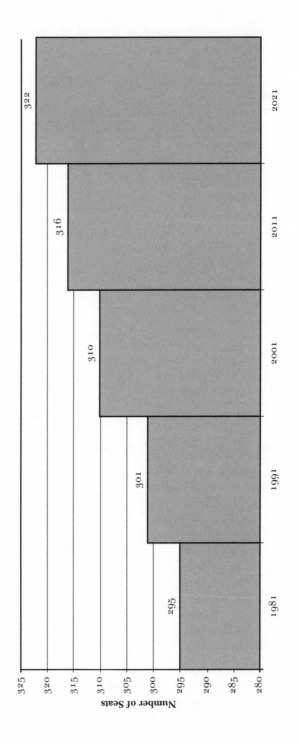

Sources: Elections Canada, *Representation in the Federal Parliament* (Ottawa: Chief Electoral Officer of Canada, 1993), and Satistics Canada, CANSIM Matrixes 6900–6910.

Figure 11.5
Provincial Representation in Commons Applying the Redistribution Formula Actual, 1981–91, and Projected, 2001–21

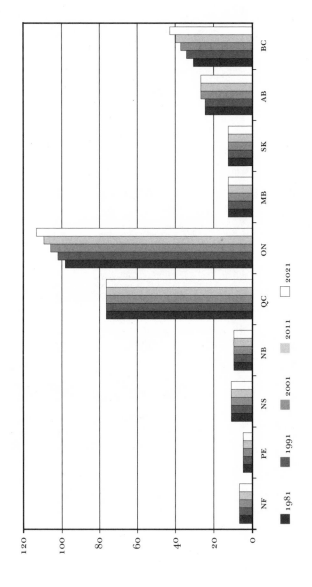

Sources: Elections Canada, *Representation in the Federal Parliament* (Ottawa: Chief Electoral Officer of Canada, 1993) and Statistics Canada, CANSIM Matrixes 6900-6910.

Figure 11.6
Federal Electoral Quotients Applying the Redistribution Formula Actual, 1981–91, and Projected, 2001–21

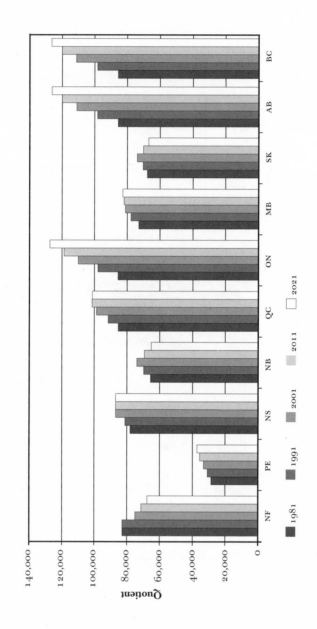

Sources: Elections Canada, *Representation in the Federal Parliament* (Ottawa: Chief Electoral Officer of Canada, 1993) and Statistics Canada, CANSIM Matrixes 6900–6910.

and Alberta, in contrast to fewer than 70,000 persons in Saskatchewan, New Brunswick, and Newfoundland seats. Prince Edward Island's 35,000 per district population would be the lowest among the provinces (see figure 11.6).

Even allowing for the possibility of inaccurate population projections, which we have noted in the past have prompted MPs to replace parts of the formula they had adopted barely a decade earlier, it is difficult to foresee any reapportionment of Commons' seats among the provinces in the next three decades that will not provoke public and political controversy about the worth of one individual's vote as opposed to another's depending upon where those voters lived. What can be done about the fact that a Canadian's vote in Prince Edward Island would be worth approximately three-and-a-half times its value in Ontario? Or that Saskatchewan can expect to have, on average, 55,000 fewer voters per federal riding than neighbouring Alberta?

It is not hard to accept the Lortie Commission's conclusion that if maintained in the years ahead, the current formula will be "a recipe for increasing the inequality among provinces" and for causing "unnecessary friction within our country."[14] Whether this friction might prompt a charter challenge to the grandfather clause (drawing on *Carter*'s "relative parity of voting power" argument) or, less likely, a reconsideration by all provinces and the federal government of the senatorial floor clause in the constitutional amending formula, remains a very open question. As noted in chapter two, for a variety of institutional and political reasons, as well as because the House of Commons performs an important federalizing role in Canada that is far less the case with lower houses in Australia and the United States, cutting back on provincial representation in the Commons is not an attractive possibility for many provinces.

An alternative to a court challenge to the grandfather clause would be parliamentary action. The Lortie Commission had recommended this when it called for an end to the grandfather provision and for a guarantee that no province slated to lose seats would do so at a rate faster than one seat per decennial redistribution. The Milliken Committee reached no conclusion on this question, which in itself is testimony to the profound political implications of trying to solve the issue satisfactorily. Instead, it recommended that, subsequent to its report being issued, another parliamentary committee be asked to "devise a new formula" for determining the size of the House.[15] No such committee had been appointed by the end of the century, six years after the Milliken report was released.

The compromises that are so much a part of designing electoral policies have led to this impasse. It is difficult to see how further compromises aimed in the opposite direction are within reach, but it could well be that a combination of four factors will lead Parliament to act. They are (1) public outrage with the growing interprovincial spread in average district size consequent to each redistribution; (2) the threat of a legal challenge and the uncertainty about how the courts might choose to further define section 3 of the charter and the principle of relative parity of voting power; (3) the genuine concern shared by many MPs about the needlessness of an increasingly larger House of Commons with each succeeding decade; and (4) the possible attraction of the Lortie proposal to cushion the effects of ending the grandfather clause and, in effect, replacing it with a guarantee that no province would be cut by more than one seat per decade. Together, these factors could lead to the replacement of the grandfather clause and at least modest reductions in the interprovincial variances in district population size with the passage of time.

Regardless of the outcome on the grandfather clause, the formula for allocating Commons seats to the provinces may well have to be revisited given the changing demographics of at least two provinces. By 2031 it is entirely possible that Saskatchewan will have been over-taken by Nova Scotia as Canada's sixth largest province.[16] If that is the case, and if Nova Scotia does not in the interval see an increase in its population that would warrant additional ridings, it will by 2031 have a greater population than Saskatchewan but three fewer commons seats. This same problem was addressed by Parliament in 1952 when Alberta, with a larger population than Saskatchewan for the first time, would have been assigned fewer Commons seats were it not for the adoption of a new feature in the formula. It lasted until 1974 when it was replaced by the amalgam method. The "Alberta clause," as it was dubbed, guaranteed that no province would have fewer electoral districts than another province containing a smaller population. It is conceivable, given the demographic shifts from one decade to the next and the possibility that nothing will be done to end the senatorial and grandfather protections, that some such provision as the Alberta clause will have to be added in the years ahead.

The Nova Scotia/Saskatchewan illustration merely reinforces the general point about the problematic nature of designing a formula that will satisfy all (unanticipated) conditions. The Lortie report was mindful of that difficulty. It found the most attractive alternative to rest in what it called "a return to our roots."[17] By that it called on Parliament to restore the kind of formula that had been put in place in 1867. Canada's original formula had been based, after a protracted and bitter debate over representational entitlements for elections to the new Parliament, on the seemingly simple proposition that there should be proportionate representation among the provinces in the House of Commons. Lortie's recommendation was to return to that fundamental principle. It called on Parliament to select one province as the "base province" (the royal commission chose Quebec and pegged its Commons representation at seventy-five members), and to assign seats to all other provinces relative to Quebec's population/seat ratio. The only exceptions would be to enable the senatorial floor provision of 1915 to continue and to ensure a one seat-per decade cushion to prevent any province from suffering massive seat losses. As reasonable and straightforward as the Lortie proposal is, no action had been taken on it by the early twenty-first century. The "return to the roots" proposal may well offer the best solution for Parliament to adopt when it next looks at the allocation of Commons' seats to the provinces.

As a general proposition, it can safely be said that, based on the record to date and seeing their own interests at stake, MPs will return to the issue of how constituencies are designed and who does the designing. That could come as soon as the post-2001 census federal redistribution. But equally, based on the work of the Milliken Committee in 1994–5 and the debate on C-69, it can be said that many MPs will be genuinely inspired to seek ways to improve the process and revamp the legislation that governs it. Self-interest is not the only, nor is it necessarily the primary, motivation that leads elected officials to question an act that bears so directly on their political fortunes. When these two motivations coincide, as they did federally in the 1990s when revisions would have materialized were it not for the stand-off with the Senate, the Electoral Boundaries Readjustment Act will almost certainly be revisited.

In all likelihood, the issues that will surface will be similar, if not identical, to those that so preoccupied the Procedure and House Affairs Committee in 1994–5. There will inevitably be MPs who will object to what commissions have done to their ridings. Some will find fault with the commissioners, others with the process. These are natural reactions for the understandable reason that members *are* proprietorial about what they see as their riding. After all, each individual member won an individual district and is intent to put his or her personal stamp on it to enhance future electoral prospects. The interest that members take in the shape, size, complexion, and name of their riding will never abate. They, their riding executives, and principal election organizers will continue to keep a watch on redistribution commissions and to appear at public hearings when they sense that their political survival or the "interests of their community" may be at stake. In light of the participation of MPs at the public hearing stage of consultations, the utility and appropriateness of holding a separate parliamentary objection stage "for members only" remains open to serious question. That MPs were ready in Bill C-69 to forego that privilege and to dispense with the parliamentary objection stage serves as a hopeful sign of how they will resolve that issue when they next have to address it.

Outstanding issues to be resolved, many of them addressed either in the Lortie report or by the Milliken Committee, will almost certainly include the following: lowering the variance limits from their current +/−25 percent levels; abolishing the extraordinary circumstances clause in the EBRA; creating a special category, possibly even a negotiated list, of isolated and sparsely populated northern seats that would be established with more generous population variances; reintroducing a relative rate of growth clause to enable population shifts to be factored into constituency design; ensuring quinquennial redistributions when population growth or changes warrant them; stating more explicitly what it is that MPs expect the concepts of community of interest and effective representation to mean; and finally, opening up the appointment process to allow interested potential commissioners to apply to the Speaker. That is a tall order. Reaching agreement on all, or many, of these issues will not be easy, for the views that elected members hold about their roles as representatives can be expected to remain as dominant and as varied in the future as they have been in the past.

If the EBRA is eventually amended to replace the 25 percent variances with limits in the order of 15 percent, to drop the extraordinary circumstances clause, to add a population growth provision, to ease out the grandfather clause, and to make no special allowance for northern seats, it could be said that the representational views of urban metropolitan, suburban, and fast-growth provinces have prevailed. If, on the other hand, the frequency of redistributions were kept at ten years, special northern seat allowances were established, the current variance limits were left unchanged, and the extraordinary circumstances clause were kept, then the MPs from rural, isolated, and slower or minimal growth parts of the country would have predominated. The lead-up to Bill C-69, combined with the changing demographics of the country, suggest that the former group will eventually be successful over the latter. If so, the authors of the revised act can claim with some justification that the changes they will have introduced merely followed the lead taken earlier by the federal boundaries commissions when from one decade to the next they designed constituencies that moved gradually closer to their province's average population.

The history of the EBRA suggests that the growing *intraprovincial egalitarianism* in constituency populations that marked the work of the electoral boundary commissions over a forty-year period stands in marked contrast to the increasing *interprovincial inegalitarianism* explicit in the federal legislation determining the number of members from each province. It is true that commissions have created isolated and territorially large seats with small populations, but with time these have become fewer in number (in spite of Parliament's exhortative and statutory interventions) as the share of seats with populations closer to provincial quotients has grown. For their part, MPs have moved in a different direction from the commissioners. By piling the grandfather clause on top of the senatorial floor, they added to the hurdles of achieving a measure of population parity in ridings across the country. Thus an obvious paradox of Canada's redistribution derives from the fact that the ten different federal commissions have accepted an increasingly uniform standard for the construction of their constituencies *within* the provinces, at the same time that the national legislative body has adopted a formula for determining membership in the commons which has the practical effect of treating the provinces differentially. It will test the ability of MPs in the years ahead to see if they too can bring their electoral boundaries legislation in step with what federal commissions have achieved since the act was introduced.

REFORMING REPRESENTATIONAL BUILDING BLOCKS

To reform a political institution has a pleasant ring about it. It conveys improvement, progress, and an ultimately fairer and more democratic political system for all citizens. Yet not all political institutions are amenable to being reformed, or at least being reformed in a fashion that the great majority of citizens would want. Nor do all reforms once implemented necessarily spell improvement and progress. What this book has tried to show through a case study of one institution, is that certain conditions or variables lend themselves to the reform and improvement of a representational building block. Based on Canada's experience with electoral boundaries readjustments in the last half of the twentieth century, we can draw some conclusions about what those conditions are. There may be an even wider application of several variables beyond an analysis of electoral boundaries readjustments. It is possible, for example, that in the on-going debate in Canada about reforming a different and possibly even more controversial institutional building block, the plurality vote electoral system, the application of these variables can help to shape the analysis of that issue and to understand the failure, by century's end, to have reformed it.

It is self-evident that reforms of a representational building block will not proceed without the *agreement of political elites*. Prime ministers, premiers, cabinets, and, ultimately, a majority of the elected members must be on side. Without that, legislated institutional reform is not possible. The impetus for the change would come from the wide acceptance of a recognized and easily understood *problem* with the then current institutional arrangements. There was little misunderstanding about what the problem was with government-controlled redistributions. The driving force behind reform of the electoral boundaries readjustment process in Manitoba, Quebec, and Canada, came from the inherent and patently obvious unfairness of the methods of designing constituencies then in use. It was readily understood that electoral districts were created at irregular intervals and that they were skewed in favour of some citizens and against others. The starkness and the simplicity of the issue gave it a *resonance* with public opinion, the metropolitan media, and the opposition parties.

The national media, social scientists, and bureaucratic and political elites provided the means whereby the *solution* was advanced and news of the reform was *transmitted* from one jurisdiction to another. *Federalism* provided the institutional framework within which that transmission took place. At the same time, federalism enabled the various governments to adopt a model of the reform that they judged to be *appropriate to their respective jurisdiction.* The easy fit of the reform with the parliamentary and legislative systems served to *allay any possible concerns* about the appropriateness of turning to an imported solution to a Canadian problem. Because the diffusion of the institutional experiment was largely successful, there was no cause to look beyond independent electoral boundary commissions to search for another alternative. These are the variables that account for reform of representational building blocks in Canada. Those who are looking at ways of changing the plurality vote method of elections now used at both the federal and provincial levels might choose to keep this checklist at hand as they pursue their objective.

"Nobody's perfect," is the closing line in Billy Wilder's classic comedy "Some Like It Hot." How apt, not least because we can say it applies to institutions as well as to humans. No institution is perfect, but some clearly are better than others. For the reasons discussed throughout this book, the introduction of the independent, non-partisan electoral boundaries commission in Canada is a definite improvement over what had existed before. But it is not perfect. Nor will it ever be. The membership of commissions and the maps they design will continue to prompt varying degrees of controversy and criticism from the politicians, the media, and the public. In keeping with a long Canadian tradition, the ridings that commissions design will still depart from strict equality of the vote, in some cases markedly so, although the degree to which they do so will never again be as considerable as it was before the shift away from government-directed redistributions. No matter how much clarification is offered by elected assemblies and courts, the statutes and guidelines setting out the list of factors to be used in the construction of ridings will still have an elusive and imprecise quality about them. But that is precisely why arms'-length institutions, in the great majority of cases led by a member of the judiciary or a senior electoral official whose competence includes exercising discretion and judgment in as fair an equitable manner as possible, are preferable to elected politicians to carry out the task. As a result of these improvements, the process generates a credibility it would not otherwise have and the product that comes out of it, imperfect as it will continue to be, will remain preferable to the alternative.

APPENDIX A

Decennial Boundary
Readjustment Process (Canada)

PRELIMINARY STEPS

1. Allocation of Seats EBRA sections 13 and 14

After the 10-year census, the Chief Statistician provides the Chief Electoral Officer with population data for each province and territory broken down by electoral districts and enumeration areas.

Using these figures and the formula in sections 51 and 51A of the *Constitution Act,* 1867 the Chief Electoral Officer calculates the number of seats to be allocated to each province and territory.

2. Establishment of Commissions EBRA sections 3, 4, 5 and 6

The members of the boundaries commissions are selected and appointed by the Speaker of the House of Commons and the appropriate chief justice.

Within 60 days from the time that the Chief Statistician supplies the population data to the government and to the Chief Electoral Officer, electoral boundaries commissions must be established and charged with fixing the boundaries of new electoral districts.

The commissions are officially established by the Governor in Council (Cabinet).

DEVELOPMENT OF PROPOSALS

3. Public Hearings EBRA section 19

Newspaper advertisements are published containing maps of the proposed electoral boundaries, as well as the time(s) and location(s) of public hearings, at least 60 days before the first hearing is scheduled.

A commission must hold at least one public hearing before completing its report.

During the hearings, interested individuals, groups and members of parliament may appear to express their views on the commission's proposals, after notifying the commission in writing of their intention to do so.

4. Completion of Reports EBRA section 20

No later than one year after receiving the population data, each commission must complete its report on the new electoral districts.

The Chief Electoral Officer may grant an extension of up to 6 months if necessary.

REVIEW OF REPORTS IN PARLIAMENT

5. Participation by M.P.s ("Objections Stage")
EBRA sections 21 and 22(1) (2)

Each commission's report is sent through the Chief Electoral Officer to the Speaker of the House of Commons, who must ensure that it is tabled and referred to a committee designated to deal with electoral matters.

Written objections, each signed by at least ten members of parliament, may be filed with the committee within 30 days of the tabling of a report.

The committee has 30 days, longer if the Commons is not sitting, to discuss any objections to a report and return it to the Speaker.

FINALIZING OF BOUNDARIES

6. The Results of Reports to the Commissions
EBRA subsection 22(3) and section 23

The reports are returned to the commissions, accompanied by the minutes of the House of Commons Committee. The commissions decide whether or not to modify their reports.

7. Representation Order ("R.O") EBRA sections 24 to 27

The Chief Electoral Officer drafts a "representation order" ("r.o.") describing and naming the electoral districts established by the commissions and sends the document to the cabinet.

Within five days of receiving the draft r.o., the cabinet must publicly announce the new boundaries in a proclamation which is to be published in the *Canada Gazette* within another five days from that date.

The new boundaries cannot be used at an election until at least one year has passed between the date the representation order was proclaimed and the date that parliament is dissolved for a general election.

Source: Adapted from Elections Canada, *Representation in the Federal Parliament* (Ottawa, 1993), 13–15.

APPENDIX B
Chronology of Redistribution Related Events, 1993–7

June 1993   Boundary Commissions appointed under the provisions of the Electoral Boundaries Readjustment Act, 1986.

Jan./Feb. 1994   Boundary Commissions release their proposals for new electoral maps and anticipate public input on them.

18 March 1994   Bill C-18: An act to suspend the operation of the Electoral Boundaries Readjustment Act is introduced in the House of Commons (passed in House of Commons, 13 April 1994).

19 April 1994   Order of reference is adopted by House of Commons that instructs Standing Committee on Procedure and House Affairs to prepare and bring in a bill respecting the system of readjusting the boundaries of electoral districts.

25 May 1994   Bill C-18 is amended by Senate and referred back to House of Commons.

9 June 1994   Bill C-18, Motion on Senate amendments is agreed to by House of Commons and sent to Senate (Royal Assent on 15 June 1994).

Sept. 1994   Commissions table their reports with the Chief Electoral Officer.

Nov. 1994   Procedure and House Affairs Committee tables its report with Reform dissenting opinion.

16 Feb. 1995   Government introduces Bill C-69 based on Procedure and House Affairs Committee Report (House gives assent to Bill C-69 on 24 April 1995).

8 June 1995   Bill C-69 is amended in Senate and referred back to the House of Commons.

20 June 1995	Bill C-69, House of Commons passes motion rejecting all but one Senate amendment.
22 June 1995	Suspended process resumes (Speaker tables reports of Boundary Commissions); Members have thirty days to submit complaints about the reports.
19 Nov. 1995	Procedure and House Affairs Committee makes recommendations to boundary commissions for further changes to the proposed electoral map based on M.P. complaints. Some of these changes are subsequently made.
21 Sept. 1995	Procedure and House Affairs Committee sends letter to the Senate.
8 Jan. 1996	New electoral boundaries are proclaimed and come into force on dissolution (27 April 1997).
2 Feb. 1996	Bill C-69, died on the Order Paper when Parliament prorogued.
2 June 1997	Federal Election held under new electoral boundaries.

Source: Adapted from Richard W. Jenkins, "Untangling the Politics of Electoral Boundaries in Canada, 1993–1997," *American Review of Canadian Studies* 28 (Winter 1998), 520 (reprinted with permission).

Interviews

AITKIN, DON, Research School of Social Sciences, Australian National University; Canberra, 11 July 1984.

ALBERT, MADELEINE, research assistant, Elections Quebec; Quebec City, 18 January 1999.

AREND, SYLVIE, professor of political science, Glendon College, York University, and member, Ontario Federal Electoral Boundaries Commission, 1990s; Toronto, 11 May 1999.

ARMSTRONG, BRIAN, chief electoral officer, Northwest Territories; telephone, 5 April 2000.

ATWELL, YVONNE, MLA, Nova Scotia, Halifax; 23 September 1998.

AUCOIN, PETER, member, Nova Scotia Federal Electoral Boundaries Commission 1990s, and research director, Lortie Commission; Halifax, 24 September 1998.

BALASKO, RICHARD D., chief electoral officer, Manitoba, and member, Manitoba Boundaries Commission 1998–9; telephone, 22 February 2000.

BILODEAU, ROGER J.A., professor of law, University of Moncton, and lawyer for SAANB; Moncton, 25 September 1998.

BLAKE, DON, professor of political science, University of British Columbia; principal technical consultant, Fisher Commission; and research director, Yukon Commission 1990s; Vancouver, 10 February 1999.

BODNAR, MORRIS, MP, Saskatoon-Dundurn (1993–7), Saskatoon; 14 November 1999.

BOURASSA, GUY, professor of political science, University of Montreal, member, Quebec Federal Electoral Boundaries Commission 1990s;

and member, Quebec provincial commission, 1980s and 1990s; Montreal, 20 January 1999.

BRUTON, Jim, research director, British Columbia Electoral Boundaries Commission; Vancouver, 10 February 1999.

CARTY, Ken, professor of political science, University of British Columbia; and principal technical consultant, Fisher Commission; Vancouver, 10 February 1999.

CASTONGUAY, Nelson, former chief electoral officer and representation commissioner, Canada; Ottawa, 11 June 1984.

CHAREST, Hon. Jean, MP, Sherbrooke, and leader of Progressive Conservative Party of Canada; Saskatoon, 16 November 1995.

CHARTIER, Jean, directeur des affaires juridiques, Office du Directeur général des Elections du Québec; Quebec City, 18 January 1999.

CLICHE, Hon. Mr Justice Vital, Quebec Superior Court, and chair, Quebec Federal Electoral Boundaries Commission, 1990s; Montreal, 20 January 1999.

DIXON, Hon. Mr Justice Russell A., Court of Queen's Bench of Alberta, chair, Alberta Federal Electoral Boundaries Commission, 1990s, and chair, Alberta provincial commission, 1980s; Calgary, 9 February 1999.

ERICKSON, Lynda, associate professor of political science, Simon Fraser University, and member, British Columbia Federal Electoral Boundaries Commission, 1990s; Vancouver, 11 February 1999.

EVANS, Ken, electoral commissioner, Western Australia; Ottawa, 25 June 1999.

FJELDHEIM, O. Brian, chief electoral officer, Alberta; Edmonton, 26 March 1999 and 22 February 2000.

GIBBINS, Roger, professor of political science, University of Calgary and president, Canada West Foundation; Calgary, 4 February 1999.

GERRARD, Hon. Jon, MP, Portage-Interlake (1993–7); Saskatoon, 12 July 1998.

GIRARD, Jacques, directeur général des Elections du Québec, and président de la Commission de la réprésentation électorale; Quebec City, 18 January 1999.

GRAESSER, Mark W., professor of political science, Memorial University, and member and vice-chair of federal electoral boundaries commission for Newfoundland in 1990s; St John's, 9 June 1997.

HAMILTON, Keith, lawyer and commission counsel for Yukon electoral boundaries commission, 1991; Vancouver, 11 February 1999.

HARPER, Stephen, president, National Citizens' Coalition, and MP, Calgary West (1993–7); Calgary, 9 February 1999.

HARRIS, Jack, MLA, Newfoundland and Labrador; St John's, 9 June 1997.

HÉBERT, Raymond, professor of political science, St Boniface College, and member, Manitoba Federal Electoral Boundaries Commission, 1990s; Winnipeg, 27 November 1998.

HINZ, Reinhard, service de la division territoriale, Commisssion de la représentation électoral du Québec; Quebec City, 18 January 1999.

HORSMAN, Anne, lawyer for SAANB; Moncton, 25 September 1998.

HUBAND, Hon. Mr Justice Charles R., Manitoba Court of Appeal, and chair, Manitoba Federal Electoral Boundaries Commission, 1990s; Winnipeg, 26 November 1998.

HUGHES, Colin A., electoral commissioner, Australian Electoral Commission; Canberra, 7 July 1984.

JENKINS, Richard W., legislative assistant to Peter Milliken, MP; Vancouver, 11 February 1999.

JOHNSON, Linda M., deputy chief electoral officer, British Columbia; Victoria, 11 August 1999.

JONES, David, legal counsel, Newfoundland and Labrador Department of Justice; telephone, 11 February 1997.

KLUGMAN, R.E., MP (Australia), and chair, Joint Select Committee on Electoral Reform; Canberra, 13 July 1984.

KNOPFF, Rainer, professor of political science, University of Calgary; and member, Alberta Federal Electoral Boundaries Commission, 1990s; Calgary, 9 February 1999.

LANDES, Ron, professor of political science, St Mary's University, chair, Nova Scotia Federal Electoral Boundaries Commission, 1990s, and member, Nova Scotia provincial commission, 1990s; Halifax, 24 September 1998.

LESAGE, Carol, Elections Canada; Saskatoon, 9 November 1991.

LÉSSARD, Marc-André, professor of sociology, Laval University, and member, Quebec provincial commission; Quebec City, 18 January 1999.

LYSYK, Hon. Mr Justice Kenneth M., Supreme Court of British Columbia, and chair, Yukon commission, 1990s; Vancouver, 11 February 1999.

MALEY, Michael, Australian Electoral Commission; Canberra, 12 July 1984.

MARSHALL, Hon. Mr Justice William W., Court of Appeal of Newfoundland, and chair, Newfoundland Federal Electoral Boundaries Commission, 1990s; St John's, 9 June 1997.

MCKENZIE, Hon. Mr Justice Lloyd G., Supreme Court of British Columbia, and chair, British Columbia Federal Electoral Boundaries Commission, 1990s; Vancouver, 10 February 1999.

MEEKISON, J. Peter, professor emeritus of political science, University of Alberta, and commissioner, Royal Commission on Aboriginal Peoples; Saskatoon, 10 November 1998.

MILLIKEN, Peter, MP, Kingston and the Islands, and chair of Commons Committee on Procedure and Elections; Ottawa, 6 June 1998.

MUFFETT, David, Australian electoral officer for Queensland; Brisbane, 5 July 1984.

NUGENT, Brian, Australian electoral officer for New South Wales; Sydney, 24 July 1984.

OUELLETTE, Roger, professor of political science, University of Moncton, and member, New Brunswick Federal Electoral Boundaries Commission; Moncton, 25 September 1998.

PATTERSON, Bob, chief electoral officer, British Columbia, and member, British Columbia provincial commission; telephone, 21 September 1999 and 22 February 2000.

PELLETIER, Réjean, professor of political science, Laval University, and member, Quebec Federal Electoral Boundaries Commission, 1990s; Quebec City, 17 January 1999.

PRUD'HOMME, Charland, member, Manitoba Federal Electoral Boundaries Commission, 1980s; Winnipeg, 9 June 1984.

RUFF, Norman, associate professor of political science, University of Victoria, and member, British Columbia Federal Electoral Boundaries Commission, 1990s; Victoria, 11 August 1999.

SANCTON, Andrew, professor of political science, University of Western Ontario, member, Ontario Federal Electoral Boundaries Commission 1990s and early 1980s; London, Ontario, 3 May 1999.

SAX, Herschell, senior policy advisor, Register and Geography Directorate, Elections Canada; Ottawa, 12 September 1996 and 7 February 2000.

SMITH, Jennifer, professor of political science, Dalhousie University, member, Nova Scotia Federal Electoral Boundaries Commission, and member, Nova Scotia provincial commission 1990s; Halifax, 24 September 1998.

TARDI, GREGORY, legal counsel, Elections Canada; Ottawa, 30 June 1999 and 19 May 2000.

THOMAS, Paul, professor of political studies, University of Manitoba, and member, Manitoba Federal Electoral Boundaries Commission, 1990s; Winnipeg, 27 November 1998.

TIDMAN, Hon. Mr Justice Gordon A., Supreme Court of Nova Scotia, and chair, Nova Scotia Federal Electoral Boundaries Commission 1990s; Halifax, 23 September 1998.

TURNBULL, Hon. Mr Justice Wallace S., Court of Appeal of New Brunswick, and chair, Nova Scotia Federal Electoral Boundaries Commission; Saskatoon, 15 October 1998.

WELLS, Loren A., assistant chief election officer, Elections Ontario; telephone, 1 October 1998.

YOUNG, Kevin, research director, Manitoba Electoral Boundaries Commission 1998–9; Winnipeg, 26 November 1998.

Notes

1 The classic twentieth-century works on representation are A.H. Birch,
  Representative and Responsible Government: An Essay on the British Constitu-
  tion (Toronto: University of Toronto Press, 1964), and Hanna Fenichel
  Pitkin, *The Concept of Representation* (Berkeley: University of California
  Press, 1967).
2 The term "riding" is far more commonly used by Canadians interchangeably with both "constituency" and "electoral district" than it
  is by any other nationals. Its first listing in the *Canadian Oxford Dictio-*
  nary is as a Canadian word meaning "a district whose voters elect a
  representative member to a legislative body; a constituency or electoral
  district." Its etymology is Old English ("thriding") from Old Norse
  ("thrithjungr," or "third part.") It was used specifically in the United
  Kingdom until the local government reorganization act of 1974 to
  refer to the three administrative units into which the county of York-
  shire was divided: East Riding, North Riding, and West Riding. One
  interpretation sometimes given to the origin of "riding" holds that it
  was the term used to refer to the distance a horse could carry its rider
  in one day.
3 Ken Carty, "The Electoral Boundary Revolution in Canada," *American Review*
  of Canadian Studies 15 (Autumn 1985), 273–87.
4 John Kingdon, *Agendas, Alternatives and Public Policies,* 2nd ed. (New
  York: HarperCollins, 1995) esp. chaps. 7–9. See also Leslie A. Pal, *Public*
  Policy Analysis: An Introduction (Toronto: Nelson, 1992), chap. 6.

CHAPTER TWO

1 In the United States "the terms *districting, redistricting, apportionment,* and *reapportionment* are treated as equivalents in common parlance. Technically, however, *apportionment* and *reapportionment* involve the allocation of a finite number of representatives among a fixed number of pre-established areas. *Districting* and *redistricting,* on the other hand, refer to the processes by which the lines separating legislative districts are drawn. Thus, state legislatures *redistrict* their states after they know the number of seats that have been *apportioned* to each state from among the 435 seats in the United States House of Representatives." Charles Backstrom, Leonard Robins, and Scott Eller, "Issues in Gerrymandering: An Exploratory Measure of Partisan Gerrymandering Applied to Minnesota," *Minnesota Law Review* 62 (July 1978), 1121, n.1.

2 Norman Ward, *The Canadian House of Commons: Representation,* 2nd ed. (Toronto: University of Toronto Press, 1963), 27. On Canada's most famous gerrymander, see R. MacGregor Dawson, "The Gerrymander of 1882," *Canadian Journal of Economics and Political Science* (hereafter *CJEPS*), 1 (May 1935), 197–221. For an account of Governor Gerry's role in establishing the "gerrymandered" seats, see Robert G. Dixon, *Democratic Representation: Reapportionment in Law and Politics* (Toronto: Oxford University Press, 1968), 459ff. On one occasion in the nineteenth century provincial seats were redistributed without having been gerrymandered by the government in its own interests: see Graham White, "'Christian Humility and Partisan Ingenuity,' Sir Oliver Mowat's Redistribution of 1874," *Ontario History* 73 (December 1981), 235–6.

3 On Northern Ireland, see D.J. Rossiter, R.J. Johnston, and C.J. Pattie, "The Partisan Impacts of Non-partisan Redistricting: Northern Ireland 1993–95," *Transactions of the Institute of British Geographers* (1998), 455–80. The American Congress adopted a Voting Rights Act in 1965 and subsequently amended it twice to protect the voting rights of Southern blacks and other racial minorities. Following its amendment in 1982 the act became the basis for most lawsuits from which court-ordered affirmative gerrymandering resulted. On affirmative gerrymandering in the United States, see Bernard Grofman, Arend Lijphart, Robert B. McKay, and Howard A. Scarrow, eds., *Representation and Redistricting Issues* (Toronto: D.C. Heath and Co., 1982), esp. chaps. 8 and 9; David Lublin, *The Paradox of Representation: Racial Gerrymandering and Minority Interests in Congress* (Princeton: Princeton University Press, 1997); and David T. Canon, *Race, Redistricting, and Representation: The Unintended Consequences of Black Majority Districts* (Chicago: University of Chicago Press, 1999).

4 Explanations of the Gini Index are found in Hayward R. Alker, *Mathematics and Politics* (New York: Macmillan, 1965), chap 3, and Alker and

Bruce M. Russett, "On Measuring Inequality," *Behavioral Science* 9 (July 1964), 207–18. I am indebted to Duff Spafford who simplified the method of calculating the Gini Index. The Gini ratio may be calculated according to the following formula:

Gini = [n + 1 − 2(Σsi/Σxi)]/(n−1)

where: n = number of constituencies;

Σsi = (Σs1 + Σs2 + Σs3 + ... Σsn);

Σxi = total population.

5 Anthony A. Peacock, "Equal Representation or Guardian Democracy? The Supreme Court's Foray into the Politics of Reapportionment and Its Legacy," in Mark Rush, ed., *Voting Rights and Redistricting in the United States* (Westport, Conn.: Greenwood Press, 1998), 41.

6 Bernard Grofman, Lisa Handley, and Richard G. Niemi, *Minority Representation and the Quest for Voting Equality* (Cambridge: Cambridge University Press, 1992), esp. chap. 5.

7 The priority value is determined by multiplying the population of a state by a multiplier. That multiplier equals 1 divided by the square root of n(n − 1). For the second seat n = 2, for the third n = 3, and so on until the appropriate number of multipliers has been calculated. I am grateful to Munroe Eagles of SUNY Buffalo for having provided this information.

8 Technically, the national quotient is established for the provinces by using as the divisor the number of commons seats either in 1976 or in the 33rd Parliament (1984–8),whichever is less. The only difference between the two comes from the three fastest-growing provinces of Ontario, British Columbia, and Alberta. They received in the redistribution of the 1980s a total of thirteen additional seats from what they had had in the previous redistribution. Their "floor," as it were, remains their representation in 1976. For the other seven provinces it remains the level of 1976 and of the 33rd Parliament – both were the same. The formula is:

PC − PT/(282 − 3) = NQ

PP/NQ = nPS

nPS + SCS = tPS

where:

p = population

P = province

C = Canada

T = territory

NQ = national quotient

nPS = number of provincial seats

SCS = special clause or "add-on" seats

tPS = total provincial seat entitlement

9 Number 55 of *The Federalist Papers* (1787–8), Clinton Rossiter, ed. (New York: New American Library edition, 1961), 341.

10 Carolyn Tuohy, *Policy and Politics in Canada: Institutionalized Ambivalence* (Philadelphia: Temple University Press, 1992).

11 On Manitoba, see Doug Nairne, "Filmon would drop 6 MLAs," *Winnipeg Free Press*, 24 August 1999, 1, and PC party of Manitoba press release, "Gary Filmon: Strong Leadership, Bright Future" (Winnipeg, 23 August 1999), 2. On Alberta, see "Klein may cut ridings," *Globe and Mail*, 10 May 1999, A5, and province of Alberta press release, premier's office, "Premier Announces Review of Provincial Electoral Representation," (Edmonton, 29 October 1998). Information on the Saskatchewan study provided by the study's author, Jack Stabler, Department of Agricultural Economics, University of Saskatchewan. Those most likely to agree that Saskatchewan had about the right number of MLAs were the unemployed (60.6 percent), university graduates (56.7 percent) and under twenty-four-year olds (54.6 percent). Those most likely to agree that Saskatchewan has too many MLAs were elementary school graduates (54 percent) and those with trade school or technical diploma education (53.7 percent). (Margin of error +/–3.5 percent, 95 times out of 100.) (N = 970).

12 British Columbia, Electoral Boundaries Commission, *Report to the Legislative Assembly of British Columbia* (3 December 1998), 37–40, and *Amendments to the December 3, 1998 Report to the Legislature of British Columbia* (3 June 1999), 11–15. In the Saskatchewan provincial election of 1999 the NDP government was returned with twenty-nine seats and the two opposition parties, the Saskatchewan party and the Liberal party, won twenty-five and four seats respectively. Although two seats were later subject to judicial recounts, and the opposition parties ended up with twenty-six and three seats respectively, the tie led the NDP to form, unexpectedly, a coalition government with the Liberals to avoid the possibility of a defeat on the floor of the legislature and a subsequent election.

13 Ontario Progressive Conservative party, "Common Sense Revolution," (Toronto, 3 May 1994), 8. The Reform party advocated a smaller Commons based on a fixed number of 265 MPs with additional members as required to fulfill the "senatorial floor" minimum for each province. For the redistribution of the 1990s this would have meant, by their estimates, a Commons of 273 members rather than 301. The reduction was justified by Reform in the following terms: "A smaller house offers considerable cost savings, less government and fewer politicians – and clearly this is what Canadians want." (House of Commons, Procedure and House Affairs Committee, Appendix A, "Dissenting Opinion," to proposed amendments to the Electoral Boundaries Readjustment Act [Bill C-69], 25 November 1994, No. 33: 37–8).

14 *The Federalist Papers* (1787–88), No. 55, 342, and No. 56, 346.

15 I am grateful to Graham White of the University of Toronto for sharing his views with me on this subject. The topic is further explored in my "The Size of Canada's Parliament: An Assessment of the Implications of a Larger House of Commons," in Peter Aucoin, ed., *Institutional Reforms for Representative Government* (Toronto: University of Toronto Press, 1985), 1–39.

16 In the twentieth century, all but one of the single-party sweeps of provincial legislatures occurred in the Atlantic provinces between 1935 and 1993:

Prov	Year	No. Seats Won by Government	% Votes Won by Government
NFLD	1959	31 of 34	58
PEI	1935	30 of 30	58
	1989	30 of 32	59
	1993	31 of 32	54
	1987	58 of 58	60
NB	1945	28 of 30	53
NS	1959	63 of 65	55
Alta	1963	60 of 63	55

17 Canada, *Parliamentary Debates on Confederation of British North American Provinces, 1865* (reprinted Ottawa: King's Printer, 1951), 39.

18 Canada, House of Commons, *Debates* (13 March 1939), 1808.

19 The "theories masquerading as principles" are described in Ward, *The Canadian House of Commons*, esp. chap. 2 and part II; see also his articles, "The Redistribution of 1952," CJEPS, 19 (August 1953), 341–60, and "A Century of Constituencies," *Canadian Public Administration*, (herafter CPA) 10 (Spring 1967), 105–221.

20 David Smith, "Party Government, Representation and National Integration in Canada," in Aucoin, ed., *Party Government and Regional Representation in Canada*, 1–68; and R.K. Carty, "Three Canadian Party Systems," in Carty, ed., *Canadian Political Party Systems: A Reader* (Toronto: Broadview Press, 1992), 563–86.

21 The "horse-trading" reference comes from Norman Ward, who gives a full account of the 1952 special committee that was composed of thirty-seven MPs representing the four parties in the House. The Liberal government had twenty-two members on the committee and an effective working majority on all its regional sub-committees. See Ward, "The Redistribution of 1952."

22 The origins of leadership review are discussed in my *Do Conventions Matter? Choosing National Party Leaders in Canada* (Montreal: McGill-Queens University Press, 1995), 37–41.

23 This issue is discussed further in J.R. Mallory, "Amending the Constitution by Stealth," *Queen's Quarterly*, 82 (Autumn 1975), 394–401.

24 On the question of an independent commission in 1864–7, see Joseph
   Pope, ed., *Confederation: Being a Series of Hitherto Unpublished Documents
   Bearing on the British North America Act* (Toronto: Carswell Co., 1895),
   147–8; for some of the early calls for changes in the system, see Canada,
   House of Commons, *Debates* (14 April 1903), 1207–12; Gerald Halabura,
   "Diefenbaker and Electoral Redistribution: Principle or Pragmatism?"
   (MA thesis, University of Saskatchewan, 1992), chap. 1; and House of
   Commons, *Debates* (10 March 1964), 760.

25 For more on pre-independent boundary commission redistributions at
   the provincial level, see R.V. Stewart Hyson, "New Brunswick's Electoral
   Redistribution of 1990–94: A Structural Approach to Redistribution Pol-
   icy" (Ph.D. dissertation, Department of Political Science, Carleton Uni-
   versity, 1999), chap. 3; Harvey E. Pasis, "The Inequality of Distribution
   in the Canadian Provincial Assemblies," *Canadian Journal of Political
   Science,* (hereafter *CJPS*) 5 (September 1972), 433–6; and Harvey E.
   Pasis, "Electoral Distribution in the Canadian Provincial Legislatures," in
   J. Paul Johnston and Harvey E. Pasis, eds., *Representation and Electoral
   Systems: Canadian Perspectives* (Toronto: Prentice-Hall, 1990), 251–3.

26 Ward, *The Canadian House of Commons,* 53 (emphasis in original).

27 Mallory, "Amending the Constitution by Stealth," 397.

28 M.L. Balinski and H.P. Young, "Parliamentary Representation and the
   Amalgam Method," *CJPS* 14 (December 1981), 797–812.

29 The population projections from StatsCan are included in my brief and
   testimony to the House of Commons, Privileges and Elections Committee, 19 November 1985, 19:6–7. The projection of 369 seats in 2001 is
   found in Elections Canada, *Representation in the Federal Parliament,*
   (Ottawa, 1993), 7.

30 Canada, Electoral Boundaries Readjustment Act, RS 1985, C E-3. As we
   will see in chapter 8, a challenge launched in British Columbia in 1987
   to the act's formula for allocating seats was unsuccessful at both the trial
   and appeal levels. The city of Vancouver and Ian Waddell, MP, had
   sought to overturn the method for determining the number of seats to
   which each province was entitled. The courts concluded that Parliament has the power to establish a representation formula without first
   obtaining the consent of the provinces and that absolute proportionate
   representation need not be adhered to in calculating the number of
   Commons' seats allocated to the various provinces.

31 The twenty add-on seats would have meant a Commons of 302 members were it not for the fact that the "rounded results" of the application of the national quotient to each province's population reduced the
   available number to 278 from 279 seats. In the post-1981 census redistribution, the application of the same formula had worked the opposite

way. It led to a "rounding up" by one seat, from 279 to 280, prior to the addition of the three territorial and twelve "add-on" seats.

32 For a summary of the kinds of concerns expressed about the American decennial census of 1980, see Allan Murray, "Redistricting Still Plagued by Confusion," *Congressional Quarterly Weekly Report* 39 (10 January 1981), 69–73. See also Margo J. Anderson and Stephen E. Feinberg, *Who Counts? The Politics of Census-Taking in Contemporary America* (New York: Russell Sage, 2000).

33 Ward, "A Century of Constituencies," 105. The number of seats to which a province was entitled (and the number it received) on entry into Confederation was: Manitoba one (four), British Columbia two (six), Prince Edward Island five (six), Alberta three (four) Saskatchewan four (six), and Newfoundland six (seven).

34 Michel L. Balinski and H. Peyton Young, *Fair Representation: Meeting the Ideal of One Man, One Vote* (New Haven: Yale University Press, 1982).

35 This is not to say that those states facing the prospects of a reduced number of congressional seats after a decennial reapportionment do not launch a major political and legal offensive against reductions in their entitlement. Challenges to census "undercounts" of large metropolitan areas are frequent. From a state's standpoint, not only is the size of its congressional delegation hanging in the balance, but many transfer payments from Washington are determined by a state's census population. The fate of one attempt in Congress to alter the reapportionment formula is described in Alan Murray, "Reapportionment: The Politics of N(N-1)," *Congressional Quarterly Weekly Report* 39 (28 February 1981), 393.

36 P.B. Waite, ed., *The Confederation Debates in the Province of Canada, 1865* (Toronto: McClelland and Stewart, 1963), 115.

37 1 July 1999 population estimates from the United States Bureau of the Census, and Statistics Canada: California, 33,145,121; Texas, 20,044,141; United States, 272,690,262; Ontario, 11,513,800; Quebec 7,345,400; Canada, 30,491,300.

CHAPTER THREE

1 James Bryce, *The American Commonwealth*, 2nd ed. (London: Macmillan and Co., 1891), 344–5.

2 The principal articles on diffusion of innovations are Jack L. Walker, "The Diffusion of Innovations among the American States," *American Political Science Review* (hereafter *APSR*), 63 (September 1969), 880–99; Virginia Gray, "Innovation in the States: A Diffusion Study," *APSR* 67 (December 1973), 1174–85, followed by "Comments" by both Walker and Gray, 1186–93; and Dale H. Poel, "The Diffusion of Legislation

among the Canadian Provinces: A Statistical Analysis," *CJPS*, 9 (December 1976), 605–26.

3 See my *The Selection of National Party Leaders in Canada* (Toronto: Macmillan of Canada, 1973), 67–8.

4 One of the members of the Barbeau Committee, Norman Ward, recorded the background to the committee's recommendations in his "Money and Politics: The Costs of Democracy in Canada," *CJPS* 5 (September 1972), 340.

5 See my *Do Conventions Matter? Choosing National Party Leaders in Canada* (Montreal: McGill-Queen's University Press, 1995), chaps. 11 and 12, esp. 248 and 264.

6 M.S. Donnelly, *The Government of Manitoba* (Toronto: University of Toronto Press, 1963), 17 and 78–80.

7 "An Independent Commission," *Winnipeg Tribune*, 21 October 1954, 6.

8 Donnelly, *Government of Manitoba*, 79. Urban voters were those who resided in metropolitan Winnipeg and the city of Brandon.

9 CCF leader Lloyd Stinson. See his *Political Warriors: Recollections of a Social Democrat* (Winnipeg: Queenston House Publishing, 1975), 158.

10 Conservative leader Erick Willis, speech to the Manitoba legislature, 26 February 1954; Provincial Archives of Manitoba (hereafter PAM), "Special Select Committee on Redistribution, 1954–56," G246.

11 "The Fourth Session," *Winnipeg Free Press*, 7 February 1949, 15. Within weeks of the newspaper's suggestion, an amendment to the redistribution bill calling for the establishment of such a commission was introduced by an Independent member of the legislature. It was defeated by a vote of 34–17. See "Bill to Boost Membership of House Gets 2nd Reading," ibid., 19 April 1949, 1.

12 The events leading up to the establishment of the committee, including a reference to the public support (especially in Winnipeg) for an independent, non-partisan commission, are described in Stinson, *Political Warriors*, 158–61. See also Harold Jansen, "The Single Transferable Vote in Alberta and Manitoba" (PH.D. dissertation, Department of Political Science, University of Alberta, 1998), 216–24. A brief submitted to the legislative committee by the powerful Winnipeg Chamber of Commerce was typical of Winnipeg business, labour, and civic organizations. It urged legislation establishing a three-member commission of judges to redraw constituency boundaries following each decennial census. See Brief, 13 September 1954, in PAM, "Special Select Committee on Redistribution, 1954–56," G246.

13 The books were David Butler's *The Electoral System in Britain, 1918–1951* (London: Oxford University Press, 1953) and Norman Ward's *The Canadian House of Commons: Representation* (Toronto: University of Toronto, 1950). Letters from Robert Menzies to Lloyd Stinson, MLA, dated

23 January 1953, and from James McGirr (former premier of New South Wales) to Charland Prud'homme (chief electoral officer of Manitoba), dated 13 July 1954. PAM, "Special Select Committee on Redistribution, 1954–56," G246.

14 W.L. Morton and Murray Donnelly brief, entitled "Redistribution," 16 October 1954. PAM, "Special Select Committee on Redistribution, 1954–56," G246.

15 Manitoba's experience with proportional representation is described in Donnelly, *Government of Manitoba*, 75–8; Jansen "The Single Transferable Vote," chaps. 4–8; Dennis Pilon, "Proportional Representation in Canada: An Historical Sketch," paper presented at the annual meeting of the Canadian Political Science Association, St John's, Newfoundland, 8–10 June 1997, and "The History of Voting System Reform in Canada," in Henry Milner, ed., *Making Every Vote Count: Reassessing Canada's Electoral System* (Peterborough: Broadview Press, 1999), 111–21; and Harry Charles John Phillips, "Challenges to the Voting System in Canada, 1874–1974" (PH.D. dissertation, University of Western Ontario, 1976), chaps. 4, 5, and 6. Western Canadian experience with preferential voting is discussed in T.H. Qualter, *The Election Process in Canada* (Toronto: McGraw-Hill, 1970), 130–37.

16 Pilon, "Proportional Representation in Canada," 36.

17 Michael Best, "PR in Winnipeg," *Winnipeg Free Press*, 7 September 1954, 19.

18 Michael Best, "Electoral Reform in Practice," *Winnipeg Free Press*, 13 April 1955, 23.

19 Ibid.

20 Brief Submitted by the Winnipeg Chamber of Commerce to the Special Select Committee on Redistribution of the Manitoba Legislature, dated 13 September 1954, 4. PAM, "Special Select Committee on Redistribution, 1954–56," G246.

21 Ibid.

22 Stinson, *Political Warriors*, 160. It was clear as well, to Stinson at least, that the cost of obtaining independent commissions was the sacrificing of the proportional electoral system, even though he claimed his party preferred it "as the most scientific and accurate method of reflecting the wishes of the voters" (p. 160).

23 SM 1955, c. 17. A statute passed two years later (Electoral Divisions Act, SM 1957, c. 18) became the basis of the present legislation.

24 Electoral Divisions Amendment Act, SM 1968, c. 21. Years cited are those in which the commission's report was completed. In all cases the legislation establishing the new boundaries was enacted the following year.

25 The 25 percent limits, tried briefly in Great Britain in the mid-1940s, were found "to be far too rigid and to produce results which in some

instances cut right across local unities." They were dropped from the factors to be considered by British commissions in 1946. See Butler, *The Electoral System in Britain*, 214.

26 Kent Roach, testimony to House of Commons, Committee on Procedure and House Affairs, 6 July 1994, 20:72.

27 Electoral Divisions Act, RSM 1987, C. E.40, ss. 12 (1) and (2). In 1998 the commission held hearings in seven locations throughout the province at which a total of sixty-one representations were made. In addition, written submissions were received from an additional 140 individuals and organizations. See Manitoba, *Report of the 1998 Electoral Divisions Boundaries Commission* (Winnipeg, 1998), 5.

28 Electoral Divisions Act, RSM 1987, C. E.40, s. 11(1).

29 Australia, Commonwealth Electoral Act 1918, Part III, s. 19. The section also included, as subsection (e), a reference to "State Electoral boundaries."

30 *Star Weekly* (Toronto), 30 April 1955, 11. See also Michael Best, "From Voters to People," *Winnipeg Free Press*, 15 January 1955, 18.

31 Paul Fox, ed., *Politics: Canada*, 1st ed. (Toronto: McGraw-Hill, 1962), 249, 264–6.

32 Fernand Grenier, Jean Hamelin, Vincent Lemieux, Yves Martin, André Raynauld, and Harold M. Angell, *Étude préliminaire à la révision de la carte électorale de la province de Québec* (Québec, 15 janvier 1962), 37 (hereafter Grenier Report).

33 Qualter, *The Election Process in Canada*, 106.

34 According to the Electoral Divisions Act the commission's report is submitted to the president of the Council (the premier) who, in turn, submits it to the Legislative Assembly (RSM 1987, C. E40, s. 10(2)). If the legislature is not in session at the time the final report is submitted to the premier, as was the case in December 1998, the premier's office releases the report to members of the legislature, with copies available from Elections Manitoba for the press and for public distribution (Young interview).

35 Between Manitoba in the 1950s and Quebec in the 1970s, Parliament adopted the Electoral Boundaries Readjustment Act in 1964. As well, with the approval of the legislature, the government of Ontario in 1962 appointed a three-member commission to advise the legislature on a new electoral map. In each of the following two decades a similar approach was taken (by a resolution presented by the government and adopted by the legislature) to redistributions by an advisory three-member independent body. Unlike Manitoba, Quebec, and Canada, Ontario has never passed a statute mandating a periodic redistribution by a committee whose composition was spelled out in the legislation. Ontario's remains to this day a strictly ad hoc arrangement. The extent to which redistribution is at the discretion of the government of the day

was made obvious in 1996 when Queen's Park adopted the recently-completed federal redistribution as the provincial redistribution for the 1990s. In 1965 the province of British Columbia established its first independent electoral boundary commission, a three-member body under the chairmanship of H. F. Angus of the University of British Columbia political science department. Like Ontario, British Columbia passed no standing legislation calling for the periodic establishment of a redistribution commission.

36 "The 'silent gerrymander' results from inaction. Without a reallocation of legislative seats the number of representatives of areas of growing population remains constant as does the representation of areas of relative decline in population." V.O. Key Jr, *American State Politics: An Introduction* (New York: Alfred A. Knopf, 1963), 65.

37 Grenier Report, 9.

38 Data computed from Quebec, Legislative Assembly, *Report on the General Election of* 1960 (Quebec: Queen's Printer, 1960), Appendix v, and Grenier Report, 9–11.

39 Manning J. Dauer and Robert G. Kelsay, "Unrepresentative States," *National Municipal Review* 44 (December 1955), 571–5. Dauer-Kelsay is a simple arithmetic measure which cannot make allowance for cross-constituency partisan or representational linkages or voting in accordance with non-geographically based identities. See Robert G. Dixon, Jr, *Democratic Representation: Reapportionment in Law and Politics* (New York: Oxford University Press, 1968), 272. Data computed from Quebec, Legislative Assembly, *Report on the General Election of* 1960 (Quebec: Queen's Printer, 1960), Appendix v, and 1871 Census of Canada, Table v, "Population of 1861 and 1871, compared by electoral districts within their present limits" (Ottawa: I.B. Taylor, 1873), 422–4.

40 *Baker* v. *Carr,* 369 US 186 (1962). At that time 27 percent of Tennessee's population could elect a majority of the state Senate, and 29 percent control the House. With the introduction of the one person, one vote principle and the intervention of the courts to interpret and enforce it, the figures had changed to 49 percent and 47 percent respectively by 1965. See Dixon, *Democratic Representation,* 622.

41 The election was fought on an electoral map that had been revised a year earlier. Following the recommendations of a special legislative committee, the legislature approved the addition of thirteen new seats (eleven in the metropolitan Montreal area) to bring the new legislature to an all-time high of 108 members. Two independent candidates were also elected in 1966.

42 Paul Stevens and John Saywell, "Parliament and Politics," John Saywell, ed., *Canadian Annual Review for* 1966 (Toronto: University of Toronto Press, 1967), 64.

43 See BNA Act (1867), s.80, the second schedule of the act, and J.-C. Bonenfant, *Rapport de la Commission permanente de la réforme des districts électoraux* (mars 1972), as included in "La carte électorale depuis 1791" (Québec: Élections Québec, octobre 1990), 8–10.

44 Figures computed from Quebec, *Report of the Chief Electoral Officer* 1966 (Quebec, 1966), Appendix V, and Canada, *Census of Canada* 1870–71 (Ottawa: Department of Agriculture, 1873), vol. I, table I.

45 J.-C. Bonenfant, "Québec," in John Saywell, ed., *Canadian Annual Review for* 1970 (Toronto: University of Toronto Press, 1971), 230.

46 The committee's hearings on electoral reform got under way early in 1971 with an opening statement from the premier, Robert Bourassa, outlining the electoral questions he wanted the committee to review. One of the essential ones was to design a new and fair way of readjusting electoral boundaries. Québec, Assemblée nationale, Commission permanente de l'Assemblée nationale, *Journal des débats*, 2nd session, 29th Législature (19 janvier 1971), B-521.

47 By the same token the Parti Québécois, who had just been elected to the legislature for the first time, had a clear interest in pushing for reform of the electoral system. The plurality system had badly penalized them. Their 23 percent of the vote converted into only seven seats. Once in office after the 1976 election, the PQ examined the possibility of changing the electoral system, even issuing a green paper on the Reform of the Electoral System, *One Citizen, One Vote* (Québec: Éditeur officiel, 1979). Nothing ever came of that or any other review; Quebec continues to this day to use the first-past-the-post electoral system.

48 Québec, Assemblée nationale, Commission permanente de l'Assemblée nationale, *Journal des débats*, 2nd session, 29th Législature (4 mars 1971), B-521. For the testimony of M. Drouin on the federal electoral boundary readjustment process and his experience as a member of the Quebec commission, see ibid. (28 janvier 1971), B-274–5.

49 Ibid. (12 juillet 1971), vol. XI, no. 74, 3568.

50 Statutes of Quebec, c. 7, "An Act Respecting the Standing Commission on Reform of the Electoral Districts" (1971). Quebec's commission has on occasion made generous use of the "exceptional reasons" clause. Of the 122 ridings approved in time for the 1981 election, for example, thirteen fell beyond the 25 percent limits. In addition, since 1972 the Îles-de-la-Madeleine constituency has enjoyed a legislatively protected status and has been guaranteed a seat of its own in the Assembly. Its 1998 electoral population was 10,364, compared with a provincial average of 42,283 for the remaining 124 seats.

51 John C. Courtney and David E. Smith, "Registering Voters: Canada in a Comparative Context," in Michael Cassidy, ed., *Democratic Rights and*

Electoral Reform in Canada, vol. x of the Research Studies for the Royal Commission on Electoral Reform (Toronto: Dundurn Press, 1991), 421–5.

52 Between October 1971 and January 1973, the Union Nationale had called itself Unité-Québec. For an account of the events in the legislature in 1972, see J.-C. Bonenfant, "Québec," in John Saywell, ed., *Canadian Annual Review for* 1972 (Toronto: University of Toronto Press, 1974), 160–1. The Union Nationale surfaced once again, when it won eleven seats in the election in 1976. It has since disappeared from Quebec's political scene.

53 Statutes of Quebec, c. 57, "An Act Respecting Electoral Representation" (1979), ss. 3, 4, 6, 7, and 8. In 1982 the commission established 3,108 precincts in the province. Since 1982 the Commission de la représentation électorale has also been responsible for establishing municipal electoral districts. In practice, however, the municipalities normally draw their own electoral districts, with the commission serving only as a final arbiter in the event of a dispute.

54 Statutes of Quebec, c. E-3.3, "The Election Act" (1989), with subsequent amendments (1990–7). A consolidated version published by le Directeur général des élections du Québec, "Extracts of the Election Act: Electoral Representation," updated 1 September 1997. The number of electors in Quebec increased from 3.4 million in 1970 to 4.7 million in 1989. In 1998 it was 5.3 million. In June 1999 the National Assembly unanimously approved legislation suspending the then-current redistribution for twelve months. Although no clearly stated reasons for suspending the redistribution were given, the possibility was raised by MNAs of public consultations being held on Quebec's electoral system. Bill-1 "An Act respecting the obligation to establish one's identity before voting and amending other legislative provisions pertaining to elections" suspending the Election Act stipulated that the commission's preliminary report, which was to have been completed by November 1999, was due no later than 1 January 2001. The National Assembly introduced the 122 to 125 range in 1987. The commission proposed 124 seats in 1987 but settled on 125 the following year.

55 In his celebrated nineteenth-century study of American politics, *Democracy in America,* Alexis de Tocqueville was one of the first to discern the influence and "peculiar magisterial spirit" of lawyers (and the courts) upon American society. See *Democracy in America* (New York: Vintage Books, 1955), I: 282. The United States Supreme Court, although called upon as early as 1932 to overturn state redistricting proposals, avoided finding for any plaintiffs until 1962, on the grounds that redistricting was a "political question." With *Baker* v. *Carr* the "political thicket" was opened. See Dixon, *Democratic Representation,* chap. 5.

56 See Courtney and Smith, "Registering Voters," 365 and 395. Legislation adopted by the Parliament of Canada in 1996 brought door-to-door enumeration to an end federally and approved the establishment of a registry of electors to be maintained continuously by Elections Canada. The 1997 federal election was the last under the former system of enumeration.

CHAPTER FOUR

1 Diefenbaker had had five years to act and he had done nothing. In the lead-up to his party's success in the 1957 general election he had promised, if elected, "to put redistribution in the hands of a non-partisan commission to eliminate the abuses of the past." See Gerald M. Halabura, "Diefenbaker and Electoral Redistribution: Principle or Pragmatism?" (MA thesis, Department of Political Studies, University of Saskatchewan, 1992), 44–5. On the 1962 Commons debate, see Canada, House of Commons, *Debates*, 9 April, 2645–52; 10 April, 2668–80; and 17 April, 3040–9.

2 Peter Newman captures the mood of mutual political distrust and animosity in his *The Distemper of Our Times: Canadian Politics in Transition 1963–1968*. (Toronto: McClelland and Stewart, 1968). Appendices F and G of that book reprint exchanges between the prime minister (Lester Pearson), senior Liberals, and the chief electoral officer about the implications for the timing of the post-1963 election of the independent electoral boundary adjustment process (pp. 498–508).

3 Robert Thompson, leader of the Social Credit party, gave support to the proposal but did not participate as actively in the parliamentary debate on the bill as the other three party leaders and, in particular, their house leaders.

4 Canada, House of Commons, *Debates*, 10 March 1964, 741 and 761, and 17 April 1964, 2294.

5 Stanley Knowles in House of Commons, *Debates*, 10 April 1964, 760. There were, as well, several favourable references to Ontario's then current experiment with a redistribution under independent commissioners. See ibid., 17 April 1964, 2289 and 2294.

6 Ibid., 9 April 1962, 2649.

7 J.W. Pickersgill, Secretary of State, ibid., 10 December 1963, 5635.

8 See ibid., 12 November 1964, 10032–9, and 13 November 1964, 10055–7.

9 *Baker* v. *Carr*, 369 US 186 (1962). For the comments of two MPs who acknowledged the importance of *Baker* v. *Carr* without giving its fundamental principle their whole support, see John Diefenbaker, House of Commons, *Debates*, 9 April 1962, 2645, and 26 November, 1963, 5127–9,

and Douglas Fisher, 12 October, 1962, 479–80. On the case itself, see Robert G. Dixon, Jr, *Democratic Representation: Reapportionment in Law and Politics* (New York: Oxford University Press, 1968), esp. 119–38.

10 The debates on redistribution and electoral boundary commissions covered some 450 pages of *Hansard* from the final session of the 24th Parliament (1961–2) to the end of the second session of the 26th Parliament (1964–5). The quotations in this paragraph and the next are taken from those debates. More on the background to the passage of the EBRA is in Norman Ward, "A Century of Constituencies," *CPA* 10 (Spring 1967), 105–21; W.E. Lyons, "Legislative Restricting by Independent Commissions: Operationalizing the One Man-One Vote Doctrine in Canada," *Polity I* (1969), 428–59; Lyons, *One Man-One Vote* (Toronto: McGraw-Hill 1970), chaps 1–2; T.H. Qualter, "Representation by Population: A Comparative Study," *Canadian Journal of Economics and Political Science* 33 (May 1967): 246–68; and Qualter, *The Election Process in Canada* (Toronto: McGraw-Hill 1979), chap. 3.

11 Castonguay interview. References to Mr Castonguay's Australian study are found in House of Commons, *Debates*, 4 June 1963, 653; 4 July 1963, 1825; 26 November 1963, 5111; and 16 April 1964, 2267–8. Castonguay's report to the government described Australian redistributions at the federal, not state level. Those of the states differ from one another and from the federal process.

12 James Jupp, *Australian Party Politics* (Melbourne: Melbourne University Press, 1966), 2.

13 I am mindful of Robert Hughes's point about Australia: "Parts of the Pacific, especially Tahiti, might seem to confirm Rousseau. But the intellectual patrons of Australia, in its first colonial years, were Hobbes and Sade." His reference is to eighteenth-century settlement; mine is to nineteenth- and twentieth-century electoral theory and practice. See Robert Hughes, *The Fatal Shore* (New York; Vintage Books, 1986), 1.

14 Patterson interview. Federal legislation in 1934 had established a permanent voters' list with an annual revision. It proved to be unsatisfactory and was abandoned in 1938 in favour of the previous system of door-to-door enumerations held during the early days of an election campaign. See John C. Courtney and David E. Smith, "Registering Voters: Canada in a Comparative Context," Royal Commission on Electoral Reform and Party Finance," in Michael Cassidy, ed., *Democratic Rights and Electoral Reform in Canada* (Toronto: Dundurn Press, 1991), vol X: 351.

15 Studies of the Australian electoral redistribution include Colin A. Hughes, "The Case of the Arrested Pendulum," in Howard R. Penniman, ed., *The Australian National Elections of 1977* (Washington: American Enterprise Institute for Public Policy Research, 1977), 305–10; Hughes, "Fair and Equal Constituencies: Australia, Jamaica and the United

Kingdom," *Journal of Commonwealth and Comparative Politics* 16 (November 1978), 256–71; Hughes and Don Aitkin, "The Federal Redistribution of 1968: A Case Study in Australian Political Conflict," *Journal of Commonwealth Political Studies* 8 (March 1970), 18–39; and Hughes and Dean Jaensch, "Judicialisation of Electoral Redistributions: The Commonwealth and South Australia, " *Politics* 15 (May 1979), 60–70. A helpful review of the Australian electoral system is found in Don Aitkin and Brian Jinks, *Australian Political Institutions,* 2nd ed. (Brisbane: Pitman Publishing, 1982), 123–39. The Australian Electoral Commission's (hereafter AEC) *Electoral Newsfile* is published several times a year and often includes up-to-date information on redistributions in Australia.

16 Details of the government's original bill, the proposed amendments, and the debates in the House are given in Ward, "A Century of Constituencies," 112–16. The phrase, "as nearly as may be" had first appeared in Mr Diefenbaker's 1962 electoral boundaries proposal (Bill c-87). It appears to have been taken in a slightly modified form from Manitoba's 1955 legislation that includes constructing constituencies "as nearly as possible" similar in population size. See RSM, c. 17, 1955.

17 National Archives of Canada (hereafter NA), RG 89, vol. 7, file 2, "Conference Re: Electoral Boundaries Readjustment Act," Saint John, New Brunswick, 17 December 1964, 25.

18 In 1974 four private members' public bills aimed at amending the EBRA made it through the first hurdle (second reading in the Commons), were referred to the Standing Committee on Privileges and Elections, but were ultimately unsuccessful in changing the legislation: Bills c-316, c-366, c-369, and c-370.

19 Ward, "A Century of Constituencies," 113.

20 NA, RG 59, vol. 6, "Meeting of Commission Chairmen, Ottawa, August 28, 1965," 2.

21 Hughes and Jaensch, "Judicialisation of Electoral Redistributions," 60.

22 Hughes interview. The two-tiered process suggests a further judicial analogue – the appellate court. By statute the chairman of the Australian electoral commission must be a judge. He takes no part in the initial (Redistribution Committee) stage, but together with the five other members of the Augmented Commission he hears appeals against the proposed maps before making the final decision on the electoral boundaries.

23 Commonwealth Electoral Act 1918, incorporating all amendments made to 30 June 1980, s. 25(2)(a)(b).

24 AEC, "Electoral Newsfile" (no. 80), January 1999, 1.

25 Commonwealth Electoral Act 1918, Memorandum Showing the Commonwealth Electoral Act 1918, As Amended by the Commonwealth Electoral Legislation Amendment Act 1983, s. 25S.(3)(a). The

expression "eye of the needle" is that of the former Australian electoral commissioner, Colin Hughes.

26 Aitkin, Hughes, Klugman, Maley, Muffett, and Nugent interviews.

27 AEC, "Fact Sheet 19 – Redistribution," 16 April 1999.

28 Ibid., *1984 Redistribution: Forward Projections of Enrolments Report* (Canberra, 1988), 3, 11, and 14.

29 Ibid., "Electoral Newsfile," January 1999, 4. As there are no checks to ensure that the 3.5 percent tolerance limits are not exceeded midway through the redistribution cycle, it remains a moot point what, if anything, their violation might actually mean.

30 See David Carter, "Implementation of the Election Expenses Act" in J.-P. Gaboury and J.R. Hurley, eds., *The Canadian House of Commons Observed* (Ottawa: University of Ottawa Press, 1979), 85–109.

31 F. Leslie Seidle provided an early account of the role that the Ad Hoc Committee played in shaping the application of and the early amendments to the new election expenses legislation and in provoking the National Citizens' Coalition to launch the first of its two successful challenges to limitations placed on third-party advertising in elections: See Seidle, "The Elections Expenses Act: The House of Commons and the Parties" in John C. Courtney, ed., *The Canadian House of Commons: Essays in Honour of Norman Ward* (Calgary: University of Calgary Press, 1985), 123–30.

32 Hughes, "The Case of the Arrested Pendulum," 307.

33 NA, "Conference Re: Electoral Boundaries Readjustment Act," 2 and 19.

CHAPTER FIVE

1 Eagles, "Enhancing Relative Vote Equality in Canada: The Role of Electors in Boundary Adjustment," Royal Commission on Electoral Reform and Party Financing (hereafter RCERPF), *Drawing the Map: Equality and Efficacy of the Vote in Canadian Electoral Boundary Reform* (Toronto: Dundurn Press, 1991), XI: 176.

2 John C. Courtney and David E. Smith, "Registering Voters: Canada in a Comparative Context," RCERPF, Michael Cassidy, ed., *Democratic Rights and Electoral Reform in Canada* (Toronto: Dundurn Press, 1991), X: 422.

3 Canada, Electoral Boundaries Readjustment Act, RS 1985, C. E-3, S. 15 (1) (a) and (2) (b).

4 Canada, House of Commons, Committee of Procedure and House Affairs, 6 July 1994, 20: 12–13.

5 RCERPF, *Reforming Electoral Democracy* (Ottawa, 1991), I: 159–69.

6 Bourassa interview.

7 David Docherty, *Mr. Smith Goes to Ottawa: Life in the House of Commons* (Vancouver: University of British Columbia Press, 1997), 190–2.

Docherty also notes that in the subsequent parliament (1993–7) in which large numbers of Liberal, Bloc Québécois, and Reform members were elected for the first time, the rookie MPs placed "helping individuals" midway in the five issue list, after "protecting riding" (no. 1) and "keeping in touch" (no. 2). As a large component of the rookie MPs in that Parliament was made up of the Bloc Québecois and Reform parties, the shift in ordering is perhaps not surprising. The BQ was preoccupied with Quebec issues, principally sovereignty, and they focused even more than members normally do on their ridings; part of the Reform's populist mantra was to make MPs better listeners to the concerns of their constituents.

8 Canada, House of Commons, Committee of Procedure and House Affairs, 7 June to 25 November 1994, in particular 7 July 1994. Also Bodnar, Charest, Gerrard, Harper, and Milliken interviews.

9 Testimony of the Chief Electoral Office for Canada, House of Commons, Committee of Procedure and House Affairs, 9 June 1994, 16:27.

10 Data gathered from Chief Electoral Officer, *Official Voting Results* 36th *General Election* 1997 (Ottawa, 1997); Statistics Canada, *Age, Sex and Marital Status* (Ottawa: Supply and Services Canada, 1992), 1991, Census of Canada, catalogue number 93–310), tables 3 and 4; and Statistics Canada, *Immigrant Population by Place of Birth and Sex, Showing Period of Immigration, for Canada, Provinces, Territories, and Census Metropolitan Areas*, 1996 Census.

11 The 1986 formula, without the application of the grandfather and senatorial floor provisions, would have yielded the following results based on the 1996 census and (in parentheses) the 1997 electoral list: British Columbia 36 (33); Ontario 104 (101); Quebec 69 (74); New Brunswick 7 (8); Nova Scotia 9 (10); and Newfoundland 5 (6). The increase in Atlantic Canada and in Quebec would have lowered the number of additional seats from 23 to 15.

12 Klugman interview, and summary of the Australia "The Case for Yes" committee for the 1974 referendum (chief electoral officer: Canberra, 1974), 11 (emphasis added).

13 Australia, "The Case for No" committee for the 1974 referendum (chief electoral officer: Canberra, 1974), 12–13.

14 Information provided in e-mail communications from Anthea Wilson, Information Section, Australia Electoral Commission, 29 February 2000.

15 Jane Bagets and Tina W.l. Chui, *Focus on Canada: Canada's Changing Immigrant Population* (Scarborough: Statistics Canada and Prentice Hall Canada, 1995), 10–11.

16 Canada, House of Commons, Committee on Procedure and House Affairs, 7 July 1994, 19:107, 108 and 110; and *Debates*, 16 March 1995, 14.

17 Quotation from David Docherty, e-mail to the author, 3 May 2000.

18 NA, RG 59, vol. 7, file 2, "Minutes of Electoral Boundaries Commission for the Province of New Brunswick," 17 December 1964, 39; ibid., vol. 4, "Minutes of Electoral Boundaries Commission for the Province of Alberta," 27 February 1965, 1. The $180 per week secretary of the first federal Alberta commission was Ivan L. Head, later special assistant to the prime minister (Pierre Trudeau) for foreign affairs and president of the International Development Research Centre.

19 These holdings are part of RG 59.

20 Elections Canada, "Background: Redistribution – 301 New Electoral Districts" (Ottawa, January 1997), EC 90820.

21 The judges with whom interviews were conducted were unanimous in their support for a meeting such as that organized by Elections Canada (Cliche, Dixon, Huband, Marshall, McKenzie, Tidman, Turnbull interviews). Elections Canada sees the meeting of all chairs at the beginning of the process as important enough to its success that they are giving consideration to expanding it to a two-day conference with all commissioners in attendance (Sax interview).

22 Walter Bagehot, *The English Constitution* (London: World Classics, 1928), 67.

23 Sax interview.

24 Testimony of Carol Lesage to House of Commons, Committee on Procedure and House Affairs, 9 June 1994, 16:26.

25 Patterson, Balasko, and Fjeldheim interviews.

26 For a brief description of digital mapping and GIS, see Hugh Calkins and Monroe Eagles, *Geographic Information Analysis and Human Capital Research* (Buffalo: SUNY Buffalo, 1996). I am grateful to Herschell Sax, senior policy adviser, Register and Geography Directorate, Elections Canada, for providing information about digital mapping in Canada.

27 British Columbia, *Report to the Legislative Assembly of British Columbia* (3 December 1998), 10.

28 Attempting to establish what Quebec spent for identical items is extremely difficult. They were either covered by Quebec's office of the chief electoral officer or they were presented in expenditure summaries in such a way as to make comparisons impossible. See Commission de la représentation du Québec, "La carte électoral du Québec: Rapport des dépenses" (Québec, octobre 1992).

29 The province of Ontario, of course, held no redistribution in the 1990s; it simply adopted the 103 federal constituencies as its own. Based on the $1.6 million that the redistribution of the 1980s cost the province, the savings realized from not holding a boundary adjustment in the 1990s would likely have been in the order of $2 million.

30 W. Ivor Jennings, *The British Constitution* (Cambridge: Cambridge University Press, 1958), 14–15. The last twelve two-member seats in the British

Parliament (all university based) were eliminated by the Representation of the People Act of 1948.

31 John Courtney, "'Theories Masquerading as Principles': Canadian Electoral Boundary Commissions and the Australian Model" in John C. Courtney, ed., *The Canadian House of Commons: Essays in Honour of Norman Ward* (Calgary: University of Calgary Press), tables 6 and 9, pp. 150 and 153.

32 RCERPF, *Reforming Electoral Democracy*, 1: 167. A valuable source for tracing the history of Canadian constituencies, their name changes, and their electoral history is Library of Parliament, *History of the Federal Electoral Ridings, 1867–1980* (Ottawa, 1983), 4 vols.

33 See RCERPF, *Reforming Electoral Democracy*, 1: 168.

34 In its attempt to implement the Lortie Commission's recommendation calling for fewer hyphenated district names, the Saskatchewan electoral boundary commission had, in 1994, created a Qu'Appelle seat. On the recommendation of the local MP, that was changed by Parliament in 1998 to Regina-Qu'Appelle. Similarly Saskatoon-Rosetown was changed to Saskatoon-Rosetown-Biggar in 1997 by way of a private members' bill.

35 Ontario's Representation Act, 1996 reads: "s. 4 (1) If only the name of a federal electoral district is changed, the name of the corresponding provincial electoral district undergoes the same change at the same time. (2) However, if the federal change of name takes place after a writ for an election is issued in the corresponding provincial electoral district, the provincial change of name does not take place until the day after polling day."

36 RCERPF, *Reforming Electoral Democracy*, 1: 168.

37 The Saskatchewan commission's comments addressing the MPs' objections to the constituency names are found at Federal Electoral Boundaries Commission for the Province of Saskatchewan 1995, "Disposition by the Commission Pursuant to s. 23(1) of the *Electoral Boundaries Readjustment Act* of Objections Filed by Members of the House of Commons with Respect to the Commission's Report Dated August 24, 1994" (Ottawa, 1995), 5–6.

38 RCERPF, *Reforming Electoral Democracy*, 1: 169.

CHAPTER SIX

1 Much of the information in this chapter is based on interviews with several past and present election officials at both the federal and provincial levels, elected members, chairs and members of recent federal, provincial, and territorial commissions, research directors of provincial commissions, and Canada's former representation commissioner: Atwell,

Aucoin, Blake, Carty, Castonguay, Chartier, Cliche, Dixon, Erickson, Gerrard, Girard, Harris, Landes, Johnson, Lesage, Lessard, Lysyk, McKenzie, Patterson, Pelletier, Sax, Smith, and Thomas interviews.

2 The few exceptions include Thomas Stefanson, whose brother was a cabinet minister in the Filman PC government, and who was known as a lifelong Conservative at the time of his appointment to Manitoba's 1985 federal commission, and Frederick Driscoll, a University of Prince Edward Island historian and former PC provincial cabinet minister at the time of his appointment to the federal PEI commission in 1993.

3 Representation Commissioner Act, RSC 1963, c. 40.

4 Canada has had five chief electoral officers since the post was first created in 1920: Oliver Mowat Biggar (1920–7); Jules Castonguay (1927–49); Nelson Castonguay (1949–66); Jean-Marc Hamel (1966–90); and Jean-Pierre Kingsley (1990–).

5 The sixteen were: Mark Graesser (Newfoundland); Roger Ouellette (New Brunswick); Peter Aucoin and Ronald Landes (Nova Scotia); Frederick Driscoll (PEI); Guy Bourassa and Réjean Pelletier (Quebec); Andrew Sancton and Sylvie Arend (Ontario); Raymond Hébert and Paul Thomas (Manitoba); Phillip Hansen (Saskatchewan); Fred Engelmann and Rainer Knopff (Alberta); and Lynda Erickson and Norman Ruff (British Columbia). One political scientist who served on a federal boundaries commission (1983) and was, a decade later, elected to Parliament, was Ted McWhinney of British Columbia. He holds the distinction of being the first boundaries commissioner with a social science background to serve later as an MP. His commission's recommendations were never enacted as, in 1985, replacement commissions were named across Canada and the work was undertaken once again.

6 John C. Courtney, Peter MacKinnon, and David E. Smith, *Drawing Boundaries: Legislatures, Courts, and Electoral Values* (Saskatoon: Fifth House Publishers, 1992).

7 Ron Fritz, Rainer Knopff, Norman Ruff, and Andrew Sancton were appointed; John Courtney declined.

8 Canada, *Report of the Royal Commission on Electoral Reform and Party Financing* (Ottawa: Minister of Supply and Services, 1991), 4 vols., and *Research Studies* (Toronto: Dundurn Press, 1991), 29 vols.

9 Peter Aucoin (research director), Lynda Erickson, Réjean Pelletier, and Paul Thomas.

10 See, for example, Canada, Chief Electoral Officer, *Report of the Chief Electoral Officer on the 36th General Election* (Ottawa, 1997), 5.

11 Kingsley, in evidence to the House of Commons, Procedure and House Affairs Committee, *Minutes of the Proceedings*, 9 June 1994, 16:29.

12 Lysyk interview.

13 Ted McWhinney (Liberal), *Minutes of Proceedings and Evidence of the Stand-ing Committee on Procedure and House Affairs,* no. 16, 9 June 1994, 17 (emphasis added).

14 The two NWT commissioners in 1994, Bob McQuarrie and Jim Currie, had had substantial involvement with the aboriginal communities in the north. In keeping with its advocacy of separate aboriginal electoral dis-tricts (AEDs) to increase the number of native Canadians in Parliament, the Lortie Commission recommended that, where more than one aboriginal district was to be created in a province, a special boundaries commission should be set up for the purposes of determining its bor-ders. It would be composed of a judge as chair plus two aboriginals appointed by the Speaker. See RCERPF, vol. 2, 150.

15 Commission members were Ron Landes (chair), the Honourable Denne Burchell, Alphonsine Saulnier, Jennifer Smith, Carolyn Thomas, and Sherman Zwicker.

16 "Terms of Reference" of the *Report of the Select Committee on Establishing and Electoral Boundaries Commission* (July 1991), as included in Provincial Electoral Boundaries Commission, *Effective Political Representation in Nova Scotia: The* 1992 *Report of the Provincial Electoral Boundaries Commission* (Halifax: March 1992), 13.

17 The 1991 census shows 10,825 Nova Scotians as being of Black origin, 7,530 as being aboriginal, 34,005 as having French as their mother tongue and 5,125 giving a multiple response of both French and English. The population with aboriginal origins and/or Indian registra-tion is given as 22,160; of these 16,455 lived off an Indian reserve. A Black leader claims the census data are low. She estimates Nova Scotia's Black population at between 20,000 and 30,000, of whom possibly 3,000 lived in her riding, Preston, the province's smallest district (Atwell interview). Statistics Canada, *Profile of Census Divisions and Subdivisions in Nova Scotia,* 1991 Census, parts A and B, catalogue numbers 95–312 and 95–313, table 1, and *Profile of Canada's Aboriginal Population: Aboriginal Data,* 1991 Census, catalogue number 94–325, table 4.

18 Ibid., 28 and 29. The smallest seat, Prescott, had a population of 8,700 or roughly one-half the provincial average of 17,300 per district. The remaining forty-seven seats ranged from between 13,200 and 20,700, with over one-half (forty-five) in a population range of 16,000 to 19,000. No agreement could be reached with Nova Scotia's Native com-munity to add a fifty-third seat to the legislature reserved for a Native member to be elected in a province-wide vote of Nova Scotia Natives.

19 Landes interview, Halifax, 24 September 1998 (emphasis added).

20 Nova Scotia was not alone in seeking to guarantee a Native seat in the legislature. Attempts in New Brunswick in the 1980s and 1990s at enhancing aboriginal representation in the provincial legislature

through agreement with the Native community on the construction of electoral districts also failed.

21 Hanna Fenichel Pitkin, *The Concept of Representation* (Berkeley: University of California Press, 1967), 61. See also A.H. Birch, *Representative and Responsible Government: An Essay on the British Constitution* (Toronto: University of Toronto Press, 1964), 14–17.

22 Realistically, the only demographically-defined groups that would have the critical mass sufficient to warrant specially-constructed constituencies would be linguistic and racial (and, in rare instances, religious) minorities. So long as the single-member district remains the defining unit for parliamentary and legislative representation in Canada, constructing seats to enhance the prospects of women being elected would be impossible because of the relatively even distribution of population by gender across the country as a whole.

23 Girard and Chartier interviews, Quebec City, 18 January 1999.

24 *MacKinnon v. Prince Edward Island* (1993), 101 DLR (4th) 397.

25 Ibid. (emphasis added), and *Reference re: Provincial Electoral Boundaries* (*Carter* reference) [1991] 5 WWR 1 (SCC), 81 DLR (4th) 23.

26 *Carter* reference, 23.

27 Keith Archer, "Conflict and Confusion in Drawing Constituency Boundaries: The Case of Alberta," *Canadian Public Policy* 19 (June 1993), 185 and 189.

28 Newfoundland's 1993 commission was also able to reach a unanimous set of recommendations even though the three parties in the House of Assembly had each named one non-legislative supporter to sit on the five-member body.

29 Previous commissions had generally respected urban municipal boundaries as a matter of choice. There had been no statutory obligation to do so.

30 Rainer Knopff and F.L. Morton, "Charter Politics in Alberta: Constituency Apportionment and the Right to Vote" in John C. Courtney, Peter MacKinnon, and David E. Smith, *Drawing Boundaries: Legislatures, Courts and Electoral Values* (Saskatoon: Fifth House, 1992), 102.

31 Mr Justice Cory in *Carter* reference, 28. See also Robert G. Richards and Thomson Irvine, "Reference Re Provincial Electoral Boundaries: An Analysis" in Courtney, MacKinnon, and Smith, *Drawing Boundaries*, 53 and 57, and Knopff and Morton, "Charter Politics in Alberta: Constituency Apportionment," in ibid., 102–4.

32 Larry McCormick, MP, in House of Commons, Procedure and House Affairs Committee, *Minutes of the Proceedings of Meetings* 90–97 (24 October–28 November, 1995), 53:55.

33 Cliche, Lessard, and Pelletier interviews. Quebec's permanent commission has also seen the river as a major divide within the province which is not to be crossed in the construction of seats.

34 *Report of the Federal Electoral Boundaries Commission for the Province of British Columbia* (Ottawa, 1994), 41 (emphasis added).

35 Erickson interview.

36 *Report of the Federal Electoral Boundaries Commission for the Province of Saskatchewan* (Ottawa, 1994), 2. By contrast, after "it got a lot of flak" at public hearings in 1994 for proposing to scrap Calgary Centre, the federal commission for Alberta reinstated the old district in a slightly modified form. The Bow River cuts straight through the riding, but that prompted no concerns with the public. Convinced that the district served as the "hub of a wheel" for the rest of Calgary's constituencies, the commissioners concluded that with a stable, downtown population in which the populations north and south of the river shared a genuine community of interest, the district made "a ton of sense." Dixon interview and *Report of the Federal Electoral Boundaries Commission for the Province of Alberta* (Ottawa, 1994), 7.

37 See Archer, "Conflict and Confusion," 186. The 1990 Electoral Boundary Commission Act of Alberta went so far as to *instruct* the provincial commission to propose forty multi-municipality districts. Five of these districts were to include parts of four named cities and adjacent rural municipalities. That section of the act was repealed in 1995. Alberta's federal commission of the 1990s deliberately rejected the possibility of constructing "rurban" seats on the grounds that there were no shared communities of interest that would include both rural and urban electorates, and that the rural parts of any such "rurban" seat would be swamped by the larger urban parts (Knopff interview).

38 The Ontario Representation Act of 1996 means that the province has effectively forfeited the final authority to determine provincial maps to the federal commissions as the electoral boundaries of the province have been deemed by the statute to have been established in accordance with the terms of the federal act.

39 David J. Bercuson and Barry Cooper, "Electoral Boundaries: An Obstacle to Democracy in Alberta" in Courtney, MacKinnon, and Smith, *Drawing Boundaries,* 120.

40 A majority recommendation of a three-member independent commission (chaired by political scientists H.F. Angus) was bypassed by the British Columbia government in favour of a minority recommendation. The issue revolved around the replacement of three-member constituencies in Vancouver with (as the majority suggested) single-member seats. The government acted on the recommendation of the minority commission member favouring two-member districts. See British Columbia, *Report of the Commission of Inquiry into Redefinition of Electoral Districts* (Victoria: Registrar of Electors, 1966), 5 and 47 ff; Patterson interview; and Paul Phillips, "British Columbia" in John Saywell, ed., *Canadian Annual Review*

for 1966 (Toronto: University of Toronto Press, 1967), 140–1. British Columbia's opposition leader charged that the bill (which passed in a recorded vote of 26 to 15) had been designed by "Mr. Gerry and Mr. Mander" (ibid.).

41 F.F. Schindeler, "Ontario" in John Saywell, ed., *Canadian Annual Review for* 1965 (Toronto: University of Toronto Press, 1966), 124, and *Canadian Annual Review for* 1966 (Toronto: University of Toronto Press, 1967), 90.

42 Jones interview.

43 British Columbia, Electoral Boundaries Commission Act, RS 107, S. 12 (3). In the British Columbia provincial redistribution of 1998–9, twenty-three of the seventy-five MLAs took advantage of the opportunity to meet with the commission in Victoria prior to the preparation of the preliminary set of maps, and eight appeared before it in advance of the final report. In the ridings, twenty-nine MLAs (several of whom had previously met with the commission in Victoria or were to meet with them at the final set of MLA hearings) appeared at one of the riding-level public meetings held in the province.

44 House of Commons, Procedure and House Affairs Committee, *Minutes of the Proceedings of Meetings* 90–97 (24 October–28 November, 1995), 53:20.

45 RCERPF, *Reforming Electoral Democracy*, 1: 164–7. See also Andrew Sancton, "Eroding Representation-by-Population in the Canadian House of Commons: *The Representation Act, 1985*," *Canadian Journal of Political Science* 23 (September 1990), 448.

46 Melissa Williams's premise that members of historically marginalized groups can best give voice to their concerns and expect a greater measure of trust in their members when they share, let us say, the same racial heritage is based on her argument that mediation is at the core of representation. Mediation, in turn, is based on three dynamic elements: legislative decision-making, legislator-constituent relations, and the aggregation of citizens into representational constituencies. See Melissa Williams, *Voice, Trust, and Memory: Marginalized Groups and the Failings of Liberal Representation* (Princeton: Princeton University Press, 1998), esp. chaps. 1, 4–7.

CHAPTER SEVEN

1 Paul Zed (Liberal, Fundy-Royal), testimony to the House of Commons Subcommittee on Proposed Electoral Boundaries for the Eastern Provinces of the Standing Committee on Procedure and House Affairs, 3 October 1995, 13.

2 Public participation, legislative objections, and government-initiated suspensions have not been restricted to the federal arena. Several

provinces have either suspended the boundary readjustment exercise once it got underway or amended the boundaries readjustment act to change the process in anticipation of a forthcoming redistribution. For example, at the beginning of the 1990s and then again at the end of that decade, Quebec's National Assembly voted to suspend the redistribution. In 1991 a six-month suspension followed the appearance of "busloads" of people attending public meetings in the Gaspésie in protest against the commission's proposal to reduce the region's representation in the legislature. The commission's subsequent decision to construct the same number of seats in the region as previously may have solved the crisis of the moment, but with the continuous outflow of population from the area and the population shifts in the province as a whole, the solution was clearly only temporary. By the time of the 1998 election, eighteen of Quebec's 125 ridings had populations outside the +/-25 percent range and again would have required substantial reconfiguring in the planned 1999 redistribution. That was suspended for twelve months during which time a legislative committee examined the larger question of Quebec's electoral system.

3 Prud'homme interview, and John C. Courtney, "'Theories Masquerading as Principles': Canadian Electoral Boundary Commissions and the Australian Model" in John C. Courtney, ed., *The Canadian House of Commons: Essays in Honour of Norman Ward* (Calgary: University of Calgary Press), table 2, 145.

4 Sancton interview.

5 Arend and Sancton interviews, and *Report of the Federal Electoral Boundaries Commission for the Province of Ontario* (Ottawa, 1994), 14.

6 Arend interview. Since 1 January 1998 Metro Toronto has become the new City of Toronto.

7 Bourassa, Cliche, and Pelletier interviews.

8 Covering 452,146 square kilometres, the next largest federal seat in a province is Manitoba's Churchill riding. The two largest seats in the country are Nunavut, with 2.8 million square kilometres, and Western Arctic, with 1.25 square kilometres.

9 Canada, *Report of the Federal Electoral Boundaries Commission for the Province of Quebec* (Ottawa, 1994), 53 and 54.

10 The removal of one seat from the east end of Montreal was far easier and "provoked less concern with the public" than did the removal of one seat from the Gaspésie (Pelletier and Cliche interviews.).

11 Canada, *Report of the Electoral Boundaries Commission for the Province of Newfoundland* (Ottawa, 1987), 6, and "Supplementary Minority Report of the Electoral Boundaries Commission for the Province of Newfoundland, 1987" (Ottawa, 1987), 1–4.

12 *Report of the Electoral Boundaries Commission for the Province of Newfoundland*, 7.

13 Two were by the same individual (an MP) who appeared in different towns. Five written submissions were received as well. *Report of the Federal Electoral Boundaries Commission for the Province of Newfoundland* (Ottawa, 1994), 6.

14 Ibid., 3.

15 Erickson interview.

16 *Report of the Federal Electoral Boundaries Commission for the Province of British Columbia* (Ottawa, 1994), 2.

17 Ibid., 3.

18 Ibid., 1.

19 Ruff interview.

20 *Report of the Federal Electoral Boundaries Commission for the Province of British Columbia*, 3–4.

21 Erickson interview.

22 Richard W. Jenkins, "Untangling the Politics of Electoral Boundaries in Canada, 1993–97," *American Review of Canadian Studies* 28 (Winter 1998), 519. An account of the 1993–4 suspension is also given in Louis Massicotte, "Electoral reform in the Charter Era," Alan Frizzell and Jon H. Pammett, eds., *The Canadian General Election of 1997* (Toronto: Dundurn Press, 1997), 175–8.

23 Letter of Mr Justice W. W. Marshall to Jean-Pierre Kingsley, 31 May 1994, 5.

24 *Report of the Federal Electoral Boundaries Commission for the Province of Newfoundland* (Ottawa, 1994), 2.

25 "We do not think that Bill C-18 had any significant impact on the participation in the hearings, though some of the submissions came in late." *Report of the Federal Electoral Boundaries Commission for the Province of British Columbia*, 2.

26 Bourassa interview. Professor Bourassa was comparing participation at the federal level (1994 being his first federal commission) with his long experience as a provincial electoral boundaries commissioner.

27 *Report of the Federal Electoral Boundaries Commission for the Province of Ontario*, 2.

28 Aucoin, Hébert, Knopff, Landes, Marshall, Ouellette, Thomas, and Turnbull interviews. The federal commission in Alberta noted the low level of public interest in their proposals in 1994: "A total of 16 formal representations were received at the seven public hearings that were held. This is not a large number ... In all, 57 members of the public attended our hearings [of whom] 30 expressed their views to the commission. Representations were made by four sitting members of

parliament and by two candidates in the [1993] election. [As well], 22 letters were received." *Report of the Federal Electoral Boundaries Commission for the Province of Alberta* (Ottawa, 1994), 3.

29 Turnbull interview.

30 Data on the numbers and categories of participants are from my "'Theories Masquerading as Principles,'" tables 2 to 5, pp. 146–8.

31 N's on "types of arguments presented at hearings" in Canada's first three redistributions varied from a low of 957 in 1965 to a high of 1,421 in 1973. Single submissions frequently included more than one type of argument to bolster their case. Data on types of issues raised at public hearings for the first three federal redistributions are found in ibid., tables 6 to 8, pp. 150–2.

32 Massicotte, "Electoral Reform in the Charter Era," 177.

33 *Report of the Federal Electoral Boundaries Commission for the Province of Saskatchewan* (Ottawa, 1987), 6.

34 Norman Ward, "A Century of Constituencies," CPA 10 (Spring 1967), 115.

35 Munro Eagles and Ken Carty, "MPs and Electoral Redistribution Controversies in Canada, 1993–96," *Journal of Legislative Studies* 5 (Summer 1999), 77.

36 Ibid., 78–9. Details of the survey are given in Munroe Eagles, "The Political Ecology of Representation in English Canada: MPs and their Constituencies," *American Review of Canadian Studies* 28 (Spring-Summer 1998), 53–79.

37 Eagles and Carty, "MPs and Electoral Redistribution Controversies," 81 and 88.

38 House of Commons Committee on Procedure and House Affairs, "Consideration of Objections to the Reports," 53:23–5.

39 Ibid., 53:25 (emphasis added).

40 House of Commons Committee on Procedure and House Affairs, "Consideration of Objections to the Reports," 53:50 (emphasis added).

41 Sancton interview.

42 Ibid.; Federal Electoral Boundaries Commission for the Province of Ontario, "Disposition of Objections," 8 December 1995, 3. In addition to the changed maps, one constituency name in Ontario was altered by the commission in its disposition of parliamentary objections.

43 Turnbull interview, and *Report of the Federal Electoral Boundaries Commission for the Province of New Brunswick* (Ottawa, 1994), 5.

44 Ouellette interview, and *Report of the Federal Electoral Boundaries Commission for the Province of New Brunswick*, 18 and 19.

45 Ouellette interview.

46 Paul François Sylvestre, *Nos parlementaires* (Ottawa: Éditions l'Interligne, 1987), 15–20, and Arend interview. Professor Arend researched the

election of francophone members of Parliament as part of her preparation for the commission's work.

47 NA, RG 59, vol. 6. "Minutes of Meeting – May 15, 1966, of the Electoral
   Boundaries Commission for Saskatchewan," 1. The author was one of
   three Saskatchewan commissioners in the 1985–87 redistribution. The
   other commissions to have left their constituencies unchanged were the
   four Atlantic provinces and the Northwest Territories.

48 Harper interview.

49 Arend interview.

50 A constitutional amendment in 1943 postponed the redistribution of
   the 1940s until the first session of Parliament after the Second World
   War.

51 The bills and their dates of introduction into the Commons were: C-208
   (5 July 1973); C-74 (1 October 1985); C-67 (1 May 1992); and C-18
   (21 March 1994).

52 Jenkins, "Untangling the Politics," 523.

53 The Reform proposal also allowed for a small increase in the House size
   as a result of the constitutional obligations imposed by the senatorial
   floor guarantee. See Appendix A, *House of Commons Committee on Procedure and House Affairs*, report of 25 November 1994, 33:37 and 39
   (emphasis added).

54 The full report of the committee to the Commons appears in ibid.,
   33:5–11.

55 It was Stephen Harper's view that "as the process unfolded" during the
   time of the Milliken Committee's consideration of reforms to redistribution, and as the early objections of many MPs were fully aired, the great
   majority of them eventually came to accept the view that the existing
   legislation, while it could be improved in a number of respects, had not
   worked badly. Harper interview.

56 Harper interview. Richard Jenkins, legislative assistant to Peter Milliken
   at the time, argues that Harper "gives the wrong impression ... The
   [Milliken] committee was not made up solely of people who were
   opposed to the current maps or whose interests would clearly be served
   by bypassing a redistribution" (e-mail to the author from Jenkins,
   3 April 2000).

CHAPTER EIGHT

1 Of the vast literature on redistricting in the United States, three books
  published at different times and exploring related, but nonetheless distinct aspects of the issue can be consulted: Robert G. Dixon, *Democratic
  Representation: Reapportionment in Law and Politics* (New York: Oxford
  University Press, 1968); Bernard Grofman, Arend Lijphart, Robert B.

McKay, and Howard A. Scarrow, eds., *Representation and Redistricting Issues* (Lexington: Lexington Books, 1982); and Mark E. Rush, ed., *Voting Rights and Redistricting in the United States* (Westport: Greenwood Press, 1998).

2 Bernard Grofman, "What Happens After One Person-One Vote? Implications of the United States Experience for Canada" in John C. Courtney, Peter MacKinnon, and David E. Smith, eds., *Drawing Boundaries: Legislatures, Courts, and Electoral Values* (Saskatoon: Fifth House Publishers, 1992), 156.

3 *Shaw* v. *Reno* is discussed in Daniel Lowenstein, "Race and Representation in the Supreme Court" in Rush, ed., *Voting Rights and Redistricting*, 67ff.

4 Dixon, *Democratic Representation*, 7.

5 Rush, ed., *Voting Rights and Redistricting*, 3.

6 Scarrow, "'One Man-One Vote': Tracing its Roots and Consequences" in Courtney, MacKinnon, and Smith, eds., *Drawing Boundaries*, 183.

7 McLachlin, J. in *Reference re: Provincial Electoral Boundaries* (*Carter* reference) [1991] 5 WWR 1 (SCC), 81 DLR (4th) 13 (hereafter cited as *Carter*, with citations from WWR).

8 *Campbell* v. *Canada (Attorney General)* [1988] 2 WWR 650, and 4 WWR 441. An attempt a decade earlier by an MP challenging the federal Ontario electoral boundaries of 1976 was equally unsuccessful. Keith Penner launched a case, heard in both trial and appeal divisions of the Federal Court, against the 1976 Ontario redistribution on the grounds that the boundaries commission had failed to give sufficient reasons for removing one seat from northern Ontario. The judges ruled against the plaintiff on the grounds that to restrain the representation commissioner from completing the draft representation order within the statutory time period would place the validity of the redistribution in question. The appeal citation is: *Penner* v. *The Representation Commissioner for Canada*, [1977] 1 FC 147 (TD).

9 *Dixon* v. *British Columbia (Attorney General)* [1989] 59 DLR (4th) 247 (hereafter cited as *Dixon*).

10 Norman Ruff gives a full account of the background to the *Dixon* case and the basis for the court's decision in 1989 in "The Right to Vote and Inequality of Voting Power in British Columbia: The Jurisprudence and Politics of the Dixon Case," in Courtney, MacKinnon and Smith, eds., *Drawing Boundaries*, 128–47.

11 *Dixon*, 261 (emphasis in original), 257 and 262. It is conceivable that section 15 of the charter would have been more natural than section 3 for purposes of analysing questions of equality of the vote and their links to variations in constituency size. For that to have happened the

petitioner would have had to have established under section 15 its standing as a disadvantaged group.

12 Ibid., 257. The court concluded that as a section 3 violation had occurred, "it is unnecessary to consider whether it also violates other sections of the Charter," (p. 270). The petitioners had also brought their action under sections 2(b), 7, and 15.

13 Ibid., 258–70.

14 Ibid., 258–70 and 283.

15 *Reference re Provincial Electoral Boundaries,* [1991] 3 WWR 1 (hereafter cited as *Carter* SCA).

16 *Carter* SCA, 598, 608, 593, and 594.

17 Ibid., 627.

18 *Reference re Provincial Electoral Boundaries,* [1991] 5 WWR at 7, 13–14, and 16 (hereafter cited as *Carter* SCC). A useful distinction between the two alternative interpretations of the right to vote that were at the crux of the *Saskatchewan Reference* case were drawn by Stewart Hyson, "The Electoral Boundary Revolution in the Maritime Provinces," *The American Review of Canadian Studies* 25 (Summer and Autumn 1995), 286.

19 *Carter* SCC, 12–15.

20 Ibid., 12–13 (emphasis added).

21 Ibid., 12–15 and 20.

22 Ibid., 3, 24 and 25.

23 Rainer Knopff and F.L. Morton, *Charter Politics* (Toronto: Nelson), 336. A thorough analysis of the two Alberta reference cases is found in Ronald E. Fritz, "Drawing Electoral Boundaries in Compliance with the Charter: The Alberta Experience," *National Journal of Constitutional Law* 6 (1996), 347–82.

24 The criteria were: (1) area of more than 20,000 square kilometres; (2) total surveyed area of more than 15,000 square kilometres; (3) more than 1,000 kilometres of highways within its boundaries; (4) more than 150 kilometres distant from the legislature; (5) contained no town larger than 4,000 people; (6) had sustained a significant loss of population due to economic factors; and (7) community of interest would be significantly and negatively affected by compliance if the district contained a higher population.

25 *Reference re Electoral Boundaries Commission Act,* [1991] 86 DLR (4th), 451.

26 1991 *Alberta Reference case,* 453.

27 Fritz, "Drawing Electoral Boundaries," 365.

28 Ibid., 369. Two other cases (one challenging a provincial redistribution in Nova Scotia, the other a federal redistribution in New Brunswick) also alleged "inadequate reflection of a community of interest" in a new set of boundaries. The injunctive relief was denied, a "common theme

in the judicial decisions" being the balance of convenience favouring the holding of a general election. See Ronald E. Fritz, "Challenging Electoral Boundaries under the Charter: Judicial Deference and Burden of Proof," *Review of Constitutional Studies* 5 (1999), 24–5.

29 *Reference re: Electoral Divisions Statutes Amendment Act* [1994], 119 DLR (4th), 11.

30 Application for leave to appeal the court decision was filed along with an application requiring the Alberta government to pay the expenses of the Alberta Civil Liberties Association and the town of Lac la Biche. The funding application was turned down, and as a result the appeal was abandoned.

31 *MacKinnon* v. *Prince Edward Island* [1993] 101 DLR (4th), 392.

32 It is correct, as Ron Fritz notes, to express puzzlement over the Prince Edward Island trial court ruling. It is reasoned and structured as if it would overturn the boundaries, rather than accept them. See Fritz, "Challenging Electoral Boundaries," 19.

33 *Friends of Democracy* v. *Northwest Territories (Attorney General)* [1999], 171 DLR (4th), 551–69.

34 The other two seats, Deh Cho and Hay River North, with populations 46 and 26 percent below the variance respectively (Brian Armstrong, NWT chief electoral officer, 5 April 2000). On an earlier redistribution in the NWT and the impact that charter-based litigations have on the "consensual government" model of the territory and on the options available for redistribution of territorial seats, see Graham White, "Northern Distinctiveness, Representation by Population and the Charter: The Politics of Redistribution in the Northwest Territories," *Journal of Canadian Studies* 28 (Autumn 1993), 5–28.

35 *Dixon*, 256. The generous interpretation that the Supreme Court (unlike the Saskatchewan Court of Appeal) accorded to section 3 in *Dixon* had the effect of shifting an examination of the burden of proof for an infringement of a guaranteed right from section 1 to section 3. According to Ron Fritz, "by defining the Charter-protected 'right to vote' as meaning the 'right to effective representation,' which includes 'parity of voting power' and myriad other factors, Justice McLachlin seems to have introduced into her section 3 analysis considerations that one would have ordinarily expected to be covered in a section 1 analysis." Fritz, "Challenging Electoral Boundaries," 29–30.

36 *Report of the Royal Commission on Electoral Boundaries for British Columbia* (Victoria, 1988), 4.

37 Ron Fritz correctly reminds us that the issue with respect to the legislated limits is whether "the mere fact that boundaries fall within +/−25 percent necessarily insulates the boundaries from a successful challenge" (Fritz communication with the author, 10 April 2000). As noted

in this chapter, the court ruled that any deviation has to be "justified on the ground that they contribute to better government."

38 Knopff and Morton, *Charter Politics*, 336.

39 Yukon, *Electoral District Boundaries Commission Report* (Whitehorse, 1991), 2.

40 *Carter* scc, 12–13.

41 *Dixon*, 413.

42 Ibid., 400. Duff Spafford's recalculations for British Columbia show the minimum level of support at 40.9 percent, not 38.4.

43 Duff Spafford, "'Effective Representation': Reference Re Provincial Electoral Boundaries," *Saskatchewan Law Review* 56 (1992), 207. I am grateful to Duff Spafford for sharing with me his insight into this difference between *Dixon* and *Carter*.

44 Ibid, 207.

45 A word check of *Dixon* shows one entry for "minority" (drawing on a citation to legislation passed with respect to the right to support minority dissentient education), and one reference each to Australian High Court decisions referring, in passing, to "community pressures" and "community of interest." See *Dixon*, 398 and 411.

46 See Committee for Aboriginal Electoral Reform, *The Path to Electoral Equality* (Ottawa, 1991), reprinted as part 3 of vol. 4 of RCERPF, *What Canadians Told Us*, 228–96; RCERPF, *Reforming Electoral Democracy*, vol. 1, 171 ff., and vol. 2, 139 ff.; New Brunswick Representation and Electoral District Boundaries Commission, *Towards a New Electoral Map for New Brunswick* (first report, July 1992,) 9; and Nova Scotia, *Effective Political Representation in Nova Scotia: The 1992 Report of the Provincial Electoral Boundaries Commission* (Halifax, 1992), 13.

47 Alan Stewart, "Comment on *Dixon v. Attorney General of British Columbia*," *Canadian Bar Review* 69 (1990), 356.

48 Ibid.

49 Nova Scotia, *Effective Political Representation*, 12–13; and Saskatchewan, Department of Justice, News Release No. 93–249, "Constituency Boundaries Act Introduced" (Regina, 14 May 1993), 1.

50 *Carter* scc, 15–16.

51 Robert G. Richards and Thomson Irvine, "Reference Re Provincial Electoral Boundaries: An Analysis" in Courtney, MacKinnon, and Smith, eds., *Drawing Boundaries*, 62.

52 Ronald E. Fritz, "The Impact of the Canadian Charter of Rights and Freedoms on Drawing Electoral Boundaries in Canada," paper presented at the Conference on Boundaries in the Canadian Experience, Edinburgh, Scotland, 3 May 1996, 7.

53 Mr Justice Guy of the Manitoba federal commission. NA, RG 59, vol. 6, "Memorandum: Re Meeting of Commission Chairmen, Ottawa, August 28, 1965" (31 August 1965), 3.

CHAPTER NINE

1 The two-seat redistribution in the Northwest Territories has not been included in this chapter's analysis.
2 Canada, *Report of the Federal Electoral Boundaries Commission for the Province of Manitoba* (Ottawa, 1994), 17, and *Report of the Federal Electoral Boundaries Commission for the Province of Nova Scotia* (Ottawa, 1994), 2. Manitoba's expression was "a license to be used without *clear* justification" (emphasis added).
3 Canada, *Report of the Federal Electoral Boundaries Commission for the Province of Saskatchewan* (Ottawa, 1994), 4.
4 *Nova Scotia Report*, 4.
5 Electoral Boundaries Commission Act, ss 1986–87, c. E-6.1, s. 20 (b) (i).
6 Dixon, Knopff, Erickson, McKenzie, Huband, and Thomas interviews (Winnipeg, 26 and 27 November 1998).
7 *Manitoba Report*, 17, and *Alberta Report*, 5 and 11.
8 Three provinces specifically referred to their inability to use population growth in constructing seats: British Columbia (in its *Disposition of Objections*) and Saskatchewan and Ontario in their 1987 *Reports*.
9 Bill c-69 [1994–95], s. 19 (2) (b) (iii).
10 Section 13 of the EBRA adopted in 1964 listed "sparsity, density or relative rate of growth of population of various regions" of a province as conditions that could render a departure necessary or desirable from the rules calling for equality of population.
11 See, for example, *Report of the Chief Electoral Officer on the 36th General Election* (1997), 6.
12 *Report of the Federal Electoral Boundaries Commission for the Province of Ontario* (Ottawa, 1994), 16, and *Report of the Federal Electoral Boundaries Commission for the Province of Quebec* (Ottawa, 1994), 54 and 58. Arend, Bourassa and Sancton interviews, and correspondence with Andrew Sancton, 10 July 1998.
13 *Carter* SCC, 13.
14 Sancton interview.
15 Bourassa, Cliche, and Pelletier interviews, and *Report of the Federal Electoral Boundaries Commission for the Province of Quebec*, 58.
16 Erickson, McKenzie, and Ruff interviews.
17 The province got its money's worth out of adopting the federal maps. The same boundaries were later adopted as the basis for the new wards for the reconstituted city of Toronto. Each federal district was bisected by one line drawn by the city council to create twice as many wards as there were federal/provincial electoral districts!
18 *Report of the Ontario Commission on the Legislature (5th Report)* (Toronto, 1975), 47 (emphasis added). According to the commission:

No one has really made the arguments and popularized them in the parties, that bigger and bigger government should be matched by a bigger legislature. This is the argument the Commission wishes to make to the Legislature and to the citizens of Ontario. As we see it, the primary difficulty in getting acceptance for the enlargement relates more to the political psychology of the Province and the defensive (even the inferiority) complex of our politicians.

We can foresee the outcry about more drones to draw on the honey-pot of the taxpayers' moneys, and reiterations that we already have too many politicians and too much politicians – and too much politics – what we really need is more efficiency and less politics (p. 49).

19 The bill went through second reading on 30 October and received royal assent on 9 December 1996. It was accepted and referred to committee at second reading stage in a recorded vote of 68 to 30. There were occasional references to effective representation throughout the debate. The expression, as was made clear several times, was borrowed from the Camp commission, not *Carter.*

20 Commission de la représentation électorale du Québec, *The Electoral Map of Quebec* (1992), 4.

21 Nova Scotia Provincial Electoral Boundaries Commission, *Effective Political Representation in Nova Scotia: The Report of the Provincial Electoral Boundaries Commission* (March 1992), 12–13 (emphasis added).

22 As noted in chapter 3, Dauer-Kelsay establishes through an ordinal ranking of constituencies by size the smallest percentage of an entire population that could theoretically elect a majority of a legislature. See Manning J. Dauer and Robert G. Kelsay, "Unrepresentative States," *National Municipal Review* 44 (December 1955), 571–5.

23 Ron E. Fritz, "The Impact of the Canadian Charter of Rights and Freedoms on Drawing Electoral Boundaries in Canada," paper presented at the Conference on Boundaries in the Canadian Experience, Edinburgh, Scotland, 3 May 1996, 16.

24 T.H. Qualter, *The Election Process in Canada* (Toronto: McGraw-Hill, 1970), 81.

25 Donald C. MacDonald, "Intense political battles loom over redistribution in Ontario," *Toronto Star,* 21 September 1994, A24.

26 Graham White, "Downsizing Democracy" (unpublished, 1995).

27 The 905 area refers to the arc around Toronto that is defined by the 905 telephone area code from Burlington to Durham. For the purposes of this analysis it does not include the Hamilton and Fort Erie areas. I am grateful to Loren Wells, assistant chief electoral officer (acting) for Ontario for her assistance. For a description of the Toronto bedroom suburbs included in 905, see Jonathon Gatehouse, "Long's instinct tells him to play to '905' voters," *National Post,* 27 April 2000, A6.

28 Quotations from two confidential interviews, Quebec City, 18 and
    19 January 1999. Citations from the Election Act, c. E-3.3, s 14
    (amended 1991) and Commission de la représentation électorale du
    Québec, "Opening Notes," Montreal, 2 and 3 December 1991, 1. The
    1998 provincial election saw the return of the PQ government with
    seventy-six seats and the Liberals to opposition with forty-eight even
    though the Liberals won a larger share of the popular vote than the PQ
    (43.55 percent to 42.87 percent). The Action démocratique du Québec
    won one seat and 11.81 percent of the popular vote. Those results also
    contributed to the recognized need among the parties for consultations
    on the voting system and electoral representation. Quebec's second sus-
    pension of the electoral boundaries readjustment process in the 1990s
    resulted from the National Assembly's unanimous approval of the appro-
    priate legislation in June 1999. The suspension was scheduled to end on
    1 July 2000.

29 I am indebted to Louis Massicotte for sharing these perceptions with
    me.

30 Robert Finbow, "Nova Scotia: Politics" in David Leyton-Brown, ed., Cana-
    dian Annual Review for 1991 (Toronto: University of Toronto Press,
    1998), 186; Landes and Smith interviews; and Nova Scotia Provincial
    Electoral Boundaries Commission, Effective Political Representation, 12.
    Jennifer Smith and Ron Landes note that the legislature's select commit-
    tee "grafted on" the Carter decision to the report it had largely finalized
    before the decision was released in early June 1991. They speculate that
    this was done in order to "avoid a constitutional challenge." Smith and
    Landes, "Entitlement versus Variance Models in the Determination of
    Canadian Electoral Boundaries," International Journal of Canadian Studies
    17 (Spring 1998), 34, n16.

31 The account by Smith and Landes (vice-chair and chair of the Nova
    Scotia commission respectively) is helpful in describing the entitlement
    system their commission designed for determining the allocation of
    seats among the province's counties, see ibid., 19–36.

32 The Nova Scotia legislature established no population variances in set-
    ting up the commission. For its part, the commission chose not to adopt
    a "rigid standard," but noted instead that in previous, non-independent
    commission redistributions, there had been an established practice of
    allowing up to a 33 percent variance inside existing counties. The
    1991–2 commission sought to aim for something approaching parity
    (+/–15 percent) for all but the protected constituencies. Smith and
    Landes, "Entitlement versus Variance Models," 20, and Nova Scotia Pro-
    vincial Electoral Boundaries Commission, Effective Political Representation,
    5, 18 and 40.

33 Aucoin, Landes, and Tidman interviews.

34 Government of Saskatchewan, Department of Justice, Press Release
No. 93–249, 14 May 1993. The NDP led by Roy Romanow defeated the
Conservative government of Grant Devine in 1991, winning a rare
majority of the popular vote and fifty-five seats. The Conservatives and
the Liberals won ten and one seats respectively.

35 In 1986 the 9.9 percent of the votes won by the Liberals translated into
one seat. For an account of the 1986 election, see Jim Miller,
"Saskatchewan," *Canadian Annual Review for* 1986 (Toronto: University of
Toronto Press, 1990), 322–6.

36 Justice Minister Bob Mitchell, second reading of the Constituency
Boundaries Act, 1993, in *Debates and Proceedings of the Saskatchewan Legislature 1993* (20 May 1993), 1851.

37 Saskatchewan, *Final Report of the Constituency Boundaries Commission* 1993
(Regina, 1993), 5.

38 Two seats were constructed in each of those cities to include parts of the
surrounding rural area and bedroom suburbs.

39 Dave Traynor, "Use federal seats to draw Saskatchewan electoral map:
PCs," *StarPhoenix* (Saskatoon), 20 May 1993, A8.

40 The 1999 share of votes for the NDP, Saskatchewan Party, and Liberals
respectively was: 38.7, 39.6, and 20.2 percent.

41 Duff Spafford, "'Effective Representation': Reference Re Provincial Electoral Boundaries," *Saskatchewan Law Review* 56 (1992), 205.

42 "Drawing Electoral Boundaries in Canada: Current Representation
Dilemmas," paper presented to the Geographic Information Systems and
Political Redistricting: Social Groups, Representational Values, and Elec-
toral Boundaries Conference, SUNY (Buffalo), 24–26 October 1997, 31.

43 Andrew Sancton, e-mail to the author, 13 April 2000.

44 Canada, House of Commons, Bill C-69, "An act to provide for the establishment of electoral boundaries commissions and the readjustment of
electoral boundaries," (1994–95) s. 19 (1).

45 Keith Archer, "Conflict and Confusion in Drawing Constituency Boundaries: The Case of Alberta," *Canadian Public Policy* 19 (June 1993), 178
and 179.

CHAPTER TEN

1 *Reference re Provincial Electoral Boundaries* [1991] 3 WWR 1.

2 *Reynolds* v. *Sims* [1964] 377 US 565–66.

3 According to Warren Baillie, chief electoral officer for Ontario and vice-
chairman of the province's redistribution commission in the 1980s, the
Ontario commission had decided at the outset of its deliberations that
effective representation would be its guide. The commission wanted to
work toward what he called "fair and effective representation." See

Baillie's remarks to the Conference of Canadian Election Officials, Ottawa, 25 June 1999.

4 Jennifer Smith and Ron Landes, "Entitlement versus Variance Models in the Determination of Canadian Electoral Boundaries," *International Journal of Canadian Studies* 17 (Spring 1998), 23.

5 W.L. Morton and Murray Donnelly brief entitled "Redistribution," 16 October 1954, PAM, "Special Select Committee on Redistribution, 1954–56," G246, 2–3.

6 In the 1983–4 redistribution in Newfoundland the legislation permitted departure from the rule of roughly equal population size districts on grounds of the "special community or diversity of interests of the inhabitants." This contrasted with a decade later when a cabinet order-in-council established a one-member commission without reference to community of interest. The Newfoundland terms and principles are set out in parts I–III of *The Report of the Electoral Boundaries Commission*, MC 95–0153, 26 April 1995.

7 Quebec, Election Act, RSQ, c. E-3.3, approved 22 March 1989 (updated 1 September 1997), c. 1 s. 15.

8 See, for example, Manitoba for "community or diversity of interests," *Report of the 1998 Electoral Divisions Boundaries Commission* (Winnipeg, 1998), 4; Saskatchewan, for "community of interests," *Constituency Boundaries Commission 1993 Final Report* (Regina, 1993), 4; and British Columbia for "community interests," *Electoral Boundaries Commission Report to the Legislative Assembly of British Columbia* (Victoria, December 1998), 144. For the federal reference, see Canada. Electoral Boundaries Readjustment Act, RS 1985, c. E-3, s. 15 (2) (a).

9 Robert Bork, *The Tempting of America: The Political Seduction of the Law* (New York: Free Press, 1990), 88–9.

10 Jane Jacobs is a leading exponent of the preservation and recognition of neighbourhood in large metropolitan areas. See, in particular, her *The Death and Life of Great American Cities* (New York: Random House, 1961).

11 House of Commons, Committee on Procedure and House Affairs, 6 July 1994, 20:33.

12 Alan Stewart, "Community of Interest in Redistricting" in Doug Small ed., *Drawing the Map: Equality and Efficacy in Canadian Electoral Boundary Reform*, vol. XI of the RCERFP research studies (Toronto: Dundurn Press, 1991), 151.

13 Ibid., 151–3.

14 See ibid., 147ff, for a brief discussion of the controversial subject of neighbourhood in urban studies.

15 I am grateful to Lisa Young of the University of Calgary for sharing these thoughts with me.

16 Stewart, "Community of Interest in Redistricting," 145–6. The difference between the two 1987 turnout figures is significant at $p < .05$.

17 The United States Supreme Court accepted that fact in a 1997 case. Signalling that highly arbitrary lines with little relationship to traditional political entities can contribute to a dilution in the concept of community of interest, the court upheld a Georgia redistricting plan favouring the use of counties in non-metropolitan areas. The plan was said to provide "ample building-blocks for acceptable voting districts." *Abrams* v. *Johnson*, 117 USSC 1997, 1940.

18 Stewart, "Community of Interest in Redistricting," 153–4. The link between an individual's identifying with a defined locality and the construction of larger electoral units has been challenged recently in Ontario. The massive rearrangement of municipal boundaries in that province in the 1990s, which has had the effect of creating fewer but larger municipalities, will force future Ontario boundaries commissions to split many more municipalities to create federal and provincial ridings than has been true in the past.

19 I am grateful to David Docherty of Wilfrid Laurier University for sharing this insight with me.

20 Cliche and Marshall interviews. A third commissioner, who had served on both the federal and provincial commissions in Nova Scotia in the 1990s, said that the concept of community of interest presents commissioners with a "carte blanche." They are free to do with it what they will – or can (Landes interview). Former Reform MP Stephen Harper agreed that many boundary commissions started carte blanche and that that is a "recipe for disaster, for it antagonizes the MPs" (Harper interview).

21 Cliche interview.

22 Arend, Landes, and McKenzie interviews, and author's notes from 1985–6 Saskatchewan federal redistribution hearings.

23 Federal Electoral Boundaries Commission for the Province of Newfoundland, "Disposition of Objections," 8 December 1995, 3 (emphasis in original).

24 Canada, *Report of the Electoral Boundaries Commission for the Province of Ontario* (Ottawa, 1983), 8.

25 Stewart, "Community of Interest in Redistricting," 141.

26 RCERFP, *Reforming Electoral Democracy: Final Report* (Ottawa: Minister of Supply and Services Canada, 1991), 1: 150 and 157–58.

27 Richard W. Jenkins, "Untangling the Politics of Electoral Boundaries in Canada, 1993–97," *American Review of Canadian Studies* 28 (Winter 1998), 525.

28 Harper interview. On the party's policy orientations at the time, see Richard Sigurdson, "Preston Manning and the Politics of Postmodernism

in Canada," *Canadian Journal of Political Science* 28 (June 1994), 249–76, and Keith Archer and Feron Ellis, "Opinion Structure of Party Activists: The Reform Party of Canada," *Canadian Journal of Political Science* 28 (June 1994), 277–308.

29 House of Commons, Committee on Procedure and House Affairs, 22 November 1994, 32: 23–5. Citing Kent Roach and Kathy Swinton, Jenkins postulates that at some future date a court may well rule, given the majority opinion in *Carter*, that sociological considerations fall under the protection of section 15 of the charter. See "Untangling the Politics of Electoral Boundaries," 526.

30 Jenkins, "Untangling the Politics of Electoral Boundaries," 526.

31 Ibid., 525.

32 Committee for Aboriginal Electoral Reform, *The Pathway to Electoral Equality* (Ottawa: Committee for Aboriginal Electoral Reform, 1991), 9. The definition of Aboriginal follows that of the Lortie Commission, Statistics Canada, and other federal agencies. It is "the aggregate of the following: registered Indians, Inuit and Métis plus non-registered Indians and Canadians of multiple ethnic origins who also list themselves as North American Indian, Inuit or Métis."

33 RCERPF, *Reforming Electoral Democracy*, I: 169. The data and sources on the Aboriginal population estimates are given at 192, n2.

34 Library of Parliament Research Branch, data supplied to the author on 1 April 1999. The failure of Aboriginals to be elected to Parliament is explained in some measure by the fact that Indians were prohibited from voting, and therefore from standing for election to Parliament, from Confederation to 1960. The provinces and territories gradually legislated the same prohibition. The Inuit were denied the federal franchise between 1934 and 1950. All provinces and territories have now granted Indians the franchise, starting with Manitoba in 1952 and ending with Quebec in 1969. See Committee for Aboriginal Electoral Reform, *The Pathway to Electoral Equality*, appendix 3, 65–6.

35 Ibid., 14.

36 RCERPF, *Reforming Electoral Democracy*, I: 171.

37 Ibid., 178. AEDs have been considered, but never adopted, by at least two provinces. See Nova Scotia, Provincial Electoral Boundaries Commission, *Effective Political Representation in Nova Scotia* (Halifax, 1992), esp. appendices C, D, and E; New Brunswick, Representation and Electoral District Boundaries Commission, *Towards a New Electoral Map for New Brunswick: First Report* (Fredericton, 1992), and *Final Report* (Fredericton, 1993): and Graeme Hamilton, "N.B. chiefs like premier's offer of seats for Aboriginals," *National Post*, 3 February 1999, A3.

38 RCERPF, *Reforming Electoral Democracy*, 179, 181–2.

39 New Zealand has since moved to a mixed-member proportional system in which voters have two votes: a 'party vote' and an 'electorate (or single-member district) vote.' Five of the sixty-five electorate members are chosen by Maori voters from single-member Maori electoral districts. The remaining fifty-five members of the 120-seat House of Representatives are elected from nation-wide lists according to each party's share of the all-party votes.

40 Ibid., 185–93.

41 Roger Gibbins, "Electoral Reform and Canada's Aboriginal Population: An Assessment of Aboriginal Electoral Districts" in Robert A. Milen, ed., *Aboriginal Peoples and Electoral Reform in Canada* vol. IX of the RCERPF research studies (Toronto: Dundurn, 1991), 168, 174, 179, 181–2, and 183.

42 Lortie clearly felt compelled to counter Gibbins's arguments. Although never naming him as the target, the commission addressed each of the issues he had raised. See RCERPF, *Reforming Electoral Democracy*, I: 182–5.

43 Committee for Aboriginal Electoral Reform, *The Pathway to Electoral Equality*, 9.

44 RCERPF, *Reforming Electoral Democracy*, I: 173.

45 Tim Schouls, "Aboriginal Peoples and Electoral Reform in Canada: Differentiated Representation versus Voter Equality," *Canadian Journal of Political Science* 29 (December 1996), 743–4.

46 Population data from Canada, Royal Commission on Aboriginal Peoples (hereafter RCAP), *Perspectives and Realities* (Ottawa: Minister of Supply and Services Canada, 1996), IV: Table 7.7, 607, and Federation of Saskatchewan Indian Nations, *Saskatchewan and Aboriginal Peoples in the 21st Century: Social, Economic and Political Changes and Challenges* (Regina: PrintWest Publishing, 1997), Table 2.2, 12.

47 David Smith, *The Republican Option in Canada, Past and Present* (Toronto: University of Toronto Press, 1999), 117.

48 RCAP, *Restructuring the Relationship*, II, part 1: 377.

49 Meekison interview, and Meekison, "Aboriginal Representation," Canadian Study of Parliament Group, Rethinking Representation Conference, Victoria, 25 April 1998, 3.

50 RCAP, *Restructuring the Relationship*, II: part 1: 379, 382.

51 *Carter*, SCC, 12–13.

52 Lisa Young, "Gender Equal Legislatures: Evaluating the Proposed Nunavut Electoral System," *Canadian Public Policy* 23 (September 1997), 313 (emphasis in original). The proposal was not original to Nunavut. George Bernard Shaw was known to have advanced such an idea, and in a 1992 resolution to the Newfoundland Assembly (which was not adopted), Jack Harris, an NDP member of Newfoundland's House of

Assembly, called for gender-equal two-member seats for his province (Harris interview); see also Rudy Plaitel, "Inuit endorses gender-equal legislature," *Globe and Mail,* 27 January 1997, A6. In her *Canadian Public Policy* article, Young makes it clear that in contexts outside Canada's north there are other institutional reforms (notably some version of proportional representation) that would be almost as effective and subject to considerably less controversy than dual-member ridings for increasing female representation.

53 The defeat of the gender-equal proposal in Nunavut (by a vote of 57 percent to 43 percent) signalled several hurdles that such a proposal would have to overcome before it would be found acceptable to a large and diverse electorate. Those who campaigned against the Nunavut plan argued that it offended the democratic rights of citizens to have the freedom to vote for whomever they wished regardless of gender, and that it amounted to a put-down of women who wanted to make it into politics in their own right. Still others saw it in a similar light to the Charlottetown Accord: it suffered the same fate because it amounted to an attempt by an out-of-touch political elite to tell voters what was good for them. See Brian Laghi, "Eastern Arctic residents reject gender-equal plan," *Globe and Mail,* 27 May 1997, A2, and "Chance for place in parliamentary history shunned," ibid., 28 May 1997, A4. On two-member ridings in Prince Edward Island, see Frank MacKinnon, *The Government of Prince Edward Island* (Toronto: University of Toronto Press, 1951), 215ff. On Canada's dual-member seats, see Norman Ward, "Voting in Canadian Two-Member Constituencies" in John C. Courtney, ed., *Voting in Canada* (Toronto: Prentice-Hall, 1967), 125–9, and Morris Davis, "Ballot Behaviour in Halifax Revisited," in ibid., 130–42.

54 Two research studies carried out for the Lortie Commission examined issues of ethnicity and minority representation within the framework of existing political institutions. See Alain Pelletier, "Politics and Ethnicity: Representation of Ethnic and Visible-Minority groups in the House of Commons" in Kathy Megyery, ed., *Ethno-Cultural Groups and Visible Minorities in Canadian Politics: The Question of Access,* vol. VII of the RCERFP research studies (Toronto: Dundurn Press, 1991), chap. 2, and Daiva K. Stasiulis and Yasmeen Abu-Laban, "The House the Parties Built: (Re)constructing Ethnic Representation in Canadian Politics" in ibid., chap 1.

55 Bridglal Pachai, *Blacks* (Halifax: Nimbus, 1997), 8.

56 The first recorded mention of a Black in Nova Scotia was in 1604. See Jean Daigle, ed., *Acadia of the Maritimes* (Moncton; Chair d'études acadiennes, 1995), 2.

57 N.E.S. Griffiths, "Acadia," *The Canadian Encyclopedia,* 1st ed. (Edmonton; Hurtig, 1995), 1: 5 (emphasis added).

58 A fuller account is given in Pachai, *Blacks*, chap. 3. See also Robin W. Winks, *The Blacks in Canada: A History*, 2nd ed. (Montreal: McGill-Queen's University Press, 1997), esp. 452–6.

59 Atwell and Landes interviews, and Nova Scotia, Provincial Electoral Boundaries Commission, *Effective Political Representation in Nova Scotia: The 1992 Report of the Provincial Electoral Boundaries Commission* (Halifax: March 1992), 13.

60 Ontario federal commissioners of the 1990s were, nonetheless, mindful of the linguistic mix of constituency lines in areas with heavy francophone populations. The central parts of the city of Ottawa had lost population to the suburbs in the 1981–91 period. The possibly negative effect that this might have had on the traditional francophone representation from that area led the commissioners to add on to Ottawa-Vanier a francophone portion of the city of Gloucester (Sancton interview). All data in this section are from the 1996 census and are profiled by province and federal electoral districts. The source is Statistics Canada, 1996 Census of Population, Profile of Federal Electoral Districts (1996 Representation Order), Canada, Provinces and Territories and 1996 Census of Population, The Nation.

61 Profound differences among immigrant and non-immigrant populations can on occasion take place within the same local political setting, as in New York where 600,000 immigrant West Indians have challenged the traditional hegemony of the older American Black community in the city's Democratic party. See James Dao, "Immigrant diversity slows traditional political climb," *New York Times*, 28 December 1999, 1ff.

62 Sociologist Edward Harvey has studied ethnic communities in the Greater Toronto Area. Based on comparative census data, he has calculated that eight to eleven years are needed before immigrants have reached the national employment and income averages in Canada. Accordingly, "these immigrants and their families are too busy getting established and putting a roof over their heads to get involved in politics." See Colin McConnell, "Slowly, the face of politics changes," *Toronto Star*, 17 May 1999, 1ff.

63 A Goldfarb poll commissioned for the *Toronto Star* at the time of the 1999 Ontario provincial election found that 39 percent of respondents from ethnic communities, compared with 78 percent of all Torontonians, believed they "had an equal chance of being elected to political office." A similar question asked of Haligonians and of Halifax's Black community prior to the establishment of the Preston seat would almost certainly have found a smaller percentage of Blacks believing in their "equality of chance." The Ontario study is cited in McConnell, "Slowly, the face of politics changes," 1ff.

64 One Italian-born Toronto Liberal MP, Charles Caccia, who has a proven history of often being at odds with the government, was not taken on the trip.

65 The same tendency to socialize immigrants and visible minorities into established parties has been true, although it came somewhat later in Quebec and British Columbia, the other larger provinces, than in Ontario. An account of the new-found power of political organizers in Canada's principal urban ethnic communities is found in Edward Greenspon, "The kingmakers," *Globe and Mail*, 20 March 1999, D1ff.

66 In spite of its careful construction, the Preston seat is by no means a sure thing for a Black candidate. It is estimated that two-thirds of its population is white and one-third Black. Black candidates won in 1993 and 1998 when, respectively, Wayne Adams of the Liberals was victorious (and became the first Black to be named to the provincial cabinet) and Yvonne Atwell of the NDP won. Atwell was defeated in the provincial election the following year by a white candidate. A white had placed second in 1993 and third in 1998.

67 Court of Queen's Bench (Trial Division) Edmunston, "Notice of Action with Statement of Claim Attached," court file No. 1, 8 August 1997.

68 Bilodeau, Horsman, Ouellette, and Turnbull interviews. See also New Brunswick, *A New Electoral Map for New Brunswick* (Fredericton, 1993), 9. The commission interpreted this instruction as requiring it to, among other things, be mindful of the "linguistic and cultural realities" of the electoral districts.

69 Office of the Commissioner of Official Languages, *Investigation Report of Complaints Concerning the Redistribution of Federal Ridings Proposed by the Federal Electoral Boundaries Commission for the Province of New Brunswick* (Ottawa, July 1996), 1 and 6–7.

70 Ibid., 7–8.

71 Elections Canada, *Report of the Chief Electoral Officer on the 36th General Election* (Ottawa, 1997), 79; Bilodeau, Horsman, and Ouellette interviews.

72 The range of who might be entitled to some measure of group representation is, arguably, as vast as the topic. Two authorities on the subject would include those who in the past have experienced systematic forms of discrimination, are currently systematically disadvantaged, and those with legitimate claims on self-government. See Will Kymlicka, *Multicultural Citizenship: A Liberal Theory of Minority Rights* (Oxford; Clarendon Press, 1995), 138–51, and Williams, *Voice, Trust and Memory*, chap 6.

73 The Reform MPs minority report is found in Appendix A, *House of Commons Committee on Procedure and House Affairs*, Report of 25 November 1994, issue 33.

CHAPTER ELEVEN

1 The best account of the origins and early practices of Canada's "federalized" cabinets remains N. McL. Rogers, "Federal Influences on the Canadian Cabinet," *Canadian Bar Review* 11 (February 1933), 103–21.
2 The failure of the electoral system to become a central focus of Canada's representational debate is not because it lacks for critics. A subject of controversy over the years because of its proven capacity to translate votes into seats in a disproportionate manner, Canada's plurality vote system, apart from three short-lived provincial experiments with alternative voting and single transferable voting, has not been changed since Confederation. Why the electoral system has not been replaced by another method of election, even though many have argued that it should be, and why electoral building blocks must meet certain conditions before they can be changed, is a subject I address in "Reforming Representational Building-Blocks: Canada at the Beginning of the 21st Century" in Bill Cross, ed., *Canadian Democracy at Century's End* (Toronto: Oxford University Press, forthcoming).
3 "Transactional representation" holds that citizens are represented through the act of electoral participation regardless of the personal characteristics of the individuals chosen. See A.H. Birch, *Representative and Responsible Government: An Essay on the British Constitution* (Toronto: University of Toronto Press, 1964), 16, and Hanna Fenichel Pitkin, *The Concept of Representation* (Berkeley: University of California Press, 1967), chap. 4.
4 The Liberals' adherence to the alternation principle in selecting leaders is discussed in my *Do Conventions Matter? Choosing National Party Leaders in Canada* (Montreal: McGill-Queen's University Press, 1995), esp. 166–9.
5 On the earlier period of redistributions in Canada, see Norman Ward, *The Canadian House of Commons: Representation,* 2nd ed. (Toronto: University of Toronto Press, 1963), especially chap. 2 and Part II; "The Redistribution of 1952," *Canadian Journal of Economics and Political Science* 19 (August 1953), 341–60; and "A Century of Constituencies," CPA 10 (Spring 1967), 105.
6 John Kingdon, *Agendas, Alternatives and Public Policies,* 2nd ed. (New York: HarperCollins, 1995), chaps. 7–9.
7 Carty, "The Electoral Boundary Revolution in Canada," *American Review of Canadian Studies* 15 (Autumn 1985), 273–87.
8 Canada, Royal Commission on Electoral Reform and Party Financing, *Reforming Electoral Democracy: Final Report* (Ottawa: Minister of Supply and Services Canada, 1991), I: 153.
9 See Alan Cairns, *Reconfigurations: Canadian Citizenship and Constitutional Change* in Douglas E. Williams, ed., (Toronto: McClelland and Stewart,

1995), esp. chaps. 4 and 6; Will Kymlicka, *Multicultural Citizenship* (New York: Oxford University Press, 1995), esp. chap. 7; Charles Taylor, "The Politics of Recognition" in Amy Gutmann, ed., *Multiculturalism* (Princeton: Princeton University Press, 1994), 25–73; and Melissa S. Williams, *Voice, Trust and Memory: Marginalized Groups and the Failings of Liberal Representation* (Princeton: Princeton University Press, 1998), esp. chaps. 4 and 7. Non-Canadians who contributed to the burgeoning literature included Anne Phillips, *Democracy and Difference* (University Park: Pennsylvania State University Press, 1993), and Iris Young, *Justice and the Politics of Difference* (Princeton: Princeton University Press, 1990).

10 Alan Cairns, "Constitutional Minoritarianism" in Ronald Watts and Douglas Brown, eds., *Canada: The State of the Federation, 1990* (Kingston: Institute of Intergovernmental Affairs, 1990), 84 (emphasis added).

11 Will Kymlicka, "Group Representation in Canadian Politics" in F. Leslie Seidle, ed., *Equity and Community: The Charter, Interest Advocacy and Representation* (Montreal: Institute for Research on Public Policy, 1993), 82 and 83 (emphasis added).

12 Richard Sigurdson, "First Peoples, New Peoples and Citizenship in Canada," *International Journal of Canadian Studies* 14 (Fall 1996), 53. Sigurdson acknowledges his debt to Ronald Beiner whose discussion of the problems of citizenship appears as the introduction in Beiner, ed., *Theorizing Citizenship* (Albany: SUNY Press, 1995), 1–28.

13 I am grateful to Lisa Young of the University of Calgary for sharing these thoughts with me.

14 RCERPF, *Reforming Electoral Democracy* (Ottawa, 1991), I: 131.

15 House of Commons Committee on Procedure and House Affairs, *Report*, 25 November 1994, 33:8.

16 The extrapolation to 2031 is based on 1999 estimates of projected population from Statistics Canada, *Population Projections for Canada, Provinces and Territories, 1999–2026* (Cat. No. 91–520). (Projection 2 data, based on medium growth projections, have been used.)

17 RCERPF, *Reforming Electoral Democracy*, 131.

Bibliography

ABBREVIATIONS

ARCS *American Review of Canadian Studies*
CJPS *Canadian Journal of Political Science*
CJEPS *Canadian Journal of Economics and Political Science*
CPA *Canadian Public Administration*
CPP *Canadian Public Policy*
CPR *Canadian Parliamentary Review*
DLJ *Dalhousie Law Journal*
DLR *Dominion Law Review*
ES *Electoral Studies*
IJCS *International Journal of Canadian Studies*
LSQ *Legislative Studies Quarterly*
MLJ *McGill Law Journal*
Nfld. and PEIR *Newfoundland and Prince Edward Island Review*
NJCL *National Journal of Constitutional Law*
PO *Policy Options*
QQ *Queen's Quarterly*
RCS *Review of Constitutional Studies*
SLR *Saskatchewan Law Review*

1. Redistribution in Canada

Archer, Keith. "Conflict and Confusion in Drawing Constituency Boundaries: The Case of Alberta," CPP 19 (June 1993), 177–93.

Bailie, Warren R. and David Johnson. "Drawing the Electoral Line," *PO* 13 (November 1992), 21–5.

Balinski, M.L. and H.P. Young. "Parliamentary Representation and the Amalgam Method," *CJPS* 14 (December 1981), 797–812.

– "Fair Electoral Distribution," *PO* 4 (July/August 1983), 30–2.

Bercuson, David and Barry Cooper. "An Obstacle to Democracy in Alberta" in *Drawing Boundaries: Legislatures, Courts, and Electoral Values.* Edited by John C. Courtney, Peter MacKinnon, and David E. Smith. Saskatoon: Fifth House, 1992, 110–27.

Cameron, James M. and Glen Norcliffe. "The Canadian Constitution and the Political Muskeg of One Person-One Vote," *The Operational Geographer* 8 (1985), 30–4.

Carty, R.K. "The Electoral Boundary Revolution in Canada," *ARCS* 15 (3) (Autumn 1985), 273–87.

Coulson, Michael. "Reforming Electoral Distribution," *PO* 9 (January/February 1983), 25–9.

Courtney, John C. "The Size of Canada's Parliament: An Assessment of the Implications of a Larger House of Commons" in *Institutional Reforms for Representative Government.* Edited by Peter Aucoin. vol. 38 of the Research Studies for the Royal Commission on the Economic Union and Development Prospects for Canada. Toronto: Toronto University Press, 1985, 1–39.

– "'Theories Masquerading as Principles': Canadian Electoral Boundary Commissions and the Australian Model" in *The Canadian House of Commons: Essays in Honour of Norman Ward.* Edited by John C. Courtney. Calgary: University of Calgary Press, 1985, 135–72.

– "Some Thoughts on Redistribution," *CPR* 9 (Spring 1986), 18–20.

– "Parliament and Representation: The Unfinished Agenda of Electoral Redistributions," *CJPS* 21 (December 1988), 675–90.

– "Electoral Boundary Redistributions: Contrasting Approaches to Parliamentary Representation" in *Comparative Political Studies: Australia and Canada.* Edited by Malcolm Alexander and Brian Galligan. Melbourne: Longman Cheshire, 1992, 45–58.

– "Drawing Electoral Boundaries" in *Canadian Parties in Transition,* 2nd ed. Edited by Alain Gagnon and Brian Tanguay. Toronto: Nelson Canada, 1995, 328–48.

– "Discrimination in Canada's Electoral Law" in *Discrimination in the Law in the Administration of Justice.* Edited by Walter Tarnopolsky, Joyce Whitman, and Monique Ouellette. Toronto: Carswell, 1993, 401–10.

– "Reapportionment and Redistricting" in *International Encyclopaedia of Elections.* Edited by Richard Rose. Washington: Congressional Quarterly Books, 2000, 258-62.

- Peter MacKinnon, and David E. Smith, eds., *Drawing Boundaries: Legislatures, Courts, and Electoral Values*. Saskatoon: Fifth House, 1993 (hereafter cited as *Drawing Boundaries*).

Eagles, Munroe. "Enhancing Relative Vote Equality in Canada: The Role of Electors in Boundary Adjustment" in *Drawing the Map: Equality and Efficacy of the Vote in Canadian Electoral Boundary Reform*. Vol. 11 of the Research Studies for the Royal Commission on Electoral Reform and Party Financing. Edited by David Small. Toronto: Dundurn Press, 1991, 175–220 (hereafter cited as *Drawing the Map*).

- "The Political Ecology of Representation in English Canada: MPs and Their Constituencies," *ARCS* 28 (Spring/Summer 1998), 53–79.

- and R. Kenneth Carty. "MPs and Electoral Redistribution Controversies in Canada, 1993–96," *Journal of Legislative Studies* 5 (Summer 1999), 74–95.

Flaherty, Mark S. and William W. Crumplin. "Compactness and Electoral Boundary Adjustment: An Assessment of Alternative Measures," *The Canadian Geographer* 36 (November 2, 1992), 159.

Garner, John. *The Franchise and Politics in British North America, 1755–1867*. Toronto: University of Toronto Press, 1969.

Grofman, B. "What Happens After One Person-One Vote? Implications of the United States Experience for Canada" in *Drawing Boundaries*, 156–78.

Hyson, Stewart R.V. "New Brunswick's Electoral Redistribution of 1990–94: A Structural Approach to Redistribution Policy." Ph.D thesis, Department of Political Science, Carleton University, 1999.

- "The Electoral Boundary Revolution in the Maritime Provinces," *ARCS* 25 (Summer /Autumn, 1995), 285–99.

Jenkins, Richard W. "Untangling the Politics of Electoral Boundaries in Canada, 1993–1997," *ARCS* 28 (Winter 1998), 517–38.

Johnston, J. Paul and Harvey E. Pasis, ed., *Representation and Electoral Systems: Canadian Perspectives*. Scarborough, Ontario: Prentice-Hall, 1990.

Hearn, Peter J.T. "From Representation by Population to the Pursuit of Elegance," *DLJ* 7 (October 1983), 762–89.

Knopff, R., and F.L. Morton. "Charter Politics in Alberta: Constituency Apportionment and the Right to Vote" in *Drawing Boundaries*, 96–109.

Lyons, William E. "Legislative Redistricting by Independent Commissions: Operationalizing the One Man-One Vote Doctrine in Canada," *Polity* 1 (Summer 1969), 428–59.

- *One Man–One Vote*. Toronto: McGraw-Hill, 1970.

Macdonald, Douglas. "Ecological Communities and Constituency Districting" in *Drawing the Map*, 221–51.

Mallory, J.R. "Amending the Constitution by Stealth," *QQ* 82 (Autumn 1975), 394–401.

Pasis, H.E. "The Inequality of Distribution in the Canadian Provincial Assemblies," *CJPS* 5 (September 1972), 433–6.

– "Achieving Population Equality Among the Constituencies of the Canadian House, 1903–1976," *LSQ* 8 (February 1983), 111–15.

– "Electoral Distribution in the Canadian Provincial Legislatures" in *Representation and Electoral Systems: Canadian Perspectives.* Edited by J. Paul Johnston and Harvey E. Pasis. Toronto: Prentice-Hall Canada, 1990, 251–3.

Qualter, Terence H. *The Electoral Process in Canada.* Toronto: McGraw-Hill, 1970.

Richards, R., and T. Irvine. "Drawing Boundaries: The Saskatchewan Case" in *Drawing Boundaries,* 48–69.

Roach, K. "One Person, One Vote? Canadian Constitutional Standards for Electoral Distribution and Districting" in *Drawing the Map,* 3–93.

Ruff, Norman J. "The Cat and Mouse Politics of Redistribution: Fair and Effective Representation in British Columbia," *BC Studies* 87 (Autumn 1990), 48–84.

– "The Right to Vote and Inequality of Voting Power in British Columbia: The Jurisprudence and Politics of the Dixon Case" in *Drawing Boundaries,* 128–47.

Ruff, Norman J. and William M. Moss. "Towards a More Equitable Distribution of Seats in British Columbia," *CPR* 12 (Spring 1989), 21–3.

Sancton, Andrew. "Eroding Representation by Population in the Canadian House of Commons: The Representation Act, 1985," *CJPS* 23 (September 1990), 441–57.

– "The Application of the 'Senatorial Floor' Rules to the Latest Redistribution of the House of Commons: The Peculiar Case of Nova Scotia," *CJPS* 6 (March 1973), 56–64.

Small, David ed. *Drawing the Map: Equality and Efficacy of the Vote in Canadian Electoral Boundary Reform.* Vol. 11 of the Research Studies for the Royal Commission on Electoral Reform and Party Financing, Toronto: Dundurn Press, 1991, 175–220.

Smith, Jennifer. "The Franchise and Theories of Representative Government" in *Democratic Rights and Electoral Reform in Canada.* Volume 10 of Research Studies for the Royal Commission on Electoral Reform and Party Financing. Edited by Michael Cassidy. Toronto: Dundurn Press, 1991.

– and Ronald G. Landes. "Entitlement versus Variance Models in the Determination of Canadian Electoral Boundaries," *IJCS* 17 (Spring 1998), 19–36.

Stewart, Alan. "Community of Interest in Redistricting," *Drawing the Map,* 117–75.

Ward, Norman. "Parliamentary Representation in Canada," *CJEPS* 13 (August 1947), 447–64.

– "The Basis of Representation in the House of Commons," *CJEPS* 15 (November 1949), 447–94.

– "The Redistribution of 1952," *CJEPS* 19 (1953), 341–60.

- *The Canadian House of Commons: Representation,* 2nd ed. Toronto: University of Toronto Press, 1963.
- "A Century of Constituencies," CPA 10 (March 1967), 105–21.
- "The Redistribution of 1952," CJEPS 19 (August 1953), 341–360. Reprinted in *Politics: Canada,* edited by Paul Fox. Toronto: McGraw-Hill, 1962, 250–64.
- "A Century of Constituencies," CPA 10 (Spring 1967), 105–23.

White, Graham. "'Christian Humility and Partisan Ingenuity': Sir Oliver Mowat's Redistribution 1874," *Ontario History* 73 (December 1981), 219–38.

Winearls, John. "Federal Electoral Maps of Canada 1867–1970," *Canadian Cartographer* 9 (June 1972), 1–24.

2. Court Cases and Legal Commentaries

Charlottetown (City) et al. v. *Prince Edward Island et al.* (1996), 150 Nfld. & PEIR 91; 470 APR 91.

City of Charlottetown v. *The Government of Prince Edward Island* (1998), 169 Nfld. & PEIR 188.

Dixon v. *British Columbia (A.G.)* (1986), 31 DLR (4th) 546.

Dixon v. *British Columbia (A.G.)* (1989), 59 DLR (4th) 247.

Friends of Democracy v. *Northwest Territories (A.G.)* (1999) 171 DLR (4th) 551.

MacKinnon v. *Prince Edward Island* (1993), 101 DLR (4th) 362.

Reference re: Electoral Boundaries Commission Act (Alberta) (1991), 78 DLR (4th) 447.

Reference re: Electoral Boundaries Commission Act (1991), 86. DLR (4th) 447 (Alta CA).

Reference re: Electoral Divisions Statutes Amendment Act, 1993 (Alta.). (1994), 119 DLR (4th) 1.

Reference re Provincial Electoral Boundaries [1991] 2 SCR 158, *(sub nom. Reference re: Electoral Boundaries Commission Act, ss. 14, 20 (Sask.))* 81 DLR 16 (commonly referred to as the *Carter* decision of the Supreme Court).

Reference re Electoral Boundaries Commission Act. [1991] 86 DLR (4th) 447.

Charney, Robert E. "*Saskatchewan Election Boundary Reference:* 'One Person – Half a Vote,'" NJCL 1 (1992), 224–34.

Fritz, Ronald E. "The Saskatchewan Electoral Boundaries Case and its Implications" in *Drawing Boundaries,* 70–89.
- "Effective Representation Denied: *MacKinnon* v. *Prince Edward Island,*" NJCL 4 (1994), 207–22.
- "Challenging Electoral Boundaries under the Charter: Judicial Defence and Burden of Proof," RCS (1999), 1–33.
- "Drawing Electoral Boundaries in Compliance with the *Charter:* The Alberta Experience," NJCL 6 (1996), 347–82.

Johnson, David. "Canadian Electoral Boundaries and the Courts: Practices, Principles and Problems," 39 MLJ (March 1994), 224–48.

Knopff, Rainer and F.L. Morton. "Charter Politics in Alberta: Constituency Apportionment and the Right to Vote" in *Drawing Boundaries,* 96–109.

Morton, F.L. and Rainer Knopff. "Does the Charter Mandate 'One Person, One Vote'?" *Alberta Law Review* 30 (1992), 669–94.

Pasis, Harvey. "The Courts and Redistribution in Canada," *CPR* 10 (Autumn 1987), 8.

Richards, Robert G. and Thomson Irvine. "Reference RE Provincial Electoral Boundaries: An Analysis" in *Drawing Boundaries*, 48–69.

Roach, Kent. "Reapportionment in British Columbia," *UBC Law Review* 24 (1990), 79–102.

Spafford, Duff. "'Effective Representation': Reference Re Provincial Boundaries," *SLR* 56 (1992), 197–208.

Stewart, Alan. "Comment on *Dixon v. Attorney General of British Columbia*," *Canadian Bar Review* 69 (1990), 355–64.

Tupper, Allan. "Democracy and Representation: A Critique of Morton and Knopff," *Alberta Law Review* 30 (1992), 695–707.

3. Aboriginal Representation and Electoral Districts

Committee for Aboriginal for Electoral Reform. *The Path to Electoral Equality*. Ottawa, 1991.

Fleras, Augie. "Aboriginal Electoral Districts for Canada: Lessons From New Zealand" in *Aboriginal Peoples and Electoral Reform in Canada*. Volume 9 of the Research Studies for Royal Commission on Electoral Reform and Party Financing. Edited by Robert A. Milen. Toronto: Dundurn Press, 1991, 67–105.

Gibbins, Roger. "Electoral Reform and Canada's Aboriginal Population: An Assessment of Aboriginal Electoral Districts" in *Aboriginal Peoples and Electoral Reform*, 153–84.

Malloy, Jonathan and Graham White. "Aboriginal Participation in Canadian Legislatures" in *Fleming's Canadian Legislatures*, 1997. Edited by Robert J. Fleming and J.E. Glenn. Toronto: University of Toronto Press, 1997, 60–73.

Milen, Robert A., ed. *Aboriginal Peoples and Electoral Reform in Canada*. Volume 9 of the Research Studies for Royal Commission on Electoral Reform and Party Financing. Edited by Robert A. Milen. Toronto: Dundurn Press, 1991

Schouls, Tim. "Aboriginal Peoples and Electoral Reform in Canada: Differentiated Representation versus Voter Equality," *CJPS* 29 (December 1996), 729–49.

Small, Doug. "Enhancing Aboriginal Representation with the Existing System of Redistricting" in *Drawing the Map*. 307–48.

4. Selected Comparative Studies

Barnes, G.P. "The General Review of Parliamentary Constituencies in England (1976–83)," *ES* 4 (August 1985), 179–81.

- "The Use of Computers in Redistributing Constituencies," *ES* 6 (August 1987), 133–8.
Butler, David and Bruce Cain. *Congressional Redistricting – Comparative and Theoretical Perspectives.* New York: Macmillan, 1992.
- "Reapportionment: A Study in Comparative Government," *ES* 4 (December 1985), 197–214.
Cain, Bruce. *The Reapportionment Puzzle.* Berkeley: University of California Press, 1984.
Dixon, Robert. *Democratic Representation: Reapportionment in Law and Politics.* New York: Oxford University Press, 1968.
Hughes, Colin. "The Case of the Arrested Pendulum" in *Australian National Elections of* 1977. Edited by Howard Penniman. Washington D.C.: American Enterprise Institute, 1977.
Grofman, Bernard, Arend Lijphart, Robert McKay, and Howard Scarrow, eds. *Representation and Redistricting Issues.* Lexington, Massachusetts: Lexington Books, 1982.
Henry, Carlton. "The Impact of New Technology and New Census Data on Redistricting in the 1990s" in *Redistricting in the* 1990s: *A Guide for Minority Groups.* Edited by William O'Hare. Washington D.C.: Population Reference Bureau, 1989.
Johnston, R.J. "Constituency Redistricting in Britain: Recent Issues," in *Electoral Laws and Their Political Consequences.* Edited by Bernard Grofman and Arend Lijphart. New York: Agathon Press, 1986.
- *Political, Electoral and Spatial Systems.* London: Oxford University Press, 1979.
- "Redistricting by Independent Commissions: A Perspective from Britain," *Annals of the Association of American Geographers* 72 (December 1982), 457–70.
Lublin, David. *The Paradox of Representation: Radical Gerrymandering and Minority Interests in Congress.* Princeton: Princeton University Press, 1996.
Mair, Peter. "Districting Choices under the Single-Transferable Vote" in *Electoral Laws and their Political Consequences.* Edited by Bernard Grofman and Arend Lijphart. New York: Agathon Press, 1986.
McLean, Iain and David Butler. *Fixing the Boundaries: Defining and Redefining Single-Member Electoral Districts,* Aldershot: Dartmouth, 1996.
McLean, Iain and Roger Mortimore. "Apportionment and the Boundary Commission for England," *ES* 11 (December 1992), 293–309.
Morrill, Richard. *Political Redistricting and Geographic Theory.* Washington, DC: Association of American Geographers, Resource Publication in Geography, 1981.
Rossiter, D.J., R.J. Johnston, and C.J. Pattie, *The Boundary Commissions: Redrawing the UK's Map of Parliamentary Constituencies.* Manchester: Manchester University Press, 1999.

Rush, Mark E., ed. *Voting Righst and Redistricting in the United States*, Westport, Connecticut: Greenwood Press, 1998.

Taylor, Peter J. and R.J. Johnson. *Geography of Elections*. New York: Holmes and Meier Publishers, 1979.

Index

Aboriginal peoples: and Charlottetown Accord 222; and community of interest 217, 220, 221; and Lortie Commission 204, 217, 218–19, 220, 221, 222, 233; and Marchand committee 168, 217, 218, 220, 225, 233; representation on and by boundary commissions 101, 102, 292n14; representational concerns of 168–9; and Royal Commission on Aboriginal Peoples 222–3; under-representation of 217, 310n34. *See also* Aboriginal electoral districts; individual provinces/territories

Aboriginal electoral districts (AEDs) 168–9, 204, 217–23, 233, 246

Acadians
– in New Brunswick 230–2
– in Nova Scotia 102, 185, 225–6; and application of effective representation principle 170, 175, 183, 190, 205, 226; and election of Acadian MLAS 191

Add-on constituencies. *See* redistribution formulas

Alberta
– allotment of federal seats in 25, 26, 27, 32, 251; projected 249, 251, 253, 254
– Electoral Boundaries Commission Act (1990) 115, 160–1, 166, 294n37

– electoral boundaries readjustment process in: basis of quotient, 107, 109; composition of commissions 83, 96, 107, 109, 111–12; constituency population size 32, 176, 238, 240, 252; constituency population variances 107, 109, 178, 181, 197, 252; cost of 87; court challenges to 160–2; and digital mapping 84; federal commissions' readjustments 176; frequency of 107, 109; Gini indexes 174, 179, 195, 196, 239, 240; institutionalization of 117, 161, 247; legislation for 107, 109, 166; model for 83, 109; provincial commissions' readjustments 111–12, 194, 195, 199–200; public participation and impact of 134, 136–7, 297n28
– rural/urban distinctions 160–1
– size of legislative assembly 16, 17, 18, 179, 195

Alberta clause, of redistribution formula 254

Alberta Court of Appeal, and the Alberta references 160–2

Alexander, Lincoln 229

Amalgam Method 25, 26, 71, 155, 242. *See also* redistribution formulas

Archer, Keith 111

Aucoin, Peter 76